NO ORDINARY ANGEL

THE ANCHOR YALE BIBLE REFERENCE LIBRARY is designed to be a third major component of the Anchor Yale Bible group, which includes the Anchor Yale Bible commentaries on the books of the Old Testament, the New Testament, and the Apocrypha and the Anchor Yale Bible Dictionary. While the Anchor Yale Bible commentaries and the Anchor Yale Bible Dictionary are structurally defined by their subject matter, the Anchor Yale Bible Reference Library serves as a supplement on the cutting edge of the most recent scholarship. The series is open-ended; the scope and reach are nothing less than the biblical world in its totality, and its methods and techniques the most up-to-date available or devisable. Separate volumes will deal with one or more of the following topics relating to the Bible: anthropology, archaeology, ecology, economy, geography, history, languages and literatures, philosophy, religion(s), theology.

As with the Anchor Yale Bible commentaries and the Anchor Yale Bible Dictionary, the philosophy underlying the Anchor Yale Bible Reference Library finds expression in the following: the approach is scholarly, the perspective is balanced and fair-minded, the methods are scientific, and the goal is to inform and enlighten. Contributors are chosen on the basis of their scholarly skills and achievements, and they come from a variety of religious backgrounds and communities. The books in the Anchor Yale Bible Reference Library are intended for the broadest possible readership, ranging from world-class scholars, whose qualifications match those of the authors, to general readers, who may not have special training or skill in studying the Bible but are as enthusiastic as any dedicated professional in expanding their knowledge of the Bible and its world.

David Noel Freedman
GENERAL EDITOR

THE ANCHOR YALE BIBLE REFERENCE LIBRARY

NO ORDINARY ANGEL

Celestial Spirits and Christian Claims about Jesus

SUSAN R. GARRETT

YALE UNIVERSITY PRESS

New Haven and London

Designed by Leslie Phillips.

Set in Minion by dix!

Printed in the United States of America by Vail-Ballou, Binghamton, N.Y.

LIBRARY OF CONGRESS CATALOGING-IN-PUBLICATION DATA
Garrett, Susan R., 1958–
No ordinary angel : celestial spirits and Christian claims about Jesus / Susan R. Garrett.
p.   cm. — (The Anchor Yale Bible reference library)
Includes bibliographical references (p.   ) and index.
ISBN 978-0-300-14095-8 (alk. paper)
1. Angels—Biblical teaching.   I. Title.
BS680.A48G38 2008
235'.3—dc22
2008024112

A catalogue record for this book is available from the British Library.

The paper in this book meets the guidelines for permanence and durability
of the Committee on Production Guidelines for Book Longevity
of the Council on Library Resources.

1   3   5   7   9   10   8   6   4   2

To

RICHARD D. RENNINGER

and

SHARON L. RENNINGER

with eternal gratitude

for their love and

support

CONTENTS

Acknowledgments, ix

Abbreviations, xiii

Hebrew and Greek Transliteration, xv

Introduction, 1

1 Agents of Healing, Messengers of Truth, 17

2 Angels at the Throne: Entering into God's Presence, 40

3 Falling Angels: Desiring Divinity, Wanting the World, 77

4 Satan and the Powers, 103

5 Guardian Angels, 139

6 Angels and Death, 186

Conclusion, 237

Notes, 243

Bibliography, 305

General Index, 321

Index of Modern Authors, 325

Index of Scripture and Other Ancient Writings, 328

ACKNOWLEDGMENTS

I first got the idea that it would be interesting to write a book about angels about ten years ago. When I began the research, I had no idea that the work would take so long to complete, or that it would take me so far afield from my primary specialization in New Testament studies. I have done my best to write in an informed way about areas in which I am less at home, but I do request the reader's indulgence. Still and all, ranging so widely has been a source of considerable interest and pleasure for me, as I hope the finished work will be for the reader.

I have incurred many debts over the course of my work. I especially want to thank administrators and trustees at Louisville Presbyterian Theological Seminary for their interest and encouragement, and for supporting several research leaves during the last decade. John M. Mulder, Joe Coalter, John W. Kuykendall, Dean K. Thompson, W. Eugene March, Dianne Reistroffer, and David C. Hester were all accommodating in this regard. Other colleagues at the Seminary were also helpful. Patricia K. Tull and W. Eugene March each read portions of the manuscript and generously shared their wisdom with me. Amy Plantinga Pauw read portions of the manuscript, offered many bibliographic suggestions, and patiently tutored me in theology, sometimes on walks through Cherokee Park. Marion L. Soards and Kathryn L. Johnson helped me through their friendship and general supportiveness. Librarians Angela Morris, David Scarlott, and Rick Jones assisted me with many bibliographic matters. Administrative assistant Melisa Scarlott helped me not only with the book but also with my other responsibilities (including, especially, my work as Coordinator of the Grawemeyer Award in Religion), thereby enabling me to eke out more time for research. Any number of students over the years heard me speak about my topic and happily engaged in conversation about it. Two especially fine students, Emily Rodgers and Viktoria Berlik, served as research assistants at different points. For the help of these people and all my past and present seminary colleagues and students, I am thankful.

Other institutions supported the project by offering grants or opportunities to speak about my work as it progressed. I am deeply grateful to the late Mr. Henry Luce III and the Henry Luce Foundation for awarding me a Henry Luce III Fellowship in Theology for the 1998–1999 academic year. The opportunity to take a full year for my research and to enter into theological conversation with other Luce fellows was extremely valuable to me. The Yale Divinity School invited me to deliver the Shaffer Lectures in 2002, and offered warm hospitality and stimulating conversation on that most enjoyable trip back to my old stomping ground. The Catholic Theological Union, Calvin College, and Union Theological Seminary and Presbyterian School of Christian Education gave me opportunities to lecture during the course of the research. Each of these occasions benefited me greatly.

A number of churches invited me to speak to them about angels, including the Brick Presbyterian Church in Manhattan; the Independent Presbyterian Church in Birmingham, Alabama; the First Presbyterian Church in Hope, Arkansas; and the Seven Oaks Presbyterian Church in Columbia, South Carolina. On each occasion I was warmly welcomed and treated with the greatest of respect. Such opportunities to speak to church people over the long course of my research greatly helped me to know what questions to ask in the book. In this connection I must also mention the Faith in Today's World class at Second Presbyterian Church in Louisville, which I taught each Sunday for about four years. Our conversations ranged over many of the topics covered in the book, and I am grateful for class members' enthusiastic and intelligent engagement.

Several friends/colleagues went above and beyond the call of duty by reading most or all of the manuscript and offering extensive critique and constructive suggestions. Robert M. Royalty, David E. Fredrickson, and Jaime Clark-Soles all helped in this way. Peter Smith, who was my student at Louisville Seminary and is a religion reporter for the Louisville *Courier-Journal,* offered his expert editor's eye as well as his keen sensibilities regarding both theology and popular spirituality. I thank all of these friends for generously sharing their expertise.

My editors at Doubleday and now at Yale University Press have been encouraging and helpful. I thank Andrew Corbin for accepting the book for the Anchor Reference Library, and for his patience as I labored to bring the project to completion. David Noel Freedman read the manuscript with painstaking care and saved me from many errors. Jennifer Banks, Susan Laity, and Leslie Phillips helped me with the transition of the manuscript to Yale University Press and offered expert editorial assistance. Kate Mertes prepared the indexes.

Without the support of friends and family, a project like this would bring no satisfaction. Here I must mention my dear friend and mentor Barney Jones, who was an unfailing source of strength and support until his death in 2005, and Florence Williams-Jones, whose continuing love and friendship are an inspiration. Jenni Walker-Noyes is as faithful a friend as one could ask for. My husband, Jim, and daughters, Laura and Kate, bring great joy into my life and make it all worthwhile.

My late father, Dick Renninger, was an extraordinary man. His integrity, sense of humor, and energy for life were legendary. He took pleasure in my accomplishments and thereby encouraged me to set the standard high. My mom, Sharon Renninger, has helped me in more ways than I could ever possibly acknowledge; for her deepest love and friendship I am profoundly thankful. I dedicate this book to the two of them as a token of my love and esteem.

ABBREVIATIONS

Abbreviations in the notes and parenthetically in the text for the books of the Bible; Old and New Testament Apocrypha; Old and New Testament Pseudepigrapha; and Dead Sea Scrolls are those given in the *SBL Handbook of Style* (ed. Patrick H. Alexander et al. [Peabody, Mass.: Hendrickson, 1999]). Abbreviations for secondary sources are as follows:

ABD   *The Anchor Bible Dictionary.* Ed. David Noel Freedman. 6 vols. New York: Doubleday, 1992.

ANF   *The Ante-Nicene Fathers.* Ed. Alexander Roberts and James Donaldson. 10 vols. 5th ed. Grand Rapids: Eerdmans, 1974.

DDD   *Dictionary of Deities and Demons in the Bible.* Ed. Karel van der Toorn, Bob Becking, and Pieter W. van der Horst. 2nd ed. Leiden: Brill, 1999.

HBC   *The HarperCollins Bible Commentary.* Ed. James L. Mays. Rev. ed. San Francisco: HarperSanFrancisco, 2000.

HCSB   *The HarperCollins Study Bible.* Ed. Harold W. Attridge and Wayne A. Meeks. Rev. ed. San Francisco: HarperSanFrancisco, 2006.

LCL   Loeb Classical Library

NIB   *The New Interpreter's Bible.* Ed. Leander E. Keck et al. 12 vols. Nashville, Tenn.: Abingdon, 1995.

NIV   New International Version

NRSV   New Revised Standard Version

OTP   *Old Testament Pseudepigrapha.* Ed. James H. Charlesworth. 2 vols. Anchor
           Bible Reference Library. Garden City, N.Y.: Doubleday, 1983, 1985.

RSV   Revised Standard Version

TDNT   *Theological Dictionary of the New Testament.* Ed. Gerhard Kittel. Trans. and ed.
           Geoffrey W. Bromiley. Grand Rapids: Eerdmans, 1964–1976.

TDOT   *Theological Dictionary of the Old Testament.* Ed. G. Johannes Botterweck and
           Helmer Ringgren. 15 vols. Grand Rapids: Eerdmans, 1997.

HEBREW AND GREEK

TRANSLITERATION

Transliteration of Greek and Hebrew terms follows the conventions set in the *SBL Handbook of Style.* Specifically, transliteration of Hebrew terms follows the conventions for the "general-purpose style" (omitting most diacritical marks). I have retained diacritical marks when quoting secondary sources that use them.

NO ORDINARY ANGEL

Introduction

Is this all there is? These bodies that can be injured in the blink of an eye—bodies that grow sick, that die? These jobs, schools, friends, or spouses that sometimes excite and challenge us but often do not? These unceasing worries about money, jobs, health, children, or relationships? Is this all there is? Or is there another place, another dimension to life?

These questions are as old as humanity. Some of the most ancient and enduring answers to them are found in the Bible, both in the Hebrew Scriptures, or Old Testament, and in the New Testament. Biblical authors take it for granted that there is a realm called "the heavens." In that realm God sits in glory, with other divine beings surrounding the throne. Biblical authors assume, moreover, that the heavenly realm is near to our hands as well as our hearts. Heaven intersects with earth at key places and key moments in the life of the people of God. At such key moments God's heavenly messengers, God's celestial soldiers, and at times even God venture forth from heaven to work and to be seen on earth. Jacob witnessed such an intersection of heaven and earth in his dream at Bethel: "He dreamed that there was a ladder set up on the earth, the top of it reaching to heaven; and the angels of God were ascending and descending on it. . . . And he was afraid, and said, 'How awesome is this place! This is none other than the house of God, and this is the gate of heaven'" (Gen 28:12, 17).

Questions about the heaven-earth connection may be very old, but they are as pressing today as they have ever been. Since the late twentieth century we have seen a new flourish of interest in angels, with evidence of this

1

interest displayed everywhere: on television, in book stores, in films, on the Internet, in women's magazines and in magazines devoted solely to the topic of angels, in newspapers, on jacket lapels, in gift catalogues, and in greeting card stores. Interest in angels is not new, however, but older than Christianity, and has never gone entirely out of fashion. Researchers have developed sophisticated explanations for the periodic ebb and flow of interest and belief in angels, and these explanations have merit.[1] But whatever the large-scale trends or cultural influences may be, on an individual level the topic of angels continues to command people's attention because they want to know: *Is there more to life than meets the eye?* Those who believe in the reality of angels answer this question with a resounding "yes!" They are saying that the world is not limited to what we can touch, taste, measure, or record on videotape.

Any present enthusiasm for heavenly inhabitants and their affairs contrasts with attitudes that prevailed only a few decades ago. In 1970, sociologist Peter Berger observed, "Whatever the situation may have been in the past, today the supernatural as a meaningful reality is absent or remote from the horizons of everyday life of large numbers, probably the majority, of people in modern societies, who seem to manage to get along without it quite well."[2] Perhaps Berger overestimated the disdain for the supernatural felt by people at that time. But even if he did, it seems clear that in the intervening decades, perceptions of the otherworldly have changed. Many have left the self-contained, scientifically predictable world of the late 1960s—a world devoid of supernatural powers—far behind. They have found that the world again teems with angels and other spirit-beings, who are reintroducing elements of magic and surprise into their lives. Angels (and their fallen counterparts) are again alive and well! In the space of just a few decades we have witnessed the reenchantment of the world.[3]

DO ANGELS EXIST, AND WHAT COUNTS AS EVIDENCE?

People who believe in the existence of angels can rarely convince those who do not believe, and vice versa. The parties to the debate cannot persuade one another because they cannot agree about what should or should not count as evidence for angels' reality. Should biblical stories about angels count, or should they be dismissed as reflecting an outmoded worldview? Should a claim to have encountered an angel be tallied as evidence? If so, what historical, visual, or psychological details are necessary to make such a claim persuasive? For example, if a person sees nothing unusual but alleges to have *felt* a spiritual presence, does that count? "What you call an angel let me call nervous calm," wrote Goethe to Lavater.[4] What personal or psychological factors would automatically discredit a person's claim to have had an angelic encounter? Or should *all* such claims be disbelieved, since another (this-worldly) explanation can nearly always be found?

The difficulty in knowing what to count as evidence stems from disagreement about where to begin the investigation. People who argue with one another about angels' reality begin from different starting points—and then inevitably move on to different outcomes. Their preconceptions shape their experiences; their experiences, in turn, confirm their preconceptions. For example, conservative Christian defenders of angels, such as Billy Graham, often take the biblical accounts of angels as their starting point.[5] Then they point to testimonies of people who claim to have encountered angels. The testimonies are taken to verify not only that angels exist, but also that angels' behavior and actions today resemble their behavior and actions in biblical times. *But the testimonies themselves do not reflect impartial experience.* Rather, Scripture has already informed and shaped the testifiers' very perception of angelic presence in the world.

On the other hand, as heirs of the Modernist era, many liberal Christians take as their starting point their conviction that the world is largely barren of so-called supernatural powers. The cosmos is the sterile world described by Berger earlier. Not surprisingly, the experience of such Christians conforms to their expectations. In other words, their experience is shaped from the outset by their conviction that all (or at least all lesser) supernatural beings have been extinguished from the world—discredited as the figments of an earlier, more mythological day. Biblical accounts of such beings are then reinterpreted as metaphor or moved to the outermost margins of faith. But contradiction can arise, for often the very same Christians who reject belief in gods, angels, demons, and the devil leave God (and perhaps the Holy Spirit) standing at the center of their beliefs—even though the same discrediting arguments could be applied to God/the Spirit as to the lesser beings.[6]

Finally, consider the case of the so-called "New Age" defenders of angels. They are the authors and readers of many of the books about angels that have crowded bookstore shelves in recent years. Such people have typically rejected the worldview of scientific modernism. Instead, they begin with what might be called an "enchanted-world cosmology." At the outset they assume the world to be filled with spiritual presences and inexplicable powers. Predictably, they then experience the world as filled with spiritual presences and inexplicable powers. It is not hard for such people to find heaven's gate. They need only turn inward, or sit with an open mind before a blank computer screen or before a blank sheet of paper, pen in hand. Then, immediately, the angels of God descend to make their presence felt and their wisdom known.[7] But, as with the other groups considered here, *such persons' experiences are suspect.* They are suspect because they have been fundamentally shaped by prior expectations.

So we see that different presuppositions about the world produce different types of angel experiences. I do not point this out to discredit conservatives, liberals, or New Agers, whom I freely admit to having caricatured here. Neither do I intend to raise up a new, fourth way to study angels—a way that will somehow escape the pressure-mold of its own premises. The point, rather, is that *everyone* comes at the topic of angels with certain assumptions already in place. Moreover, these assumptions are not about picayune affairs. They pertain to the very greatest questions of life: Does God exist? If so, what is God like? Does God speak to humans? If so, by what means, and what sorts of things does God say? What is the nature of reality? Are there natural laws, and can they be broken? What is our human nature?—and so on. Each of us comes to assume certain answers to these and other such questions, even if we have never given them conscious attention—just as children learn to speak their native language without any formal study of grammar. The answers we give to these questions, in turn, predispose us to perceive the world (with or without its supernatural elements) in certain ways. Such bias cannot be escaped, for it is built into the process of all human knowing. We cannot know the world unless we have words, concepts, and mental maps with which to describe it. But our words, concepts, and mental maps preshape and direct all that we perceive and how we make sense of it. We need not lament this built-in bias to all human knowing, but we do need to acknowledge it. Having recognized that there is always a bias, we can direct our efforts to tracing its contours in a given instance to discern its effects on thinking about angels.

We learn our mother tongue at our parents' knees. Similarly, we absorb many of our key opinions about God and the world from our parents, from our family of origin, and especially from the larger culture (or subculture) in which we live. It can be difficult for us to see our own opinions because we are so close to them. The effort can be like trying to get a good, critical look at ourselves without a mirror. What we need is a place where we can stand, to look at ourselves and see how our assumptions fit into the bigger picture. We can procure such a vantage point by comparing our views to the views held in other cultures. Whenever anthropologists immerse themselves in the life of another people, they embark on a process of learning *two* cultures: the host culture and their own. By trying out the words, concepts, and mental maps that another people uses to make sense of the world, the ethnographers come to a better understanding of their *own* cultural assumptions. The same principle holds when college students go abroad for a year. Provided that they have mixed with the locals, such students often come back with a new perspective on their own world. In this book, I will try to offer the footing needed to see our culture's governing assumptions about angels, by delving into the world of biblical angels and the ancient authors who wrote about them. In other words, looking into the strange world of biblical angels will enable us to discern more clearly what is distinctive (and sometimes destructive) about various modern views of divine messengers.

Popular representations of angels today arise not in a vacuum but in a culture that is preoccupied with spiritual affairs and the possibility that there are higher powers affecting the course of our mortal existence. The ways people talk about angels reflect common motifs in popular spirituality. For example, in our era angels are often said to help us mortals live life to its fullest by abandoning our driven existence and finding joy and satisfaction in the moment. But such emphasis on savoring everyday pleasures is not found only among those who talk of angels; the theme is pervasive in all varieties of popular spiritual teaching, from conservative or liberal Christian to contemporary Buddhist to New Age. As a second example, consider a story widely circulated on the Internet about a three-year-old boy named Brian who is nearly crushed to death under a garage door. Later Brian describes his near-death experience to his mother, calling the angels "birdies" because they were up in the air. "He said they were so pretty and so peaceful, and he didn't want to come back. Then the bright light came. He said that the light was so bright and so warm, and he loved the bright light so much. Someone in the bright light hugged him and then told him, 'I love you but you have to go back. You have to play baseball, and tell everyone about the birdies.'" Brian went on to explain to his mother that there is a plan for everyone's life, and the birdies help us to live according to our plan. This story reflects many typical features of popular spirituality and of near-death accounts, including the emphasis on "the plan"; because each of us has one, nothing is random, and all happens for a purpose.[8] In my analysis of popular portrayals of angels, I will endeavor to show the continuity between such talk about angels and broader themes in popular spirituality.

ANGELS IN THE BIBLICAL WORLD

Often we think we already know what the biblical sources say. We may assume that the ancient accounts and our modern beliefs about angels are more or less consistent. For example, in the book *Angels,* Billy Graham presupposes that his own view of angels matches "the biblical view." (Graham further takes it for granted that there is only one "biblical view.") As a second example, in Frank Peretti's several sagas about angels battling demons, the novelist assumes an identity between the angels he depicts and biblical angels. But in fact, modern authors—and those who read their works—hold many ideas about angels that are quite foreign to the world of the Bible.

A warning: not all will find the needed close study of the biblical texts to be an easy affair. These ancient writings do not yield their riches on this topic to the casual or hasty observer; readers of this book should likewise be prepared to read it closely and to think both critically and imaginatively! And, as if the challenges posed by the biblical accounts were not enough, much important information about ancient angel beliefs is hidden away in other, more obscure ancient texts. Consider, for example, the difficult writing known as *1 Enoch.* This document has an extraordinarily rich angelology. But *1 Enoch* is preserved in its entirety only in Ge'ez, the language of ancient Ethiopia. So, right off the bat we are at the mercy of the handful of scholars who have mastered this arcane tongue. Further, *1 Enoch* evolved over a period of time (roughly between the third century BCE and first century CE) and had multiple authors and editors. It is full of gaps, repetitions, and inconsistencies. Even short passages by a single author are written in a style that can be very hard to follow. But we must take on the challenges posed by *1 Enoch* and other such documents, for there are crucial aspects of ancient Jewish and early Christian angel beliefs that we can scarcely understand apart from them.

Biblical authors—like authors today—use stories about angels to talk not only about angelic existence but about a whole range of subjects. We will proceed farthest in our quest for understanding if we turn our eyes and ears to those other matters. So in this work, rather than focusing on the question of angels' existence, I will explore *what else* was being said and heard when ancient authors wrote about angels. What were such authors claiming about God? About God's interventions in the corporate life of God's people? About God's interventions in the lives of individuals? About human sinfulness, human perceptiveness, human ability or inability to affect the natural course of events? About humans' fate after death? And so forth. The specific questions will vary with each text in which a given angel account is found.

Bracketing the question of angels' existence is an important first step in our quest for understanding. By leaving this question open, we also keep our minds open to discover new, metaphorical dimensions of truth in stories of angels. We thereby avoid that modern tendency to, in Jeffrey Burton Russell's words, "analyze, reduce, and narrow down toward definition." Writing of heaven, Russell observes: "Moderns are used to dichotomies between true and false, fact and fiction, they are put off by comparative terms such as 'more real' or 'more perfect,' and they create a dichotomy between 'literal' and 'metaphorical.' . . . The modern assumption is that the so-called factual statement relates to 'outside reality' and that the metaphorical statement is subjective and unrelated to 'outside reality.' "[9]

But because of their vastness and richness, some realities—including heavenly realities—*cannot* be conveyed or grasped except through metaphor. Biblical authors sensed all this. "God is a poet at least as much as a scientist or a historian," Russell writes.[10] The truths that biblical authors sought to convey in their descriptions of angels overflow the words and images at those authors' disposal. In seeking to discover the metaphorical or poetic truth of their descriptions, we are not prejudging the question of angelic existence. We are not saying that angels aren't real. We are declining to focus on the finally unprovable issue of their reality or nonreality, in an effort to discern the larger meanings of stories that tell about them. As an illustration of the point, consider the prophet Isaiah's awe-inspiring vision:

> In the year that King Uzziah died, I saw the Lord sitting on a throne, high and lofty; and the hem of his robe filled the Temple. Seraphs were in attendance above him; each had six wings: with two they covered their faces, and with two they covered their feet, and with two they flew. And one called to another and said: "Holy, holy, holy is the LORD[11] of hosts; the whole earth is full of his glory." The pivots on the thresholds shook at the voices of those who called, and the house filled with smoke. And I said, "Woe is me! I am lost, for I am a man of unclean lips, and I live among a people of unclean lips; yet my eyes have seen the King, the LORD of hosts!"
>
> Then one of the seraphs flew to me, holding a live coal that had been taken from the altar with a pair of tongs. The seraph touched my mouth with it and said: "Now that this has touched your lips, your guilt has departed and your sin is blotted out." Then I heard the voice of the Lord saying, "Whom shall I send, and who will go for us?" And I said, "Here am I; send me!" (Isa 6:1–8)

Here Isaiah uses human words and images—instruments of limited capacity—to describe an encounter so rich with meaning as to defy description. What words could ever suffice to portray an encounter between an infinite God, the creator of the universe, and a weak, fallible, fragile human being? Or what words could express the marvelous truth that a mortal was selected to stand in God's presence and carry God's word to the people? In choosing his words and images, Isaiah was not writing a neutral, objective description of events, the way a lab worker might write up an observation report for an experiment whose outcome does not deeply interest him. Rather, Isaiah was describing an experience of being overwhelmed by God—an experience in which the prophet was not a detached observer but a full participant. Inevitably, that experience exceeded the capacity of the words and images that Isaiah chose to convey it.

And yet, the prophet's words and images are what are left to us. And so we proceed to translate, unpack, and explicate. We envision the scene in our mind's eye, and we ponder the symbolic import. Likely we will all agree that the account is at least partly symbolic. Surely Isaiah's lips were not physically burned—but, just as surely, he experienced himself as being purified somehow, so that his mouth would be enabled to speak God's holy words. How much else in Isaiah's account has symbolic or metaphorical import? What about the throne? What about the seraphs? What about the wings of the seraphs? It doesn't get us very far simply to say that the seraphs were or were not real. It is much more fruitful to ask what their presence as God's attendants, or their covering of their own eyes, or their purifying act means for Isaiah's overall depiction of God's majesty. *We need to fix our attention on precisely such questions of meaning.*

We always speak to one another—and God always speaks to us—in particular languages. These languages encompass more than just words. They encompass entire cultures—the fantastically complex sets of symbols, assumptions, practices, and mental maps shared by a given people. To understand what is being said and heard in an act of communication we need to know (or rely on someone who knows) the relevant language and the relevant culture. Consider Isaiah's vision once more. The words of the vision can be translated readily enough, but we quickly realize that more is needed for understanding. For example: (1) What does it mean to say that God sits on a "throne"? To answer, we need information about the understandings and practices and accoutrements of kingship—not kingship in the twenty-first century, or the sixteenth century, but kingship in the days of King Uzziah (eighth century BCE). Otherwise we will read later ideas of thrones or of kingship back into the earlier text. (2) Who or what are "seraphs"? Are they angels such as we normally think of angels today? How is it, then, that they have six wings instead of two? Here again, knowledge of Isaiah's culture helps us to grasp the scene: seraphs were winged serpents, like dragons, often depicted in ancient Near Eastern (especially Egyptian) art in association with royal thrones. (3) Why do the seraphs cover their faces? Yet again, knowledge of the culture (specifically of biblical culture) assists us. By biblical convention, God is so holy that no one can see the face of God and live (see Exod 33:20). By covering their faces, the seraphs call attention to that extreme holiness; even these supernal creatures cannot look upon God's face. No wonder the mortal Isaiah cried "Woe is me!" The point is that biblical authors were influenced as much by their culture as contemporary authors are by today's culture. In order to maximize our understanding of angels, whether biblical angels or angels of the twenty-first century, we need to view the depictions of them against the backdrop of the relevant culture. Only by doing so can we perceive nuances of the accounts and also minimize the reading of our own cultural assumptions into them.

When we view ancient depictions of angels in their cultural context, we come upon ideas that seem outmoded, strange, or mysterious to us. Consider, for example, the widespread assumption in the ancient Near East that the stars, sun, and moon are living beings. Some of the biblical authors show their familiarity with this view by depicting the celestial bodies as members of the heavenly host, fighting in God's angelic army against the enemies of Israel. As the author of Judges writes: "The stars fought from heaven, from their courses they fought against Sisera" (Judg 5:20; cf. Josh 10:12–13).[12] Or, consider Paul's statement that women should wear head coverings "because of the angels" (1 Cor 11:10). What could he possibly mean? Here it would be helpful to have still better knowledge of Paul's culture than the relatively full knowledge that we already possess. Paul has apparently adopted certain cultural assumptions that are obscure to us now about the role of angels in worship, or about the behavior of angels toward women, or about both. Is it possible, as some have suggested, that Paul supposes the angels will be sexually attracted to the sight of women's uncovered heads? We do know that the story of angels who mated with human women, told in Genesis 6:1–4, was widely known and discussed in the first century (see Chapter 3). Whenever we come upon such strange and mysterious elements of ancient angel beliefs we should note them well. They will remind us not to get too comfortable with the biblical stories—not to assume that we always know exactly what the ancient authors were talking about. Even when ideas look familiar, authors may be making assumptions and associations that we cannot understand or accept as valid.

Because the Bible was written by humans who lived in worlds so radically different from our own, we are always foreigners to it in very important ways. Therefore, we approach it best with sensitivity and respect. Consider the story of two outsiders who go to live in a small village in another country. One is loud and demanding. He insists that residents meet his needs and relate to him in the manner to which he is accustomed in his own land. The other outsider is gentle and respectful. He takes months or years to get to know the residents of the village and tries hard to understand their ways. He learns from them far more than the first visitor can ever learn, for he is receptive to wisdoms other than ones that he has always known. We face similar options as we foray into the biblical world of angels. We can barge in, demanding that the biblical authors support our preconceived ideas. Or we can look, listen, and learn. If we choose the latter course, what we see and hear may be rather different from what we expect.

The situation is, however, more complicated than the analogy suggests. For the Bible is not a village whose inhabitants all know one another and all share, more or less, the same perspectives. The various books of the Bible were written over a span of many centuries, and reflect the many cultures with which the writers came into contact. Hence the authors present diverse ideas about angels. Sometimes these ideas are simply different from one another, and sometimes they seem actually to contradict one another. As an example, consider again the issue of the heavenly host. When the author of Isaiah 40 writes of the starry host, he portrays it as created by and subordinate to God: "Lift up your eyes on high and see: Who created these? He who brings out their host and numbers them, calling them all by name; because he is great in strength, mighty in power, not one is missing" (v. 26).[13]

But in another passage from Isaiah, members of the host are set to be judged by God, suggesting that they have strayed from God:

> On that day the LORD will punish the host of heaven in heaven, and on earth the kings of the earth. They will be gathered together like prisoners in a pit; they will be shut up in a prison, and after many days they will be punished. Then the moon will be abashed, and the sun ashamed; for the LORD of hosts will reign on Mount Zion and in Jerusalem, and before his elders he will manifest his glory. (Isa 24:21–23)

In this second passage the host is *not* depicted as fully subordinate to the divine will, but as a gathering of independent gods who oppose the LORD. So God will punish them along with their earthly counterparts, the rebellious human kings. Many modern authors who survey biblical angels simply ignore such tensions in biblical depictions of the heavenly host or individual members of it. They assume that all scriptural teachings are consistent; what is said of angels in one part of Isaiah can be used to shed light on what is said in another part, what is said in Genesis can be used to shed light on what is said in Hebrews, and so forth. Another option, though, is to strive to hear *all* the different voices in Scripture—whether they be harmonious or dissonant. With respect to the example given above: many biblical scholars contend that Isaiah 24:1–27:13 (from which the second passage above is taken) was written not by the prophet who wrote Isaiah 40:26, but by another author, writing some years later.[14] The two authors' ideas about the heavenly host differ because their own backgrounds and the purposes for which they wrote differed. When we harmonize their teachings on this topic, we flatten and reduce their respective words to us. But when we strive to pick out the different voices speaking in Scripture and hear each voice in its own context, we produce a richer interpretation and better respect the integrity of the authors and first readers of the biblical texts.

Some of the most exciting recent discoveries in the study of ancient beliefs about angels pertain to the figure of Jesus. Immediately after Jesus' death his followers mined biblical and other textual traditions for imagery and language that could explain Jesus' identity and the nature of his reconciling work. Scholars are finding evidence that some important traditions that Christians adapted for this purpose were *traditions about angels*. These include various traditions about God's chief angelic mediator—a kind of right-hand angel to the deity. We see the evidence for such influence of angel traditions on ideas about Christ scattered throughout the New Testament. One of the most striking instances of such "angelomorphic" Christology (that is, Christology that has been influenced by traditions about angels)[15] occurs when Paul recalls the welcome that the Christians in Galatia extended to him on his initial visit to them. Paul writes, "Though my condition put you to the test, you did not scorn or despise me, but welcomed me as an angel of God, as Christ Jesus" (Gal 4:14). Commentators usually assume that Paul means his statement hypothetically: "You welcomed me as warmly as you would have welcomed an angel of God—indeed, as warmly as you would have welcomed Christ Jesus himself." But there is good reason to suspect that Paul is claiming that the Galatians received him "as God's angel—namely, Jesus Christ." In other words, Paul is making the startling claim that when he first preached the gospel to the Galatians, he was united with Jesus Christ (see Gal 2:20), whom Paul identifies with God's chief angel. In other passages, too, Paul's language suggests that he made sense of Jesus' person and work by likening him to angels, or even by identifying him with the chief angel of God.[16] Other New Testament authors did the same, including the authors of Luke and Acts, John, Hebrews, Jude, and Revelation.

Seeing that early Christians compared Jesus to angels, I will do likewise. I do so as one who shares the early Christians' conviction that it is Jesus, and no ordinary angel, who is the truest and best messenger from God. In my view, it is Jesus who has most perfectly revealed God's identity and God's intentions for the created world. Jesus differs from the angels in one all-important respect: he suffered and died. Moreover, that suffering and death are not incidental to the message that Jesus brings, but are its very heart. Yet, in comparing Jesus to the angels, one cannot simply pit him against them, for he is like them in some quite important ways—as early Christian authors perceived so clearly. Comparison of Jesus with angels can never be a simple matter of showing his superiority to them. So, in my analysis I will also explore what he and they have in common.

ANGELS AS THEY WERE AND ARE

A look in a bookstore or search on the Internet will quickly reveal that modern angels are thought to fill various job descriptions. They are healers, guardians, givers of praise. They are soldiers fighting for God against their fallen counterparts, namely, the devil and demonic hordes. At the hour of death they are guides who lead humans to "the other side." Biblical or other ancient depictions of angels lie somewhere behind most of these modern ideas about angelic roles. It would be fascinating to trace the lineage of various ideas as they pass through the 2,000 intervening years of the Common Era, but to do so would be an enormously complicated endeavor requiring a multi-volume work. Still, even if we cannot trace how this or that notion of angels evolved through the centuries to come to its present manifestations in culture, we can benefit from looking at the ancient counterparts to modern notions and vice versa. In the chapters to come, I will alternate between analyses of ancient and modern depictions of angels, and compare these, in turn, to portrayals of Jesus. The strategy will permit clearer perception of how each such image—be it ancient or modern—functioned, or functions, within its own cultural, historical, and theological contexts.

It is hard to know which of the recent representations of angels to address. On the one hand, it might seem to make sense to limit our study to testimonies by people who claim that they have encountered angels or have special wisdom about them. These testimonies are found on the Internet, in various published collections and magazines, and in the burgeoning number of angelic self-help books offering advice on how to make contact with angels or tap into their power.[17] In such cases, the narrators purport to tell the truth, and so their accounts might seem worthier of our attention than the fictional depictions in recent print, drama, film, and television. But the fictional accounts must be considered also, for they exercise enormous influence on the popular imagination. David Ford comments on the huge audiences for films and videos, and on the millions of readers of novels:

> They are being drawn into a fictional world, and in turn are welcoming fictional people and plots into their lives. This is something of immense importance. Taking part in this fiction-saturated culture, we discover who we are and we test our identities. We enter into the fictional world of novels, plays, films, and all sorts of other stories. But the lines between fiction and reality are not at all clear, and our hopes, fears, dreams, and conceptions of reality may be more profoundly affected by fiction than by "true stories" (if those are what historians and journalists tell).[18]

The millions of people who watched *Touched by an Angel* each week throughout its long run (and now in syndication) have been shaped in important ways by the show's stories of angels who opened blind eyes, softened hard hearts, and mended broken relationships. So also with all those who have watched Frank Capra's classic film *It's a Wonderful Life* and other, more recent angel films, or who have read Frank Peretti's apocalyptic novels about angels battling demons.[19] In the following study, I will sample all of these types of angelic representations, both fictional and nonfictional, comparing and contrasting them with biblical portrayals that correspond in some way.

The distinction between the nonfictional and fictional accounts of angels turns out to be quite a slippery one in any case, because the testimonies that people offer are fictions also—even if the reported events really happened. Much like television scriptwriters and movie producers, those who testify to encounters with angels *create* their accounts. In other words, they choose which elements of the encounter to report and how to narrate the story so as to elicit the desired response from readers or listeners. When one reads the testimonials, it quickly becomes apparent that the narrators' choices on such matters follow established conventions. For example, many accounts of miraculous angelic intervention in a time of crisis end with the disappearance of the mysterious stranger who gives the aid. He or she simply vanishes. No one, however, ever actually witnesses the disappearance, the way Alice witnessed the disappearance of the Cheshire cat. Rather, the narrator is typically distracted for a moment, and when he or she turns to say "thanks," the stranger is gone. Later efforts to track the helper down prove fruitless. The "disappearance of the angel" is a nearly indispensable feature of the modern genre of angelic encounter narratives. Narrators of such stories have been influenced not only in their narration of such experiences, *but even in their initial perception of them,* by what they themselves have seen and heard in other, earlier such testimonies—not to mention what they have seen and heard in the fictional media depictions, or what they have read or heard from the Bible.[20]

Talk of angels always points to a reality beyond that which we can see. When people today talk of angels, they are implicitly asking or asserting something about such a transcendent reality. Just *what* they are asking or asserting can vary greatly. For example, when people tell stories of guardian angels who rescue them from impending disaster, they are claiming that a higher power—Christians would say "God"—watches over them and guides their steps. Or, when people tell stories of angels who open blind eyes, they are claiming that there is a healing truth for each of our lives, a truth that can be sought and found. We can rephrase these implicit claims as questions: Does God watch over us and guide our steps? Are truth and the abundant life it brings available to us?

In each of the following chapters, I begin by highlighting issues or questions that underlie current talk of angels. Then I consider biblical, or biblical-era, angel materials that address analogous questions. Study of the ancient angel materials typically offers vantage points and openings to peer into the inner workings of the modern accounts, but the reverse will also prove to be true: the stories of modern angels will offer new perspectives on their ancient counterparts. In addressing the central questions of each chapter, I will draw on insights gained through such analytic study and comparison of ancient and modern angel talk. I write, however, not only as a scholar, but also as a Christian. Therefore I do not claim to be neutral. The questions raised by the angel materials are of deepest existential import, and my answers to them are profoundly shaped by my conviction that it is Christ who answers them best.

Can God heal us where we are broken? Can God show us the distortions in our lives—the places where we do not see things right—and give us new vision? These are the questions to be considered in Chapter 1, "Angels of Healing, Messengers of Truth." I will look at some of the biblical traditions about "the angel of the LORD," and at the angel Raphael as presented in the book of Tobit. Such angels appear to key figures in the history of Israel, to heal blindness and deliver messages from God. I will also look at very recent testimonies about angels who heal blindness, and at early Christian testimonies about Jesus, empowered by God to heal blindness and bring truth.

Where and how can we find those sacred moments we need to assure us that we are not alone? How can we come into the presence of the divine? These questions motivate many people who are now seeking or claiming encounters with angels. In Chapter 2, "Angels at the Throne," I will look at recent writings by and for such people. I will then turn to ancient Jewish and Christian depictions of humans who enter into the very place where God and angels dwell. The ancient accounts include, for example, Ezekiel's stunning vision of the Glory of God seated on a throne borne aloft by four fantastic creatures; and a vision, shared among ancient Jews living near the Dead Sea, of humans worshiping alongside angels in the heavenly sanctuary. I will conclude the chapter by looking at an early Christian version of such heavenly worship—the speaking "in the tongues of angels" in the Corinthian church—and at the Apostle Paul's counter-balancing command to *love one another.* For it is this love of God in Christ Jesus—love both given and received—that elevates *and sustains* our sense of God's presence in our lives.

How can we find our heart's desire? How can we discover the miraculous—more than that, the divine—in the midst of our everyday world? How can we learn to live each day, each hour, each moment to the full? These questions lie at the heart of several recent angel films, indeed, at the heart of much popular spirituality today. The angel films seek to answer such questions via the peculiar motif of angels' longing for human pleasures. In Chapter 3, "Falling Angels," I will look at biblical and other ancient materials that feature this motif. These include Genesis 6:1–4, the story of "sons of God" who came down to earth and mated with human women, and various postbiblical retellings. I will highlight the stark contrast between the films' celebration of desire for sensuous pleasures, and the widespread ancient conviction that desire is the root of all evil. Each perspective has both strengths and liabilities. I will conclude by suggesting that we are best served, and serve best, not by finding a happy medium between these alternatives, but by following Jesus' model in allowing God to reorder our desires.

Why are we assaulted with pain and sorrow? Why are our lives so often not what we envision for ourselves, or what we think God envisions for us? Why do we fall into patterns of behavior destructive to ourselves and others? In the view of many Christians today, any truthful answer to such questions must implicate Satan and other evil angels. In Chapter 4, "Satan and the Powers," I will look at the roles of the devil and his servants in early Jewish and Christian explanations of suffering and sin, and compare these explanations to recent accounts. Such recent accounts of Satan's activity range from the apocalyptic novels by Frank Peretti about the satanic conspiracy to take over the world, and the series of novels by Tim LaHaye and Jerry B. Jenkins about the Great Tribulation,[21] to Walter Wink's effort to redefine Satan and demons in terms acceptable even to liberal skeptics. Finally, I will reflect on how Jesus, who endured the extreme suffering and seduction of satanic assault, may be seen as God's answer to undeserved evil.

Is God looking out for us as we and our loved ones traverse the minefields of everyday life? Do we have any basis for hope that, in moments of temptation or danger, God will protect us and keep us safe? In Chapter 5, "Guardian Angels," I will demonstrate that questions such as these, answered affirmatively, motivate many recent testimonials of angels appearing on earth. I will look at the origins in ancient Israel of the notion of guardian angels and at comparable notions in the ancient Near Eastern and Greco-Roman cultures. We will see that the role played by guardian angels in the biblical materials is minimal when compared to their much greater role in patristic, medieval, and more-recent Catholic theology and practice. Finally, I will consider how the doctrine of the incarnation—God's taking on of vulnerable human flesh in the person of Jesus—both supports belief in God's presence in our material world and undercuts the notion of angels who protect us from physical harm.

Do we face death all alone? Or do we have reason to hope, indeed, to expect, divine presence with us in our hour of greatest need? Many people answer "yes" to the latter question, and specify that such divine presence comes in angelic form. A survey of popular television shows, films, and written publications about angels and near-death experiences will show just how widespread such belief in an angel (or angels) of death has become in recent years. In Chapter 6, "Angels and Death," I will explore the emergence in late Second Temple Judaism[22] of various angels associated with death. These include not only "psychopomps" (that is, angels, both fearsome and benign, who lead departing souls to the beyond), but also angels who fill out the realms of heaven and hell, acting in a great variety of roles. Consideration of these various angels and their modern counterparts will offer insight into our own culture's obsession with—and denial of—death. I will also consider the suggestion of several New Testament authors that Christians are destined to participate in the angelic realm, beginning not at some remote future date but here and now, as we live out our lives on earth. Changing *from* glory *into* glory, we escape some of the bonds characteristic of mortal life and are, like the angels, empowered to live and to love more fully.

1

Agents of Healing,

Messengers of Truth

Truth can be painful. Do I really want to see the world as God sees it? Or myself as God sees me? I do not even like to watch myself on video! How much more frightening, then, to catch even a glimpse of myself through the lens of God's camera—God, who "is able to judge the thoughts and intentions of the heart," and before whom "no creature is hidden, but all are naked and laid bare" (Heb 4:12–13). It would be so much more comfortable to go on seeing things, self included, as I want to see them.

Healing also can be painful. If I am to be healed of my psychic and spiritual distress, then I must admit that I have erred. I must own up to wrong judgments that I have made about myself or others, or to wrong deeds that I have done, or to deeds that I have left undone. If I am to be healed, then I must give up my unhealthy compulsions and dependencies. I must change. Most painful of all, I must say good-bye to the time that I have wasted and mourn its loss.

And yet, despite the pain that truth and healing may bring, I—and so many like me—seek after them! The world has shrunk, pluralism has grown, and with so many visions of reality now competing for our allegiance, truth has become ever more elusive. And yet, we go on searching high and low for truth. We long also for healing—healing of our damaged selves and damaged relationships. We say we are willing to suffer the pain that comes with change, if someone would just tell us what to do. Our desire for truth and our desire for healing are bound together. For to find the truth is to be healed of our blindness—our wrong ways of looking at ourselves, our wrong ways

17

of looking at the world, and our habit of looking in the wrong places for our heart's desire.

In these present days of the quest for truth and healing, angels have emerged in many people's lives as agents of revelation and change. Consider the case of Martha Beck, who offers memoirs of an extraordinary pregnancy in *Expecting Adam: A True Story of Birth, Rebirth, and Everyday Magic*.[1] Martha and her husband John have already adorned the walls of their cramped apartment with two Harvard diplomas apiece. As her story opens, they are graduate students in quest of Harvard PhDs. The Becks have bought, without reservation, into the Harvard ideal of the good life. Being brilliant (or looking brilliant) and working insane hours to get ahead are what matter in life. Personal concerns always have to be subordinated to these higher goals. For women students, pregnancy is viewed as personal failure. When Martha accidentally conceives Adam, who will be her second child, she is inexplicably joyful, yet determined to hide her condition from professors and peers till the last possible moment for she knows what their response will be. The pregnancy turns out to be relentlessly, almost impossibly, difficult. To make matters worse, John has to be in Asia for extended lengths of time.

Some weeks into the pregnancy, amazing things begin to happen. A woman acquaintance shows up at the door with a bag of groceries as Martha is about to collapse from dehydration and lack of nourishment. She receives mysterious aid as she and her eighteen-month-old daughter are about to succumb to smoke inhalation in the stairwell of a burning building. Later she sees a picture taken by news reporters at a moment when her anonymous helper should have been right behind her, but no one shows up on the photo. She experiences miraculous healing when the placenta pulls away from her uterine wall (a potentially fatal condition for both mother and fetus). She experiences moments of clairvoyance, when she is mentally transported to the sights and sounds that John is experiencing in Asia (later confirmed by him in conversation). And she is gradually becoming aware of *invisible beings* present all around her, guiding her and comforting her whenever she opens herself to them.

When Martha learns that the child she is carrying has Down syndrome, Harvard professors, colleagues, and medical personnel pressure her and John to abort the fetus. But Martha and John insist on having the baby (at first, she more urgently than he). And from that point forward their outlook on life begins to change. Martha has a dream in which a young man, whom she feels she has always known, tells her not to be fearful. She knows he is "Adam." (Later, after her son Adam's birth, a psychic tells Martha that he is an embodied angel—a point she does not wholeheartedly endorse, but does not refute either. She also favors the comment of a friend who tells her that angels attend Adam wherever he goes.) Most significantly, both Martha and John have moments of truth, when they see with new eyes how shallow and false are the lives of those who embody Harvard's measures of success. Martha sees through the façade of a physician who had urged her to have the abortion to the personal fear and pain that drive him. John suddenly sees the coveted office of a world-renowned professor as the small, cramped cage of an empty life. Throughout her narrative, Beck intersperses anecdotes about Adam's present life. These anecdotes are designed to show how he heals spiritual blindness, helping Martha, John, and others to see the world as a place of wonder and delight. They reject their former lives as worthless, holding only to the truth that Adam and the spirit-beings have brought.

For Beck, these beings are agents of healing and messengers of truth. They help her to turn from the dark prison of a driven existence to the light and joy of everyday life. It is not surprising that Beck should give angels such a prominent place in her story of conversion or rebirth: it is a role that they frequently play in popular American culture. Clarence Oddbody in *It's a Wonderful Life*, Monica on the long-running CBS series *Touched by an Angel*, Michael in the film by that name, Seth in the movie *City of Angels*—all of these angelic figures help people to see the world in a new way. They heal the blindness that keeps us from "seizing the day." Or consider the child-angel in the popular novella *The Christmas Box*, about an industrious young entrepreneur named Richard (played by Richard Thomas in the Hallmark television version), who neglects his wife and small child to attend to his growing business.[2] The child-angel repeatedly appears to him in a dream and, with the assistance of a human "angel," or messenger, helps Richard to see that by his overwork he is "trading diamonds for stones." So, in *Expecting Adam*, when Beck depicts her spirits as ones who help her to turn from blindness to true sight by showing her the magic of everyday life, she is tapping into deep cultural currents.

The angels of certain biblical accounts also heal human blindness and convey divine truth. In this chapter, I will examine several such accounts and briefly compare them with modern stories of angelic healing and truth-bringing. Such comparisons will help to clarify what is distinctive and compelling about each set of stories. Then I will turn to consider the New Testament portrait of Jesus as one who heals blindness and brings truth. How does Jesus' role resemble or differ from the role of biblical angels who do the same? And more importantly, how can Jesus speak to our own quest for healing and truth?

The Bible tells many stories of blindness healed, but few as engaging as the story of the prophet Balaam and his donkey. It is here that we begin.

BALAAM AND HIS ASS

The children of Israel have hiked in the wilderness for forty years and are about to cross the Jordan River to enter into the Promised Land. They are encamped on the plains of Moab. The native inhabitants fear that Israel will try to capture and destroy them. So Balak, the king of Moab, takes action. He hires the prophet (or "seer") Balaam to curse the people of Israel.[3] King Balak says to Balaam, "A people has come out of Egypt; they have spread over the face of the earth, and they have settled next to me. Come now, curse this people for me; since they are stronger than I; perhaps I shall be able to defeat them and drive them from the land; for I know that whomever you bless is blessed, and whomever you curse is cursed" (Num 22:5–6). Balaam sets out on his journey to fulfill the contract. But then the LORD's anger is kindled against Balaam, and "the angel of the LORD took his stand in the road as his adversary [Heb. *satan*]" (v. 22).[4] The donkey sees the angel of the LORD standing in the road, with drawn sword in hand. *But Balaam, the famed seer, does not see the angel.* Balaam beats the donkey for stopping. The same thing happens again. The third time the angel of the LORD blocks them at a narrow pass, and the donkey lies down under Balaam. When again Balaam beats the ass, God gives it voice. The animal asks Balaam why he is striking it and Balaam answers, "Because you have made a fool of me! I wish I had a sword in my hand! I would kill you right now!" (v. 29). The ass points out that it has not been in the habit of treating Balaam this way, and Balaam admits that this is true.

Amazingly, the miracle of the donkey's speech passes by without comment. Neither the ass nor Balaam remarks on this unusual occurrence. Perhaps the narrator wants to direct all attention to the second, greater miracle that is about to occur:

> *Then the LORD opened the eyes of Balaam,* and he saw the angel of the LORD standing in the road, with his drawn sword in his hand; and he bowed down, falling on his face. The angel of the LORD said to him, "Why have you struck your donkey these three times? I have come out as an adversary, because your way is perverse before me. The donkey saw me, and turned away from me these three times. If it had not turned away from me, surely just now I would have killed you and let

it live." Then Balaam said to the angel of the Lord, "I have sinned, for I did not know that you were standing in the road to oppose me. Now therefore, if it is displeasing to you, I will return home." The angel of the Lord said to Balaam, "Go with the men; but speak only what I tell you to speak." So Balaam went on with the officials of Balak. (Num 22:31–35; emphasis added)

The true miracle is not the donkey's speech but the opening of Balaam's blind eyes. Balaam continues on to meet Balak the king, but instead of *cursing* Israel (as the king wishes), four separate times Balaam frustrates the king by *blessing* Israel. Balaam is, in his own words, "the man whose eye is clear, . . . who hears the words of God, and knows the knowledge of the Most High, who sees the vision of the Almighty, who falls down, but with his eyes uncovered" (24:15–16). Balaam is no longer a blind seer who uses his divining rod to beat his donkey. Now Balaam sees—more than that, he *knows*.[5]

THE ANGEL OF THE LORD

The angel who blocks the donkey and then Balaam is the *mal'ak yhwh,* Hebrew for "the angel of the Lord." This angel appears at various points throughout the Scriptures.[6] In the Balaam incident, he comes to convey God's displeasure that Balaam—much like the ass—has refused to go the way that "the master" wished.[7] The narrator is not especially interested in this angel's appearance or nature.[8] Here, as in other early biblical accounts of angels, primary interest is in the sender—the Lord—and in the Lord's message. In the Balaam story, *the Lord and the angel seem virtually to be one and the same.* For example, when Balaam is healed of his blindness, the narrator notes that it was the Lord (not the angel) who opened Balaam's eyes. And, when the angel says to Balaam, "Go with the men; but speak only what I tell you to speak" (Num 22:35), he uses the pronoun "I" as if he were God, and he echoes the very words uttered by God a little earlier in the story (see v. 20).

This ambiguity as to the identity of the angel of the Lord also occurs in a number of other stories in which this figure appears. Consider, for example, the story of Hagar, the handmaiden of Sarah with whom Abraham has intercourse (at Sarah's instruction, because she herself cannot conceive). Sarah (who is called "Sarai" in this part of the narrative) grows jealous of the pregnant Hagar and mistreats her, so that Hagar runs away. But God has other plans for Hagar:

> The angel of the Lord found her by a spring of water in the wilder-
> ness, the spring on the way to Shur. And he said, "Hagar, slave-girl of
> Sarai, where have you come from and where are you going?" She said,
> "I am running away from my mistress Sarai." The angel of the Lord
> said to her, "Return to your mistress, and submit to her." The angel of
> the Lord also said to her, "I will so greatly multiply your offspring that
> they cannot be counted for multitude." (Gen 16:7–10)

The angel speaks as if he were God.[9] And when the angelic message is ended, Hagar says, "Have I really seen God and remained alive after seeing him?" (v. 13). Hagar does not distinguish between the angel who visited her and the One whom that angel represents.

Also in the story of Abraham's near sacrifice of his son Isaac, the narrator makes no clear distinction between the Lord and the Lord's angel. It was God who commanded Abraham to sacrifice Isaac, as a test of Abraham's faithfulness (Gen 22:2). It was God who showed Abraham the spot where the burnt offering should be made (v. 3). But it was the angel of the Lord who intervened at the last possible moment to stop the sacrifice, saying, "Do not lay your hand on the boy or do anything to him; for now I know that you fear God, since you have not withheld your son, your only son, from me" (v. 12). The angel's use of the first person pronoun ("You have not withheld your son, your only son, from me") guides the reader's attention away from the angel and toward God, who requested the sacrifice. Somehow, *God is fully present in the words of the angel.*

In the story of the burning bush, at first the angel of the Lord is said to be the one who appears to Moses in the flame (Exod 3:2). Soon afterward, the speaker is said to be "the Lord" or "God" rather than the angel. God (not the angel) says to Moses, "Remove the sandals from your feet, for the place on which you are standing is holy ground" (v. 5). Moses hid his face because "he was afraid to look at God" (v. 6). And so on through the rest of the story. Did the narrator forget that the angel of the Lord had already been intro-duced as the one speaking from the burning bush? The narrator appears to assume that God and God's angel are interchangeable.

How do we account for the easy alternation, in the foregoing stories and in others, between "God" or "the Lord" on the one hand and the "angel of the Lord" on the other? Scholars have devised various explanations. One theory is that the older layers of the tradition spoke without embarrassment of God appearing directly to human beings, but later editors of the stories were troubled by such assertions and therefore substituted "the angel of the Lord" in place of some but not all of the references to God.[10] Another theory is that the distinction drawn between the LORD and the LORD's angel has to do with point of view. Supposedly, biblical authors used the "angel of the LORD" whenever they were describing how God enters into the perception of a human being, but "the LORD" when they were not describing any particular interaction with humans.[11]

This frequent alternation between "LORD" and the "angel of the LORD" expresses a crucial but paradoxical truth. On the one hand, *God is so holy that humans cannot "see the face of God and live"* (Exod 19:21; 33:20; Judg 13:22). In other words, humans cannot encounter God directly. Therefore God's presence must be experienced in some other, more oblique way.[12] On the other hand, *God truly is present in these encounters,* so that when the biblical narrators referred to "God" or "the LORD" instead of to "the angel of the LORD," they were correct. It really *was* God who spoke to Hagar, Abraham, Moses, and others. To try to explain away the biblical stories' switching between the LORD and the LORD's angel misses the point that *both* halves of this paradox are true. James Kugel remarks that the angel in these stories "is not some lesser order of divine being; it is God Himself, but God unrecognized, God intruding into ordinary reality."[13]

According to Exodus, humans cannot see the face of God and live. God's holiness is so great that direct exposure to it would be fatal for weak and sinful mortals. God always remains partially hidden, always transcends our full comprehension. Thus, when Moses asks for God's name, God gives an ambiguous answer, saying something like, "I am who I am" (Exod 3:14)—as if to suggest that the name of God cannot be owned by humans or manipulated by them.[14] God first appears to Moses, not face-to-face, but concealed in a burning bush (Exod 3:2; cf. 3:6). When the Israelites under Moses' leadership reach Mount Sinai, God sets strict bounds around the mountain; any who transgress these bounds are to be put to death (Exod 19:12, 22, 24). And, when Moses later asks to behold God's glory, the prophet is permitted only a glimpse of God's back: "But," God says, "my face shall not be seen" (Exod 33:22).[15] Such pointers to God's holiness—and hence to God's hiddenness— remind us that even the prophets among us cannot fully understand the workings of God, any more than tiny infants can fully understanding the workings of their parents.

But if God remains hidden, then how can humans know God's *presence* (the second half of the paradox)? One answer is that God shows forth God's presence in a manner suited to our human limitations. In John Calvin's terms, whenever God is revealed in material and visible form, this is not because God is like that, but for our sake. In love God condescends or "stoops down" to meet humans where they are.[16] The *mal'ak yhwh* or "angel of the

Lord" is one of the means by which God has taken up contact with earthly beings. Michael Welker interprets such encounters as the infinite God becoming "finite" and "concrete" for humans' benefit. Welker compares and contrasts God's action to that of a human ruler. When a human monarch sends out messengers to the hinterlands to convey a royal decree, the monarch's power and reach are magnified: the messengers accomplish more than the monarch could ever achieve alone. But as messengers *of God,* the angels—however glorious—do not contain or convey the full majesty and infinite wisdom and power of God. The angels represent a *reduction* rather than an expansion of God's power and essence.[17] God is always greater than the messenger, greater even than the sum of all the messengers.

Then, do angels show us that God is near to us and cares for us? Or do angels prove, rather, that God is so remote that we cannot experience divine presence directly? The traditions about the angel of the Lord make both of these points. In some passages the *mal'ak yhwh* points to God's presence, and in other passages the angel reminds us of God's distance or concealment.[18] For example, as the Israelites escape from the Egyptians in the Exodus, the angel is linked to a pillar of cloud and fire that accompanies them—a sign of God's presence (Exod 14:19; as if to underscore the point, a few verses later the narrator refers not to the angel but to "the Lord in the pillar of fire and cloud" [14:24; cf. 23:23]). On the other hand, when God promises to send an angel before the Israelites as they enter into Canaan, the declaration highlights God's transcendence or distance. God says, "But I will not go up among you, or I would consume you on the way, for you are a stiff-necked people" (Exod 33:3).[19] So, the biblical stories about the angel of the Lord remind us *both* that God is partly inaccessible to us (because of God's transcendent holiness) *and* that God is present with us.

This question of how to manage the tension between God's transcendence and God's presence or immanence is a perpetual one in Christian theology. Mary Farrell Bednarowski's definitions are useful: "Broadly defined, immanence refers to the presence of the sacred or of ultimate reality within the world and its inhabitants. Transcendence, by contrast, is a concept traditionally used to designate the uniqueness and the apartness of the divine from creation, and ultimate reality from the penultimate or the transitory."[20] The terms may be academic but the issues are not. Do we understand God to be present in the world, or absent from it? Do all people have ready access to God, or must God's presence be mediated through some other figure or institution? Is the created world suffused with the divine and therefore good, or is it unworthy because it is finite and perishing? Such questions lie also at the heart of any discussion of angels. Are angels a means for the divine to be present in the world? Or do they point, rather, to God's absence from the world—the way a delegate might point to the absence of the CEO from a business meeting?

Over the centuries, emphasis on God's transcendence has often prevailed over stress on God's immanence. God has been seen as ultra-transcendent: so holy, changeless, and infinite that no way can be found to think of the Deity as actually present in or caring for the changing, perishing, created world. Thus, God's role is reduced to that of Creator at the beginning of the cosmos and Judge at the end. Today, popular authors on spirituality often claim to be correcting such a view. Terry Lynn Taylor, for example, broaches her theory of angels as a way to help us get rid of any notion of God as an "oversized parent in the sky" who will punish us for doing things that are "childish or silly." Rather, we should think of God as our partner and of ourselves as God's cocreators.[21] Neil Donald Walsch likewise rejects the view of God as "Holy Desperado"—a view that he says was imposed on him in his childhood, when Christians informed him that his mother would burn in hell because she told fortunes. Walsch responds with a portrait of God as wise and witty conversation partner—as *friend,* or even *pal.*[22] These authors rightly reject a caricature of God as unapproachable and vindictive—a caricature that forgets God's presence and fails to claim God's healing power and love. The problem is that Taylor, Walsch and others *overcorrect* the caricature and so commit the opposite theological error: they forget God's holiness, and fail to give God due honor and respect, even as they exaggerate the capacity of finite humans for moral goodness and self-determination. In short, they demote God and put humans in God's place.

But we can choose to affirm God's transcendence without buying into the portrait of God as remote and tyrannical. By saying that God is transcendent, we can signify that God transcends our finite understanding and our limited human categories—including even the categories of "presence" and "absence." Viewing divine transcendence in this alternate way opens up new possibilities for managing the tension between transcendence and immanence. Instead of trying to strike some sort of delicate balance—say, by affirming that God is 50 percent present and 50 percent absent, or that God mostly remains absent but sporadically intervenes in the world—we may instead affirm that God is both *radically transcendent* and also *radically immanent.* The figures add up to more than 100 percent. God is never fully accessible to us, not because God is remote but because God is so much *more*—more powerful, glorious, righteous, and, indeed, *present*—than we can ever imagine. [23]

Considered together, the various scriptural references to the angel of the

LORD maintain the tension between divine transcendence and divine imma-nence without sacrificing either half of the paradox. The angel is a face of the infinite God that is suited to our limitations as finite beings. God is surpass-ingly holy—so holy that God is not seen directly; indeed, God can never be comprehended fully. God's holiness and righteousness give the Deity war-rant to make demands on us and to judge us when we fall short. But God is not one who sits back to watch us make our mistakes and then to punish us. Rather, God is intimately present to us in every aspect of our lives: God undergirds us with every breath we take, every turn we make. God is nearer to us than we are to ourselves.

Scripture shows God using other means besides angels to take up contact with humanity and to make God's word known. The prophets were one such means. Different biblical authors and different prophets understood and explained the prophetic experience in various ways. For example, prophets were often viewed as bearers of God's spirit, which in some cases could be passed on to others.[24] Other prophets portrayed themselves as having stood in the midst of the divine council. For example, the Hebrew prophet Micaiah ben Imlah said, "Therefore hear the word of the LORD: I saw the LORD sitting on his throne, with all the host of heaven standing beside him to the right and to the left of him" (1 Kgs 22:19).[25] Micaiah sees the LORD speaking with the heavenly advisers who surround him—angels, in later understanding. Other prophets, including Isaiah and Ezekiel, would also speak of being present before the very throne of God (see Chapter 2). And some prophets (including Ezekiel, Zechariah, and the author of Revelation) received God's word through symbolic visions or dreams—visions or dreams so detailed and complex that interpreter-angels sometimes were needed to help the prophets decipher the meaning.[26]

The first Christians were convinced that God's decisive move to take up contact with humans came through the person of Jesus: "Long ago God spoke to our ancestors in many and various ways by the prophets, but in these last days he has spoken to us by a Son, whom he appointed heir of all things, through whom he also created the worlds" (Heb 1:1). Jews had long pondered and written about the "word"—referring not to the written words of Scripture but to God's creative, ordering principle for the cosmos.[27] But the author of Hebrews, like the author of John's Gospel, makes the decisive move of identifying this world-engendering "word" with Jesus of Nazareth (compare John 1:1–18). Some other early Christians went further still: reading the Jewish Scriptures, they concluded that even the angel of the LORD was, in reality, Jesus.[28] One can understand how they drew such a conclusion. Like Jesus—the incarnate word, in their view—the angel of the

Lord represented God's meeting of finite and sinful human beings on a level they could manage.

But the logic behind such a reading of Jesus into accounts of the angel of the Lord went deeper. Many Jews before and during the time of Jesus were deeply interested in angels. Some understood the angel of the Lord as a being completely separate from God—a sort of angelic vizier or right-hand angel, who served as head of the heavenly host and in other important capacities, including as a mediator between God and humans. Further, some Jews routinely appropriated language used in Scripture to describe the angel of the Lord and used it to characterize certain of God's attributes, including God's *word, glory, wisdom, spirit, power,* and *name*—almost as if these aspects of the Deity were themselves independent angels. In other words, quite apart from Christianity there was talk among ancient Jews of God's *word,* God's *glory,* and so forth in terms highly reminiscent of the angel of the Lord. So, when early Christian authors like Justin Martyr connected Jesus with God's word and that word, in turn, with the angel of the Lord, they were not inventing from scratch so much as adding a new layer to well-established ways of reading Scripture.[29]

When do *we* listen for a word from God? When do *we* look for an angel to appear? For many people today, the need and desire to encounter God or God's agent becomes most acute at life's crossroads, the times of crisis and transition. When life is confused, when the future is in turmoil, when hope seems lost, we turn to God. And the Bible bears witness that God often makes God's presence known at just such times. Whether through the angel of the Lord, the Spirit, the prophets, or the incarnate word, God has met the people at the crossroads. Hagar was at a crossroads, convinced that she could not live in the house of Sarai any longer. But the angel of the Lord showed her that the way out of her dilemma was for her to return rather than to run away. Some time later, when she and her child Ishmael had been cast out of the house of Abraham and Sarah and were about to die of thirst, the angel appeared again, with a promise from God that a great nation would come forth from Ishmael. And "then God opened her eyes and she saw a well of water. She went, and filled the skin with water, and gave the boy a drink" (Gen 21:17–19). Abraham was likewise at a crossroads, about to slay the very son through whom God's promises to him would be fulfilled, but the angel stayed Abraham's hand and showed him a ram to offer as sacrifice instead. At these and other such crucial moments, the Lord's angel dissolves the old, accustomed perception of reality and offers *a new way to view and move into the future.* A way that had been rejected—or never considered—becomes the path ahead.[30] But are such hope and guidance available to us now?

ANGELS AND VALUES

Here I turn our attention again to Martha Beck, whose story of her conversion from a Harvard-shaped reality to an angel-shaped one we considered earlier. She and husband, John, gave up their quest for academic and worldly success in order to follow the path toward a new goal—what we might call the goal of "seizing the day" or "living life to the fullest." As in the biblical stories whenever the angels made their presence known, Beck was at a crossroads—a moment of dire need. The angels came to her when she had to choose whether or not to abort the baby, when her life was in danger, and when she was about to give birth. But Beck's conversion was not completed with Adam's birth. For several years, she continued in a state of ill health and confusion about her goal and the means to reach it. All was finally revealed to her during an operation, when she was under general anesthesia and encountered a "Being of Light." The message delivered by this Being is worth quoting at length, for it typifies much of the current angel wisdom:

> While the surgery proceeded, the Being of Light gently explained to me that I was barking up all the wrong trees. I would not find my way back home by fasting, it told me, or by meditating, following endless lists of rules, or even dying. All those things might help, given the right conditions, but not unless I was willing to do something much more difficult. . . . It said that the way back to my real environment, the place where my soul was meant to exist, doesn't lie through any set of codes I will ever find outside of myself. I have to look inward. I have to jettison every sorrow, every terror, every misconception, every lie that stands between my conscious mind and what I know in my heart to be true. Instead of clutching around me all the trappings of a "good" person, a "successful" person, or even a "righteous" person, I have to be exactly what I am, and take the horrible chance that I may be rejected for it. I can't get home by cloaking myself in the armor of any system, social, political, or religious. I have to strip off all that comforting armor and go on naked.[31]

The good life, according to Beck's angelic revealer, is one in which she follows her own, self-fashioned set of values—whatever she "knows in her heart to be true." These values are not simply to be taken over from any established social, political, or religious system. Rather, Beck has to start viewing herself as a free-floating moral agent, disavowing all indebtedness to any larger body of people. She has to "go on naked."

Such radical individualism is a dominant cultural model in American society today. In this model, human selves are viewed as independent or unencumbered entities seeking their own best interests. But, as Robert Bellah and others have pointed out, the model has serious flaws. Above all, it obscures the many ways in which we are dependent on one another:

> We find ourselves not independently of other people and institutions but through them. We never get to the bottom of our selves on our own. We discover who we are face to face and side by side with others in work, love, and learning. All of our activity goes on in relationships, groups, associations, and communities ordered by institutional structures and interpreted by cultural patterns of meaning.[32]

We can never completely strip ourselves of our social, cultural, and institutional contexts. Beck may have given up the Harvard-influenced notion that prestige and intellect and praise will bring happiness. But she did not thereby give up all socially constructed beliefs about the good life. For, as Bellah and his colleagues point out, the very notion of the dignity, worth, and moral autonomy of the individual is "dependent in a thousand ways on a social, cultural, and institutional context that keeps us afloat even when we cannot very well describe it."[33] Nor did Beck give up all socially constructed notions of religion. For example, it is apparent enough that Beck's Mormon childhood and her exposure to various New Age cultural patterns (including, for example, that of the near-death experience) have shaped her perception of the beings who intervene in her life.[34]

Beck, like the biblical authors, tells how angel-like beings (including son Adam) dissolved her old accustomed perception of reality and offered a new way to view and move into the future. They healed her body. But much more than that, they healed her spirit. In doing so, Beck's angels imitated many of the angels of classic and recent films and television shows. Think again of angel Clarence Oddbody, who healed George Bailey of his flawed and self-destructive outlook in *It's a Wonderful Life*. Beck's angels also imitated the angels featured in book after book in the spirituality section of the local bookstore.[35] In much of this angelic self-help literature, angels are beings who work as therapists, or "life coaches," to remove hindrances, encourage self-actualization, and give us whatever it is that each of us needs to thrive. (Beck herself now works as a professional life coach.) Authors of one self-help book write, "Whether we call upon them or not, the angels are with us in our everyday lives. They're ready, willing, and delighted to help us. It doesn't matter what we're doing—meditating, shopping, driving, deep-sea diving—no task is too small, no goal too grand to merit their affectionate attention."[36] But there is no *communal dimension* to the angels' help in *Ex-*

pecting Adam, or in most of the angelic self-help literature; focus is on the self-actualization of individuals. Nor do Beck or other recent authors show awareness of how thoroughly the teachings of their angels have been shaped by modern and postmodern Western culture.[37]

Beck's angels reveal their adherence to the cultural model of radical individualism not only by the values that they teach, but also by the fact that they manifest themselves to her at all. Beck and others promote the idea that each of us is surrounded by benevolent beings, and that we can fully expect these beings to show themselves if we but open our minds to them. The biblical figure of the angel of the LORD, by contrast, was highly selective in his appearances, intervening only to direct the well-being of the people as a whole. No radical individualism here. To be sure, in the Bible, the angel of the LORD appears to individuals (Hagar, Abraham, Jacob, Moses, Balaam, Gideon, the wife of Manoah, etc.), but *always to individuals whose destiny is intertwined with that of Israel.* Hagar will be the mother of a nation, the Ishmaelites. Abraham is "Father Abraham," the patriarch of the Hebrew people. Jacob, later known as Israel, is the namesake of an entire people. Moses is the first and foremost prophet of Israel, who will lead the people out of bondage. Balaam is set to bring blessing upon Israel at a crucial point in its history. Gideon will lead the people against their Midianite oppressors. The wife of Manoah will bear a son, Samson, who will deliver Israel from the Philistines.[38]

During the latter centuries of the Second Temple era, angels became a subject of intense interest in their own right. Some Jews began to think of angels as distinct and identifiable beings with names. Whereas only two angels are named in the Hebrew Scriptures, writings from the last few centuries before the turn of the Common Era (including, for example, *1 Enoch*) name dozens of angels. Perhaps this development resulted from Israel's increased contact with the rich angelology of Zoroastrianism.[39] Or, perhaps the new attention to the heavenly world "was not really new but represents old Israelite popular religion which only finds its way into the literary sources in the postexilic writings."[40] Whatever the origin of such speculation, with so many heavenly beings crowding highways and byways, it is not surprising that some people began to suppose that angels intervened more often and in more routine situations than had been assumed in times past.

The book of Tobit, written in the fourth or third century BCE, introduces us to the angel Raphael. Raphael's name means "God heals." In the story, Raphael masquerades as a human under the alias, Azariah. His charge is a worthy young Jewish man named Tobias. Raphael has been sent to perform several tasks. The first task is to heal Tobit, the righteous father of Tobias, who had been struck blind. Raphael's second task is to aid a kinswoman of Tobias named Sarah, who has been plagued by a vicious demon named Asmodeus. This demon has killed seven husbands of Sarah on her wedding nights. By Jewish law, Tobias is next in line to wed the unfortunate Sarah (Tob 7:11). The third task to be accomplished by Raphael is for him to serve as guardian to Tobias, protecting him on a lengthy journey he must undertake to recover some of his father's money and, although Tobias does not know it ahead of time, to take Sarah as his bride.[41]

The story is told well, with plenty of opportunities for readers to chuckle at the human characters' unwitting interactions with the angel. For example, when Tobias and the still-incognito Raphael are about to set out on their journey, Tobit prays, "May God in heaven bring you safely there and return you in good health to me; *and may his angel accompany you both for your safety, my son*" (Tob 5:17; emphasis added). Near the end of the story, Azariah finally reveals that he is the angel Raphael, "one of the seven angels who stand ready and enter before the glory of the LORD" (12:15).[42] He also informs Tobit that in days past he himself had been the one who had read the record of his and Sarah's prayers for healing before the glory of the LORD (12:11–15).

When we look at how Raphael is portrayed in Tobit, we can see evidence for the emergence of new ideas about angels, some of which are still prevalent today. The angel of the LORD as depicted in the Hebrew Scriptures had been very elusive—here one minute and gone the next. But Raphael (like today's film and television angels) sticks around for a while. He has a name and a job description: he is one of the seven from God's innermost circle.[43] In that capacity he carries the prayers of the righteous before God. On earth he serves as a guardian to protect people from harm. He heals blindness and rids a young woman of a terrible demonic affliction. At one point in the story he miraculously travels to Egypt, and returns before his own presence is missed—traveling, as some say today, "at the speed of thought." Finally, Raphael is sent by God to solve problems that beset a few individuals, rather than to intervene in the course of the whole people of God. So, here in Tobit we seem to find a biblical angel who resembles many of the angels depicted in recent films, television shows, and angelic self-help books, in that he helps and directs an individual and his loved ones, rather than the whole nation of Israel.

But when we look closely we also note differences. The most important is a contrast in "values" (to use current jargon). Raphael's vision of the good life is not the one upheld by Beck's near-death angel, or by so many of the angels that we read or hear about today. To be sure, then—as now—the prize that the angel offers is God's approval and the divine reward of prosperity or well-being. But in Tobit, the way to obtain that prize is *by walking the path of obedience to God's law*. God's approval goes not to those who "go on naked"—that is, to those who refuse to acknowledge the authority of cultural or communal norms. Rather, divine approval and aid go to those who fulfill communal expectations by revering and honoring God, observing the Jewish festivals and upholding the laws pertaining to food and purity, marrying women from their own tribe, exercising self-discipline, and—above all—giving alms.[44] "For almsgiving saves from death and purges away every sin. Those who give alms will enjoy a full life, but those who commit sin and do wrong are their own worst enemies" (Tob 12:9–10). By obeying Torah, Tobit repeatedly shows that he is wholly devoted to the upward call of serving God. Not only does he perform great acts of almsgiving, but he even ventures out to bury Israelites whom the foreign occupiers of the land had killed and cast aside, thereby risking his own punishment or execution at the oppressors' hand.

We can't dismiss the emphasis on almsgiving and on burying fellow Israelites as incidental to the narrative, for this emphasis is key to the author's understanding of God and the angels who serve God. By paying so much attention to acts of charity, the author makes the point that all actions (human, angelic, divine) must follow the rules and values of that author's own community. Tobit is viewed as righteous because he strengthens the community by upholding its weaker members even when all his family and his neighbors fail to do so. Sarah is righteous because, through her sexual purity, she upholds the honor of her father and guards the property rights of her family.[45] God is righteous because God answers the entreaties of these two who have helped to maintain the social fabric. Raphael is righteous because he works to support communal norms by driving the antisocial demon out of the country, and by arranging a marriage for Tobias and Sarah that respects the communal norm of endogamy (marriage within the clan, tribe, nation).[46] So, although Tobit, Tobias, and Sarah play no role in major events in Israel's history, they perfectly embody the ideals of the people as a whole. Their eyes are focused squarely on God and they are wholly devoted to serving God.

In sum, in Tobit's world, the angel upholds the cultural standards of the author who portrayed him. Analogously, the angels portrayed today typically uphold the ideals of popular spirituality ("radical individualism," "seizing the day," "living life to the fullest," and so forth) prevalent in late twentieth and early twenty-first century U.S. culture.

HEALING, TRUTH, AND JESUS

The angel of the LORD and the angel Raphael are preeminent among the biblical figures who heal blindness and set people on a new and better course. But they are not the only ones who do so. In the New Testament, it is Jesus who commands our attention as healer and source of truth. Jesus represents both God's presence or immanence (Matt 2:23) and the fullness of God's transcendent glory (Matt 17:1–8; 2 Cor 4:4–6). Luke tells us that Jesus spoke words of the prophet Isaiah to announce the shape of the mission he was about to undertake: "The Spirit of the LORD is upon me, because he has anointed me to bring good news to the poor. He has sent me to proclaim release to the captives and recovery of sight to the blind, to let the oppressed go free, to proclaim the year of the LORD's favor" (Luke 4:18–19; cf. Isa 61:1–2; 58:6). Luke is careful to show how Jesus fulfilled his mandate literally, releasing those who were physically bound and healing those who were physically blind. But Jesus' words as reported by Luke overflow this literal meaning. Each item in the mandate points beyond any particular instance of literal, physical fulfillment to the radically new and transforming character of encountering Jesus. An encounter with him brings change as radical as freedom to captives, as astonishing as sight to the blind.

Among the New Testament healing stories, Mark's account of Jesus' two-stage healing of the blind man at Bethsaida is especially rich in its symbolism. Jesus lays hands on the man, but at first he sees only indistinctly. He says, "I can see people, but they look like trees, walking." So Jesus touches him again, "and he looked intently and his sight was restored" (Mark 8:22–26). The story foreshadows Peter's progress—or, rather, his lack of progress—in understanding. A few verses later, Peter confesses Jesus to be "the Christ," but then rebels when Jesus predicts his own death. Like the blind man after Jesus' first touch, Peter sees—but not yet clearly. He still does not comprehend that Jesus is to be a *suffering* Messiah. Not until after Jesus' death and resurrection will Peter receive the second touch, the one that will give him full sight. In the meantime, Jesus says, Peter is "setting his mind not on divine things but on human things" (vv. 31–33).[47]

In Luke's Gospel, Jesus sometimes operates in angelic ways. For example, Crispin Fletcher-Louis shows how in Luke's story of the call of Peter and the miraculous catch of fish Jesus is portrayed much like an angel (Luke 5:1–11). Peter had been working all night and had caught no fish, but when Jesus told him to put out the nets into the deep water Peter obediently did so and "caught so many fish that their nets were beginning to break" (v. 6). When Peter saw this, "he fell down at Jesus' knees saying, 'Go away from me,

LORD, for I am a sinful man!'" (v. 8). Fletcher-Louis points out that Jesus' instruction about where to find what Peter is seeking, Peter's awe, his sense of shame before Jesus, and Jesus' words of assurance ("Fear not") are all best explained by analogy to biblical stories of angels.[48]

Or, consider Luke's story of the Transfiguration, when the eyes of three disciples are opened to glimpse Jesus in his heavenly glory. Some ancient Jews believed that all the righteous will be made like angels at the end time. Accordingly, many recent commentators have said that the Transfiguration accounts are designed to help the disciples—and us as readers—anticipate such end-time glory. But Fletcher-Louis argues that the more relevant background material may be found in Jewish stories about heavenly angels, or in stories about a few ultrarighteous persons who become angels *before* the end time. The Transfiguration reminds Fletcher-Louis of the description of God's principal angel found in Daniel 10, the transformation of Enoch to an angel as reported in noncanonical documents, and the coming of the angelic son of man on the clouds of heaven as described in Daniel 7 and alluded to elsewhere in the New Testament.[49]

Luke's account of the road to Emmaus has also been influenced by earlier accounts of angels. As the two disciples were walking along the road, "Jesus himself came near and went with them, but their eyes were kept from recognizing him." Jesus and the disciples conversed. Afterward, when he was at table with them, "he took bread, blessed and broke it, and gave it to them. Then their eyes were opened, and they recognized him; and he vanished from their sight" (Luke 24:30–31). John E. Alsup notes the extent to which scriptural narratives such as the appearance of the angels to Abraham at the oaks of Mamre in Genesis 18–19 and the account of Raphael as Tobias' traveling companion in Tobit 5–12 stand behind this story of the Emmaus road.[50] In Tobit, for example, Raphael acts incognito, as Jesus will on the Emmaus road. After Raphael reveals his identity, he ascends to heaven "and they could see him no more" (Tob 12:21; compare Luke's account of Jesus' ascension in Acts 1:9). In the Genesis story of Abraham, heavenly beings allegedly on a journey "are entertained by mortals who seem unaware of their guests' identity."[51] But even more than such narrative details, it is the central event in the account of the Emmaus road—Jesus' healing of blindness—that evokes biblical stories of angels. Jesus, like the angel of the LORD in the story of Balaam and elsewhere, dissolves the old, accustomed way of looking at things. Once the disciples' eyes have been opened they will never see the same way again.

Jesus' greatest healing is that of Saul, the Pharisee—later known as the Apostle Paul (Acts 9:1–19; 22:6–16; 26:12–18). Saul has been ferociously pursuing Christians and dragging them to prison. He is convinced that the new Christian movement, called "the Way," runs counter to the purposes of God. But when Saul is traveling on the road to Damascus, a bright light from heaven flashes around him and he falls to the ground. He hears a voice say to him,

> I am Jesus whom you are persecuting. But get up and stand on your feet; for I have appeared to you for this purpose, to appoint you to serve and testify to the things in which you have seen me and to those in which I will appear to you. I will rescue you from your people and from the Gentiles—to whom I am sending you *to open their eyes so that they may turn from darkness to light.* (Acts 26:15–18; emphasis added)

When Saul rises, he can see nothing. Others have to lead him by the hand. "For three days he was without sight, and neither ate nor drank" (Acts 9:9). Before healing Saul, Jesus must first show him how blind he really is! Three days later a disciple lays hands upon Saul and "something like scales" fall from his eyes. Saul's eyes then open onto a new world—a world where he knows Jesus as Lord and himself as Jesus' servant. Like Balaam, Saul has been given a new perception of reality; the old perception fell along with the scales. The "Way" that he once rejected has become the path before him.[52]

In the letter to the Philippians, Paul writes about how coming to know Jesus has changed his life. After listing out all his qualifications and accomplishments in Judaism he writes, "Yet whatever gains I had, these I have come to regard as loss because of Christ. More than that, I regard everything as loss because of the surpassing value of knowing Christ Jesus my Lord. For his sake I have suffered the loss of all things, and I regard them as dung, in order that I may gain Christ" (Phil 3:7).[53] By his own account, Paul had been zealous but moving in the wrong direction. Jesus turned him around and set him on the path toward a new goal, "the goal for the prize of the heavenly call of God in Christ Jesus" (Phil 3:14). Paul's ideas about what mattered in life changed. "Dung" or "filth"—those are the strong words he now uses to describe what he once regarded as his great successes in life. Today it still takes the strongest words we can find to describe how Christ can transform us. We struggle to find images that are up to the task. Luke spoke of "blindness healed" and "bonds broken." The author of John's Gospel spoke of "second birth." Today, David Ford speaks of a "shift in the boundaries of our being."[54]

The Jesus who transformed the disciples on the road to Emmaus, who transformed Saul to Paul, and who transforms us is the *crucified* Jesus. Here

is the greatest difference between Jesus and the angels. For angels, not being
of flesh, do not know the weaknesses of flesh. But Jesus—though he lives—is
always, first, the Human One. Fletcher-Louis shows how, in the Emmaus
Road story, Luke counters his own angelomorphic portrayal of Jesus by insisting that he ate a piece of fish. It was axiomatic in Jewish antiquity that
angels do not eat—or at least they do not eat earthly food. By showing Jesus
eating, Luke makes the point that his identity cannot be reduced to that of
an angel: he is divine like the angels, but he is also human.[55] His experience
as a human epitomizes the trials that humans must endure. Jesus is the one
who knows in his own person not only what it means to be hungry, but also
what it means to be mocked, falsely accused, beaten, betrayed, and utterly
forsaken. He is the one who knows what it means to have his faith and obedience tested to the utmost. Because he has lived through such trials, Jesus
understands our trials in a way that no ordinary angel ever could. But he
does not offer us an easy way out of such trials—only a way through them.

The self-help angels say: "BE SPECIFIC AND ASK BIG."[56] But Jesus says of
Paul: "I myself will show him how much he must suffer for the sake of my
name" (Acts 9:16). To us Jesus says: "Whoever does not take up the cross and
follow me is not worthy of me" (Matt 10:38). When we take up the cross we
commit everything we have and are to the quest for God and God's righteousness. The self-help angels serve individual wants and desires, and make
no demands. They urge us to ask for their aid in getting what we think we
require. But the crucified and risen Jesus heals us by *reordering* our desires.
He brings to the surface the "desire that lives beneath all desires and that
only God can satisfy."[57] This one desire, which overwhelms all others, is the
desire for God—what Paul calls "the heavenly call of God in Christ Jesus."
Christ fills our mind and heart with this desire until every other desire pales
by comparison. Jesus said, "The kingdom of heaven is like a merchant in
search of fine pearls; on finding one pearl of great value, he went and sold all
that he had and bought it" (Matt 13:45). So too we who would follow Jesus
"sell all that we have." We exercise control over what we own. When we "sell
all," we relinquish that control. We say, "Jesus, this property, this family, this
career, this life are no longer mine. They are yours." And we have made a
good exchange. We have purchased the pearl of great price.

David Ford writes of the longing in our day "for something magical, the
quick fix, the miraculous touch or medicine, the dramatic release." Occasionally that kind of miracle does happen. Certainly many of the recent angelic interventions reported in the media qualify as miraculous, quick-fix
solutions. Ford notes that Jesus, too, gave quick-fix help by healing people
and feeding them. "But the thrust of his teaching," Ford writes, "was to get at

the roots of evil and suffering, and his message of the kingdom of God was about a healing that involved love, trust, compassion, forgiveness, and radically inclusive hospitality. He faced the fact that that sort of healing can only be offered by those who embody it, whatever the cost."[58] Jesus embodied such healing in his own life and death—a death that Ford calls the "healing exchange" at the heart of Christian faith and worship. As Jesus' disciples we are called to follow him, to live and die like him, and so to become like him the "balm for all wounds."[59] Mysteriously, our own healing begins when we commit to living our lives for him so that others might be healed.

CONCLUSION

The word "angel" means "messenger." In popular culture, angels often serve as messengers who bring healing truth. They come to those who suffer from spiritual, psychological, or emotional blindness and cause the scales to fall from their eyes. The angels open up a new way to view and move into the future. Attention in many or most of the modern accounts of angelic epiphanies is on healing the individual's distress. Angels enable individuals to attain personal satisfaction and fulfillment—for example, by teaching them that happiness is not found in the things that the world views as markers of success, but in the magic of everyday life.

In the Bible, too, angels are messengers—messengers sent by God. The "angel of the Lord" not only speaks the truth, but enables people to receive it. The angel opens Balaam's blind eyes and thereby enables him to discern that God's intent is not to curse Israel but to bless it. The angel relieves Hagar of despair and helps her to see that the way out of her dilemma in Sarah's house is, remarkably, to return to it. The angel answers all Moses' protests about his inadequacy for the task God has given him, and tells the prophet that he will be given the right words at the opportune time: "Who gives speech to mortals? Who makes them mute or deaf, seeing or blind? Is it not I, the Lord? Now go, I will be with your mouth and teach you what you are to speak" (Exod 4:11–12). Moses was finally persuaded that he had a part to play as servant and leader in the divine plan for God's people. Other biblical figures—including Gideon, Abraham, Hagar, the wife of Manoah, and Jacob—were shown by the angel of the Lord that they, too, had important roles to play, either as leaders or as parents. The angel was God's agent to serve these people, not for the sake of their individual happiness or fulfillment, but so that they could in turn serve God and the people of God.

The biblical figure of the "angel of the Lord" shows us that God is both beyond or hidden from us and also present to us. An angel or some other mediator is necessary, in the biblical view, for no mortal can look directly upon God's countenance. God is too vast, too holy for our feeble human minds to comprehend fully. Unmediated, God's holiness would consume us. And yet, angels also convey that God is here with us, concerned about the welfare of God's people, and willing to intervene to set them on the right path. Through the angels, the infinite God takes up contact with finite human creatures. The angels—glorious and wise and powerful though they may be—convey God's presence but not the fullness of God's glory. They demonstrate God's willingness to meet humans where they are.

We have seen how some popular authors who write about angels use them as a corrective to a view of God as remote, harsh, and judgmental. These authors claim that God is not a tyrant but our friend. For such authors, angels represent the *immanence* or immediate presence of the divine in our world. The message is that God is good, the world is good, and we ourselves are also good. But, in reacting against the caricature of God as distant and unapproachable, these authors overestimate the human capacity for righteousness and fail to give God due honor. It is more helpful to stress both the *radical immanence* of God and also the Deity's *radical transcendence*. In affirming God's immanence we mean that God is intimately present to each of us and indeed to all the created world. In affirming God's transcendence we mean, not that God is outside the world, but that God radically exceeds all our finite human capacities and attainments and our understandings of power, glory, righteousness, wisdom, service, presence, and love.

Both ancient and modern depictions of angels convey the moral values important to particular authors and readers. In the angelic self-help literature of recent years, angels are invoked as ones who heal and guide individuals to a higher level of self-actualization. As in the Bible, the angels in such recent presentations serve as agents of healing and messengers of truth. The truth they convey generally pertains to problems with personal relationships, attitudes, and assumptions about the purpose of life and the achievement of individual happiness. Martha Beck's Being-of-Light told her that she must not look to established religion or any other institution for truth but must instead listen to the voice within her. But even our innermost voices speak to us using the languages and conceptual models we have learned from our culture and social institutions in which we live, work, and play.

Angels depicted in the Bible and in other ancient Jewish and Christian sources openly uphold God's values as understood in the particular times and places of those who authored the depictions. Not only the messages that such angels convey but also the times and places of their appearances reflect a commitment to communal norms and to the flourishing of the community rather than to the flourishing of the individual only. In other words, in the scriptural accounts, when the angels make their presence known, it is not to just any individuals, but to those whose destiny is intertwined with the future of *the whole people of God.* Angels guide such persons as Moses, Abraham, Hagar, and Jacob onto a new path—a path not previously seen or imagined. Through such appearances, the angels shape the destiny of the whole people, that they might obey God and uphold the values of God.

For Christians, Jesus is the agent of healing and messenger of truth par excellence. New Testament authors depict Jesus as the one who heals people's physical bodies and their broken or blinded spirits. These ancient authors recognize the similarities between Jesus' work and that of angels, and sometimes portray Jesus in angel-like terms: as when Jesus appears in heavenly or angelic glory at the Transfiguration, or when he appears to the disciples on the road to Emmaus and then vanishes from their sight. Jesus, like biblical angels, conveys God's truth through the words he speaks. But, unlike the angels, Jesus also reveals God's truth by the fleshly life he lived. He obeys God throughout agonizing trials, he labors for "the least of these," he feeds the hungry and sets the captives free, he stands up for truth and righteousness even when it will cost him his life. In his living, in his dying, and in his living again Jesus is the salve that heals our blindness and our wounds. He heals, paradoxically, by calling us to follow him in a life of service—a life devoted to bringing to others the message of God's truth and the healing balm of God's forgiveness and God's love. The miracles of healing that Jesus effects are not always quick-fix solutions but they are miracles nonetheless—as any who have been healed by him can attest.

The question of the extent and modes of God's presence in the world lies at the heart of any discussion of angels, as we have seen. In the next chapter, we turn to consider in more depth how biblical and modern authors have depicted their experiences of coming into God's presence, and the roles ascribed to angels in those remarkable encounters.

2

Angels at the Throne

Entering into God's Presence

IN SEARCH OF THE SACRED

How can we know that God exists? Where can we find those sacred moments we need to assure us that we are not alone? We want to encounter the Holy. We want to transcend the limitations of our physical sight and our physical bodies. We want to be transported outside ourselves. We yearn to find ourselves caught up in something much greater, much more beautiful than what we have known before.

America is and always has been a nation of religious seekers. But by some accounts the quest for experience of the divine has reached new, epic proportions—what has been called a "Third Great Awakening." The chief impulses behind this widespread flourishing of spirituality have not come from institutionalized, mainstream religion. For many people caught up in the quest the emphasis has not been on finding God within the gathered body of God's people.[1] Rather, the sacred is being pursued through more individualized means: through encounters with nature, for example, or through prayer, meditation, or other consciousness-altering means. Much energy in this new awakening is devoted to opening the "inward doors of perception" so that people might experience a higher consciousness, a more intense level of reality. Many are seeking or claiming "peak experiences" or "sacred moments"—moments of heightened awareness of the Holy, which they seek to integrate into everyday existence to sanctify all of earthly life.[2] Such peak experiences take various forms, but, for some, they are taking the form of encounters with angels.

40

Narrators from the biblical era also report sacred moments experienced by the characters whose stories they tell. Such experiences occur in dreams and in visions, in moments of spiritual and bodily transport. In the most astonishing accounts, characters enter into the very throne room of God, where angels dwell, to hear messages from God or to participate with the angels in the celestial worship of God. What can we learn from these extraordinary accounts? How do they resemble and differ from the peak experiences claimed by many today? And how can the ancient accounts of such experiences inform the living of everyday life in the present era?

In this chapter, I will begin by looking at modern stories in which angels serve as bearers of God's presence. Then I will consider several analogous biblical and noncanonical ancient narratives, including visions of the heavenly throne room or temple and accounts of early Jewish and Christian worship. Through this study of certain ancient and modern depictions of angels, we can perhaps learn something about what it means to be "caught up in the Spirit"—given over to the reality of God, whose greatness, hospitality, and love elicit our deepest devotion.

ANGELS AND DIVINE PRESENCE IN POPULAR THOUGHT

Martha Beck's experience of being "touched by angels" during her pregnancy (recounted in her book *Expecting Adam,* discussed in Chapter 1) was unique in its details. Nonetheless, in general terms her experience followed a well-attested pattern of unusual coincidences, paranormal occurrences, and full-blown angelic epiphanies that compel the one experiencing them to reevaluate his or her life and then to live it in a new and fuller way. Beck's experience occurred in stages. An initial epiphany awakened her senses and filled her with a sense of overwhelming, transforming love. For her, it was like being given "a whole pan of brownies." But it wasn't enough; she yearned for more. She wore herself out trying to trigger a repeat of the experience. Several years later she finally got what she wanted: an encounter with a being-of-light, who instructed her to stop looking for fulfillment from sources outside herself (see Chapter 1, p. 28). For Beck this second encounter was another "pan of brownies."

Eileen Elias Freeman, author of several popular books on angels, tells of a life-changing encounter with her guardian angel when she was just five years old. She had been an unusually fearful child—afraid of many things, but especially of death. After her grandmother died her fears reached an all-time high, until she refused to sleep at night. Then, her angel appeared. It emerged out of a silvery mist as a human-like figure, bathed in light. The angel told her that she should not worry about her grandmother, who was happy in heaven with her loved ones. "Always remember, there is nothing to be afraid of," her angel continued. In that single, transforming moment Freeman was released from her many fears. "The angel had subtly changed more than my perception of death—he had altered my whole fearful approach to life." As Freeman grew, her memory of that early experience sustained her. "It was solace when life became sad. It was encouragement at dark moments. It was joyful affirmation whenever I felt the light and love of God filling my life. It was a constant reminder of God's love for me."[3]

The early meeting with her guardian angel was not Freeman's last such encounter. In 1979, that angel and others began to speak to Freeman. She reports that they taught her a number of things about the angelic hierarchy and about angels' nature and abilities. In her first such revelatory experience, Freeman was sitting in her living room one evening when she "began to sense the presence of God in an unusual way." Gradually she became less and less conscious of her surroundings, and was drawn deep inside her own heart or soul, where she reports that she "saw the shadow of God, so bright I could not look at it." The vision filled her with light and peace. "It seemed as though all of the conflicting thoughts and duties and attitudes we all must deal with daily had been evened out, smoothed away; and I was so utterly tranquil I have no words to describe it." After awhile, Freeman reports, she heard a voice coming from within the center of her being. The voice said, "I am Enniss, servant of God, and your guardian by divine grace; and you are my ward in this world."[4] It was the first time Freeman's angel had ever disclosed his name to her, but she knew intuitively that the name was right. Three other angels also identified themselves to her at that time. Moved by her mystical experience, Freeman began to spend considerable time each day "in solitary prayer and meditation, not trying to analyze, but just to be open to grace." She writes that she would often receive "what I believed and still do believe, were insights from God through Enniss about the dimension called heaven and the angelic beings who help us humans in our quest to live in the fullness of that dimension."[5]

Betty Eadie also experienced a revelation of heaven and angelic beings, and years later reported her insights in a *New York Times* best seller, *Embraced by the Light,* billed as "the most profound and complete near-death experience ever." Jesus stood at the center of Eadie's vision, which occurred when she slipped into the state of death following an operation. But three angels also played a prominent role in her experience, as the ones who guided her to the Master. She learned that before her own incarnation at birth, she had spent eternities with these particular angelic beings. Moreover, she was later informed, spirits from "the other side" regularly help humans in their progression on the path to enlightenment. The three monk-like angels who had been her eternal friends conveyed Eadie to Jesus, who in turn welcomed her with the most unconditional love she had ever felt. "I felt his enormous spirit," Eadie writes, "and knew that I had always been a part of him, that in reality I had never been away from him. And I knew that I was worthy to be with him, to embrace him."[6] Jesus proceeded to reveal to Eadie all knowledge about the nature and purpose of earthly life, suffering, and death. She comments, "The word 'omniscient' had never been more meaningful to me. Knowledge permeated me. In a sense it *became* me, and I was amazed at my ability to comprehend the mysteries of the universe simply by reflecting on them."[7] For example, Eadie learned that almost everything that happens on earth, even that which is seemingly evil, happens for a purpose. "The hand of God, and the path we chose before we came here, guide many of our decisions and even many of the seemingly random experiences we have."[8] Eadie learned how we actually *choose* many of the painful or bad things that happen to us, and how we can draw on the powers of heaven to be healed. Above all else, Eadie learned we are to love God and one another, for "greater joy will come to us through love than in any other way."[9] After learning these things, Eadie was returned to life and consciousness, for her time was not yet come.

Beck, Freeman, and Eadie are all seekers, searching for light and peace. Each comes at the search from a different angle. Though raised as a Mormon, Beck seeks not the God of Mormons, but a nameless divine force operating within her being. Freeman is a Catholic and sees her God as the Judeo-Christian God and her angel as her assigned guardian angel. Eadie is part Sioux Indian, with both Catholic and Methodist upbringing; in her early life, caretakers had terrified her with images of God as demanding and judgmental. She perceives the loving God of her vision to be Jesus Christ. Despite their differences, Beck, Freeman, and Eadie all seek and find sacred moments in the form of encounters with angels who assure them that all is right with God, that they are loved, and that inner tranquillity is within their grasp. Moreover, all three have become convinced that angels routinely help mortals to live in the fullness of the heavenly dimension. Freeman, for example, insists that angels care for each of us ceaselessly and are in constant touch with us. We cannot force them to appear to us in visible form, she contends, but we can and should establish rapport with them by seeking God and the things that are above. She recommends simple methods of prayer and meditation to help open our minds and hearts to divine guidance. When we open ourselves in this way, there is no helpful task that is too menial for the angels to perform.

Other authors are likewise confident that we can tune into angelic wisdom by meditative means, and are bolder and more elaborate than Freeman in describing the necessary techniques for making contact and conversing with one's angel(s). For example, authors of the popular volume *Ask Your Angels* outline a lengthy four-step procedure for angel-consultation, designated "the GRACE process." The four steps are "Grounding," "Releasing," "Aligning," and "Conversing." The final "E" in the acronym stands for "Enjoying (The Angel Oracle)." It is an alternative, quick-response method of divination using angel-tarot cards, said to be perfect for those times when you are "too caught up in the chaos of your life to sit down and dialogue with your angel." The four steps of the (full-length) GRACE process are designed to help one move out of an ordinary state of mind into "Higher Mind." When we are in a state of Higher Mind, the authors explain, we can meet the angels on their customary frequency of vibration, which is finer than ours.[10]

Alma Daniel, Timothy Wyllie, and Andrew Ramer, the authors of *Ask Your Angels,* view human beings as part and parcel of the divine. An angel named "LNO," the "kick-ass" guide or guardian to Alma Daniel, explains the human condition:

> Within each human is the divine spark, the God That Is. Through the soul's descent into physical matter, that spark becomes covered over, hidden, yet it remains within each human individual—and indeed within each living thing. Our function is to ignite the spark within, to fill you not with "our" thoughts, but to connect you with the know-ingness that you already possess. You forget. Humans forget because the descent into matter lowers consciousness and brings about for-getfulness.[11]

LNO's explanation coheres with a theory (broached later in *Ask Your Angels*) that each person's angel is actually his or her Higher Self, which became separated at the time of embodiment. "From this standpoint, meeting your angel is reconnecting with another part of yourself."[12] In other words, according to this theory the angels encountered through the GRACE process are indeed a figment (or a fragment?) of each person's imagination—but that is not a bad thing. Such ambiguity regarding the spirits' identity or separateness from the human(s) with whom they communicate is typical for the New Age phenomenon of channeling, communicating with spirit entities.[13]

Belief in the essential unity of the Higher Self with the divine pervades not just *Ask Your Angels* but a number of recent best-selling books on angels (and on popular spirituality in general). In theological circles, such belief would be called a form of monism, the notion that an ultimate or absolute reality encompasses and transcends everything that exists. This outlook is characteristic of various religious and philosophical traditions from the East, including Hinduism. In some western variants of monism (such as the one presupposed in *Ask Your Angels*), God is said to be located within the self, so that "if I go deeply enough or high enough within myself, I will find God."[14] Thus, Neale Donald Walsch reports in *Friendship with God* that God told him: "There is only One of Us. You and I are One," and that the soul is "the part of Me that is closest to you," so that to know God, "all you have to do is truly know your own soul."[15] And various authors refer to humans as cocreators with angels, or even cocreators with God. Such close identification of the human self with the divine helps to account for the psychologizing of spirituality—the "turning of attention away from the world and into the never-ending realms of the psyche"[16]—evident in so many of these best-selling books, including *Ask Your Angels*. The psychotherapeutic steps of the GRACE process put one in touch with one's angel(s) *and* with one's Inmost or Higher Self, which are seen as more or less the same thing.

There is another "ism" besides monism at work in *Ask Your Angels, Embraced by the Light, Expecting Adam,* and some other recent books on angels: it is gnosticism, or at any rate a modern version (or versions) of that very ancient school of thought. The ancient gnostics were a Christian-influenced sect dating back to the mid-second century CE or perhaps somewhat earlier. Gnostics told elaborate stories of creation that drew on then-popular interpretations of Plato as well as the biblical book of Genesis. According to these gnostic accounts of creation, the physical world was not created by the highest, transcendent God, but by a lesser deity, the Demiurge. To counter this unauthorized process of creation by the Demiurge, the highest God provided humanity with a spark of the divine substance. Gnostics claimed that *gnosis* (literally "knowledge") of these origins and of their own true spiritual nature would help to free them from bondage to the physical world, and ultimately enable them to achieve salvation by returning to the Kingdom of Light.[17]

Rather than adopting wholesale the elaborate creation myth of ancient gnosticism, modern gnostics zero in on the ancient claim that humans are spiritual creatures now bound by material existence, but still possessing a spark of the divine. In both ancient and modern gnosticism, it is *gnosis*— acquaintance with ourselves and with God—that can lead us from bondage of the flesh into spiritual freedom. Modern gnostics claim that when we acquire the requisite knowledge, we are actually regaining what we already knew in a previous spiritual life, but forgot at the time of our descent from spiritual to bodily existence.[18]

In the modern versions of gnosticism, any notion of sin—of human failure to live up to divine standards for life—is minimal. Instead of sin there is *ignorance,* for which the solution is *knowledge.* Thus, while on her heavenly tour, Betty Eadie is made to see how often she had wronged people and how her wrongs had a ripple effect on others. But rather than chastising or judging her for her wrongs, Jesus told her that she is judging herself too critically. "You're being too harsh on yourself," he says. He then shows her how she had never really made any mistakes; even her harmful actions toward others had been pre-arranged (in some cases by angels) to bring Eadie to "higher levels of knowledge." [19]

Like the modern authors surveyed here, biblical authors attest that God *seeks us out.* And, in the person of the LORD's angel, God meets key biblical characters where they are. But the encounter with God or God's angel typically produces in such characters, not a sense of well-being and peace, but—at least initially—an awareness of their own frailty or of their own sinfulness. Let us begin the study of such encounters with the stories of Jacob.

JACOB AND THE ANGELS

Jacob is fleeing from his twin brother, Esau, who threatened to kill him for tricking their father, Isaac, into blessing him instead of Esau (Gen 27:41–45). On his way to Haran, Jacob stops for the night at Bethel and lies down, using a large stone for his pillow. He dreams of a ladder or a stairway extending from earth up into heaven (28:10–17). Perhaps the stairway resembled the Mesopotamian structures called ziggurats, stairways attached to temple towers that priests would ascend and descend, carrying communication from heaven to earth and back.[20] In Jacob's dream, not priests but angels traverse up and down the steps. What were the angels on that stairway to heaven doing? Centuries later, rabbis would speculate that the angels wanted to compare the earthly, human Jacob to the image of Jacob engraved on God's heavenly throne: "And he [Jacob] dreamt . . . and the angels who had accompanied him from his father's house went up to announce to the angels on high: 'Come and see the righteous man [Jacob] whose likeness is set upon the divine throne, the one whom you have wanted to see.' Then the holy angels of God 'went up and down to gaze upon him.'" (*Frg. Tg. Neoph.,* Gen 28:12)[21] The biblical account itself gives no hint of the angels' motive. Still, their presence in Jacob's dream is meaningful. Their easy going and coming seem to signify the nearness of the heavenly realm.[22]

Heaven is nearer, even, than the image of the stairway suggests. Jacob, asleep, dreamily ponders the silent, marching angels. And even as he dreams, God comes to stand beside him. Not angels but God! Not far away but at his head![23] The LORD had made a covenant with Jacob's grandfather, Abraham, and had carried that covenant on through Jacob's father, Isaac. Now the LORD folds Jacob into the covenant. God speaks to Jacob and tells him that his descendants will be as numerous as the dust of the earth.[24] God promises to bring Jacob back into the land from which he now flees and to abide with him throughout the time of his troubles. Neither in this incident nor prior to it has Jacob actively sought God. James L. Kugel comments, "Jacob has done nothing in particular to bring about this dream vision and is in fact frightened by it; if it were up to him, he would presumably have chosen to do without it."[25] But when God seeks Jacob and finds him, Jacob is moved to speak and act. Filled with awe, he declares that God is present. He worships God, upends his stone pillow as a memorial, and vows his loyalty to God. By his actions Jacob lays claim to the promises he has just heard. He names the place Bethel, for "House of God." God has seized Jacob and moved him from ignorance of God's presence to awareness.

The author of Genesis refers to several more encounters of Jacob with both God and the angels (32:1–2, 22–32; cf. 35:9–15). In one of these mysterious episodes Jacob is left alone, and a man wrestles with him until daybreak. When the wrestling match comes to a draw, this unidentified "man" puts Jacob's hip out of joint and demands that Jacob let him go. Jacob, who had wrestled his brother Esau once for priority in birth order and again, years later, for their father's blessing, now refuses to let the mysterious person go until he grants a blessing.

> Then the man said, "You shall no longer be called Jacob, but Israel, for you have striven with God and with humans, and have prevailed." Then Jacob asked him, "Please tell me your name." But he said, "Why is it that you ask my name?" And there he blessed him. So Jacob called the place Peniel, saying, "For I have seen God face to face, and yet my life is preserved." (Gen 32:28–31)

Who was this so-called man? Was he an angel? Why did he fight Jacob? What did he want? How did Jacob know that this being was someone powerful enough to grant a blessing? And what is the meaning of Jacob's conclusion that now he has "seen God face to face"? Because it leaves so many questions unanswered, this story of Jacob's wrestling prompted reflection and speculation even in biblical times. In the eighth century BCE, the biblical prophet Hosea comments on the story:

> In the womb he [Jacob] tried to supplant his
>   brother,
>   and in his manhood he strove with God.
> He strove with the angel and prevailed,
>   he wept and sought his favor,
> he met him at Bethel,
>   and there he spoke with him.   (Hos 12:3–4)[26]

The second and third lines of the above passage are parallel, describing the same incident: Jacob's striving with God and his striving with the angel are, in Hosea's view, one and the same event. In the previous chapter we looked at biblical portrayals of the angel of the LORD and noted how authors often identified this figure with God. So also, this man who wrestled Jacob should be identified with God. Jacob perceives the identity of his opponent and therefore he declares, "I have seen God face to face, and yet my life is preserved."

How relevant are Jacob's angel encounters for us today? Can we too be convinced of heaven's nearness? Can we too be seized by God? Can our state of "not knowing" give way to assurance of God's presence? On the one hand, we ought to hesitate before generalizing from these incidents. As we saw in Chapter 1, the biblical authors limit appearances of the angel of the LORD to individuals who are representative for the nation as a whole. And no one is more representative than Jacob, that is, "Israel"—the very namesake of God's people. By appearing to Jacob, God was directing the future of God's whole people. Why should that nation-sized theophany cause us to expect that God will appear to us in the routine of our merely life-sized lives?

And yet, the Bible bears witness in this passage and in many others that God's presence can be known. For God is nearer to us than we are to ourselves:

> You know when I sit down and when I rise up;
>   you discern my thoughts from far away.
> You search out my path and my lying down,
>   and are acquainted with all my ways.
> Even before a word is on my tongue,
>   O LORD, you know it completely.
> You hem me in, behind and before,
>   and lay your hand upon me.   (Ps 139:2–5)

The psalmist proclaims that we need not search high and low for God, because wherever we are, God is already there. God does not just intrude occasionally and then withdraw till the next time, but is present to us always, in every aspect of our lives.[27] Jesus will press the point: not only is God present wherever we go, but God diligently seeks us out (see, for example, John 14:23; Luke 15:4–9).

Back to Jacob. Some early Jewish readers perceived the extraordinary status or character of the patriarch and took it a step further, declaring that Jacob/Israel was, in fact, the chief angel of God. According to this view, Jacob-the-man (as known from Genesis) was but a human incarnation or embodiment of a heavenly, angelic Jacob. The *Prayer of Joseph,* a first-century CE Jewish text, has the angel Jacob/Israel make several spectacular declarations about himself: he is "firstborn of every living thing to whom God gives life" (v. 3), "archangel of the power of the Lord" (v. 7), "chief captain among the sons of God" (v. 7), and "first minister before the face of God" (v. 8).[28] Such claims for Jacob by ancient Jews are interesting for many reasons, including the light they shed on early Christian ideas about Jesus. Jesus was also an erstwhile mortal, who likewise was viewed by some as "firstborn" and as "chief" among those who minister before the face of God (see, for example, Col 1:15–20; Heb 1:6).

The *Prayer of Joseph* probably emerged from a Jewish mystical tradition that developed in the first centuries CE, which in its later forms came to be known as merkabah mysticism. The term *merkabah* is the rabbinic (Mishnaic) designation for the throne on which the prophet Ezekiel envisioned the "likeness of the glory of the LORD" (Ezek 1:26–28).[29] The merkabah mystics sought and claimed for themselves the experience of visionary ascent and entry into the heavenly court of God. But even before merkabah mysticism was well-established, Ezekiel's breathtaking glimpse of divinity provoked many Jews and Christians to intense reflection about whether and how humans might enter into the presence of God.

EZEKIEL'S VISION

Ezekiel's throne vision deserves to be approached with humility and respect, or even fear and trembling. Respect is due because of the exalted and difficult content of the vision. Here Ezekiel ventures to tell of the mysteries of the divine presence, using dreamlike images, and writing in a literary style that is difficult to translate. The vision does not open its secrets to the casual reader. But respect is also due because of the history of the interpretation of the passage. Among the first Christians, the vision commanded close attention—indeed, it was a central influence on the development of early thinking about the identity and nature of Christ. Among rabbis both before and after Jesus' day, this awesome account occasioned not only great interest but also, in interpreter David Halperin's words, "nervous suspicion that often seems to cross the border into fear."[30] Ordinary people were warned away, or even prohibited, from interpreting it. Therefore, I myself approach this vision with an acute sense of modesty, realizing how very faint is any light that I may shed.

Ezekiel was a priest who had been exiled from his home in Jerusalem. He was deported to Babylon with King Jehoiachin and a number of palace and temple officials and craftspeople in 597 BCE, when Jehoiachin surrendered to the army of Nebuchadnezzar II. Many inhabitants remained behind in the land of Judah, and this splitting and scattering of the population raised profound questions, including questions about the nature of God's relationship to Jerusalem and to the Temple there. As a priest, Ezekiel had believed that God's permanent address was the inner sanctum—the Holy of Holies—in the Jerusalem Temple. Indeed, Ezekiel seems to have presumed that the Temple was the closest one could come on earth to paradise—to "the world in its ideal state, the world as its creator hoped it would be."[31] In the Temple, worshippers experienced a sense of God's presence: hence the psalmist's assertion that "The God of gods will be seen in Zion," and that "a day in your courts is better than a thousand elsewhere" (Ps 84:7, 10). But for those forced to leave the country in the Exile, conviction that the Temple was the special place of God's presence became inadequate. For how could the exiles worship a God who lived so far away? There were other questions provoked by the Exile: How long would it last? Would there be an opportunity to return? And who were the rightful members of the household of God—the exiles such as Ezekiel, or the ones who had remained behind in the land?[32]

As prophet, Ezekiel felt called to address these questions. But his mandate to do so was in doubt because some supposed that true prophecy could occur only in Jerusalem. Trying, perhaps, to counter such doubt about his right to prophesy, Ezekiel relates how God seized or possessed him, transporting him in visions of God to various locations. Thus Ezekiel makes the point that, despite where he happens to be, he sees only what God shows him and speaks only what God tells him to speak.[33]

On the fifth day of the fifth year of the Exile (593 BCE), when Ezekiel was among the exiles by the river Chebar in Babylon, he experienced God's call to prophesy. "The heavens were opened, and I saw visions of God" (Ezek 1:1). He saw a great cloud approaching, but it was no ordinary storm cloud; it had "brightness around it and fire flashing forth continually" (v. 4). In the cloud were four extraordinary living creatures, roughly human in shape, but each with four wings arranged in a square with wings touching. Each of the creatures had four different faces—those of a human, a lion, an ox, and an eagle—so that the square could be facing north, south, east, and west all at once. The creatures could move in all of these directions. Beneath the creatures were interconnected sets of wheels within wheels that had eyes all around. Spreading over the creatures was a firmament or dome made of crystal, and on the dome rested something like a throne, made of sapphire. Ezekiel continues:

> And above the dome over their heads there was something like a throne, in appearance like sapphire; and seated above the likeness of a throne was something that seemed like a human form. Upward from what appeared like the loins I saw something like gleaming amber, something that looked like fire enclosed all round; and downward from what looked like the loins I saw something that looked like fire, and there was a splendor all around. Like the bow in a cloud on a rainy day, such was the appearance of the splendor all round. This was the appearance of the likeness of the glory of the LORD. When I saw it, I fell on my face, and I heard the voice of someone speaking. (Ezek 1:26–28)

The voice addresses Ezekiel and commands him to go to the rebellious house of Israel—to both the fellow exiles in Babylon and those who remained in Israel itself—and warn them that God would judge them most harshly unless they repented. Note how Ezekiel uses words such as "appearance" and "likeness" with great frequency in this vision. By this means the prophet reminds us that what he saw was so extraordinary that it defied precise description.[34]

Further on in Ezekiel, the author will identify the four living creatures bearing up the sapphire throne as "cherubim." We know the cherubim from elsewhere; they are winged beings above which God is enthroned (see 2 Sam 22:11 [= Ps 18:10] and Ps 99:1). Sculpted cherubim adorned the cover of the Ark of the Covenant, and the wings of huge, gold-plated cherubim spanned the Holy of Holies in Solomon's Temple.[35] But if God is enthroned above the cherubim, then wouldn't the being borne up by them in Ezekiel 1 likewise have to be God—or one very closely identified with God? Ezekiel implies that the cherubim have now left the Jerusalem Temple and transported the LORD to the place of exile.

How did a prophet know and show that his message was from God? When Moses was on the mountain, the people themselves witnessed the thunder, the cloud, and the fire. They heard the trumpet blast. Other prophets prior to Ezekiel demonstrated the authenticity of their message by describing an encounter with the Lord in the heavenly court. But in this first astounding vision of Ezekiel, he is transported neither to the mountaintop nor to the council room of God. Instead, the dais with the very throne and being of the Holy One is transported to Ezekiel in his place of exile.

The cherubim that flanked the Ark of the Covenant in the Jerusalem Temple were pieces of statuary, made of olivewood overlaid with gold (1 Kgs 6:23–28). Grand though they must have been—they spanned the whole width of the inner sanctum—for impressiveness they fell short of the fantastic, living, four-faced creatures of Ezekiel's first vision. In a later vision, Ezekiel will find himself present in the Jerusalem Temple and will watch as the temple cherubim make way for the divine throne borne by the heavenly cherubim:

> Then the glory of the Lord rose up from the cherub to the threshold of the house, the house was filled with the cloud, and the court was full of the brightness of the glory of the Lord. The sound of the wings of the cherubim was heard as far as the outer court, like the voice of God Almighty when he speaks. (Ezek 10:3–5)[36]

In this vision Ezekiel presumes much more than he says. For one thing, he presumes that the Temple with all its human-crafted furnishings is but an imperfect representation of a God-made sanctuary, a sanctuary inhabited not by statues but by living beings.[37] Ezekiel's privilege is to see past the inanimate structures to the divine reality. With inner sight he perceives the *living* cherubim, the throne that they bear, and—most astonishing of all—the very presence of the glory of the Lord of Israel.

In the vision in Ezekiel 9–10, the glory of the Lord departs from the Jerusalem Temple. That is bad news for Jerusalem, for the departure signals the impending destruction of the Temple and the city owing to the great sin of the people. But there is a way in which the departure is also good news. For by recounting it, Ezekiel affirms that God is not tied to one location. It was not in the Jerusalem Temple but by the river Chebar in Babylon where Ezekiel first witnessed the throne-chariot and the Lord's glory. The four creatures faced the four corners of the world, and the firmament they bore up was like the firmament or dome of the heavens: *the whole of the earth and the whole of the heavens are God's home.*

Ezekiel continues to hold that God is specially bound by covenant to the people of Israel. In the latter part of the book, Ezekiel foretells how the rebellious people of Israel will be reconciled to God, not because they deserve it, but by God's act of pure grace. Israel remains, in Ezekiel's view, the chosen people of God. But, at the same time, the prophet makes it clear that God is sovereign over *all* the earth. God uses the nations (including Babylon) as tools to accomplish divine purposes. The glory of the Lord is manifested wherever God chooses, for God is all-present and all-seeing, as the psalmist proclaims:

> If I ascend to heaven, you are there;
> > if I make my bed in Sheol, you are there.
> If I take the wings of the morning
> > and settle at the farthest limits of the sea,
> even there your hand shall lead me,
> > and your right hand shall hold me fast.
>
> (Ps 139:8–10)

Understood in context, an important part of Ezekiel's message is the assurance that God's glory—God's presence—cannot be contained by a building or confined to a place.

Even early readers took Ezekiel's vision out of context, probing it for what it disclosed about the arrangements of heaven. Such readers were fascinated by the four living creatures, who carry the firmament upon which the divine throne rests. They were entranced by the living wheels, with their eyes all around. The Hebrew text of Ezekiel 3:12–13 hints that the living creatures and the wheels are distinct angelic choirs who extol the deity in antiphonal praise. Later writers, both Jews and Christians, will incorporate details from Ezekiel's description of these creatures and their song into fresh revelations.[38] But, intrigued as they were by the living, traveling throne, prophets and mystics in the centuries following Ezekiel's vision were captivated most of all by the one who sat on that throne—the "likeness of the glory of the Lord." For here was a mysterious and utterly awe-inspiring figure who seemed to represent God's very self—in human form.

THE GLORY OF THE LORD

In what sense did Ezekiel behold the Lord? And if indeed it was God, then why did the prophet choose his words so cautiously—claiming only that he saw the *likeness* of the *glory* of the Lord? The attention given in Chapter 1 to the figure of the angel of the Lord will help us with this question. In many biblical narratives the angel of the Lord is like an alter ego or a mask that God chooses to show to mortal beings. Moreover, biblical and later authors sometimes borrowed traditions about the angel of the Lord to describe certain attributes of God—writing as if those attributes were themselves distinct angelic beings separate from God. "Glory" (Heb. *kabod* or Gk. *doxa*) was one such attribute or hypostasis.[39] It was the designation given to God's appearance more than once during the Exodus, as when Moses was on the mountain:

> Then Moses went up on the mountain, and the cloud covered the mountain. The glory of the LORD settled on Mount Sinai, and the cloud covered it for six days; on the seventh day he called to Moses out of the cloud. Now the appearance of the glory of the LORD was like a devouring fire on the top of the mountain in the sight of the people of Israel. (Exod 24:15–17)[40]

In this passage from Exodus and in others (including others in Ezekiel), *the "glory of the LORD" is a visible manifestation of God's invisible presence.* So when Ezekiel says that he witnessed "the likeness of the glory of the LORD" upon the throne, it is nearly, but not entirely, accurate to say that he witnessed the LORD.[41]

Ezekiel writes that the likeness of the glory "seemed like a human form." There was biblical precedent for God's glory appearing in human form. In Exodus, when Moses said to God, "Show me your glory, I pray," the LORD covered Moses with a "hand"; Moses was allowed to see the LORD's "back" as the LORD passed by (Exod 33:18–23). Already in this intriguing passage from Exodus we are seeing the influence of traditions about the angel of the LORD. "Yahweh himself, the angel of God, and his Glory are peculiarly melded together, suggesting a deep secret about the ways God manifested himself to humanity," observes Alan Segal.[42] Ezekiel seems likewise to have merged ideas about the LORD's *glory* with ideas about the LORD's *angel.* By blending traditions in this way, Ezekiel manages to show God's transcendence balanced by God's accessibility. Ezekiel does not look directly on God's face, or even directly on the face of the glory—rather, he sees the *"likeness* of the glory." Thus God's transcendence is safeguarded. Yet the prophet knows himself to be in God's very presence. That is why he falls on his face—because the presence overwhelms him.

Some later authors interpreted the glory on the divine throne in Ezekiel's vision not as an aspect of God but as distinct angelic being. The book of Daniel (written around 164 BCE[43]) is one of the earliest works to interpret Ezekiel's depiction in this way. Daniel 7 describes not a throne but thrones and not one but two majestic figures: the "Ancient of Days" (= God), and "one like a son of man" (or "one like a human being" [Dan 7:13]). The author of Daniel probably identified this figure with the angel Michael, and may be implying that he took a seat on one of the thrones.[44]

By Jesus' day, Ezekiel's depictions of the "likeness of the glory of the LORD" and other biblical descriptions of God in human form—including the various traditions about the angel of the Lord, and the depiction of the one like a son of man from Daniel 7—had coalesced for many Jews into images of a *chief heavenly mediator* (see above, pp. 11–12, 26–27). This mediator, it was believed, is no ordinary angel, but represents or participates in God's own being in some mysterious way—much as in Exod 23:21, where the angel of the Lord is said to bear God's very name.[45] Philo, the first-century Egyptian Jewish philosopher and theologian, treats the heavenly mediator (whom he identifies as the *logos* or "word"), as scarcely distinct from God at all, but more like an aspect of God that acts as an independent person. Ancient rabbis would most often identify this chief angel-like being as *Metatron* (perhaps deriving from Greek words meaning "one who stands after or behind the throne"). Apocalyptic writers from the Hellenistic and Roman eras named him variously the son of man, Melchizedek, Adoil, Eremiel, Yahoel, and Michael.[46]

Early Christians added a new layer to the pattern of interpreting God's glory as an angel-like figure: they identified the glory with Jesus of Nazareth, raised from death to the right hand of God. Segal regards such identification as the central feature of earliest Christianity, and as especially pivotal for Paul, who experienced ecstatic visions and apparently claimed personally to have witnessed Christ "the Glory."[47] In 2 Corinthians, Paul reminds his readers that they likewise behold the divine presence, for God "has shone in our hearts to give the light of *the knowledge of the glory of God in the face of Jesus Christ*" (2 Cor 4:6; emphasis added). The Hebrew Scriptures insisted that mere mortals could not look upon God's face; now, Paul informs us, we *can* look upon the face of Jesus Christ. And that face reflects God's glory as though in a mirror.[48] In Revelation, the visionary John of Patmos also identifies the risen Jesus with the divine presence, using images culled from Ezekiel and Daniel and then creatively recombined:

> I saw one like the Son of Man, clothed with a long robe and with a golden sash across his chest. His head and his hair were white as white wool, white as snow; his eyes were like a flame of fire, his feet were like burnished bronze, refined as in a furnace, and his voice was like the sound of many waters. In his right hand he held seven stars, and from his mouth came a sharp, two-edged sword, and his face was like the sun shining with full force. (Rev 1:13–16)

For the seer John, the risen Jesus is none other than "the appearance of the likeness of the glory of the Lord," seen by Ezekiel so long before.[49]

The traditions about a supreme angel-like being who shares in God's glory were used to explain not only Christ's *resurrection and exaltation to heaven* (as in the quotations above from 2 Corinthians and Revelation), but also Christ's *preexistence.* The author of Hebrews writes that Jesus "is the reflection of God's glory and the exact imprint of God's very being" (Heb 1:3). Paul wrote of Christ as one who, before being "born in human likeness" had been "in the form [Gk. *morphē*] of God" (Phil 2:6, 7). Segal observes that by using the term *morphē,* Paul implies that before the incarnation Christ had the form of a divine body identical with the glory.[50] The letter to the Colossians gives a still fuller exposition of Christ's existence and role before the incarnation:

> He is the image of the invisible God, the firstborn of all creation; for in him all things in heaven and on earth were created, things visible and invisible, whether thrones or dominions or rulers or powers—all things have been created through him and for him. He himself is before all things, and in him all things hold together. (Col 1:15–17)

The assertions made here call to mind the exalted descriptions of the angelic Jacob in the *Prayer of Joseph* (see p. 49), Philo's exalted language about the *logos,* or "word," as the agent of creation, and the Gospel of John's naming of Jesus as "Word become flesh," the one through whom all things came into being (John 1:3, 14).

According to the author of John, even in the days before Jesus' mortal life, the preexistent Christ had made God's glory known. The evangelist implies that the prophet Isaiah's great vision of "the Lord sitting on a throne, high and lofty" (Isa 6:1) was a vision of none other than Jesus (John 12:41; cf. 8:58).[51] The thought is echoed in the fourth-century "Liturgy of St. James," put to music in a well-known hymn. The first stanza of the hymn enjoins all mortals to keep silence, in expression of reverence at the incarnation:

> Let all mortal flesh keep silence,
> And with fear and trembling stand;
> Ponder nothing earthly minded,
> For with blessing in His hand,
> Christ our God to earth descendeth,
> Our full homage to demand.

The fourth stanza then alludes to Isaiah's vision of the heavenly throne, with its angelic attendants all around:

> At His feet the six-winged seraph;
> Cherubim, with sleepless eye,

Veil their faces to the presence,
As with ceaseless voice they cry,
Alleluia, Alleluia,
Alleluia, Lord Most High![52]

In the hymn it is God who is on the throne—but it is also Christ. The Christ who descended to earth (stanza one) is the same glorious figure who long before had been witnessed by Isaiah, encompassed and acclaimed by the angelic host (stanza four).

So, traditions about angels helped the earliest Christians to understand Jesus as the preexistent and resurrected Lord. The lines of influence intersect and double back and then intersect again, and so are hard to trace. Here are a few of these lines of influence:

- Ezekiel drew on beliefs about the "angel of the LORD" and the "glory of the LORD" in order to describe "the likeness of the glory of the LORD," a human-like figure.
- The author of Daniel deployed the traditions about the angel of the LORD again, together with a fresh appropriation of images from Ezekiel.
- New Testament authors drew on the glory traditions from Ezekiel and Daniel (and on then-current interpretations of those traditions referring to a chief angelic mediator) to interpret Christ in both his preexistent and his resurrected states.

Early Christian authors did not *call* Jesus an angel, for he was different and much more than an angel. As the author of Hebrews wrote, Jesus had "become as much superior to angels as the name he has inherited is more excellent than theirs" (Heb 1:4). But it is fair to say that *traditions about angels lie at the heart of the earliest claims for Jesus as the preexistent and resurrected Lord.*

If angel-traditions have influenced early views of Jesus' *preexistence* and of his *resurrection,* have such traditions also influenced understandings of Jesus' incarnate, earthly life? As noted in Chapter 1, the evangelists suggest that Jesus does not wholly conceal the glory even during his earthly ministry. It shines through most brightly at the Transfiguration. But the evangelists are careful not to overexpose Jesus' glory in their depictions of his mortal life. Instead they stress Jesus' lowliness and humility and servanthood. By this emphasis they show us what divine love and divine presence look like in the human realm: like the deepest sort of sharing, the deepest sort of giving. In Jesus' incarnation he gave up the glorious form of God, exchanging it for a far more humble and vulnerable human body. And then he gave his body as well. Jesus' life and death traced a pattern, not of striving after glory, but of costly self-donation.[53] By looking at Jesus' manner of living and dying, we discern that God's presence, love, and glory are manifested especially in and through fleshly life. Jesus took on human flesh—and then put his flesh entirely at risk.

In the narratives about the angel of the Lord, God is portrayed as stooping down to compensate for our human limitations. Protestant theologian Jürgen Moltmann calls this stooping down "God's self-humiliation, God's indwelling."[54] God stooped down in the person of the angel who appeared to the ancients of Israel. God lowered Godself to be in the pillar of cloud and fire that accompanied the Israelites in the wilderness; later, God's presence or *shekinah* dwelt on the mercy seat of the Ark of the Covenant. God dwelt in the glorious one, the one "like a human being," witnessed by Ezekiel. And in the early Christians' conviction, God lived—and lives—among us in Jesus, the very reflection of God's glory, who gave up his godly form to be born as a human being. In all these ways, God has made Godself present to humanity by a movement of self-giving, self-opening, self-sharing. Later I will contend that as humans we enter into awareness of God's presence when we give *ourselves* wholly to God in return. For, as philosopher Ralph Harper wrote in his exquisite book *On Presence,* both human and divine presence "need two." "You cannot practice presence all by yourself. There must be a mutual dependence, an exchange."[55] God loves us and wants our love in return. Only when the giving goes both ways can God's desire for us expand into full presence.

I'M OK, GOD'S OK

How are modern accounts of God's presence similar to the ancient accounts? How are they different? For Beck, Freeman, and Eadie, to enter into the presence of the divine is to be flooded with a sense of love, acceptance, and tranquillity. They insist that before God there is *no need for fear*. As noted in Chapter 1, they—like many other recent authors and spiritual teachers—are striving to counter what they see as a perverse and damaging emphasis in our Judeo-Christian culture on God as tyrant and judge. Consider the remarks of Barbara Mark and Trudy Griswold, authors of *The Angelspeake Book of Prayer and Healing:* "God has received so much bad publicity that it's no wonder so many people are afraid of Him. From our earliest years we have been taught to fear Him. We have been told He is angry and that we are sinners, and as sinners we are not worthy of Him. Furthermore, God punished sinners. He kicked Adam and Eve out of the Garden of Eden for making one mistake." [56] But, such authors insist, there is no cause for fear. God loves but does not judge; God sees that our mistakes derived from inadequate knowledge and, in any case, helped us or others to progress on the spiritual path. Coming into the presence of the divine—whether directly or as mediated through angels—is like coming into the presence of a best friend who always listens and never criticizes.

By contrast, ancient accounts—varied as they are—stress God's awesomeness. To come before God is not to experience a sense of relaxation, a letting down of one's guard. Rather, it is to enter into awareness of one so powerful, so pure, so great that *one senses one's very life to be at stake.* Hence Hagar's wonder after encountering the angel of the LORD: "Have I really seen God and remained alive after seeing him?" (Gen 16:13b). And Jacob: "I have seen God face to face and yet my life is preserved" (Gen 32:30b). At the theophany on Mount Sinai, the awesomeness of God is symbolized by fire, smoke, trumpet blast, and thunder; the holiness and power of God, by the threat to human life:

> Now Mount Sinai was wrapped in smoke, because the LORD had descended upon it in fire; the smoke went up like the smoke of a kiln, while the whole mountain shook violently. As the blast of the trumpet grew louder and louder, Moses would speak and God would answer him in thunder. When the LORD descended upon Mount Sinai, to the top of the mountain, the LORD summoned Moses to the top of the mountain, and Moses went up. Then the LORD said to Moses, "Go down and warn the people not to break through to the LORD to look; otherwise many of them will perish." (Exod 19:18–21)

Centuries later, Isaiah beheld the LORD sitting on the divine throne, high and lofty, and declared: "Woe is me! I am lost, for I am a man of unclean lips, and I live among a people of unclean lips; yet my eyes have seen the King, the LORD of hosts!" (Isa 6:5). At the sight of God's glory, the prophet Ezekiel fell upon his face; at the end of his vision he sat, overwhelmed, for seven days (Ezek 3:15). At times, encounters with Jesus also produced such effects, for some perceived in Jesus the presence of God. When Jesus caused a miraculous catch of fish, Peter declared: "Go away from me, Lord, for I am a sinful man!" (Luke 5:8). When the risen Christ appeared to Saul, Saul fell to the ground, unable to see, and then addressed Jesus, saying: "Who are you, Lord?" (see Acts 9:3–5). The encounter with the angel left Jacob wounded; the encounter with Jesus left Saul blind.

In these and other such passages, the fear that people exhibit before God is not panic over impending punishment, but rather a sense of reverence, humility, and awe before one who is so much greater than the paltry human self. For the human is made of flesh, with a heart that is prone to seek its own good rather than the good that God intends, and with a mind that cannot by itself begin to comprehend how God undergirds all that is. In a hymn, one of the Dead Sea sectarians expresses this awareness of human limitation before the Deity:

> What then is man that is earth, that is shaped [from clay] and returns to the dust, that Thou shouldst give him to understand such marvels and make known to him the counsel of [Thy truth]? Clay and dust that I am, what can I devise unless Thou wish it, and what contrive unless Thou desire it? What strength shall I have unless Thou keep me upright, and how shall I understand unless by (the spirit) which Thou hast shaped for me?" (1QH 10.3–6).[57]

As the passage conveys so well, the relationship between God and those who fear God is asymmetrical; the latter depend upon God for life and breath and understanding in a way that God does not depend on them.

For those who know God, fear is always balanced by trust, for God is good. Moment by moment, God gives us what we need and far more. "Do not be afraid," Moses tells the frightened people at Mount Sinai (Exod 20:20). After appearing to Gideon, the (angel of the) Lord says: "Peace be to you; do not fear, you shall not die" (Judg 6:23). And to Daniel: "Do not fear, greatly beloved, you are safe. Be strong and courageous!" (Dan 10:19). The Apostle Paul writes to Christians in Rome: "You did not receive a spirit of slavery to fall back into fear, but you have received a spirit of adoption" (Rom 8:15). If God is for us, Paul continues, who could possibly be against us? "He who did not withhold his own Son, but gave him up for all of us, will he not with him also give us everything else?" (8:31–32). In all of these contexts, the one who genuinely strives to do right is freed from anxiety, for he or she knows that God is "slow to anger and abounding in steadfast love." And yet, for biblical authors, *trust* in God never slips over into *chumminess* with God. For God remains God: the giver, sustainer, and judge of all life, patient and loving, but rightly claiming our best energy, worship, and love.

At some point in life each of us comes face to face with our own weaknesses. It may happen in a time of suffering. It may happen in the midst of a fit of anger. It may happen when I find myself succumbing, yet again, to temptation. Whatever the specific occasion, at such a moment I see with perfect clarity that I am not leading the life I want to live. How do I make sense of this weakness, and how do I cope? The new spirituality insists that the problem lies not with *me* but with all the baggage that I carry around—some of it a direct inheritance from my Judeo-Christian culture. Actually, I myself am OK. In fact, I am divine! The divine power to remake myself lies already within. Spirit guides or angels, consulted via meditation or channeling, will help me to dump the baggage so that the divine in me will finally be unburdened enough to strut its stuff. And, as for punishment for my shortcomings and errors, I needn't fear, because God is OK, too! God is not a punishing tyrant, but a friend, who recognizes that my mistakes resulted from ignorance, and who bestows knowledge as an antidote. God even uses my mistakes to work out the divine plan for my life. "All things work together for the good."[58]

Such an understanding of the human self and of God differs from the views of biblical authors. For ancient Jewish and early Christian authors, God is far greater than the human self, indeed far greater than we can ask or imagine. And, left to my own devices, I am not "OK." Far too often I do not do the good I want, but the evil I do not want—or perhaps I simply do nothing at all. But the solution to this dilemma does not lie in my claiming to be God. Rather, it begins with my acknowledging my own weakness, my inability to meet God's high standard of righteousness—and then continues with my resting in the firm assurance of God's GRACE. For God *is* slow to anger and abounding in steadfast love. More than that, God generously gives me the power to do what I cannot do on my own. When I enter into awareness of God's presence, I enter into the sphere of God's power. It is not power to hurt or rule over others, but power to live a new and rich life. It is power to live joyfully, because God has forgiven me for my sins and set me free to live in true fellowship with others. It is power to live wisely, to understand something of God's ways in the world.

Christian theologians affirm that God is present within the innermost depths of the human self. Moltmann, for example, asserts that as the Holy Spirit, God is present "in a special way, not in the way of his general omnipresence, but in the way of his self-revelation. . . . The creative energies of God's eternal life are overflowing our mortal life which becomes then wholly living from within." He comments on Psalm 31:8: "Thou hast set my feet in a broad room."

What is this "broad room" and "wide open space" except the unbelievable nearness of the infinite God in the Spirit, which surrounds us from all sides!? "Thou surroundest me from every side and holdest thy hand over me," says Psalm 139:5. If divine presence surrounds us from all sides, we can unfold our lives free and unhindered. We can live "in God" and move and dwell "in God." Here God is not only a transcendent person, to whom we can speak, but at the same time a life-space, in which we can live.[59]

Saying that God is present in the world and active in our mortal lives may sound suspiciously like the angel-book writers' talk of "God in us." And yet there are important differences. For in a Christian understanding, the creature is not the creator. The human self is not God. Moreover, the Spirit is most characteristically active, not in us as isolated individuals, but in us as we commune with others. The Spirit creates, as Moltmann says, a "life space" in which we can live. The Spirit in the world and in us is God's gift of presence, graciously bestowed; it is not a constituent part of us and we cannot own it or manipulate it. God remains sovereign, immanent in *but also transcending* the earthly order, and neither God nor any angel is subject to human beck and call. The divine presence occurs on God's terms, not on our own. Although our awareness of the divine presence brings peace and light, that very light shines also on our own inadequacies. And, once our souls have opened up to perceive the greatness and the graciousness of God, we naturally respond by turning, in worship and praise, to the One who created us.

WORSHIPPING WITH ANGELS

In 1985, Howard Storm nearly died—or perhaps he did die—from a perforated duodenum. As he was crossing over the threshold of death, he experienced a visionary transport of his soul—first to a netherworld where he was afflicted and beaten by demonic beings, and then, when he cried out to Jesus for help, to heaven. There is more about such near-death experiences in Chapter 6. Pertinent here is the effect of the experience on Storm's subsequent life: soon thereafter, he began to worship with angels. Before his near-death experience, Storm had disdained organized religion. But during his long and painful journey back to health, he ventured into a church, and there he was instantly overwhelmed by the presence of a multitude of angels filling the upper part of the sanctuary:

> The worship had just begun with the congregation singing the opening hymn when we entered the sanctuary. A few feet inside I saw on the ceiling of the church hundreds of angels basking in praise of God. They were a golden color and radiated golden light around them. The unexpected sight of the angels unleashed powerful emotions of awe of God from inside me. I did the only thing I could do in that circum-

stance, which was to throw myself down on the floor. Prostrate on the carpeted aisle I thanked God and praised God profusely.[60]

Despite his wife's reluctance to go back to that (or any) church after Storm's outburst, he did return, and eventually went on to become an ordained minister in the United Church of Christ.

Storm's angel-filled worship experience is unusual for a Protestant. To be sure, some Protestant hymns and numerous Christmas carols make direct or indirect reference to worshipping angels—"Angels we have heard on high" and so forth. And, as New Testament scholar Victor C. Pfitzner points out, those who celebrate the ancient liturgy of the Western Mass (including Catholics and some Lutherans) routinely declare their partnership in worship "with angels and archangels and with all the company of heaven."[61] Still, one wonders how many who sing or say these words actively perceive themselves to be in the company of angelic presences.

The belief that humans are partners in worship with both angels and saints is especially strong in Eastern Orthodox Christianity. In the Orthodox view, "the true locus of the Church's worship is heaven itself."[62] The author of one recent Orthodox catechism explains this conviction, relating it to the importance of icons in helping worshippers to sense the heavenly dimension:

> Because the Liturgy of the Church takes place in heaven, it is celebrated in the presence of all the angels and Saints. Traditional Orthodox temples are filled with icons of the Saints, often covered from floor to ceiling. These icons sacramentally manifest to us the literal presence of the Saints. That is why, upon entering a temple, we venerate the icons. We are greeting the members of our heavenly family as we would greet the members of our earthly family upon entering a room.[63]

In this view, true worship has its locus *in heaven*—even as believers stand physically before painted icons in an earthly time and place.[64]

Many ancient Jews and early Christians were deeply interested in the perpetual worship of God carried out by angels in the heavenly sanctuary. Much as in the modern Orthodox experience, the boundaries between earthly, human sanctuaries and the celestial temple tended to blur: some of the faithful professed to be able to enter into the heavenly angelic liturgy, even as they worshipped here on earth. Thus the anonymous author of a hymn from the Dead Sea Scrolls marvels, "Thou hast cleansed a perverse spirit of great sin that it may stand with the host of the Holy Ones, and that it may enter into community with the congregation of the Sons of Heaven." [65] This is an astonishing claim! As biblical scholar Martha Himmelfarb points out, other Jewish writings had alluded to humans attaining a place among the angels after death, or at the end of days. And some texts had described how ancient greats—Moses, Enoch, and others—were carried up to heaven and transformed into the brightness or likeness of angels. But the Dead Sea sectarians insisted that they could experience such marvelous events *already in this earthly life.* [66]

When Old Testament authors permit us glimpses into the heavenly precincts, they most often show us, not a place of worship, but a divine council room, patterned after a royal court. The divine council is a place where the business of governance is carried out. In the first two chapters of Job, for example, all the heavenly beings come to present themselves before God. As Carol Newsom observes, "The image is one of divine beings reporting to God, receiving commissions to execute, and reporting back from their missions." [67] God makes a point of commending Job's faithfulness to one of their number, called the *satan,* and this being's accusatory response gives the story a legal cast: God's throne room is the court, God is the judge, and the *satan* is the prosecuting attorney (see Chapter 4). Psalm 82 also paints a courtroom scene, but now it is other deities who are judged: God is said to "take his place in the divine council," and to hold judgment "in the midst of the gods." Similarly, the literature of ancient Mesopotamia, Ugarit, and Phoenicia attests to belief in an assembly where gods and goddesses come together to make decisions that direct the course of the cosmos and its inhabitants. Arrayed beneath this tier of divinity are still lesser, messenger gods—the equivalent of biblical angels. [68]

In the Second Temple era, however, temple imagery came to dominate in descriptions of heaven (though court imagery also continued to be used). Himmelfarb argues that Ezekiel's throne vision initiated a shift of emphasis in descriptions of the divine council and its setting, from heavenly council room to celestial temple. Ezekiel had come to understand the earthly Temple in Jerusalem as so defiled that it was no longer a fit resting place for the glory of God. Therefore God abandoned the Temple for a chariot even before the Temple's destruction. Thus God was now divorced from the earthly Temple; the true dwelling place for God's glory was instead an eternal, heavenly temple (of which the earthly Temple was a mere copy). [69] In the centuries following Ezekiel, the preeminence of the celestial temple over the earthly structure became widely assumed, and temple imagery became common in depictions of heaven.

However heaven is described, the Hebrew Scriptures consistently show its inhabitants *giving God honor and acclaim.* For example, the heavenly beings who present themselves before the LORD in Job 1–2 are showing their obeisance, acting as loyal clients toward their patron. When Isaiah glimpses the LORD "sitting on a throne, high and lofty," the setting is the Jerusalem Temple (overlaid with the heavenly reality). Seraphs, winged servants, are in attendance above God:

> Each had six wings: with two they covered their faces, and with two they covered their feet, and with two they flew. And one called to another and said:
>> "Holy, holy, holy is the LORD of hosts;
>> the whole earth is full of his glory."
> The pivots on the thresholds shook at the voices of those who called, and the house filled with smoke. (Isa 6:2–4)

In Psalm 97:7 the gods are depicted "bowing down before God." In Daniel 7:10, God is envisioned upon the throne, with "a thousand thousands" serving him, and "ten thousand times ten thousand" standing to attend him. Psalm 148 commands inhabitants of earth to join in a cacophony of praise to be offered by all created beings, including the angels and the celestial bodies:

> "Praise the LORD!
> Praise the LORD from the heavens;
>> praise him in the heights!
> Praise him, all his angels;
>> praise him, all his host!
> Praise him, sun and moon;
>> praise him, all you shining stars!"   (vv. 1–4a)

All must praise the Lord, the psalmist continues, "for his name alone is exalted; his glory is above the earth and heaven" (v. 13).

As the image of heaven shifted, so did the image of angels. Earlier eras saw them as messenger-deities and as warriors fighting in the angelic army or host of God, but the late Second Temple era increasingly saw angels as priests: they offer praise and (bloodless) sacrifice in the heavenly temple, carry the prayers of the faithful to heaven, and even intercede on humans' behalf. Consider the following passage from the *Testament of Levi:*

> In the uppermost heaven of all dwells the Great Glory in the Holy of Holies superior to all holiness. There with him are the archangels, who serve and offer propitiatory sacrifices to the Lord in behalf of all

the sins of ignorance of the righteous ones. They present to the Lord a pleasing odor, a rational and bloodless oblation. (*T. Levi* 3:4–6)[70]

Even more striking is the fragmentary work from Qumran known as *Songs of the Sabbath Sacrifice.* This work, which is heavily indebted to Ezekiel, purports to describe the Sabbath worship and the sacrifices offered by angelic priests in the celestial temple. Near the opening of one fragment of this text, for example, the "holy ones" (angels) are said to have become, in God's eyes, "priests of [...] attendants of the Presence in the inner chamber of His glory, in the assembly belonging to all the gods of [...] divinities."[71]

This assumed priestly function of angels also made its mark on early Christian ideas about Christ and Christian worship. In the view of the Apostle Paul, whose descriptions of Christian worship are the earliest we possess, angels play a role when Christians come together to praise and magnify God. In one text he gives enigmatic instruction that, during worship, women must keep their heads covered (or their hair bound up; the text is not entirely clear), "because of the angels" (1 Cor 11:10). Whatever this ambiguous directive means, it presumes angelic presence.[72]

In another passage, which follows his instructions for worship, Paul critiques those "who speak in the tongues of mortals *and of angels,* but do not have love" (1 Cor 13:1; emphasis added). He has already referred to this speaking in "various kinds of tongues" as one of the special abilities or gifts bestowed by the Holy Spirit. In contrast to prophecy, such ecstatic speech was not intelligible to all; it required persons to whom the Spirit had specially granted the gift of interpretation. Light is shed on the phenomenon by the *Testament of Job,* a Jewish text stemming from around the time of Paul that depicts the three daughters of the restored Job as speaking in angelic tongues. When, for example, the first of Job's daughters wrapped herself in a special cord given her by Job, "she took on another heart—no longer minded toward earthly things—but she spoke ecstatically in the angelic dialect, sending up a hymn to God in accord with the hymnic style of the angels" (*T. Job* 48:2–3).[73] Antoinette Clark Wire suggests that some in the Corinthian church of Paul's day, including some women, may have understood themselves "as like the angels in speech or knowledge." Angels were sometimes viewed as mediators of God's word; therefore, Christian prophets might conceivably "claim to understand, see, and speak like angels."[74] Paul downplays the gift of tongues but he does not deny it. On the contrary, he thanks God that he speaks in tongues more than any of the Corinthians (1 Cor 14:18). He and they share a basic assumption that the worship of God *by humans* and the worship accorded *by angels* are closely intertwined.

Angel traditions have shaped Paul's understanding not only of Christian worship but of the entirety of Christian life. For, as we have seen, by Paul's day biblical and later traditions about the angel of the LORD had coalesced into widely held belief in a chief heavenly mediator, whom Paul knows as the "glory of God" and identifies with Jesus Christ. At the heart of Paul's gospel was the news that Christians are of one spirit with this heavenly figure—this "man from heaven"—and that all who are united with Christ are transformed into his image or likeness: "Now the Lord is the Spirit, and where the Spirit of the Lord is, there is freedom. And all of us, with unveiled faces, seeing the glory of the Lord as though reflected in a mirror, are being transformed into the same image *from one degree of glory to another;* for this comes from the Lord, the Spirit" (2 Cor 3:17–18; emphasis added). Here Paul (like other ancient authors) presumes that beholding God changes one to be more like the angels, and more like God.[75]

Writing after the time of Paul, the author of Hebrews depicts Christ as the heavenly high priest, a priest "after the order of Melchizedek." Probably the author supposes that the "Melchizedek" of Genesis 14:18–19 and Psalm 110:4 was an angel. As a high priest of this angelic order, Jesus is able to enter the celestial Holy of Holies, and there to offer the definitive sacrifice for humankind—a sacrifice of his own blood. But it is not only Christ who enters into the heavenly temple. In a manner of speaking, Christian worshippers do also:

> But you have come to Mount Zion and to the city of the living God, the heavenly Jerusalem, and to innumerable angels in festal gathering, and to the assembly of the firstborn who are enrolled in heaven, and to God the judge of all, and to the spirits of the righteous made perfect, and to Jesus, the mediator of a new covenant, and to the sprinkled blood that speaks a better word than the word of Abel. (Heb 12:22–24)

This picture of humans and angels joined in festal gathering is not merely anticipation of what will happen after death or at the end of time, for throughout the letter, the author has taken pains to show that already Christians may enter into the divine presence. By his death Christ has *already* opened access into the heavenly sanctuary (see Heb 4:16; 8:1; 9:12, 24). The angels worship Jesus (see 1:6), and Christians should see themselves as *joining with the heavenly throng in offering praise.*

The book of Revelation includes some of the most striking images of heavenly worship of God and of Christ. The setting of the author's vision alternates between earth and heaven. Earth is the scene of vast and terrible judgment. Meanwhile, in heaven Christ, "like a lamb that has been slaughtered," shares God's throne and receives the veneration of gathered angels and martyrs.

> After this I looked, and there was a great multitude that no one could count, from every nation, from all tribes and peoples and languages, standing before the throne and before the Lamb, robed in white, with palm branches in their hands. They cried out in a loud voice, saying, "Salvation belongs to our God who is seated on the throne, and to the Lamb!" And all the angels stood around the throne and around the elders and the four living creatures, and they fell on their faces before the throne and worshiped God, singing, "Amen! Blessing and glory and wisdom and thanksgiving and honor and power and might be to our God for ever and ever! Amen." (Rev 7:9–12)

This worshipping multitude consists of faithful believers who had been killed in the great ordeal described in the rest of the vision (see Rev 7:14). But still-living "saints" (believers) also participate in the heavenly worship through their prayers, which rise up before God like the smoke of heavenly incense (see Rev 8:4).[76] Thus the worship on earth and the worship in heaven are one. Not all Christian leaders affirmed the truth of John's vision, however. When an author wrote in Paul's name to Christians in Colossae—a city in the vicinity of the seven churches of Revelation—he admonished them to disregard any who were encouraging them to "self-abasement" and "worship of [or by] angels" (Col 2:18). The heretics targeted here may well have been John and others in his circle.[77]

We will never know just what it was like for the earliest Christians to worship with the angels—to be "raised up with Christ and seated with him in the heavenly places" (Eph 2:6). Did they envision their mundane surroundings transfigured into the splendor of the heavenly sanctuary, as did Isaiah and Ezekiel? Did they perceive visible angels hovering over their earthly place of assembly, as did Howard Storm? Did they fall into a motionless or lightly swaying trance, as do some modern "channels" of angelic and other higher spirits? Did they raise their arms in the air, as do some charismatic and Pentecostal Christians? Were they flooded with a sense of freedom and joy as they left all earthly concerns behind—"taking on another heart" and "ceasing to be minded toward earthly things," like the daughters in the *Testament of Job*? About these and many other such questions we remain in the dark. What we can know is this: in worship, early Christians—like some Jews of their day—numbered themselves among the vast heavenly throng privileged to enter into the very throne room of God to pour forth their adoration and praise.

THE SACRED AND THE EVERYDAY

In a *Washington Post* column, writer and Sunday school teacher Marta Vogel details her search for a church that would satisfy her craving for sacred moments.[78] Vogel had been raised in the church but left it as an adult. When her eldest child was six months old she found herself yearning to go back. She told her husband, "I want to lose myself, to not be able to think about whether Cheerios are on sale at the grocery store or whether I need to call the plumber to fix the downstairs bathroom." She was looking for a time each week set apart from the mundane, a time that would shift the balance of her life so that she was not so much "of the world." She was looking, she writes, "to feel a lump in my throat, a swelling in my chest." As she chronicles her search, she repeatedly speaks of seeking reverence, but from her account one could argue that she was, rather, seeking *presence.* For what is reverence but the awed response of one who recognizes that she has entered into the realm of the holy—the presence of the divine?

Vogel never does find a church that fully satisfies her need. She laments the lack of quiet and mystery at nearly every church she visits, complaining that they are more like committee meetings than like anything resembling a spiritual experience. "There was lots of activity, plenty of social activism, discussions of homosexuality and racism, but few moments of silence and little or no reverence." Repeatedly the secular world invades what she had hoped would be sacred time and sacred space. The Quakers do an adequate job of setting the worship service off from "roof repairs and coffee hour sign-ups"—but they lack the "candles and darkness and mysterious music" that Vogel deems essential to worshipping with "reverence." She finally joins a Methodist church but says that she feels disappointed almost every Sunday because "reverence is in short supply."

In expecting that worship be a time set apart from the bustle and worries of everyday life, Vogel reflects a struggle in Western culture with the disappearing boundary between the secular and sacred. To many it seems as though the secular in our 24/7 culture has swallowed up the sacred entirely. We are "too much of the world" because the world is everywhere and always in our face. Vogel suggests that much of what is considered New Age (not to mention drugs and other such escapes) may be a response to this perceived lack of opportunities for sacred moments. I would expand Vogel's point: not just New Age spirituality but also much of popular Christian spirituality struggles with this lack. But whereas Vogel wants to reassert the boundary between the secular and sacred by deliberately setting sacred times apart from everyday life, many others are insisting that we cultivate a different sort of awareness, a spirituality that sees everyday life as itself sacred. In this alternate approach, holy moments do not happen only in times apart—when Moses is on the mountaintop, for example. Any place and any time offer opportunities to enter into awareness of God's presence.

This attention to the spirituality of everyday life has been especially popular in feminist writings, in part because women—even upper-middle-class and professional women—so often lack the luxury of "times apart." Jewish ethicist Laurie Zoloth-Dorfman critiques theologies that depict the spiritual quest as a solitary (and usually male) disdain for the ordinary, in pursuit of the holy. Such depictions usually pay no attention to the matter of who is supporting the quest. Zoloth-Dorfman writes that texts like those about Moses and Jacob "always leave me muttering about who is watching the four-year-olds near the water, who is bouncing the babies to sleep at the edge of the gathering, who is washing the plates after dinner, who is dyeing the cloth for the sacred raiment." God must also be present in the interruptions that characterize so much of women's—and all our—lives.[79]

The need to discern the sacred in everyday life also helps to fuel much popular angel literature. The authors of the angel books assure us that angels are always present, always making themselves felt, attentive to the smallest details, and as near as one's own breath; they represent the immanence of the divine. And, although Beck, Freeman, and Eadie all encountered angels in extraordinary peak moments, these and other such authors tell us that we can benefit from angels' presence at any moment or place. There is no need for arduous training or long withdrawal to a mountaintop or a desert. Nor, the authors imply, is there need to participate in communal worship, for the spiritual quest is a private endeavor. The journey heavenward is a journey out of the entanglements and mutual labeling that characterize human relationships, and into the deepest or highest part of the naked soul, where God is found. Established religion may even hinder the spiritual quest by imposing rules and structure, which cause us to lose sight of our own oneness with the divine.[80]

Nearly 2,000 years ago, the need for boundaries and structure was a point of dispute between the Apostle Paul and the Corinthian congregation. Some in that church worried that too many rules would hinder communion with the divine. Paul, for his part, anticipated by nearly 2,000 years Marta Vogel's concern that there be propriety—and not too much talk—in worship. He informs the Corinthians that when they run all over each other's lines (1 Cor

14:27–31), or when they fail to share provisions at their love feasts (11:20–22), they are showing a fundamental lack of respect for one another. When all speak in angelic tongues and none interpret, they fail to impress their visitors, who leave thinking not that God was present but that the Christians are crazy (14:23–25). Proper ordering of worship is, in Paul's view, yet one more way of expressing divine love, which is the mark of God's own Spirit in our lives (see Rom 5:5). The gift of angelic tongues is meaningful only if it is exercised with love for fellow worshippers and attention to their needs. Love is the means by which Christians may sustain a sense of God's presence in their lives. Love trumps participation in the angelic liturgy.[81]

Paul embraced the mystical dimension of Christian experience. He had received a direct revelation of Jesus Christ (Gal 1:11–12). He had ascended mystically to the highest level of heaven, where he had heard things too holy to be repeated (2 Cor 12:2–4; cf. Acts 22:17–22). And he had often spoken in angelic tongues (1 Cor 14:18).[82] But Paul insisted that spiritual seeking must never obstruct concrete expressions of mutual love in the context of community. *For Christians, spiritual seeking is chiefly a communal and not a private endeavor.* This is because the Holy Spirit resides in the midst of God's gathered people, where it is actively working to reorder relationships. The more socially prominent Corinthian Christians—Paul calls them "the strong"—were fixated on the special privileges that they expected because of their superior social standing and education. Paul tells them to give up their perks and privileges when it will benefit their brothers and sisters in Christ. The strong coveted ecstatic transport, but Paul says, "Honor the weak." They sought angelic rapture, but Paul says, "Suffer when others suffer, and rejoice when they rejoice" (1 Cor 12:26). Christians, Paul wrote, are privileged to behold nothing less than the image of God's glory: they do so not at the divine throne but in the unveiled faces of the members of the reconciled community. Beholding the glory of the Lord *in one another,* they are transformed into the same image (2 Cor 3:18). Their transfigured faces and relationships exemplify God's work of new creation, in which the forces that alienate us from God and from one another are subjected to the power of love.[83]

So, love is for Paul—and is it not for us as well?—the means for sustaining an everyday sense of the presence of God. I say an "everyday" sense because love and its expressions are carried out not chiefly in sacred times, times apart, but in the ebb and flow, the giving and receiving, the injuring and forgiving of everyday life. Still, Christian love is like ecstatic worship or transport, in that such love also is a kind of surrender to a power much greater than oneself—the power of Christ's love for us. Paul writes, "The love of Christ controls us, because we are convinced that one has died for all; therefore all have died" (2 Cor 5:14). This "love of Christ" is Jesus' love for us, which he expressed by dying "for all." But we who serve Christ express our love for him by dying also—dying to the idols, the passions, the desires that formerly dictated our thoughts, words, and actions. Now another force—Christ's love—controls us. Our desires are reshaped as we learn to desire what Christ desires: not only our own flourishing, but also the flourishing of others.

Sacred time, time spent apart in prayer and in communal worship, does have a crucial place in this new spiritual economy. These are times when we come before our holy and transcendent God in praise and thanksgiving. But such times are not the only times when God can be known. Rather, time in worship and time apart replenish us for life lived in the world. Ralph Harper points to Jesus, who could give so freely to God and to others "because his life was made up of regularly alternating periods of solitude and society. He would go away by himself, to pray, to be with the Father." Harper suggests that Jesus' frequent withdrawals in prayer were for him times of entry into the heart of Being, and that his giving was in turn an overflowing of the fullness of the glory that he encountered there. "We do not see God; we do see God's glory. Jesus' disciples saw him enter a cloud on the mount of the Transfiguration, and when he came out of the cloud, 'his face shone like the sun' (Matt. 17:2). He had been near 'the power and the presence' (2 Pet. 1:16)."[84] And so it is for us. In times of worship and prayer we encounter the fullness of glory. This divine love transfigures us, and overflows into our daily lives.

In the matter of divine presence, then, sacred time and everyday time are complementary, but not mutually exclusive. In each sort of time we are invited to love God, who has first loved and desired us. In each sort of time our love for God opens us to God's presence. In each sort of time we learn to know God and to trust that the one who sees all faults will neither mock nor condemn but embrace us and transform us into the image of the glory of the Lord.

Yet there is a darker side to the matter at hand that cannot go unmentioned. From Jesus' example we see that not only experiences of God's presence, but also times of God's seeming absence, belong to the life of faith. "Though self-donation often issues in the joy of reciprocity, it must reckon with the pain of failure and violence."[85] On at least one occasion, Jesus' retreat was a means by which he prepared himself for such an experience: he withdrew to pray on the night of his arrest, before the crucifixion. Praying in Gethsemane, Mark reports, Jesus submitted himself to God's will, even as he implored God to take away the cup of suffering that he knew would soon be his to drink. Through his time of prayer Jesus was fortified for the trials that lay ahead. In those trials, Jesus, who had known God in the closest possible fellowship, could no longer see God's face. Hence, his cry from the cross: "My God, my God, why have you forsaken me?" (Mark 15:34). Jesus' act of self-donation had become "a cry before the dark face of God."[86] He had entered into the void in human experience where God cannot be found. But Jesus did not cease to trust in God: even his cry of dereliction was uttered in the form of a prayer.[87]

There is more to be said about trials of faith—about the nature and meaning of those times in life when the believer's trust in God and reliance on God are pressed to the limit (see Chapter 4). For now, I observe only that for us, as for Jesus, times of withdrawal to pray can nourish us so that we can persevere through the hour of trial.

CONCLUSION

Many spiritual seekers today long to find holy times and places. Angels are key players in some best-selling accounts of sacred moments or peak experiences, the authors of which tell us that angels will help us to live *all* of life in a different way. Angels help humans in their quest to progress on the path to enlightenment and to live in the fullness of the heavenly dimension. According to such reports, we can and should establish rapport with our angels, through meditation and by opening our souls to their constant presence. When we do so, the angels convey wisdom consistent with the themes of much best-selling spirituality: themes such as the essential oneness of our Higher Selves with God, the divine/angelic wish to heal our every hurt and answer our every desire, and the absence of any need to fear God's judgment or feel guilty for wrongs done. We needn't fear God, we are told, because God isn't a Holy Desperado after all. Moreover, we needn't feel guilty because there really is no such thing as sin, but only ignorance; mistakes made in ignorance actually help each person to fulfill the divine plan for his or her life.

Biblical authors, too, stress God's incredible nearness. When Jacob dreams of angels ascending and descending on a stairway to heaven, he perceives that God is in that very place. And when he wrestles with an angelic being, the mysterious "man" is near enough to wound Jacob physically. When Ezekiel witnesses the "likeness of the glory of the Lord," he is far away from God's preferred dwelling place in Jerusalem. Hence this stunning vision conveys God's nearness or accessibility even in a location as remote as Babylon.

Ezekiel's vision also conveys God's transcendence: though truly present, God can be glimpsed only in and through the mediating, human-like figure on the throne. Like many biblical authors (but unlike the modern writers surveyed above), Ezekiel is awed and humbled by the grandeur of God's presence. Such humility before God is always appropriate, because humans fall short of God's intentions for them: they are prone to worship false gods and to commit acts of injustice. God is a just God, and wise humans "fear" God in the sense that they recognize and revere God's righteousness and are moved to repentance. But they also know that God is slow to anger and abounding in steadfast love. Therefore, fear of God is to be balanced by trust in God's essential goodness and mercy.

In the centuries following Ezekiel, ancient Jewish authors seized upon his dazzling vision, redeploying nearly every detail in fresh visionary accounts of heaven. The "likeness of the glory of the LORD" began to be ascribed independent or quasi-independent identity, as a chief mediator between God and humans. Earlier biblical stories of God appearing in human guise fed these emerging beliefs about a divine mediator. The influential biblical stories included not only passages about the angel of the LORD but also texts about God's word, glory, wisdom, power, spirit, and name. Generalizations about the emerging chief mediator-figure are risky, for the ancient texts do not all agree on this figure's names or roles, or on how separate the mediator is from God. In Daniel, for example, the "one like a son of man" is an angel-like being who is presented before God and who may even sit on a distinct throne. In Philo's thought, the *logos* seems to operate as an angel, though it participates fully in God's own being and seems scarcely separate from God. In early Christian thinking, Jesus—preexistent, living as a mortal, and now resurrected—is this chief mediator between God and humanity. Indeed, he bears the image of the glory of God.

During the latter part of the Second Temple era, heaven was increasingly envisioned as a temple, where God sits enthroned, surrounded by angels. Only a few of the worthiest mortals—hand-picked prophets and holy men such as Abraham, Enoch, and Isaiah—are depicted in writings from this era as having been able to enter into God's presence in the heavenly sanctuary. Apocalyptic visions ascribed to these figures build on the accounts in the Hebrew Scriptures of the divine glory, above all on the vision of "the likeness of the glory of the LORD" in Ezekiel 1.[88] Among the Dead Sea sectarians, access to the divine presence in the heavenly sanctuary may have been somewhat more routine. The sectarians read and preserved texts that purported to describe the angels' heavenly liturgy, and they marveled that God had permitted them, lowly as they were, to stand alongside the host of the angels and enter into communal worship with them.

Like the Dead Sea sectarians, early Christians understood themselves to be in the presence of the holy angels. The faithful believed that their earthly worship paralleled or intersected with the angels' heavenly worship of God and of the Lamb. New Testament authors speak of humans raised up to the heavenly heights, of prayers ascending to heaven like the smoke of incense, and of angels descending to be present among those who gather in earthly assemblies. When Christians envision the throne, they see Jesus present there, either standing alongside God or perhaps seated on a throne of his own. He is not an angel—or at least he is no ordinary angel. Jesus represents the very glory of God. He is "the reflection of God's glory and the exact imprint of God's very being" (Heb 1:3). In the person of Jesus, God has stooped down to make God's presence known.

In Paul's letters to the Corinthian church, we catch a glimpse of how early Christians disagreed about this matter of entry into divine presence. The so-called strong in Corinth—those with greater wealth, education, and other privileges—prided themselves on the ecstatic experience of speaking in "the tongues of angels." They held that the capacity to speak in tongues was a badge of honor, granted only to the superspiritual. Paul countered with an insistence that *all* Christians are possessed by the Spirit of God. And the greatest mark of the Spirit's presence is not participation in the angelic liturgy but *love manifested in community.* When we as Christians behold Christ's face reflected in one another, we are transfigured to become more like him, just as the ancient visionaries who ascended to the throne became like the heavenly angels. Becoming more like Christ, we give of ourselves in love by honoring and serving the weak rather than by holding on to the privileges that set us apart. Thus the mark of our transformation "from one degree of glory to another" is love, and the mark of love is self-lowering in service of the weak.

If the strong obeyed Paul by lowering themselves to be in solidarity with the weak, this would have leveled status differences and enabled a new type of fellowship. In such a fellowship all are brothers and sisters, made one in Christ Jesus, bound to one another in love. Only this sort of community fully reflects the image of Christ, who in the incarnation gave up his godly status and bound himself to us in love. But talk about "lowering the self" does not appeal to everyone today. It runs counter to some feminists' sensibilities, for example. Their argument (a valid one in my opinion) is that the charge to lower oneself has too often been made to those who have no status or sense of self-worth in the first place. Paul was not speaking, however, to the socially weak but to the strong. In his envisioned new community, the weak actually *rise* in status (see especially 1 Cor 12:24).

Talk about "lowering the self" also runs counter to the sensibilities expressed by proponents of the new spirituality. Such proponents emphasize self-help, self-affirmation, self-fulfillment, and a lone ranger model for encountering God—the strong and fearless individual goes it alone, needing and wanting help from no one. But Christians affirm that we do, indeed, need one another, for the Holy Spirit is active in the midst of God's gathered people. The Spirit is working among us to remake us into the image of the God who gave up divine form so as to be in solidarity with weak and suffering humanity. The Spirit is kindling in our midst the fire of love for God and for all the children of God. Giving and receiving love is what sustains our awareness of God's presence from day to day.

The scriptural and other ancient reports of visions of God, the glory of God, and the angels around God's throne are like the image of sunlight reflected on glass. The reports do not offer us real presence—but they can give us an idea of what real presence is like.[89] By contrast, in times set apart for God and in day-to-day living and giving with brothers and sisters we *can* catch a glimpse of the real thing: of life as it will be when God has completed the work of restoration begun in Jesus and is finally "all in all" (1 Cor 15:28). The church anticipates this full restoration. The church is a place where the Spirit of God has taken up residence, and where all are being transformed, both as individuals and in their relationships to one another. Though broken and imperfect, the church is a place where we taste the divine life, the life of God's New Creation. Acutely aware of our weaknesses and failures, we look to the day when all will be perfected in love.

In this chapter I have written about the boundary between the everyday world and the realm of the sacred. I have written about reports of humans who crossed that boundary, ascending to heaven where they beheld the angelic host and entered into God's very presence. Now I will turn to focus on reports of angels who crossed over the boundary in the opposite direction. These angels, described in Genesis 6 and elsewhere, forsook the celestial realm for earthly pleasure. Their legacy has been extraordinary. Millions have seen them as "fallen angels"—evil spirits or demons who are a chief source of wickedness and cause of alienation from God. Satan, the Prince of Darkness, is often viewed as their instigator and head. But in recent years the "fallen" (or "falling") angels have been viewed differently: as loving beings who yearn for the simple pleasures of mortal existence, and who by their yearning teach humans to value those pleasures anew. In the next chapter I will compare several ancient and modern accounts of these angels, to try to discern what their angelic desire and its consequences can teach us about the yearning of our own hearts.

3

Falling Angels

Desiring Divinity, Wanting the World

How do we find our heart's desire? How do we control the desires that threaten to undo us? How do we tell the difference between the good desires and the bad ones? Can we train ourselves to desire only the things that are approved by God? And if we could ever truly manage to desire only what is good, would having that single focus help us to live in a fuller, more satisfying way? To speak about the ordering of our desires is to address fundamental questions about the meaning and purpose of life.

The emotion of desire wields tremendous power over us. Whatever the longing, once stirred to life it can alter our inner landscape with astonishing thoroughness and speed. Desire can shift moral boundaries that we thought were immovable, commandeering our thoughts and dictating our actions. Ancient philosophers and physicians knew well the force exercised by desire, and warned of it in the strongest terms. Desire was something to be fought, mastered, and feared. But today the common cultural wisdom seems to be the exact opposite: we don't fear desire, we cultivate it! Never has desire exercised more power than in the consumerist economy of the present era. As David Ford points out, vast economic resources are devoted to the arousal and sustaining of our desires.

> Our economy and culture are like a machine manufacturing and orchestrating the desires of millions of people. The most obvious way this happens is through the entertainment industry, advertising, and mass democratic policies. Our whole civilization would collapse if people started desiring in very different ways. Therefore, massive

forces are focused on making sure that that does not happen. These are the forces behind the compulsions, and it is difficult and sometimes dangerous to resist them.[1]

Ironically, even the spiritual publishing industry is a "force behind the compulsions." It, too, would collapse if people stopped desiring to improve their lot by purchasing books and other aids to spiritual self-help. Some such aids offer spiritual rationales for conspicuous consumption (angels tell people to "BE SPECIFIC AND ASK BIG!").[2] Some explain how we can escape the prison of misplaced wants—and go on to sell thousands (and even hundreds of thousands) of copies, thereby prompting their authors to apologize for their financial success.[3]

Filmmakers have used angels to address questions about desire. Movies such as *Wings of Desire, City of Angels, Michael,* and *The Preacher's Wife* have all featured angels who yearn for the pleasures of human life.[4] In the films, the angels' desire prods human characters in the story (and viewers in their turn) to examine and reorder their own priorities. After all, if angels want what we have, then perhaps we ought to stop taking so much of it for granted! This plot device predates the films mentioned above. The 1948 movie *The Bishop's Wife* (of which *The Preacher's Wife* is a remake) already featured Cary Grant as the winsome angel, Dudley.[5] Dudley was attracted to one of his human charges, Julia (played by Loretta Young), and envious of her husband, an Episcopal bishop (played by David Niven). Whereas *The Bishop's Wife* observed the rules of traditional morality—Julia flees when she learns of Dudley's feelings for her, and he vows never to see her again—several of the more recent films do not. Instead, the recent films revel in the very fact of angelic desire.

This motif of angelic desire is quite ancient. Genesis 6:1–4—an exceptionally difficult passage—tells of divine beings or angels (literally "sons of God") who looked upon human women and found them to be fair, then came down to earth and mated with them. Each of the films mentioned above goes back, if indirectly, to this account. Ancient authors told and re-told the Genesis story of the lustful angels, and transformed it in each re-telling. For example, one very ancient account identifies the Nephilim, or giants, mentioned in Genesis as the offspring of the angelic-human unions; when the giants die, evil spirits come forth from their bodies.[6] Another ancient version claims that it is not the angels who desire intercourse, but the human women: they use their feminine wiles to charm their heavenly visitors.[7] But the most interesting and significant transformation of the story occurred over the course of centuries, as the account of the angels' descent became tightly intertwined with the story of the angel Satan, whose desire to be first among God's creatures reputedly led to his own fall from grace and to Adam's fall as well.

In this chapter, I will consider both ancient and modern stories of angels who looked at the earth and wanted what they saw. These are stories about angels (and humans) who are enticed by their desires to transgress the boundaries separating different spheres of existence: heaven and earth, spirit and flesh, divinity and humanity, immortality and mortality. In the ancient accounts the angels and those who follow them are condemned; in the modern tales they are portrayed as heroes. The stories and the ways in which they differ provoke many questions—questions about the boundaries that are crossed, about the angels' desire for what lies beyond those boundaries, and about whether and how we ourselves might ever manage our own overwhelming desires. To address these questions I will consider not only the stories of angels who incarnate in human flesh, but also the story of Jesus. According to one early Christian writer, Jesus' incarnation was not a fulfillment but a giving up of desire: though in the form of deity, Christ did not grasp or clutch his equality with God but willingly relinquished it to take on lowly human form. Then, in his earthly life, Jesus experienced the full force of fleshly desire, but chose to subordinate his own longings to the desire of God.

THE SONS OF GOD AND THE DAUGHTERS OF MEN
(GENESIS 6:1–4 AND RETELLINGS)

BOUNDARIES CROSSED

In Genesis, God seems determined to keep the divine and human realms separate. God forbids Adam and Eve to eat from the tree of the knowledge of good and evil because, when they do, they will become like God (Gen 3:5). God worries that they may go on to become still more God-like: "See, the man has become like one of us, knowing good and evil; and now, he might reach out his hand and take also from the tree of life, and eat, and live forever" (3:22). So God banishes Adam and Eve from the Garden of Eden, and places cherubim and a flaming sword as guardians protecting the tree of life. Later, humans build a great city and a tower "with its top in the heavens," and God comes down to inspect. Taking note of how all earthly peoples speak a single language, God realizes that the city and tower are just the beginning. Henceforth "nothing that they propose to do will now be impossible for them" (11:6). And so, to ward off further encroachment on divine prerogatives, God scatters them abroad and confuses their languages (11:1–9).

In Gen 6:1–4, angels—called "sons of God"—are the ones who transgress the divide between heaven and earth: "When people began to multiply on the face of the ground, and daughters were born to them, the sons of God saw that they were fair; and they took wives for themselves of all that they chose. Then the LORD said, 'My spirit shall not abide in mortals forever, for they are flesh; their days shall be one hundred twenty years'" (vv. 1–3). The illicit sex prompts God to declare that humans will not be immortal. Their finitude will distinguish them from the gods.[8] But then the narrator volunteers another piece of information: "The giants [Heb. *nephilim*] were on the earth in those days—and also afterward—when the sons of God went into the daughters of humans, who bore children to them. These were the heroes that were of old, warriors of renown" (v. 4). It is not clear how the presence of the giants relates to the mingling of the angels and women. Are we to understand that the *nephilim* were the offspring of the intercourse between angels and women? Presumably they were; otherwise, why mention them? But the author is not particularly interested in the giants' origin. Instead, this story and the following one focus on showing that God is still in control. God limits the human lifespan, and soon afterward God sends the Great Flood to blot out human wickedness.

Why did the sons of God leave the heavenly realm? Because, according to Genesis, the human women were beautiful. The angels were driven by desire. Note that these angels seem to have been fully embodied creatures, able to do the deed. They did not need to fall off any buildings beforehand, or to trade their armor of immortality for a moment's pleasure. According to Genesis, their coming to earth was not a fall but a descent, done voluntarily and without fanfare. But God disapproves of their action and "is immediately on the spot with his word of judgment."[9] God solemnly declares, "My spirit shall not abide in mortals forever, for they are flesh; their days shall be one hundred twenty years" (Gen 6:3).

God's reasoning here is obscure. Why should the cross-species intercourse, initiated by angels, lead to *human* mortality? The sequence in *Wings of Desire* and *City of Angels* seems to make more sense; in the films, it is the *angels* who become mortal when they succumb to desire. But the contrast drawn in Genesis 6:3 between human "flesh" and divine "spirit" gives a clue to a deeper logic. The proper balance between flesh and spirit had been established at the time of creation, when God first breathed divine breath into human flesh (Gen 2:7). Now, with the influx of the angels' own life principle into the world via intercourse, the balance has been disturbed. By moving to limit the human lifespan, God repairs the breach in the wall around heaven. Humans will not be gods after all. Flesh and spirit will stay in proper balance.

In popular thought today, flesh (or body) is generally viewed as material, whereas spirit (or soul) is understood to be nonmaterial. This material/nonmaterial dualism is taken for granted in the angel films. Thus, in *Wings of Desire* and *City of Angels,* the angels are spirit-beings with no capacity to experience physical sensation. This premise underlies the most charming scene in *Wings of Desire,* in which the actor Peter Falk as a former angel, now become human, describes the pleasures of hot coffee and a smoke to an angel, Damiel, whom Falk senses but cannot see. But ancient peoples did not view the categories of flesh and spirit in this way. Flesh was thought to differ from spirit, but the difference had nothing to do with the material/nonmaterial distinction that is so widely assumed today. Indeed, as Dale Martin points out, most ancient theorists regarded spirit as itself material—it was viewed as "a kind of 'stuff' that is the agent of perception, motion, and life itself." [10] In ancient Jewish writings, "spirit" pointed to an aspect of life that partakes of the divine and so is undying or eternal, whereas "flesh" signified the mortal or perishing aspect of living, breathing creatures. Thus God says in Genesis, "My spirit shall not abide in mortals forever, for they are flesh; their days shall be one hundred twenty years" (6:3). And in *1 Enoch* we read that the angels who mated with human women were once "spiritual, (having) eternal life, and immortal in all the generations of the world" (15:6). [11]

Even though it is not ancient, the opposition between material flesh and nonmaterial spirit is widely assumed in Western culture. Popular spiritual authors, gurus, and workshop leaders presuppose such dualism of flesh and spirit—even as they struggle to counter what they regard as an epidemic of separation. "Separation" as used by such teachers refers to an overemphasis on a half of the dualism, for example, to excessive stress on human rationality or the things of the spirit/mind to the exclusion of body/earth-awareness. [12] The angel films contribute to the agenda of empowering people to move out of separation and into a more holistic life. In the films, nonmaterial angels defy separation by becoming material. As spirits who incarnate in human, or human-like, bodies, they unite spirit and flesh, and show their human charges how to do likewise. So, for example, the harried minister in *Preacher's Wife* follows the angel Dudley's example and learns to pay attention to his lovely wife and child; in *Michael* a cynical reporter takes archangel Michael's lead and learns to savor sex and sugar. The angels in these films are not depicted as transgressing forbidden boundaries, instead, they are breaking down walls that inhibit the fullness of life.

KNOWLEDGE REVEALED

There is another boundary at stake in the ancient accounts and modern films about descending angels: the boundary that protects divine knowledge.[13] In *1 Enoch,* when the angels leave heaven to mate with human women, they take heavenly secrets with them and reveal them to the women. This classified information is deeply attractive to humans, but also destructive: it includes mining and metallurgy, which lead to the production of weapons of war, and the arts of jewelry and cosmetics, which lead to fornication:

> And Azaz'el taught the people (the art of) making swords and knives, and shields, and breastplates; and he showed to their chosen ones bracelets, decorations, (shadowing of the eye) with antimony, ornamentation, the beautifying of the eyelids, all kinds of precious stones, and all coloring tinctures and alchemy. And there were many wicked ones and they committed adultery and erred, and all their conduct became corrupt. (*1 En.* 8:1–2)

Also revealed are secrets of sorcery and astrology.[14] These angelic revelations wreak havoc upon the earth and are later condemned as "the rejected mysteries" (*1 En.* 16:3). On the other hand, *1 Enoch* does not take any general stand against special revelation; there are approved mysteries as well. In this document, Enoch is escorted through the heavens by revealing angels, and is himself eventually transformed into a heavenly being. The approved heavenly knowledge is given to Enoch through the course of his celestial journeys—knowledge that brings not destruction but salvation. For example, revelations about the stars and planets enable correct observance of the religious calendar (see chaps. 72–82). Revelations about other features of the cosmos give welcome evidence that God will judge the wicked and reward the righteous (see chaps. 17–19 and 21–32).[15]

In the films the angels also convey heavenly wisdom. Their revelations concern how to achieve personal wholeness by attending to the flesh as well as the spirit—to the affairs of the heart as well as the affairs of the human protagonists' (highly rational, workaholic) minds. In these films spirituality is achieved not through monastic seclusion or prayer (otherworldliness), but through holistic celebration of the blessings and pleasures of human life. The message is to "taste and see that the world is good!" Thus Nicholas Cage as the angel Seth persuades Maggie Rice, played by Meg Ryan, to *savor* the pear she is eating; John Travolta as Michael looks out over a field at sunrise and quietly marvels at "how beautiful it all is," as the track for "What a Wonderful World" plays softly in the background. Where is the sacred to be found? In the midst of the everyday. This is the special knowledge that the film-angels share.

The theme of "knowledge revealed" is also quite pronounced in popular written works on angels, including accounts of near-death experiences. Such accounts typically reflect a gnostic-type worldview: material existence imprisons and stupefies individuals, causing them to forget their indwelling divinity and potential for spiritual freedom. Only knowledge—not factual knowledge but interior revelation—can awaken humans from their torpor, enabling them truly to know themselves and their own divinity (see pp. 45–46). In many accounts of near-death experiences, angels help with this process of waking or sobering people up: they convey the needed "revelatory impulses, designed to fan the fallen spark of the human spirit into the blaze of gnosis."[16] In some accounts, such as Betty Eadie's *Embraced by the Light* or Howard Storm's *My Descent Into Death*,[17] angels do much more. Like interpreting angels of old, they explain the entire moral order: "the way things work in both the world of spirit and the everyday world of form that we, the living, currently inhabit."[18] The purpose of their revelation is to enable those of us who are stuck on the fleshly plane of existence to discover our true spiritual (divine) essence. Allegedly, this discovery will help us to live in a fuller way.

A gnostic perspective dominates, for example, a book by emergency and trauma physician Michael Abrams. In *The Evolution Angel,* Abrams recounts conversations that he had with angels while he was attending the deaths of his patients. He learns that angels are numerous and various, but nevertheless they are one. "There is no distinct 'me,' " the angel tells Abrams at the time of the death of Amy, an eight-year-old girl. "I shift and change, merging, flowing in and out of the others."[19] The angel goes on to explain the divinity of all creation, of "every subatomic particle, every molecule, every rock, every star, every animal, every plant, every human being, and every angelic being."[20] Angels and humans are all a part of the oneness of divine Spirit, and exist only as *apparent* "fragments of the one light."[21] This revealed knowledge is presented as therapeutic for humans. It will help them to develop an "angelic mind-set"—an outlook "characterized by perfect positivity, optimism, and love" and harboring not even a trace of "discouragement, fear, judgment, and malice." The person with an angelic mind-set is "invariably cheerful, easy going, and perfectly accepting of others."[22]

In summary, in the biblical and other ancient accounts of descending angels, a clear boundary separates divinity from humanity. This boundary has been established by God, who has very definite ideas about how angels—and humans—should conduct their affairs. From the heavenly side the boundary is permeable, albeit problematic. Angels are not prevented from descending to earth and partaking of fleshly pleasures, but they do pay for their actions. The boundary can also be crossed from the earthly side, but only rarely, only by the exceptionally righteous, such as Enoch, and only with God's full initiative or, at least, full compliance. More typically, divinity and humanity are separate and remain so. But in modern films about descending angels and accounts of near-death experiences, the situation is viewed quite differently. Now the dividing wall between divinity and humanity is not just permeable but nonexistent or illusory, like a holographic image. Angels or humans can pass through it unhindered. For angels, mixing with humans and revealing heavenly mysteries or wisdom do not bring punishment, because these are the angels' assigned tasks. Likewise for humans, crossing the boundary between mortality and divinity brings not punishment but reward. To come to know themselves as divine is for humans finally to discover their own true nature, which they had never known, or had once known but long ago forgot.

MOTIVES AND CONSEQUENCES

In the ancient accounts, misplaced desire led the angels to meddle. In Genesis, apparently, this desire was chiefly physical lust: the sons of God wanted to have sex with beautiful women. But did the author suppose that there were other desires at work, too? Did the angels also want power, or autonomy from God? Was their descent an attempt at mutiny? Ancient readers speculated on these questions. Although not explicit in Genesis, the motif of rebellion against God enters the legend of the descending angels very early. In *1 Enoch* 6–11, written in the third century BCE,[23] the angels (called "watchers") recognize the evil nature of what they are about to do and make a pact not to back out. They say, " 'Let us all swear an oath and bind everyone among us by a curse not to abandon this suggestion but to do the deed.' Then they all swore together and bound one another by (the curse)" (6:4). Afterward, the giants born to the human women work mayhem and destruction on the earth. The earth's inhabitants cry out in protest to God, who sends the angel Asuryal to tell Noah that the Flood is coming. God also authorizes the angels Raphael, Michael, and Gabriel to destroy the marauding giants and to bind the sinful watchers "under the rocks of the ground" until their final destruction on the Day of Judgment (see 10:1–15). But the ghosts of the dead giants (viewed as demons) continue to corrupt humans, causing all kinds of sorrow (see 15:8–12).

By having God pass judgment against the sinful angels, *1 Enoch* transforms their voluntary *descent* (as in Genesis) into a catastrophic *fall from grace.* Formerly, the angels who mated with human women "were spiritual, (having) eternal life, and immortal in all the generations of the world" (*1 En.* 16:6). Henceforth they "will not be able to ascend into heaven unto all eternity," but will "remain inside the earth, imprisoned all the days of eternity" (14:5). In chapters 17–19, Enoch is led on a tour of earth and the underworld. The climax of the journey is when they reach the deep pit where stars that wander off course and the fallen angels are punished.[24] The scene underscores God's sovereignty and righteousness in judging sinners. Evil will not run unchecked! The author of the New Testament book of Jude also makes the point that God does not permit sinners to go unpunished: "And the angels who did not keep their own position, but left their proper dwelling, he has kept in eternal chains in deepest darkness for the judgment of the great day" (v. 6).[25]

Why do ancient authors insist that angels must "keep their own position?" And why does their "leaving their proper dwelling" merit such severe judgment? By contrast, in the movies, when angels "leave their proper dwelling" they are not judged. In *City of Angels,* Seth learns that God has given angels, like humans, free will. Hence Seth can simply choose to fall into mortality, with all its attendant limitations and sorrows as well as joys, apparently without incurring divine disapproval. But in the view of ancient readers/authors, the descent of the angels in Genesis 6:1–4 was not simply the free choice of beings who have every right to set their own agenda. The angels were refusing to obey God. Their refusal constituted rebellion, and their rebellion threatened the entire cosmic order—just as the insurgence of an underclass in a hierarchical society threatens the social order.[26] What would happen if *everyone* in such a society decided to act in a way that defied his or her social station? Chaos would ensue.

In the Bible and in much ancient Jewish and early Christian literature, God is portrayed as one who rewards humility and punishes arrogance. God is a God of reversal: as Mary proclaims in Luke's Gospel, God has "exalted those of low degree; he has filled the hungry with good things" (1:52–53 RSV; cf. 1 Sam 2:1–10, especially vv. 5–7). The reversal-motif penetrates to the very core of Israel's identity: the Hebrews were the lowest of the low, slaves in Egypt at the time when God chose them to be God's own people. The motif of reversal penetrates also to the core of Christian identity: Jesus emptied himself, taking the form of a servant, being born in human likeness and humbling himself by dying on a cross. Therefore God exalted him and gave him "the name that is above every name" (see Phil 2:5–11). As Gary Anderson observes, in the Bible "bending the knee portends exaltation not humiliation."[27] But divine reversal works in two directions; not only does

God raise the lowly, God also lowers the arrogant and proud, those who would put themselves in the place of God. As Mary further proclaims in Luke's Gospel, God "has scattered the proud in the imagination of their hearts, he has put down the mighty from their thrones" (1:52). In ancient understanding, when the angels made a pact to go down to earth, their "going down" was also an attempt to "move up"—arrogantly to assume God's role as the one who orders the universe. That was why they had to be punished.

DAMNATION BY ASSOCIATION: OTHER ERRANT ANGELS

The "sons of God" (or angels) in Genesis 6:1–4 were damned not only because of their own actions but also by association: early on, they were linked in the popular mind with other celestial figures who overstepped their place and so were punished. The author of Isaiah 14 portrayed the King of Babylon as a rebellious deity or star, whom God cast down to earth for his arrogance.

> How you are fallen from heaven,
>> O Day Star, son of Dawn!
> How you are cut down to the ground,
>> you who laid the nations low!
> You said in your heart,
>> "I will ascend to heaven;
> I will raise my throne
>> above the stars of God;
> I will sit on the mount of assembly
>> on the heights of Zaphon;
> I will ascend to the tops of the clouds,
>> I will make myself like the Most High."
> But you are brought down to Sheol,
>> to the depths of the Pit.   (vv. 12–15)

Ezekiel 28–32 includes similar oracles of judgment against rulers who exalt themselves as if they were gods and so are cast down to the pit. In one of these, the King of Tyre is compared to a celestial being who had been in the very presence of God (see Ezek 28:11–19). Perhaps Isaiah's and Ezekiel's imagery of rebellious celestial beings or stars who are then punished in the deep pit at the base of the mountain of God already influenced the portrayals in *1 Enoch* of the rebellion and punishment of the angels.[28] In any case, the passages in Isaiah and Ezekiel about rebellious rulers cast down because of their lust for power ("I will raise my throne above the stars of God") and *1 Enoch*'s several accounts of errant angels would soon be intertwined in the popular view.

Both sets of traditions would become elements in a powerful new story about a figure called *Satan,* erstwhile member of God's heavenly council. The Old Testament texts that explicitly discuss the figure of the *satan*[29] do not say anything about his having been expelled from heaven. Nonetheless, ancient readers made that inference, based on the texts from Isaiah, Ezekiel, *1 Enoch,* and elsewhere. Indeed, the word *day star* in Isa 14:12 would one day be translated as *Lucifer* ("light bearer") in the Latin, thereby giving Satan one of his most enduring names and linking this passage to him irrevocably. By New Testament times, many assumed that Satan had led a host of fellow angels in rebellion. God had cast Satan out of heaven because of his arrogant will to power. Satan's desire was to be preeminent in all things, to have a throne above the heights, to be like God.[30]

I will have much more to say about Satan in Chapter 4. In the remainder of this section I will address only the single question, why did Satan rebel? Ancient Jews and early Christians told different stories to answer this question, but a common thread runs through them: God favored humanity (or Israel, or Adam, or Christ) over the angels. Satan rebelled at this inversion of the normal order of things. According to this order, the firstborn (or first created, as the case may be) by rights would inherit the greater share of the parents' blessings. As it turns out, in the Bible this rule of primogeniture was sometimes violated: Abel, the second-born, received God's approval for his sacrifice, whereas the firstborn Cain did not. Jacob, the younger twin, inherited all that should have accrued to his older brother Esau. And Joseph was favored by his father, Jacob, over his older brothers. Gary Anderson suggests that a similar break from the usual norm happens when God favors humans—late arrivals in the sequence of creation—over angels.[31] Most of the angels accepted God's preference for the ones created in God's image. But not Satan, the greatest and most glorious of all God's angels, the "signet of perfection, full of wisdom and perfect in beauty" (Ezek 28:12). According to the ancient document the *Life of Adam and Eve,* when Michael instructed the angels to worship the newly created Adam, Satan replied, "I do not worship Adam." And when Michael pressured him, Satan continued, "Why do you compel me? I will not worship one inferior and subsequent to me. I am prior to him in creation; before he was made, I was already made. He ought to worship me" (*LAE* 14:3).[32] This theme of Satan's arrogance and resentment is hinted at already in the gospel accounts of Jesus' temptation. In Luke 4, Satan leads Jesus to a high place and shows him the kingdoms of the world:

> And the devil said to Jesus, "To you I will give their glory and all this authority; for it has been given over to me, and I give it to anyone I

please. If you, then, will worship me, it will all be yours." Jesus answered him, "It is written, 'Worship the Lord your God, and serve only
him.'" (vv. 6–8).

Why else would Satan have made such an offer, if not from jealousy and a
sense of foreboding over the worship that Christ would one day receive? It
was worship that Satan, the ruler of this world, believed ought to be his. Rabbinic authors tell a different but related story, of the angels' resentment and
protest when God chose to give the Torah to humans rather than to them.[33]
In these and other such stories, Satan/the angels act out of the jealousy born
of desire. They want the privileges that humans—Adam, the Israelites, or
Jesus—had been given. They want the power and prestige that come with
being first.

A WELL-ORDERED COSMOS

I have tried to show that, in ancient understanding, *desire* motivated the angels to come down to earth. In some accounts it was desire for sex with beautiful human women, and in other accounts, desire for preeminence over
God's other creatures (or even over God). Ancient readers viewed the angels' descent as an act of disobedience or rebellion. The angels had contested
the divine ordering of the cosmos. They "did not keep their own position,
but left their proper dwelling" (Jude 6). When they descended they were
simultaneously attempting to ascend—to usurp God's right to determine
their lot.

The notion that the cosmos is divinely ordered, down to the most minute
detail, runs through *1 Enoch*. The text includes extensive tours of the heavens,
in which Enoch is shown everything from the storehouses of the winds to
the appointed courses of the stars. The descriptions of cosmic order demonstrate God's sovereign control over and careful measuring of all that happens in the world. Carol Newsom compares the display of God's heavenly
realm before Enoch to the practice by ancient monarchs of displaying their
riches and military might to visiting dignitaries. She cites the story of King
Hezekiah, who wanted to impress the ambassadors of Merodach-Baladan:
"Hezekiah welcomed them; he showed them all his treasure house, the silver,
the gold, the spices, the precious oil, his armory, all that was found in his
storehouses; there was nothing in his house or in all his realm that Hezekiah
did not show them" (2 Kgs 20:13). When Enoch tours the heavens, it is as an
emissary between the earthly and heavenly realms. Just as Hezekiah's display
demonstrated his value as an ally, God's display of the heavenly realm before
Enoch shows him that God is an efficient administrator and a forceful and

effective judge.[34] God's ordering and control of the cosmos are stressed in other sections of *1 Enoch* as well. For example, the Book of Heavenly Luminaries, a section of *1 Enoch* dating to about 110 BCE,[35] describes the waxing, waning, and movement of the moon in great detail, and then comments that the luminaries (including the stars) "do not leave from the fixed stations according to the reckoning of the year," and "scrupulously render service to the fixed positions in the cosmos" (*1 En.* 75:1–2). God, through the angel Uriel, regulates all the luminaries' motion.

Though the heavenly surveys in *1 Enoch* center on what we might identify as the province of the natural sciences (for example, the source and movements of the winds, moon, and stars), there is high moral significance in all that is revealed. Cosmic order is here correlated with social order. Because God had *commanded* the stars to move a certain way, their deviation from the appointed course was not just a curiosity—an aberration from something like natural law. Rather, it was viewed as a moral transgression worthy of eternal punishment. God has single-handedly organized the economy of the cosmos. The arrangement is hierarchical, with each creature having its proper place and function. In such a context, the story of the descending or falling angels points to what is wrong with the world: some creatures stubbornly refuse to recognize their created purpose or place.[36]

By contrast, the popular angel films show little interest in a divine order for the world. In the films, angels' mingling with humans compromises no rank structure and brings no punishment. Why don't the angels in the films have to pay a price for their actions? Surely because in the laissez-faire West in these first decades of a new millennium, consensus about the proper ordering of society has all but vanished. We no longer share convictions about appropriate social roles or the consequences when role boundaries are transgressed. A half century has made the difference: in *The Bishop's Wife* (1948), the angel's desire for the beautiful woman is quite evident (though expressed with gentlemanly decorum). Angelic desire is denied, however, for the greater good of upholding social norms. Propriety wins out over the chemistry of mutual attraction. But what agreement is there about the meaning of social propriety today? While the recent angel films stop short of promoting adultery, other restrictions from the post-WW II era have all but disappeared. (*The Preacher's Wife*, a remake of *The Bishop's Wife*, is the conservative exception here.) The films serve as social commentary much as *1 Enoch* did, but the world they reflect is one in which the old moral order has nearly eroded away.

In the ancient accounts, the angels' desire was their undoing—the cause both of their descent and of their fall from grace. But the filmmakers who retell the angels' story invert the ancient moral valuations. Desire now has become the angels' salvation—the driving force behind their (and their charges') escape from the blandness and separation of superrational existence into the unqualified pleasure of a more holistic life.

DESIRE AS DELIGHT AND DANGER
CELEBRATING DESIRE AND ITS FULFILLMENT

The newest crop of film-angels long to partake of the tactile or fleshly pleasures of earthly existence. These angels crave robust, full-bodied sensory experience. *City of Angels* works its spell by evoking a vicarious yearning for such robust experience in us, the viewers, and then satisfying it. Watching the film, we feel Seth's intense, aching desire for the attractive surgeon, Maggie Rice. At one point the camera lingers in close-up on Maggie's face as a tear runs down her cheek. Through Seth's eyes we drink in the silky texture, the substance, the *fleshliness* of her skin. Later, we witness Seth's momentous "fall" into human form, his exhilaration at the change, his unfettered joy at his union with Maggie. From opening scene to final credit, this film celebrates the passion of desire and its fulfillment.

And why not celebrate desire? Like those who write the screenplays, we view the passion of desire as a sweet—or at least a bittersweet—companion. We see its role as temporary but indispensable. Temporary, because the thought of living for days or months or years with unfulfilled desires strikes us as intolerable. But delay *sweetened by desire*—that is another story. Without the technique of delay there would be no romantic comedies, no foreplay, no Victoria's Secret catalogs. In postmodern American culture we can scarcely imagine that desire, in and of itself, could ever be inherently wrong or destructive. Surely desire is a good thing; it is a form of hope, and who could say anything bad about hope? It is hard for people in our culture to get riled up about the problem of desire, because we simply don't see it as a problem. In fact, our situation is quite the opposite—we *want* to hold onto our desires, even the illicit ones. We want to hold on to them because to yearn is to enjoy a kind of virtual reality: an imagined future, as vivid as the images of celluloid reality that fill our heads. To relinquish desire is to abandon a vision of circumstances that promise to bring joy and to fill the hungry heart.

There could scarcely be a view more at odds with ancient sensibilities. The writings from ancient Judaism and early Christianity *lament* the destructive power of lust or desire—and not only sexual desire. Desire of any kind, it was assumed, quickly grows from a tame amusement into a difficult and deceptive master. When we cater to desire, instead of diminishing, it becomes bolder and taunts us with still more outrageous demands. Once our better self falls under desire's control, this new overseer of our soul coerces us to act against our best and most noble intentions. The author of the New Testament book of James describes the pernicious working of desire in terms that sound like an allegorical reading of the story of the falling angels: "But one is tempted by one's own desire, being lured and enticed by it; then, when that desire has conceived, it gives birth to sin, and that sin, when it is fully grown, gives birth to death" (Jas 1:14–15). So, too, the feminine objects of the angels' desire had conceived and given birth to the sinful giants, who brought lawlessness upon the earth and finally gave birth to demons who in turn wrought death. Philo of Alexandria, a first-century Jewish author, explains that passions must be bridled like a defiant horse, or they will carry one away into impassable abysses from which there is no escape (*On the Special Laws* 4.79). According to Philo, Moses himself denounced desire as "a battery of destruction to the soul, which must be done away with or brought into obedience to the governance of reason, and then all things will be permeated through and through with peace and good order" (*On the Special Laws* 4.95).[37]

Philo and the author of James were neither prudish nor extremist for their day. Among ancient writers, the passions were widely viewed as devious and destructive movements of the soul. Rhetorically, they were portrayed as diseases to be healed through moral asceticism or education, or as athletic or military opponents against whom the wise or virtuous person must struggle.[38] First-century orator Dio Chrysostom depicts the Cynic Diogenes warning of pleasure, using still another metaphor: Diogenes styles pleasure as a dangerous woman who arouses one's passions and then takes one captive. So perilous is she that the strongest man is not the one who conquers her by force but the one who can keep the farthest away from her.

> For it is impossible to dwell with pleasure or even to dally with her for any length of time without being completely enslaved. Hence when she gets the mastery and overpowers the soul by her charms, the rest of Circe's sorcery at once follows. With a stroke of her wand pleasure coolly drives her victim into a sort of sty and pens him up, and now from that time forth the man goes on living as a pig or a wolf. (*Discourses* 8.24–25)[39]

So when James and Philo lament the power of desire to damage the soul, they are simply voicing the common sense of their own era.

Not only philosophers and orators but also physicians of the ancient world reflected on the problem and the dangers of desire, especially sexual passion. Today we are inclined to think of passionate desire as primarily a mental or emotional state, but ancient medical writers (and also more popular writers, including the authors of ancient love spells) represent desire as "frankly physiological."[40] In Dale Martin's words, "It was part of the common sense of Greco-Roman culture that desire constituted an internal burning, the smoldering of the inner body's fire."[41] The burning of desire, it was supposed, must be kept at just the right level or it could have disastrous consequences for such vital physiological processes as the production of sperm and conception. For example, in the view of Soranus, an ancient gynecologist, the heat of a woman's excessive passion could burn up the deposited male seed entirely, and thereby prevent conception from taking place.[42] So when ancient persons portrayed philosophers as "physicians of the soul" who could heal the "disease" of lust and other passions gone to excess, their metaphor correlated closely with the best medical wisdom of the day. Indeed, the metaphor was scarcely metaphorical: excessive desire wasn't *like* a disease—it *was* a disease.

Among those early Jews and Christians who believed in Satan's existence and role as the tempter, the problem of desire had still another dimension. The devil, it was believed, eagerly exploits human desire for his own evil purposes. His habit of doing so goes all the way back to the beginning: Acting through the serpent, the devil tapped Eve's desire for the forbidden fruit. And by no means does Satan limit his assaults to the weak or the wicked. On the contrary: the righteous are the devil's targets of first choice. He tempted Abraham (according to one ancient account) by exploiting the patriarch's desire to preserve the life of his son Isaac; he tempted Job via Job's wish to end his own terrible affliction; he tempted Jesus by offering bread at the end of a forty-day fast.[43] On account of Satan's habit of attacking at the point of greatest desire, the Apostle Paul recommends that husbands and wives not abstain from sex for too long, "so that Satan may not tempt you because of your lack of self-control" (1 Cor 7:5). Moreover, as the case of Job makes abundantly clear, affliction also provokes a form of desire: the desire for preservation of the flesh, and for relief from suffering. Hence Satan's penchant for violent assault on life and limb. By such means he arouses his victims' desire for relief and their consequent vulnerability to his suggestions. In the cultural context of the first century, to celebrate *desire* would have been to celebrate *misery*.

ORDERING DESIRES AND ORDERING THE WORLD

When we watch the angel films, the motif of the angels' desire directs our attention to the objects of that desire, inviting us to marvel at the beauty of the world. The angels in these films are strangers in a strange land, seeing the earth for the first time. Their perspective helps both the human characters in the films and also us as viewers to look at that world afresh. We see anew the wonder of the material realm. In *City of Angels,* Seth always asks each departing soul what he or she liked best about mortal life: a little girl says flannel pajamas with feet; a man says the wind on his face. While still an angel, Seth can kiss Maggie, but he cannot feel it. He can swim in the ocean, but he cannot relish the water slipping over his body. When cut with a knife, he does not feel pain, nor does he bleed. But after he has fallen into human embodiment, which he did by falling, literally, off a building, he becomes able to partake of fleshly pleasure—and also able to be injured, to lose someone he loves, and to die.

This dualistic portrayal of nonmaterial spirit versus material flesh correlates with another dualism that is taken for granted in popular spirituality today, that of scientific rationalism versus emotional/bodily ways of knowing. As a spirit, Seth knows that his life, though eternal, is incomplete: He wants the wholeness of spirit *and* flesh, and he takes a literal leap of faith in order to pursue that wholeness.[44] As a surgeon, Maggie Rice does *not* know that she is caught in the prison of scientific rationalism, a worldview in which all is believed to be subject to rational analysis and control. Not until one of her patients dies unexpectedly does the sacred canopy of this worldview tear. At that moment Maggie sees, with inner sight, Seth peering through. Before that happens, Maggie lives a life characterized by separation. Like William Hurt's character in *Michael,* like Martha Beck in her Harvard days, and even like George Bailey in *It's a Wonderful Life,* Maggie is out of touch with her physical and emotional self. She is all head and no heart—ironically so, since she is a heart surgeon. Not only does Maggie fail to *pursue* her heart's desire, but she doesn't even *know* her heart's desire. She needs to learn how to live in the fleshly moment and seize the day. Seth's desire for her and attention to her world open her eyes to a new way of seeing. His incarnation triggers her own, and for a brief time the two of them—making love, holding one another by a foggy lake in the early morning—symbolize the pop spiritual ideal of holistic pleasure, of flesh and spirit fully joined.

By celebrating desire, *City of Angels* taps into the insatiable desire—for connection, fullness, love?—that is a facet of the human condition as we know it. Augustine, the great fifth-century theologian, famously identified this desire as a yearning for God.

> Great are you, O Lord, and exceedingly worthy of praise; your power is immense, and your wisdom beyond reckoning. And so we humans, who are a due part of your creation, long to praise you—we who carry our mortality about with us, carry the evidence of our sin and with it the proof that you thwart the proud. Yet these humans, due part of your creation as they are, still do long to praise you. You arouse us so that praising you may bring us joy, because you have made us and drawn us to yourself, and our heart is unquiet until it rests in you.[45]

The desire to praise God, Augustine believed, is an instinct left over from humanity's innocence before its fall into sin at the time of Adam's transgression. But this good instinct is compromised by the human sinfulness that has prevailed ever since the Fall. Humans desire to praise God—but they also desire to have their own way in the world. For his insight into this duplicity or contradiction at the center of the human condition, Augustine depended on the Apostle Paul.[46] Paul had observed how those who love the law know what is good and yearn in their inner selves to attain it (just as Augustine would later say that they yearn to praise God). But even the best of humans find themselves unable to live up to all their good intentions.

The angel films promise that our insatiable yearning can be satisfied—not in the hereafter, but in the here and now. It can be satisfied when we enter into another way of living in the world—a way characterized not by separation, nor by repression of desire, nor by grasping for power, but by attentiveness, presence, and relationship. Seth, a messenger from another plane of existence, fans the fallen spark of Maggie's spirit that it might blaze into knowledge of the fullness of life. He invites her (and us as viewers) to notice "what lies up close and underneath but is rarely seen," and to find our salvation in that seeing.[47] But just what is it that she and we are to perceive more clearly? The beauty of nature? The texture and sweetness of a ripe pear? The brevity and preciousness of mortal life? Certainly all of these. The insights of Paul and Augustine suggest, however, that we must also perceive *the contradiction in which we are caught, between wanting God and wanting what we want*. When we come to see ourselves as ensnared in such contradiction, we are rejecting the tenet of pop spirituality that humans are divine, fundamentally good, and already well on the way to perfection. We are confessing that we are frail and fallen creatures who can scarcely live up to our own expectations, let alone God's expectations for us. We are conceding that there is indeed a separation, a boundary, between the goodness, greatness, steadfastness, and infinite love of God and the paltry human self. And we are recognizing that, although we yearn to cross that boundary and enter into full communion with God, we cannot do it on our own power alone.

Sallie McFague agrees with Augustine's insight into the human desire for God. She writes, "It's alright to be excessive: one can't love God *too much*. It's a relief to finally find the proper object of insatiable desire." But rather than emphasizing the transcendence of God in the way that Augustine does— stressing God's distance or separation from us because of our sin—McFague stresses God's radical immanence or presence in the world. "One doesn't have to hold back; the *sanctus* is the proper primary prayer; we were made to glorify God—and it feels good to do so. But once again, it is not an either/ or—God or the world. The incarnation has taken on a whole new meaning for me: it means God is forever and truly the God with and for the flesh, the earth, the world." [48] For McFague, "looking more closely" and "seeing things as they really are" mean recognizing that God is the source and sustainer of everything. God is available all the time; it is we who have to make ourselves available to God by becoming conscious of God's presence. "To say God is always present is simply to acknowledge that God is reality, the breath, the life, the power, the love beneath, above, around, and in everything." [49] McFague argues that the recognition of God's radical immanence is desperately needed to counter the religion of consumerism—an economic system that depends on rampant desire, and that is wreaking ecological havoc on the planet. Consumerism is ultimately based on a distorted view of God as removed from the world, and of humans as unconnected from one another and superior to the natural world.

Although McFague downplays the boundary dividing creation from God, she does insist that there is a divinely given order to the world. But it is not, as the consumerist mentality holds, an order that revolves around human beings with their ever-burgeoning desires. She describes her own dawning awareness of this divine order:

> Things are neither chaotic nor ordered in relation to me and my wants. Everything is ordered by God and in relation to God. Reality "makes sense," not according to worldly standards (nor mine), but in terms of the love that created everything and wants it to flourish. . . . Such reality has order and harmony; the disorder and confusion come when we fail to acknowledge this order and try to reorder things around ourselves. [50]

"Reordering things around himself" was the sin of Satan, according to the legends, and the reason for his expulsion from God's presence. Instead of desiring communion with God, Satan desired *to be* God—and falsely supposed that all the world ought to give him worship and honor. "Reordering things" is likewise the sin of consumerist economies. When we define humans as consumers we falsely suppose that all the world was created to satisfy human wants.

The entertainment and advertising industries encourage us to suppose that we can find our deep satisfaction in the material goods of this world or in sexual relationships. But most of the desires promoted by our economy and culture are sinful according to McFague's definition, because they displace God as the true center of all created life and put us in that central place. "Sin is centering life in the self, trying to establish the self in itself for itself. Sin is living a lie: it is living contrary to God's ordering of things."[51] Sin distorts and perverts our sense of what really matters in life. "The seven deadly sins are indeed deadly because they contribute to disorder and perversion. Caught in the nets of pride, envy, lust, greed, and so on, we cannot imagine a different rendering of the good life, of what matters." Only when we gain a proper sense of the divine order—and hence, of the God-given meaning and purpose of our lives—can we order our desires in a way that will bring us deep and lasting contentment.[52]

This submission of ourselves to an order in which God is at the center also reorders our lists of the things in life that we want most intensely. Reordering our desires is not the same as eradicating them, or repressing them because we think we are not worthy or fear that they can never be fulfilled, nor is it the same as puritanically rejecting every form of pleasure. To reorder desires we must face them and understand them: how they arise, how they are stimulated, how they can and cannot be satisfied. We must know where the boundaries are—the boundaries that are essential for ourselves and others to thrive, and the boundaries that are destructive of such thriving. We must acknowledge the force of our desires and when those desires coax us to overstep the essential boundaries, figure out how to cope.

But to some, the notion that we can reorder our wants may seem ludicrous. How can we control or change any strong passion, whether it is desire, anger, jealousy, fear, or hatred? Such emotions, when at their maximum force, seem more like things that happen *to* us. And of all the emotions, desire may be the most challenging, because desire promises great things, desire assures us that satisfaction will come when we turn the fantasies it proffers into reality, desire is pleasurable in itself. To master desire, one must be convinced—and maintain the conviction over time—that it would be a good thing to do so. This is no easy task. Desire can indeed be a defiant horse that "carries one away into impassable abysses from which there is no escape."

Philo and other first-century Jews believed that, if trained in the discipline of the Mosaic law, human reason could reign in rampant desire. Writing at about the same time, Paul disputed that the law could exercise such control. Even those who know and love the Mosaic law find themselves unable to resist "another law" that seems to be at work in us. Rather, Paul insists, it is the Spirit of Jesus Christ who can finally empower us to escape from the grip of "covetousness" (desire). But Paul's assertion is not true in a simple or automatic way. Christ's Spirit does not offer effortless protection from the dangers of desire. If it did, there would not be so many Christians—lay and clergy alike—who succumb when they are tempted. How, then, might Paul's assertion be true?

DESIRING DIVINITY, WANTING THE WORLD

Christ, like the cinematic angels, became incarnate. But there was a difference. Unlike the angels, in becoming human Christ was not *pursuing* the objects of his desire but *giving them up.* The act of incarnation was itself a giving up, a relinquishing of inestimably precious equality with God that Christ had and could have kept. Likewise, as the mortal Jesus, Christ enacted a pattern of self-giving, relinquishing all desires for his own comfort, power, and glory to pursue the desires of God.

We see this pattern of self-giving played out in the New Testament theme of Jesus being tested. He was tested by Satan in the wilderness: offered bread when hungry, promised glory and honor, challenged to prove his relationship to God. He was tested by his human enemies, and even by his own followers when they failed to understand God's plan and sought to divert Jesus from it. Each of these tests played on a particular human desire. By persevering throughout his trials, Jesus made the choice to pursue the way of God rather than the way of his own desiring.

And Jesus did experience the strongest possible desires. The movie *The Last Temptation of Christ*[53] caused an uproar when it came out because it suggested that Jesus may have experienced sexual desire. Actually, in the movie Jesus desires not sex but continuing life. In the scene in which Jesus is on the cross, Satan comes to him in the form of a little girl and tells him that God doesn't want him to suffer so. The words provoke a vision of his life as it might have been—with a wife, a family. This vision of ordinary life is the "last temptation" to which the film's title refers.

The Gospels portray Jesus as desiring mortal life. Once when Jesus speaks of his own impending death, Peter rebukes him, saying, "God forbid it, Lord! This must never happen to you!" (Matt 16:22). For Jesus, Peter's words were a test from the devil. "Get behind me, Satan," he said to Peter, "You are a stumbling block to me" (v. 23). Peter's words were a test of Jesus' obedience because Jesus wanted to go on living—but knew that God's path would lead him to the cross. Jesus wanted God, but he also wanted the life of this world. In the Garden of Gethsemane on the night before his death, he prayed for God to take away the cup of suffering, but submitted himself to God's will. The prayer that Jesus prayed—"Not what I want, but what you want" (Mark 14:36)—did not extinguish his yearning to live, but *gave him the strength to choose for God even in the face of so powerful a contrary desire.*

In the Genesis account of the descending angels, God had worried that divine spirit and human flesh be kept in measured ratio. But not so with Jesus Christ. Christians hold that, though Jesus was human, the full might and glory of the transcendent God were present in him: "And the Word became flesh and lived among us, and we have seen his glory, the glory as of a father's only son, full of grace and truth" (John 1:14). Here "word" (Gk. *logos*) stands for the power and creative agency of God. For first-century readers of the Fourth Gospel, the term may have had angelic connotations, since there was precedent for connecting *logos* to the angel of the LORD (see Chapter 2, pp. 55, 74). But by insisting that the human Jesus was the divine word incarnate, John's Gospel makes it clear that Jesus' time on earth was not merely the fleeting visitation of an angel. When the angel Raphael materialized in the story of Tobit, he "really did not eat or drink anything" but only gave the appearance of doing so (Tob 12:19). Jesus, by contrast, *became* flesh. As a mortal he was subject to desire, even as he was subject to suffering and death.

For Christians, the incarnation that took place in Jesus of Nazareth is the pivotal event in all of history. It is the peerless example of God's stooping down to be present in and with the world. But there is a flip side to the incarnation, for *here the human also became divine.* Over the course of his struggle against the forces of sin, Jesus showed himself perfected, elevated beyond anything that could ever be accomplished by human powers alone. Thus he showed us what divine existence looks like when lived on the human plane. The good news is that, through the Spirit, Christ works to perfect us also— helping us to accomplish more than we ever could by our human powers alone. We are not divine—the claims of many popular spiritual authors notwithstanding. But, united with Christ by the Spirit *we are raised up to know God in a fuller and more intimate way.*[54]

The incarnation is also the ultimate proof that we do not have to deny the flesh in order to live a spiritual life. The notion that we have to choose between loving the things of God and the things of this world has a long and distinguished pedigree. For example, Augustine said that we are called to a higher, inner experience of God in the depths of the soul, purified from all distraction by the concrete stimuli of this world. Augustine claimed that his own love for God was not a love for the beauty of bodies, nor for the rhythm of time, nor for "the radiance of light, so dear to our eyes." Rather, Augustine's love for God was a love for "a light and a sound and a perfume and a food and an embrace" that are not in the world but only to be discovered through prayerful introspection.[55]

But Augustine doesn't get the last word here. As Jürgen Moltmann observes, "The nearness of God makes this mortal life worth loving, not something to be despised."[56] Indeed, loving the world is an expression of our love for God who created it and who came to dwell here in Jesus' flesh. "When I love God," Moltmann writes, in direct response to Augustine, "I love the beauty of bodies, the rhythm of movements, the shining of eyes, the embraces, the feelings, the scents, the sounds of all this protean creation. When I love you, my God, I want to embrace it all, for I love you with all my senses in the creations of your love."[57] Jesus also loved the world, and the life of this world. It is true that he withdrew to the mountaintop to pray—but he also drank wine, fed hungry people, healed broken bodies, and cried over the death of a loved one and over the impending destruction of his own body.

So we are free to love God and to love the world—indeed, we are called to do so. But loving the world does not mean satisfying our every desire. Unlike the angels who came down to earth, Jesus entered into the power and glory of God not by *acquiring* but by *relinquishing* all objects of his own desiring. So also today, we find abundant life not by acquisition (whether of material goods, power and control, desired relationships, or prolonged life), but by loving God and by opening ourselves to God's love for us. The paradox is that putting God before our other desires leads to our finding our true treasure, just as it led Jesus to resurrection. The treasure is not material but heavenly, stored "where neither moth nor rust consumes and where thieves do not break in and steal" (Matt 6:20).

Desiring God does not prevent us from being seized by other desires that seem too strong to resist—hence, our acute and ongoing need for forgiveness. As David Ford observes, we seem to be made for excess, and some seem to be more made for excess than others.[58] In ancient Jewish and early Christian tradition, it is those with a passion for God—Abraham, Job, Jesus—whom Satan would most like to pull aside. Love for God offers no magical protection against the temptations of desire, and Paul seems to have recognized this. Although he taught that we have every hope of perseverance (see Rom 5:1–11) and that God allows no temptation too great to be endured (see

1 Cor 10:13), Paul also exhorted members of a church to restore a member who has transgressed, acting in a spirit of gentleness and self-scrutiny lest they themselves be tempted (Gal 6:1; cf. 2 Cor 2:6–8). Yes, the Spirit gives us power to persevere. But God graciously forgives us and restores us if and when we, in spite of the Spirit's presence with us, fail to do so.[59]

In *City of Angels,* when the immortal, spiritual angel chooses to become human, he falls off a tall building and into mortal, fleshly life. The scene is a visually stunning portrayal of one being's leap of faith. To leap, Seth had to trust that what he would get would equal or better what he was giving up. The image is apt for the kind of trust that God requires of us. We can hold nothing back. We have to relinquish control. Relinquishing control means letting go of our many desires, trusting that the God of life will keep us from falling into destruction, stand us on our feet, and usher us into a new and abundant life in which we come to embrace, at last, "the desire that lives beneath all desires and that only God can satisfy."[60]

CONCLUSION

What do angels want, and what do their longings tell us about our own desires? In ancient accounts of the angels who descended to mate with human women, the angels wanted sex, or autonomy from God, or even, in the case of Satan (whose story became wrapped up with the story of the errant angels) power and glory greater than those of God. *Desire* caused the angels to transgress the boundary between heaven and earth. In pursuing the objects of their desire the angels set their own agenda, rejecting the lordship of Almighty God and putting themselves in God's place. Furthermore, their willful actions provoked immense human suffering: Demonic spirits eventually issued from their sexual union with the daughters of the earth, and the angelic revelation of forbidden knowledge led to all manner of catastrophe for humans. For all these reasons (by the ancients' logic), the angels' action merited severe and eternal punishment.

It is no wonder that unchecked desire should be the source of so much anguish in these stories, for it was common knowledge in the ancient world that desire was the root of all evil, a fearsome adversary, scarcely to be mastered except by the very strongest athletes of virtue. In the medical sphere also, desire had to be strictly monitored and bounded, lest the "internal smoldering" flare out of control, with unfortunate physiological consequences.

Modern films about angels who long for human pleasures reveal a vastly different attitude to the emotion of desire. In these pictures, the motif of angelic desire is used to direct audience attention to the blessings and pleasures of everyday life and love. In the films, the angels are driven by their longing for fleshly pleasures to cross over the boundary between heaven and earth—to incarnate as fleshly beings. For them, desire is the avenue not to disaster but to salvation, both for themselves and for their human charges.

The modern stories presuppose a dualism of nonmaterial spirit and material flesh. But the spirit/flesh opposition also functions symbolically in these films to represent the assumed split in Western culture between scientific rationalism ("head") and earthly/bodily ways of knowing ("heart"). The angels teach the human characters to live a holistic life—a life that embraces both spirit *and* flesh, head *and* heart. For example, the movie *Michael* features a cynical reporter for a tabloid magazine. Michael teaches the reporter to tune into feelings (his own and others'), and to love. Thus the film counters the phenomenon called, in many strands of popular spirituality, "separation." Separation designates a mind-set that exalts rational thinking, and that sees humans as separate from the rest of the created order and from the divine. Those who criticize the mind-set of separation allege that we erect boundaries where none need be: between heaven and earth, soul and body, culture and nature, thought and matter, divinity and humanity. The angels in the films (and in some popular writings) help humans to see that the boundaries are permeable, even illusory.

Theologically, the counterpart to the mind-set of separation is an overemphasis on God's transcendence. Such overemphasis can breed the conviction that God is removed from the world and that humans are autonomous agents, with rational minds to subdue and dominate godless creation. Sally McFague blames such a perspective for the rise of consumerism, a way of life that assumes that all the world was created to satisfy human wants. She counters by stressing God's immanence in creation: "God is reality, the breath, the life, the power, the love beneath, above, around, and in everything."[61] Our salvation—and our liberation from our ravenous desires for the produce of the earth—happens when we come to see that it is not humans with their wants but God who is at the center of the cosmos. McFague's message overlaps with that of the angel films and popular spiritual authors, insofar as she, too, downplays the boundaries between God and creation, spirit and flesh. But she stresses (more than they) our need to exercise discernment wherever desire is concerned. Desire is not the avenue to salvation: unchecked, it will lead to the destruction of the earth.

Spiritual life begins when we come to see that we are *not* divine, but are finite, fallible, and highly prone to overestimate our own capacity for goodness. There is indeed a boundary separating us from God, who created our world and who upholds it moment by moment. Apart from God's help we are powerless to cross that boundary, for though we desire God we also want what we want. We are at the whim of our many desires. The answer to our fallen condition (and hence to our separation from God) lies in seeing ourselves for what we are and in trusting, not an incarnate angel, but the incarnate *God.* Jesus crossed the boundary for us, in him God became human, and the human became divine.

As a human, Jesus struggled to overcome desire. Not only did he himself succeed, but he poured out on *us* the power to persevere in God's way, even in the midst of intense competing desires. Jesus was tested as we are—he understands our dilemma. Yet he was without sin—he showed himself as divine. Through his endurance of repeated testing, culminating in his endurance of the crucifixion, he conquered sin and death. United with the victorious and risen Christ by the power of God's Spirit, we too are empowered to accomplish what we could never do by weak flesh alone. We become able to put Christ at the center of our lives, to say "not my will but thy will be done." Christ reorders the list of desires we carry around in our heads. We do not thereby become invulnerable to the temptations of desire, but we are strengthened—and also assured of God's forgiveness if and when we fail to persevere in times of trial. We are free to love all of creation, to cherish beings of flesh, to see all about us the evidence of God's presence, glory, and love.

In this chapter I have examined themes from the story of the "fallen" or "falling" angels in several of its many versions: themes such as the dangers of desire; the nature of the boundaries between heaven and earth, between spirit and flesh; and the sin of disregarding God's order and placing oneself at the center of the cosmos. The last-mentioned was the sin of the falling angels in ancient accounts, but it was especially the sin of Satan. In Chapter 4, I will examine ancient and modern ideas about Satan, whose story (sparse in the Hebrew Scriptures) took much fuller form in the centuries before and after Christ. The early Christians characterized Satan as terribly cunning and fierce. But as we will see, they were convinced that in Jesus Christ this evil angel and all his servants had more than met their match.

4

Satan and the Powers

Evil is "the main human problem." All around us in the world are want, wretchedness, affliction, misery, and death.[1] To be sure, in our wealthy and insulated society some of us can and do pretend, for a time, that evil is somebody else's problem. We teach our children that God is in heaven and all is right with the world. We convince ourselves that if we live the right way bad things will only happen to other people, or we buy into one of the plentiful current theories that those who suffer have chosen that course for themselves—in a previous life if not this one. By these and other ruses we reassure ourselves that the cosmos is fundamentally a rational and not a random place. Affliction falls where it should rather than simply where it may. But what happens when some terrible event assaults us and thrusts us into anguish and despair?

How could a good and all-powerful God let bad things happen? Theologians and philosophers call this question, raised by our experience of evil in the world, the problem of theodicy. The word is derived from Greek words meaning "God" and "justice" (or "justify"). The question of theodicy is, How can we show that God is just, given the terrible things that happen in our world? Though a favorite topic of professional philosophers and theologians, the theodicy problem is not just an academic one. On September 11, 2001, it blasted all other problems out of its way and took center stage in national and international consciousness. But the problem also surfaces more routinely, in conversations over the morning newspaper and at break time. Priests, ministers, rabbis, and therapists confront the problem daily as they help people to cope with the shattering devastations of ordinary lives. Those who invite others into a life of faith in God have the problem of evil shoved in their faces as a defensive shield: "Well, I *would* believe in God, but how can I with so much suffering all around?"

The theodicy problem is especially acute for Christians, because they claim *Jesus as Lord*. Not only is God all-powerful and loving, Christians profess, but God's only son "has gone into heaven and is at the right hand of God, with angels, authorities, and powers made subject to him" (1 Pet 3:22). How are we to understand Jesus' alleged authority over cosmic powers when oppression, terror, war, loss through death, physical suffering, discrimination, hostility and alienation in personal relationships, addiction, abuse, loneliness (and on and on) remain so much the order of the day? God intends that creation should flourish, but on every side powers that oppose God wax while sufferers' hope wanes. If Jesus is Lord, then how can evil still triumph in the world? And—perhaps a harder question—how can evil still triumph in our very selves? For evil isn't only something that happens to us, it is something in which we actively participate! We fail to live up to God's or even our own best expectations. We fail, sometimes in spectacular fashion, and so heap suffering upon ourselves and others, including those whom we love.

Popular cultural answers to questions about evil draw massive attention and generate one best-selling book after another. Fallen angels, especially Satan, take the blame in many of these explanations. In one sense, there is nothing new about Satan's prominent place in such explanations of evil. The devil has long been charged with the awful things that happen in the world and in our individual lives. Jesus himself saw Satan as the tyrannical agent who opposed God's plan for the redemption of the world and who stood as Jesus' own chief adversary. For two millennia Christians have followed Jesus' lead, interpreting their trials as the devil's attack, and their own enemies as the devil's special allies.

What may be new is the scale on which theories of Satan's intervention are being spread, via popular novels and non-fiction books, TV evangelists, and the Internet. The Left Behind novels, written by prolific fundamentalist author Tim LaHaye and novelist Jerry B. Jenkins, have sold more than sixty-two million copies.[2] Distribution of the Left Behind series has penetrated not just the fundamentalist and evangelical churches, but also the mainline denominations. The novels depict the seven-year Tribulation following the Rapture of the church, with Satan's servant the Antichrist (a Romanian-born dictator named Nicolae Carpathia) as the chief antagonist. Before the Left Behind series there were the novels of Frank Peretti, which depict "spiritual warfare" between angelic and demonic forces played out simultaneously in the human and heavenly realms. Peretti's novels have been reprinted multiple times and are held up by many readers as authentic portrayals of the nature of opposition to God and God's people by Satan and his demonic hordes.[3] And before Peretti there was *The Late Great Planet Earth*, by Hal Lindsey. As the best-selling nonfiction work of the 1970s, the book shaped and guided the religious right during that decade and has continued to do so ever since. LaHaye, Jenkins, Peretti, and Lindsey have persuaded millions of readers that the devil has authored the current liberal social and political agenda and orchestrated the moral breakdown in society. Who knows how many others such a message has reached via TV evangelists and the thousands of purveyors of like-themed Web sites, videos, and instructional books?

Meanwhile, for decades mainline theologians and church leaders have insisted that belief in Satan is not important to authentic Christian faith. Or, if not dismissing Satan and other such powers outright, they have simply ignored those parts of the biblical and theological tradition in which the powers played a role. In turn, thousands of pastors educated in mainline seminaries have done likewise. They never speak of Satan from the pulpit, convinced that he and his demon-servants belong to an obsolete worldview. Lay people in churches led by these pastors have had several choices: follow their leaders by ignoring what the Bible (on the one hand) and the conservative media (on the other hand) say about Satan; resist their leaders' dismissal of Satan by various means, including defection to more conservative congregations or denominations; or muddle along in a state of confusion, not knowing what or whom to believe and not able to articulate any helpful answers to the problem of evil as it touches them in their own lives.

My goal in this chapter is not to argue for or against the reality of Satan and his angels as autonomous beings but to examine what the Bible teaches about these characters and explore some of the options for making sense of the teachings today. While I disagree with many of the fundamentalist premises about Satan, I think that the mainline churches and theologians have seriously erred in their inattention to biblical views on this topic. One cannot ignore all the passages in the New Testament about "the rulers, the authorities, the cosmic powers of this present darkness, the spiritual forces of evil in the heavenly places" (Eph 6:12) and end up with an intact story. Jesus' struggle against evil is central to the New Testament's message. The Gospels present Jesus as coming to "bind the strong man" and "plunder his house" (Mark 3:27; cf. Acts 10:38). The epistle to the Hebrews describes Jesus as taking on human flesh and blood "so that through death he might destroy the one who has the power of death, that is, the devil, and free those who all their lives were held in slavery by the fear of death" (Heb 2:14–15). Jesus' very purpose in coming was to destroy the devil and free his prisoners! Throughout the New Testament, the salvation Jesus offers is always conceived as salvation *from* something: namely, from the powers that compete with or actively oppose God, demanding humans' allegiance and all too often taking them captive.

I will begin the chapter by examining the portrayal of Satan and his forces in the Left Behind series. Though the novels are fiction, they reinforce and propagate a widely-held pattern for experiencing, symbolizing, and judging evil in the real world. They are transparently meant to instruct ("We are using fiction to teach biblical truth," LaHaye has said) and to advocate a particular social, religious, and political program.[4] What assumptions underlie LaHaye's and Jenkins' diagnosis of the world's ills and reckoning of them to the devil's account? In the second part of the chapter, I will give an overview of biblical teachings about suffering and evil, and ask how and when Satan and the principalities and powers entered the biblical scene. I will suggest that the scriptural accounts convey important truths. One such truth is that *the problem of sin goes back to the beginning of creation.* A second is that *sin has a tragic dimension:* though humans sin freely, there is a way in which, against their own best intentions, they are blinded, deceived. Finally, in the third part of the chapter I will consider Jesus' role as "king of angels"—the one who is enthroned over the principalities and powers, including the devil (Eph 1:20–21). What does Jesus' kingship or lordship mean today, in the broken world we know? How does he help us cope with this brokenness? To answer these difficult questions I will seek help from a few recent theologians, and take up the LaHaye/Jenkins paradigm once again. I will argue that the answer Jesus gives to the problem of evil is not a philosophical explanation but *a charge and a benediction.* Jesus' charge is that we watch with those who suffer, and confront the principalities and powers that seek to obstruct God's reign in our world and in our very selves. His benediction is a promise of real power—"power at work within us" by which God "is able to accomplish abundantly far more than all we can ask or imagine" (Eph 3:20).

A WORLD AT WAR

"LEFT BEHIND": DISPENSATIONALISTS AND THE DEVIL

Tim LaHaye and Jerry Jenkins could have taken 1 John 5:19 as a foundational premise of their multivolume story: "We know that we are of God, and the whole world is in the power of the evil one." The "we" in the Left

Behind novels refers to true Christian believers: those who have been born again into faith in Christ. The "whole world" in the novels refers to everyone else: the political, economic, and religious institutions around the globe, all of which answer to the Antichrist, Nicolae Carpathia. The "evil one" is Satan, created as highest angel but cast out on account of lust for God's place and now "an immensely powerful, unutterably malevolent spirit-being who lives to murder and deceive mankind."[5]

The first novel in the series[6] opens with the Rapture of the true church. This is the anticipated event when Jesus returns and whisks all who are born-again Christians into heaven (together with all young children, including fetuses), according to a particular interpretation of 1 Thess 4:16–17. The Rapture initiates the seven-year period of the Tribulation, which is the overarching time frame for the entire series of novels. At the end of the seven years, the Tribulation concludes with the Glorious Appearing of Christ (depicted in the twelfth and final book). The protagonists in the multivolume story are all new Christians, converted since the Rapture. Midway through the series, the new believers, called Tribulation Saints, are plainly identifiable to one another by means of the "mark of the believer" supernaturally manifested upon their foreheads. Humans who belong to Carpathia, the Antichrist, are plainly identifiable also—not just to one another but to all—by means of the "mark of the beast" tattooed by human hands on their foreheads. Once the marks have been received or taken, fates are sealed: believers are destined for eternity with Christ, nonbelievers for eternal perdition. The war between the two sides goes on, but, really, all are just biding time; the fate of each side is already set. Believers sport Uzi submachine guns and can kill nonbelievers with impunity, since the nonbelievers are damned anyway. As one Christian character points out, "In the heat of battle, killing the enemy has never been considered murder."[7] Nonbelievers can and often do kill Christians, but in doing so only hasten the believers' access to heaven. Still, there is a motive for the Christians to survive: those who endure the full seven years of the Tribulation will see Christ's Glorious Appearing.[8]

The novels include infrequent but significant angelic epiphanies.[9] Angels serve as healers, rescuers, bearers of messages from God, and comforters at the time of martyrdom. At one point an angel even pilots a jet. Satan makes a stunning appearance in the seventh book, *The Indwelling*. A converted Jewish scholar and holy man named Tsion Ben-Judah is granted a vision of the devil—the great deceiver, Lucifer. At the outset of the vision, Satan manifests himself as a glorious angel of light (brighter even than the archangel Michael who is present on the sidelines). Lucifer wheedles God:

" 'Your so-called children are beneath you, ruler of heaven,' came the persua-sive mellifluous tones of the eternal solicitor. 'Abandon them to me, who can fashion them for profit. Even after being called by your name, their natures reek with temporal desires. Allow me to surround myself with these enemies of your cause, and I will marshal them into a force unlike any army you have ever assembled.' From the throne came a voice of such power and authority that volume was irrelevant: 'Thou shalt not touch my beloved!' " When God continues to refuse Satan's demands, Lucifer vows, "I will destroy them and defeat you! I shall bear the name above all other names! I shall sit high above the heavens, and there shall be no god like me!" [10] Then the devil morphs into a hideous, raging dragon.

Ben-Judah's vision of Satan makes explicit a premise that underlies the series from beginning to end: the evil that is in the world derives from a transcendent, supernatural power. Evil cannot be explained solely by refer-ence to natural, social, or psychological factors. Rather, *Satan* has orches-trated the social, moral, and political decline leading up to the Tribulation, and will drive the persecutions of that epoch. As critic Gershom Gorenberg writes, the novels presume that "one villain is behind every crime in the de-tective story that is human history." [11] Throughout the novels, Satan blinds people as if by magic and, at least in the case of the Antichrist, indwells them by possession. Satan grants the Antichrist and those who serve him nearly unlimited resources and powers, and they are formidable adversaries for the Christians. Nonetheless, the believers steadfastly affirm the sovereignty of God in Jesus Christ, and God corroborates that sovereignty through havoc-wreaking judgments on the evildoers and astonishing, miraculous rescues of the Christian saints.

The plot of the Left Behind series is organized according to a particular interpretation of biblical prophecy known as "premillennialist dispen-sationalism," which has a long and substantial record of influence in the United States. Its originator was John Nelson Darby (1800–1882), an Irish preacher and member of the Plymouth Brethren, an evangelical Christian movement begun in Ireland in the 1820s. Darby visited the United States repeatedly in the mid-nineteenth century. His interpretive scheme is called "premillennialist" because it teaches (as do other, older but different ver-sions of premillennialism) that Christ will return before the inauguration of the "millennium"—his thousand-year reign, prophesied in Revelation 20:6. The scheme is called "dispensationalism" because of its premise that God has planned for history to fall into separate "dispensations"—sequential, nonoverlapping periods of time, in each of which God relates to and tests humans in distinct ways. [12] In Darby's interpretation, the Rapture (a term

Darby may have been the first to use with this meaning) precedes the seven years of the Tribulation.[13] The Tribulation in turn precedes the return of Christ to defeat the Antichrist's forces at Armageddon and establish the millennial dispensation.

The popularity of Darby's scenario was boosted with the publication of the Scofield Reference Bible in 1909. Cyrus Scofield, a Congregationalist pastor, had connections to Darby. Scofield was pastor of a church in Dallas, Texas. Besides authoring his dispensationalist reference Bible (the first book published by Oxford University Press ever to sell one million copies), Scofield also wrote the *Scofield Bible Correspondence Course* (still available today), and helped to found Dallas Theological Seminary, a continuing center for dispensationalist thinking. Scofield and other dispensationalist leaders of the early twentieth century lent their support to the emerging Christian fundamentalist movement, whose members took up the Scofield Bible with enthusiasm.[14]

Ultimately, Darby's approach "affected the religious beliefs of millions of people," as theologian Raymond F. Bulman notes. Such thinking even "found its way into the inner chambers of high political power." Hal Lindsey's work was popular in Ronald Reagan's White House, and Reagan himself "had drunk deeply from the draughts of dispensationalist theology and was known to express frequently his private conviction that we find ourselves at the very brink of the Last Days."[15] Reagan's infamous description of the Soviet Union as "the evil empire" should be viewed against this theological backdrop. So also should the stridently pro-Israel and anti-Palestinian stance of many fundamentalist Christians today—a stance partly conditioned by belief that the millennium can only be inaugurated once Israel is an intact nation with a rebuilt and operational Temple on the historic site in Jerusalem. This Third Temple has to be standing because, in the predicted scenario, the Antichrist is scheduled to desecrate it halfway through the Tribulation, allegedly in fulfillment of prophecy.[16]

The dispensationalist scenario impresses many who encounter it as eminently biblical because its predictions seem to be based on Scripture. Proof-texts are culled from a number of biblical books, including Isaiah, Jeremiah, Ezekiel, Zechariah, Daniel, the Gospels, 1 and 2 Thessalonians, and Revelation. And yet, despite the plentiful references to Scripture in the pages of dispensationalist theology, biblical warrant is dubious or lacking for key events and for the sequence as a whole.

LaHaye and Jenkins use their novels to advance a conservative/fundamentalist social and political agenda. The United Nations, arms control, abortion rights, ecumenism and interfaith dialogue, Catholicism, Judaism, feminism, homosexuality, and the New Age movement all come under direct or indirect attack. The novels' anti-Judaism is especially noteworthy. Such a charge may strike some readers of the novels as unfounded; after all, LaHaye and Jenkins portray some Jews sympathetically. But all the sympathetic Jews are *converted* Jews. Take, for example, Tsion Ben-Judah, who was granted a vision of Satan. Ben-Judah is "a rabbi who announces that a three-year study has led him to recognize Jesus as messiah, and who immediately begins speaking like a fundamentalist preacher." [17] In the story, he uses the Internet to become spiritual leader of opponents of the Antichrist around the world, even as LaHaye and Jenkins use Ben-Judah's character to lend scholarly credibility to their own skewed interpretation of the Hebrew Scriptures. In the tenth novel, *The Remnant*, Ben-Judah points out that Jews need to make up for the "national sin" of rejecting Jesus. Gorenberg observes, "Their choice in the last days comes down to an old one: convert or die." [18] With the Jews—as with all the people and positions that LaHaye and Jenkins oppose—there is no room for an alternate opinion. In Left Behind's dualistic universe, "Whoever is not for us is against us"—that is, whoever does not support the LaHaye/Jenkins agenda is of the devil, and will ultimately be annihilated. Conveniently, the ambiguity that characterizes life in the real world has been resolved into the clarity of the two-mark system: every person bears either the mark of the believer or the mark of the beast, and there is no mistaking the one for the other.

PUT ON THE WHOLE ARMOR OF GOD: SPIRITUAL WARFARE

Like LaHaye and Jenkins, many fundamentalist and evangelical Christians, dispensationalist and otherwise, insist that Satan and his angelic servants are presently engaged in a full-scale assault on humanity. The phrase "spiritual warfare" is often used to designate the ongoing struggle between Christians and evil forces, with the call to arms in Ephesians 6 cited as evidence:

> Finally, be strong in the Lord and in the strength of his power. Put on the whole armor of God, so that you may be able to stand against the wiles of the devil. For our struggle is not against enemies of blood and flesh, but against the rulers, against the authorities, against the cosmic powers of this present darkness, against the spiritual forces of evil in the heavenly places. Therefore, take up the whole armor of God, so that you may be able to withstand on that evil day, and having done everything, to stand firm. (Eph 6:10–13; see also vv. 14–18)

Those who teach about spiritual warfare today typically identify two arenas in which Christians struggle against demonic/diabolical activity: deliverance ministries, in which *individuals* are released from captivity to evil spirits; and mission and evangelism, in which *institutions, cities, states,* and *nations* are freed from the dominion of spirits obstructing the spread of the Gospel.[19] Clinton Arnold contends that spiritual warfare is an integral part of any authentic Christian experience. "To think that a Christian could avoid spiritual warfare is like imagining that a gardener could avoid dealing with weeds." Spiritual warfare is all-encompassing because "there is virtually no part of our existence over which the Evil One does not want to maintain or reassert his unhealthy and perverse influence.[20] But Christians can achieve victory over the enemy, Arnold explains, by living in solidarity with Christ and appropriating the power of the Holy Spirit through prayer.

Novelist Frank Peretti has probably done the most to foster current popular interest in spiritual warfare. Peretti's works, especially his earlier ones, offer cartoon-like portrayals of bat-winged, sulphurous, hideous demons and of the male, muscular, gleaming angels who fight and conquer them. The good angels are "covered" (strengthened) in their warfare by the prayers of faithful Christians. In Peretti's universe, demons cause all social problems, and the good angels' defeat of the demons causing a given ill leads to instant, dramatic cure.[21] In contrast to Peretti, other proponents of spiritual warfare de-emphasize its sensational aspects, cautiously accept some insights of modern psychology, and insist that self-examination and Christlike love—rather than the passing of judgment and accusations of demon possession—must take priority in a Christian's life.[22] Still, all commonly stress Satan's nearly ubiquitous agency behind events small and large and his ongoing assault on the human psyche.

LaHaye, Jenkins, Peretti, and many other fundamentalist and evangelical Christians today take for granted a profile of the devil that is long standing in Christian theology. This profile is based on a composite of all the biblical passages that refer to the devil, and some that originally did not, including passages in Isaiah and Ezekiel about arrogant rulers who aspired to the place of God (discussed in Chapter 3) and the story of the serpent in the Garden of Eden. Those who accept the profile typically do not prove but simply assume that all of these passages, in fact, refer to the devil.

But there are other ways to read the biblical record on the topics of evil and Satan. The Bible, written by many authors over the course of centuries, exhibits not one but several perspectives on the people, circumstances, and forces that obstruct the flourishing of God's creation. Many Old Testament writers operate without any apparent knowledge of or interest in Satan. If and when these writers come to the topic of evil, they have other explanations. Scripture's various teachings about evil are best interpreted against the backdrop of what is known of the changing historical circumstances, literary conventions, and worldviews out of which the relevant texts emerged.

BIBLICAL PERSPECTIVES ON SATAN AND EVIL

FROM BEGINNING TO END: GENESIS TO REVELATION ON EVIL

Bernhard W. Anderson ("Sin and the Powers of Chaos") offers a useful overview. He begins by noting the vast difference in outlook between opening and closing episodes of the Christian Bible. At the beginning, we have the Genesis story of the transgression of Adam and Eve, in which the emphasis falls on the humans' misuse of their God-given freedom and their consequent guilt and punishment. In Revelation, by contrast, the focus is no longer merely on sin, but on the wider dimensions of the evil that corrupts the cosmos. In Revelation the serpent has become "the archenemy of God, the leader of the hosts of chaos, who foments a rebellion that spreads through the whole creation." The Apocalypse portrays the problem of evil and deliverance from it as far-reaching and dramatic: deliverance is not only from the bondage of sin but also from "the uncanny powers of chaos, manifest in oppressive institutions (the state) or imperial ambitions, that victimize the 'meek' of the earth and plunge human history into suffering and catastrophe." [23]

How did this striking transition from Genesis to Revelation—in views of evil, and, hence, also in views of the necessary deliverance—come about? Anderson traces several phases in biblical authors' perception of evil and response to it. The story of Adam, Eve, and the serpent, like other stories in Genesis 1–11, portrays suffering as punishment for sinful rebellion against the Creator. Anderson contends that the belief in suffering as a consequence for sin underlies two of the major theological models used in ancient Israel: the covenant theologies associated with Moses and with David.

At the heart of Mosaic covenant theology (reflected especially in the first five books of the Hebrew Scriptures) is the story of God's liberation of the people from bondage and their grateful and obedient response to God's covenant stipulations in the Jewish law. The Mosaic covenant has a conditional aspect: God makes a commitment to be bound to the people and promises to bless them, but vows that disobedience by the people will destroy the relationship. God sets before them life and death, and it is up to them which they will choose: the path of obedience, which leads to blessing and life; or the path of disobedience, which leads to disaster, curse, and death (see, for example, Deut 30:15–16, 19–20). Anderson points out that this theology regarded the people as fully responsible—and therefore fully culpable—for their suffering. There was no room for any suggestion that some outside, sinister power of evil had inflicted their troubles on them. Sufferings in the political arena were interpreted as deserved punishment for sin. For example, in a time of great catastrophe the prophet Jeremiah proclaims to the people, "Your ways and your doings have brought this upon you. This is your doom; how bitter it is! It has reached your very heart" (Jer 4:18).[24]

The Davidic covenant theology strongly influenced the writing of 1 and 2 Chronicles and the work of the eighth-century BCE prophet Isaiah of Jerusalem; its foundational text is 2 Samuel 7:4–17, Nathan's prophecy to David. Through Nathan, God promises to establish eternally both the throne of David's kingdom and also the Temple in Jerusalem. Here, as in Mosaic covenant theology, the promises are conditional: though God's covenant loyalty (Heb. *hesed*) will never be removed from the people, nonetheless they will be chastised, disciplined, and purified through suffering if they fail to be obedient to God. The psalmist elaborates:

> If his children forsake my law
>   and do not walk according to my ordinances,
> if they violate my statutes
>   and do not keep my commandments,
> then I will punish their transgression with the rod
>   and their iniquity with scourges;
> but I will not remove from him my steadfast love,
>   or be false to my faithfulness.
> I will not violate my covenant,
>   or alter the word that went forth from my lips.
>   (Ps 89:30–34)

In this covenant, as in the Mosaic covenant, "people were called to responsibility before God and suffering was understood as the consequence of human failure."[25]

The strong emphasis in these two covenant theologies on suffering as just penalty for sin did trigger protest, found, for example, in Jeremiah's confessions, in the psalms of lament, and especially in the Book of Job. Indeed, Psalm 89 veers from praise for God's covenant with David to harsh lament at God's renunciation of that covenant and defiling of David's crown: "Lord, where is your steadfast love of old, which by your faithfulness you swore to David?" (v. 49). Anderson sees a similar sort of protest already in Abraham's disputation with God in Genesis 18:16–33. On the eve of destroying Sodom and Gomorrah, God tells Abraham what is about to happen to the cities, and Abraham responds by raising questions: How could God indiscriminately destroy the righteous along with the wicked? If there are even ten righteous people present, ought not a city to be saved? Abraham, Job, and the other dissenters acknowledged the depth of human sin but also asked whether the doctrine of suffering as divine punishment for sin was really enough to explain the magnitude of human pain and sorrow.[26]

This question became more urgent as Israel's historical circumstances deteriorated. The sudden death in 609 BCE of King Josiah, who had faithfully served God and followed the Law, severely tested the theory that God would reward good kings and punish bad ones. Anderson interprets the very terse report of good king Josiah's death in 2 Kings 23:29–30 as evidence that the doctrine of suffering as judgment for departure from God had been weighed in the balance and found wanting. An even greater test of the suffering/ punishment doctrine came with the fall of Jerusalem and Exile of the general population to Babylonia in 587 BCE. The author of Psalm 44 reproaches God for permitting these terrible events to occur: "You have made us like sheep for slaughter, and have scattered us among the nations," even though "we have not forgotten you, or been false to your covenant" (Ps 44:11, 17). When the disasters were of such enormity, Anderson argues, it began to seem too "sweeping" and "simplistic" to interpret them as punishment for the people's betrayal of the covenant.[27]

The prophet Habakkuk marks a transition between the older acceptance of the sin/punishment explanation for suffering and the newer mood of protest against it. On the eve of Jerusalem's fall, Habakkuk complained bitterly to God. "Why do you look on the treacherous," the prophet asked, "and are silent when the wicked swallow those more righteous than they?" (Hab 1:13).[28] In response, God promised that vindication would come—in God's own time. But God's word to Habakkuk that the righteous would eventually be vindicated did not long suffice for those in despair. As prophecy shifted into apocalyptic mode, spokespersons for God began to answer the repeated cry, "How long?" more concretely than Habakkuk. In Daniel, for example, the angel Gabriel revealed the time line for Israel's deliverance, using a method of calculation that put salvation close at hand to the author of the book and his contemporaries, who were suffering under a tyrant in the second century BCE (Dan 9:1–27).[29]

Besides assuring followers of a time limit to God's wrath, apocalyptic thinkers also provided "a new understanding of the radical power of evil."[30] To be sure, they still held the people to be sinful and dependent on God's grace. But such thinkers' emphasis shifted away from the call for repentance toward God's offer of consolation. The new perception in apocalyptic theology was that sin was "part of a much larger historical evil that holds people as victims in the grip of massive, oppressive powers over which they have no control."[31] To symbolize this tyranny of evil in society and in history, the book of Daniel reaches back into the mythic heritage that the ancient Israelites shared with their neighbors.[32] The structure of the apocalyptic vision in Daniel 7—with its four beasts that rise from the sea, only to forfeit their dominion and glory to a heavenly being—resembles a type of myth known from Ugaritic (ancient Canaanite) sources. According to one such Canaanite myth, the god Baal ("the cloud rider") defeated the powers of chaos embodied in the ocean, called Prince Yamm ("sea"); Baal then returned to the heavens as victorious king, to set up his temple and feast with the gods.[33]

Anderson contends that Old Testament apocalyptic visions of victory over the forces of chaos are not far from the portrayal of divine victory over the "beast from sea" in Revelation 13. Like the author of Daniel, so also the seer John in Revelation views the problem of evil as much greater than merely the problem of human sin: demonic powers are at work throughout the cosmos. They are powers larger than any human being, or any human institution. But Anderson's conclusion needs to be refined, for, along with the similarities of viewpoint, there is one great difference. In the Old Testament visions, there is no organized leadership of the forces that oppose God. In Daniel, although there is an angelic being at the head of the servants of God, there is no presumption of the existence of Satan or any similar archfiend to direct the forces of chaos.[34] In Revelation, by contrast, all the powers arrayed against God and God's anointed are led by one malevolent being, portrayed as a great dragon, "that ancient serpent, who is called the Devil and Satan, the deceiver of the whole world" (12:9). Though other New Testament authors use less spectacular imagery, they share John's assumption that this one being, Satan, leads the forces of evil. The question is, how and why did Satan come to rule the day?

THE SHIFT TO SATAN

The story of Satan's emergence in the late pre-Christian era as archfiend of God and God's people is intricate and difficult. Over the course of centuries, Jews had reflected on various adversary-figures known from ancient myths about combat by God (or the gods) with divine enemies. These myths circulated throughout the ancient Near East and were preserved both in independent narratives and in snippets scattered throughout the Hebrew Scriptures.[35] Adversary-figures from these myths included the rebellious angels of Genesis 6:1–4 and of subsequent legendary retellings, the dragon Leviathan, the arrogant rulers of Isaiah 14 and Ezekiel 28–32, a character named Belial (from a Hebrew word meaning "worthless, useless, productive of disorder"), and the archfiend from Zoroastrian religion (known as Angra

Mainyu or Ahriman). In the third or second century BCE, ideas about these adversary-figures began to merge with and shape developing views on the character of the *satan* (a Hebrew word meaning "accuser" or "adversary") as known from Job, Zechariah, and 1 Chronicles.

Of the three Old Testament books that mention this character, Job's story of the *satan* was the most influential on later views. In Job the heavenly *satan* appears only in the prologue (Job 1–2). He is one of the beings who surround God's throne in the divine assembly. Along with other heavenly beings (literally "sons of God"), on a certain occasion the *satan* presents himself before God:

> The LORD said to the *satan,* "Where have you come from? The *satan* answered the LORD, "From going to and from on the earth, and from walking up and down on it." The LORD said to the *satan,* "Have you considered my servant Job? There is no one like him on the earth, a blameless and upright man who fears God and turns away from evil." Then the *satan* answered the LORD, "Does Job fear God for nothing? Have you not put a fence around him and his house and all that he has, on every side? You have blessed the work of his hands, and his possessions have increased in the land. But stretch out your hand now, and touch all that he has, and he will curse you to your face." The LORD said to the *satan,* "very well, all that he has is in your power, only do not stretch out your hand against him!" So the *satan* went out from the presence of the LORD. (Job 1:7–12)

Soon Job's servants, livestock, and children have all been destroyed. But rather than cursing God, as the *satan* had predicted, Job "arose, tore his robe, shaved his head, and fell on the ground and worshipped. He said, 'Naked I came from my mother's womb, and naked shall I return there; the LORD gave, and the LORD has taken away; blessed be the name of the LORD'" (Job 1:20–21). In Job 2, the whole scene is repeated with variations: the *satan* goes before God and receives permission to harm Job (including, this time, permission to "touch his bone and his flesh"); Job suffers grievous bodily afflictions; he refuses to "sin with his lips" by cursing God.[36]

For the author and very first readers of Job, the term *satan* had been merely a role designation—"accuser" or "adversary"—rather than the name of a specific archfiend.[37] But once the archfiend idea took hold, under continuing influence of Job the word *satan* became a proper name (translated as *diabolos* ["devil"] in the Septuagint, the ancient Greek translation of the Hebrew Scriptures). Some readers from the intertestamental era then found in Job 1–2 a highly adaptable template for understanding relationships among

God, Satan, and humans in times of suffering. In the second century BCE, the author of *Jubilees* used this template when he retold the story of the testing of Abraham. The retelling echoes Job rather loudly. A heavenly adversary called Prince Mastema responds to a report concerning Abraham's merit by inviting God to order him to sacrifice his son Isaac: "And Prince Mastema came and he said before God, 'Behold, Abraham loves Isaac, his son. And he is more pleased with him than everything. Tell him to offer him (as) a burnt offering upon the altar. And you will see whether he will do this thing. And you will know whether he is faithful in everything in which you test him'" (*Jub.* 17:16).[38] Like the anonymous author of *Jubilees,* others, too, drew far-reaching conclusions from Job 1–2 about the human situation vis-à-vis the Tempter. It was inferred that:

- human righteousness and service for God may prompt satanic attack;
- Satan views his affliction of humans as a contest in which honor and authority are at stake;
- although Satan is free to attack human flesh, he cannot gain authority over a human's soul unless the person forfeits authority by cursing God;
- Satan stands in an ambiguous relationship to God, authorized by God but seeking, nonetheless, to lead God's faithful astray.

These assumptions underlie numerous references to Satan in ancient Jewish and early Christian literature, including the story of Jesus.[39]

When many people today think of Satan it is not Job that they remember but Adam and Eve. When those two ate the forbidden fruit in the Garden of Eden, was it not because Satan, in serpent-form, had seduced them? So we seem to remember—but the text of Genesis 3 never actually says so. In the Genesis account, the serpent is called the "most subtle" or the "craftiest" animal God had made, and indeed its craftiness exceeds anything seen in nature: this serpent speaks, and fashions devious arguments. The author of the passage was probably influenced by ancient Near Eastern mythological motifs that would themselves, over the centuries, contribute to the development of Satan's character.[40] At the time when Genesis was written, the archfiend Satan was not yet in view, but as centuries passed interpretations of Genesis 3 changed. Readers as early as the first century BCE inferred that the serpent in the Garden was Satan, and drew corresponding conclusions about the devil's habits and character.[41] If the story of Job had convinced them that Satan was ruthless, using violence and physical torment to get his way, then the story of the serpent in the Garden of Eden suggested that the devil could as happily employ cunning and flattery, making "beautiful presentations" that arouse and exploit the human passion of desire.[42] Both of these techniques take advantage of the human's nature as *fleshly being,* as Dietrich Bonhoeffer saw so clearly. "In temptation Satan wins power over the believer as far as he is flesh. He torments him by enticement to lust, by the pains of privation, and by bodily and spiritual suffering of every kind. He robs him of everything he has and, at the same time, entices him to forbidden happiness."[43] From Genesis, readers inferred that Satan could change form to suit his purposes, the way a chameleon changes its colors. In the garden he showed himself as a serpent, but in Corinth he appeared as "an angel of light" (2 Cor 11:14). The *Testament of Job,* a document from about the same era as Paul, depicts Satan disguised as a beggar, a bread-seller, and king of the Persians.

The new presumption that the tempting serpent was actually Satan reinforced a belief held by some Jews on other grounds: *God did not author sin, but sin was in the world from the beginning.* The author of *4 Ezra* (late first century CE)[44] makes no mention of Satan, but still traces human failure back to Adam, who was "burdened with an evil heart," as were all his descendants. In the story, Ezra complains to God about God's failure to take away "the evil heart" at the time of Adam's creation. Because God did not remove the evil heart, the Israelites were set up for failure when the law was given: "Thus the disease became permanent; the law was in the hearts of the people along with the evil root; but what was good departed, and the evil remained" (*4 Ezra* 3:22; cf. 4:30). Likewise, the Apostle Paul sees Adam as the entry point for evil into the world. As he writes in Romans 5:12, "Sin came into the world through one man, and death came through sin, and so death spread to all because all have sinned."[45]

By tracing sin back to Adam, the author of *4 Ezra* and Paul are each saying that sin is as old as humanity. Describing sin as an "evil root" and a "permanent disease" suggests that sin is not superficial. We cannot avoid it simply by choosing to do so, for, as theologian Hendrikus Berkhof observes, "Its roots lie deep in the structure of our reality."[46] And yet, despite sin's deeprootedness, Paul and the author of *4 Ezra* do not hold sin to be inherently part of the creation. Neither author blames God for the disaster wrought through Adam: "It is as if evil had come in from without, and spoiled the plan."[47] Sin and death "came in" (Paul's term) after God created humans—created them in God's own image, as creatures who were made for love but who are also free to misdirect that love or turn away from it altogether.

Later in Romans, Paul writes of sin "reigning" (5:21; 6:12) and "acting as lord" (6:14), and as one whom persons "serve as slaves" (6:6, 16, 17). Is the apostle here reinterpreting conventional beliefs about Satan as the tempter of Adam and the enslaver of all his progeny? Further, in Romans 7, Paul writes that this acting power—sin—exercises its lordship through "deception," by arousing "all kinds of covetousness" (vv. 8, 11). Is he here alluding to the work of the serpent, who deceived Eve and made her covet the forbidden fruit—an event Paul recalls elsewhere (2 Cor 11:3)? Certainly for Paul in Romans, sin acts a great deal like the serpent in the garden, and a great deal like Satan. Sin for Paul is not merely a given misdeed but a devious agent—a power that seduces people away from obedience to God, arouses covetousness and other enslaving passions, and leads humans into death. Paul's description of sin as a satan-like power underscores what Berkhof calls "the relentless force of evil."[48] Humans sin because forces larger than them blind them, deceive them, subjugate them.

By referring, however, to "sin" and "death," Paul suggests that there are other ways to construe the worldly agents working to thwart our devotion to God than by reference to Satan. Elsewhere Paul names these forces using terms such as "authorities and rulers," "elemental spirits," and even "the law." The church has tended to dislodge all these other designations in favor of the concept or figure of Satan—not surprising, Berkhof suggests, considering Satan's metaphorical and direct force.[49] Such narrowing down of all opponents to a single, nearly all-powerful adversary has had unfortunate consequences. It promotes demonizing of opponents and conspiracy theories, because all earthly adversaries are allegedly working for one boss. It also detracts from our ability to analyze the causes of—and Christ's answer to—the problem of evil—especially systemic or social evil—in our world.

The images in *4 Ezra* of an "evil heart" and an "evil seed" are standard metaphors for the *yetser hara*—the "evil inclination."[50] Many ancient Jews and early Christians supposed that all humans possess such a disposition to sin. The evil inclination, in this thinking, is *an agent of separation within the human self.* The one who follows the evil inclination sections off a portion of the mind or heart as a kind of preserve or sanctuary for drives toward idolatry, sexual immorality, self-justification, revenge, self-aggrandizement, and more—behaviors or states of mind that keep us from God. Such persons are fundamentally divided, double-minded, seeking to please God but seeking also to gratify their own passionate desires. Being rent by contrary drives, they are highly prone to succumb to temptation when it comes. They are not stable in their commitments but are like ships driven and tossed by the waves on a rough sea, plunging now one way, now another (see Jas 1:6–7).

Ancient talk about the evil inclination was often correlated with teachings about Satan. On the one hand Satan was viewed as "the great dragon" (Rev 12:9), a cosmic adversary warring in heavenly regions against God and

God's angels and manifest on earth in oppressive rulers and social systems. On the other hand Satan was viewed as the adversary within the human self. He assaults the faithful who struggle daily to walk in God's way. He acts on individual human psyches as readily as on empires. Thus one of the central texts from among the Dead Sea Scrolls explicitly correlates humans' internal struggle against the evil inclination to the cosmic warring of the "angel of truth" or "prince of lights" against the "spirit of injustice" or "angel of darkness." [51] Along similar lines, the *Testaments of the Twelve Patriarchs* teaches that the devil and the evil inclination work in tandem: "Flee from the evil tendency, destroying the devil by your good works. For those who are two-faced are not of God, but they are enslaved to their evil desires, so that they might be pleasing to Beliar and to persons like themselves" (*Testament of Asher* 3:2). [52] The notion of the evil inclination helped Jews and Christians to understand a kind of combat in which they found themselves engaged—a struggle against not only external enemies but those within their own breasts.

The ancient rabbis taught that the defeat of the evil inclination, like the defeat of the cosmic adversary, will require nothing less than world transformation. There will come a day when not only the heavens and the earth but also the human heart will be recreated: "In the coming age, I will uproot it [the evil inclination] from you, as the Bible says, 'I will remove the heart of stone from your body and give you a heart of flesh; and I will put My spirit into you.' " [53] When Paul writes in Romans of Jesus' perfect obedience (see Rom 5:18–19), he is saying that for Jesus that promised day has already dawned. Jesus alone among humans refused to follow the evil inclination; he alone was perfectly obedient to God. Moreover, Christians share in his righteousness. They do so not because they are no longer tempted, but because God graciously reckons to them the very righteousness of Christ, and because the Spirit empowers Christians to "set their minds on the things of the Spirit" and so to resist the voice of temptation. [54]

In Genesis, the serpent told Eve that if she ate the forbidden fruit, her eyes would be opened and she would "be like God" (3:5). The irony is that by instructing Eve on what to do, the serpent was putting *itself* in God's place as chief-in-command. By Jesus' day, the idea was firmly entrenched that Satan coveted God's position as ruler of all, highest of the high, and object of human worship. Isaiah 14:13–14, about the King of Babylon, was read as an indictment of Satan: "You said in your heart, 'I will ascend to heaven; I will raise my throne above the stars of God; I will sit on the mount of assembly on the heights of Zaphon; I will ascend to the tops of the clouds, I will make myself like the Most High.' " For his presumption, the King was cast down to

Sheol (Isa 14:9, 11, 15, 19). This passage (and thematically similar passages in Ezek 28–32) seemed to explain Satan's fall: he had dared to make himself equal to God, and so was cast down.[55]

In the first century CE, all the mythic strands had not yet been knit into a coherent, well-plotted, master narrative of Satan's origin as a glorious angel, his declaration of intent to make himself "like God," and his expulsion from heaven with his retinue of lesser angels. But these threads were in the process of being joined. We can see the process underway, for example, in Luke 10:18, where Jesus envisions Satan falling from heaven "like a flash of lightning" (alluding to Isaiah 14), and in Revelation 13, where the "beast from the Sea" promotes idolatrous worship of himself and of the dragon, who has been cast down with his angels (Rev 12:9) and is eventually thrown into the lake of fire (19:20).

A theory of Zoroastrian influence best explains the readiness of so many Jews of the intertestamental period to believe in a single archfiend, author of evil and "ruler of this world," Prince of Darkness and lord over a host of demons.[56] Zoroastrianism of that era taught that two rival gods—a good deity associated with light, and an evil deity linked to darkness and ignorance—battled for sovereignty over the cosmos.[57] Still, the full dualism of Zoroastrianism goes well beyond any characterization of cosmic combat in the Old or New Testament. In ancient Jewish and early Christian talk about the devil, Satan is hostile to God but remains subservient to God. *He is enemy and servant at one and the same time.* In 2 Corinthians, for example, Paul regards Satan as having evil designs on the church (2 Cor 2:11; 11:15) but also as sent by God to chastise Paul, lest he become arrogant on account of the divine visions he had experienced (12:7).[58] And even the Qumran sectarians never doubted God's ultimate triumph over the forces of evil. Zoroastrian dualism probably influenced developing beliefs about Satan, but Jews (and Christians in their turn) never went as far as full Zoroastrianism. A general commitment to monotheism and also specific language from the book of Job helped to check estimations of Satan's authority. In Job, Satan was a servant who had to *ask God for permission* to do what he did. Jewish and Christian authors assumed the same.[59]

In summary, by the dawn of the New Testament era several stunning developments in beliefs about the cosmic adversary had taken place. Satan, or the devil, had come to be regarded as a distinct and independent spiritual being, who used deceit and physical torture to tempt the righteous to disobedience. No longer was the *satan* believed to manifest himself only in heaven: he had moved into the arena of everyday life, where victims often recognized him and even conversed with him. He was viewed as ruler of the

cosmos, and lord over an army of lesser evil angels or demons. He was able
to sway people's thoughts and actions, seducing them with promises of benefit or pleasure, or coercing them with threats of torment or pain. Though
he was already master over all idol worshippers on earth, Satan's chief desire
was to lead God's righteous ones astray from fidelity to the covenant by promoting various sins, above all, idolatry, but including also cultic sins, sexual
immorality, enmity, and strife. This picture of Satan was fundamentally a
composite picture. Satan as known in the first century combined attributes
culled from an array of biblical texts and nonbiblical myths. The various
texts and traditions each made specific contributions to beliefs about the
devil's identity, aims, and modes of operation.

Why did some ancient Jews and early Christians find this emerging story
of Satan so powerful and appealing? As Bernhard Anderson suggests, perhaps the story first took hold because the magnitude of the people's suffering had become too great to understand it as solely punishment for sin. In
times of national suffering, the people sensed themselves to be not only sinners but also victims of forces beyond human control. They were victims as
an entire people, oppressed and exploited by foreign or godless rulers. Also,
as individuals they knew themselves to be victims of irresistible forces, forces
able to reach even into human psyches to blind minds and sway thoughts
and actions. Without denying their own complicity in wrongdoing and consequent guilt, their naming of Satan as adversary helped give expression to
this sense of being a victim—what Hendrikus Berkhof calls the *tragic dimension* of human sin. Further, naming Satan as adversary opened up ways
to cope. He became a known quantity—albeit an amazingly powerful one.
Had not Job defeated Satan by his patient endurance? Had not Jesus done
so—promising us power to do the same? "See," Jesus said in Luke, "I have
given you authority to tread on snakes and scorpions, and over all the power
of the enemy; and nothing will hurt you" (Luke 10:19).

And yet, there were other ways to name the enemy. New Testament authors did not always and only conceive of God's opposition as a united spirit-
force, headed up by a single wicked spirit-being. They recognized something
of the complexity of evil's operation in our world—the way evil pervades
the very structure of our reality. Their language about the principalities and
powers points to this complexity.

UNDERSTANDING THE PRINCIPALITIES AND POWERS

The New Testament is replete with vocabulary for the powers at work in this
world. This vocabulary includes not only the terms often translated "principality" and "power," but also words for authority, rulers, cosmic rulers, kings,

angels, demons, spirits, thrones, and dominions. Then there are the specific powers: Satan, sin, and death. The terms are well dispersed throughout the New Testament. Rather than engaging in detailed examination of the terms, I will make three brief summary observations, following the work of Walter Wink.[60] Later I will say more about Wink's theological reflection on these terms.

First, the language of power in the New Testament is fairly imprecise, interchangeable, and unsystematic. The same words may be used with varied meaning in different contexts, and several different words may connote the same idea. It is not that word choice is arbitrary, but that one word, a pair, or a series of words sometimes represents them all. Moreover, terms are sometimes strung together for rhetorical effect rather than for precision of reference.[61]

Second, the terms for power or the powers can refer to heavenly, spiritual realities; to earthly officeholders or structures of power; or, typically, to both at once.[62] For modern readers, it can be hard to know which meaning is intended. First Corinthians 2:7-8 illustrates this kind of ambiguity. Paul writes, "But we speak God's wisdom, secret and hidden, which God decreed before the ages for our glory. None of the rulers of this age understood this; for if they had, they would not have crucified the Lord of glory." When Paul refers to *the rulers of this age,* does he mean the human rulers who executed Jesus? Or does he mean the heavenly powers who rule from above? Likely he means both. In the New Testament's apocalyptic worldview, leaders exercise authority on the visible, earthly plane, but their actions are the reflection or outworking of events happening on an invisible, spiritual plane. These assumptions are similar to those in the book of Daniel, where earthly victory over Persia and Greece comes only when the archangel Gabriel conquers the patron angels (called *princes*) of Persia and Greece (see Dan 10:12–21). Competing heavenly forces, operating under God's sovereignty and with God's permission, determine the unfolding of history.[63]

Third, the powers are neither exclusively good nor exclusively evil.[64] They can, and often do, serve the good of the world order, as in Romans 13, where Paul writes about the need to obey political rulers because they are ordained by God. But there are also powers that work to undermine God's vision for a world of life, blessing, and righteousness, as the author of Ephesians assumes: "For our struggle is not against enemies of blood and flesh, but against the rulers, against the authorities, against the cosmic powers of this present darkness, against the spiritual forces of evil in the heavenly places" (Eph 6:12). The author of 1 John expresses a similar view: "We know that we are God's children, and that the whole world lies under the power of the

evil one" (1 John 5:19). The actions and interactions of evil spiritual forces
or agents are assumed to bear on social and political events, as in Daniel and
in the passion narratives. They bear also on individual psychic processes,
as Abraham assumes in a prayer found in the pseudepigraphic book of *Ju-*
bilees: "Deliver me from the hands of evil spirits who have dominion over
the thoughts of men's hearts, and let them not lead me astray from thee, my
God" (*Jub.* 12:20).

In the late fifth or early sixth century CE, an author purporting to be "Dionysius the Areopagite" (a man mentioned in Acts 17:34) will claim that
the power terms in the New Testament refer unambiguously to angels. He
will systematize the terms into a scheme of nine triadic choirs of angels,
arranged in a hierarchy: the seraphim, cherubim, and thrones; the dominions, powers, and authorities; the principalities, archangels, and angels.[65] By
contrast, in the New Testament the relationship between angels and all the
other powers is hard to specify. When New Testament authors use power
terms they may hint at their angelic identity but do not make such identity
explicit. For example, in Luke's Gospel Jesus says to those who arrest him,
"But this is your hour, and the power of darkness!" (Luke 22:53). Here the
expression, "power [or authority] of darkness," alludes to the angel, Satan,
who is pulling the strings of Jesus' adversaries in Jerusalem (see also 22:3).[66]
As a second example, when Paul wants to enumerate all the cosmic forces
that might try to separate Christians from the love of God, he lists "angels"
alongside "rulers" and "powers," suggesting close affinity if not equivalence
(Rom 8:38). Angels, rulers, and powers alike are spiritual forces operating in
the heavenly regions but with the capacity to influence earthly life.[67]

Angels, like the other powers, could be thought of as working for good
or for ill. Although some angels are portrayed as God's messengers and as
spirits ministering to righteous human beings, it was assumed that other angels are hostile and dangerous. Angels—some of them, anyway—are jealous
of humans because of the favor before God that the sons and daughters of
Adam and Eve enjoy. Satan is the extreme example of a jealous angel: stories
told that out of jealousy and a desire for power and veneration, he had challenged God and so been cast from heaven, along with an entourage of lesser
angels. Satan responds, according to *Life of Adam and Eve,* by assaulting the
first couple in the Garden of Eden so that *they* might be cast out of Paradise
just as *he* was cast out of heaven (see Chapter 3, p. 87). Eventually, Christians
would identify all the fallen angels in Satan's retinue as demons who now
plague them on earth.[68]

Paul alludes to the temptation in Eden in Rom 5:12, but it is the twin
powers of sin and death, not Satan, who accost Adam and so enter into the

cosmic drama. Sin and death here are like Satan but without the personality: they do the same things Satan routinely does, namely, lead God's children astray and inflict destruction and decay (see pp. 117–18). Paul believed that when Adam transgressed, God relinquished limited but very real authority to sin and death (cf. Luke 4:6). Thus God has granted to the powers sin and death—and to *all* the rulers, authorities, and cosmic powers of this present darkness—a measure of control over the cosmos. This age is "an evil age" in Paul's view, because the powers determine the outcome of many earthly events. They do so because God permits them to do so. But God does so in hope, looking ahead to that day when all creation "will be set free from its bondage to decay and will obtain the freedom of the glory of the children of God" (Rom 8:21).

Significantly, Paul does not think of God as actively plotting each evil thing that happens in the world. God does not sit in heaven saying, "infanticide for her" and "death by sword for that one." Rather, suffering comes to us at the hand of forces that oppose God and seek to undermine God's plan for all to live in peace with God and with one another. In stipulating that God does not plot evil but permits it, Paul is not implying that God *lacks the right sort of power* to intervene. He is not saying, for example, that God has power to persuade human hearts and minds and to be present with and comfort those who suffer, but not power to stop a marauding wild animal or a ravaging disease or a murderous adversary.[69] Yes, God is wholly immanent (and therefore present in our suffering), but in Paul's view God is also wholly sovereign and able to intervene at will. Paul removes God by one degree from responsibility for *causing* evil, but does not let God off the hook entirely. For reasons known only to God, the world has been "subjected to futility," Paul writes, and God is the one who did the subjecting (Rom 8:20).[70] The world is as it is because God permits it to be so.

In ancient apocalyptic circles it was widely assumed that before the end time there would be a period of heightened affliction for the righteous. (It is the scattered scriptural references to such affliction that are systematized by dispensationalists' into the doctrine of the Tribulation.) In the end-time trials, the forces that oppose God escalate their attacks on God's servants, for "they know that their time is short" (paraphrasing Rev 12:12). But the havoc-wreaking forces do not act "for no reason," as God admits to having done in the book of Job.[71] Rather, according to this view, the evil forces do their dirty work for a purpose: to aggrandize themselves and undermine God's plan to redeem the cosmos. That is why Christians' identity as "children of light and children of the day" should lead them to expect *more* suffering rather than *less* (1 Thess 5:5).

New Testament authors are not dogmatic or systematic in their assumptions about the origin of evil or the nature of the evil powers' relationship to God. Despite the prevalence of the view I have sketched above, the authors can also imply that God sends particular instances of suffering to instruct or chastise. Sometimes Satan is portrayed as the archenemy of God, serving no good purpose. Other times Satan is God's own servant for bringing about a positive result.[72] The New Testament writers' approaches to the problem of evil remain loose and ad hoc—serving their immediate pastoral or rhetorical needs rather than adhering to a grand master narrative designed to account for evil's origin.[73]

In summary, the Bible gives not one but several answers to the fundamental question of why there is so much suffering and evil in the world today. The different answers came to currency at different moments in the ever-changing historical and cultural circumstances of the people of Israel. Some explanations put the brunt of the blame on humans, claiming that any affliction suffered is a just penalty for disobedience to God's covenant. Others, written in harder times, defy the notion that human misery is always warranted punishment; some suffering is just too immense to be deserved. Throughout Israel's history, authors reached back into Near Eastern mythological lore for symbols to describe the forces that opposed God, as well as God's (contested) sovereignty. Such authors exploited lore, for example, about the monsters Rahab (Ps 89:10; Isa 51:9) and Leviathan ("the fleeing serpent . . . the twisting serpent . . . the dragon that is in the sea" [Isa 27:1]), and about heavenly warriors who fought on the High God's behalf (Deut 33:2). In the period of the Exile and afterward, authors seized on the ancient imagery as they struggled to explain the vast and powerful forces that gripped the cosmos. During the two centuries preceding the Common Era, symbolism for opposition to God crystallized around the figure of Satan— in Job a nameless functionary, but by Jesus' day a fearsome enemy of God and God's people, governor of individual souls and of empires.

JESUS, KING OF ANGELS

OPPOSITION TO JESUS BY THE POWERS

Why did Satan test Jesus? Why did the demons submit to him? Why did the rulers and authorities and powers hate him and finally crucify him? I suggest that, in the logic of the Gospels, the powers *recognized* Jesus, as surely as the servant girl recognized Peter when she said, "You also were with Jesus the Galilean" (Matt 26:69). At the very least, the powers recognized Jesus because he had endured Satan's assaults during the testing in the wilderness.

But the story line likely goes back much further. The powers recognized Jesus because *they knew that through him the world was created.* In the incarnation he is briefly made lower than the powers—but they are not fooled. They know whence he came, and they know what he is going to do to them. The demon cries out at Jesus' first exorcism, "What have you to do with us, Jesus of Nazareth? Have you come to destroy us? I know who you are, the Holy One of God!" (Mark 1:24).

I am assuming that the evangelists and other New Testament authors affirmed Jesus' pre-existence and virtual identity with the "glory" witnessed by Moses in the Exodus and by Ezekiel on the banks of the River Chebar. In Chapter 2, I briefly reviewed recent scholarly work that affirms both the prevalence in early Judaism of belief in a chief angelic mediator, identified variously with God's glory and with the "Angel of the LORD," and the early Christian pattern of identifying that glory with Christ in his pre-incarnate state.[74] In Chapter 3, I described the recurring motif in ancient Jewish sources of the angels' (or Satan's) jealousy over God's attention to ones who were created after them. Against this background, New Testament authors' claims about Christ's lordship emerge in a new light—especially the claims that he is firstborn, agent of creation, and at God's right hand.[75]

To say that Christ is firstborn and the agent of creation is to identify him with the personified figure of Wisdom, and thereby to insist that he predates the angels. In Jewish antiquity, Wisdom was widely assumed to be God's first creation, and the agent used by God to fashion the rest of the cosmos. Philo calls Wisdom "the firstborn mother of all things."[76] In common understanding, angels didn't come along until the second (or possibly even the fifth or the sixth) day of creation. By calling Christ firstborn and by insisting on his role in creation, the New Testament authors undermined any alleged claim by jealous angels, including Satan, that Christ was younger than they and therefore undeserving of worship.[77]

To say that Christ stands at God's "right hand" is to assert his authority over another, lesser power in heaven, namely, Satan. The devil's role as prosecuting attorney in God's court is first portrayed in Job 1–2 and then in Zechariah 3. This role is taken for granted by New Testament authors. In 1 Peter, the devil is *antidikos,* opponent in a lawsuit (1 Pet 5:8); in Revelation, he is the "accuser of our brethren, who accuses them day and night before our God" (Rev 12:10). But Christ has defeated Satan and so has greater authority than him—so much so that some New Testament authors portray Satan as cast out of heaven (see Luke 10:18; John 12:31; Rev 12:10–12). Thus, Paul's question in Romans 8, "Who is to condemn?" is rhetorical. The accuser has no authority against us because Jesus stands ready to plead our case before God: "Christ Jesus, who died, yes, who was raised, who is at the right hand of God, who indeed intercedes for us" (Rom 8:34).

Satan, along with his angels, is fallen from the place he once occupied. We do not have to assume that there was a battle in heaven, though Christians did sometimes think in those terms (see especially Rev 12). Some may instead have reasoned that by his perfect obedience Christ defeated the power of sin, which had sought to entice or coerce him away from God (Rom 5:19). In Revelation, the devil's expulsion from heaven comes with a loud warning of woe to the earth and sea because, having been cast out, the devil knows that his time is short. He will wield his dominion over the unsaved and continue his assaults on the saints with a vigor born of desperation.

New Testament authors are not consistent in characterizing Jesus' lordship over these rampaging powers. Some passages imply that Jesus' authority over them is already fully achieved and recognized by all. But other key passages suggest that the victory is not yet fully realized. Hebrews, for example, states, "As it is, we do not yet see everything in subjection to him" (Heb 2:8 RSV; cf. 10:12–13). And Paul writes that Jesus will hand the kingdom over to the Father only "after he has destroyed every ruler and every authority and power." He continues, "The last enemy to be destroyed is death" (1 Cor 15:24–26).[78] So the power of death is not yet subjugated, though its end has been guaranteed by Christ's resurrection. And the power of sin, the old slave master, is still on the loose. Christians do not have to obey sin, but there is always the danger—too often realized—that we will choose to do so (see Rom 6:13). In any case, sin retains immense authority over the unconverted masses of humanity. Creation groans because the fallen powers continue, seemingly unhindered, to have their way in this fallen world.

DECONSTRUCTING THE POWERS

In the past half-century, many theologians have discussed the nature of the principalities and powers. How can they help us to appropriate early Christian claims of Jesus' lordship for the twenty-first century? Here I will consider briefly the work of Rudolf Bultmann and Walter Wink and compare their analyses to that of LaHaye and Jenkins in the Left Behind series.[79] Why look to these authors? Bultmann epitomizes the modernist era's dismissal of the powers, and Wink offers the most thoroughgoing recent critical attempt to understand the principalities and powers exegetically, theologically, and sociologically. The numerical reach of the Left Behind series is staggering and its consequent potential to influence the theological and political climate in America and abroad is undeniable.

In the 1950's, theologian Rudolf Bultmann exorcised the powers and

principalities. He declared them unacceptable to "modern men," who allegedly take for granted that "the course of nature and of history, like their own
inner life and their practical life, is nowhere interrupted by the intervention
of supernatural powers."[80] Bultmann's rejection of the powers was part of his
larger program of interpreting mythological categories non-mythologically.
Specifically, he interpreted the mythological notions of Satan and evil spirits
as expressing key human insights into the nature of evil—insights that could
also be expressed in non-mythological terms. These included the recognition that humans "are often carried away by their passions and are no longer
masters of themselves, with the result that inconceivable wickedness breaks
forth from them"; and the insight that incidents of evil are not isolated or
unrelated to one another but "make up one single power which in the last
analysis grows from the very actions of men, which forms an atmosphere, a
spiritual tradition, which overwhelms every man." Hence, Bultmann concluded, "the consequences and effects of our sins become a power domi-
nating us, and we cannot free ourselves from them."[81] Thus, he accepted
the reality of evil and its transcending *of individuals,* but explained these
without recourse to any notion of forces, beings, or processes that transcend
the course of nature and of history.

By dismissing the powers, Bultmann undercuts the great potential of
the New Testament's language about them for helping us to comprehend
the spirits of rage, enmity, and domination that have captured one population after another in recent decades. In principle, Bultmann did permit the
continuing metaphorical use of language about the powers, language that
he understood as expressing a valid perception of the mysterious enslaving
power of evil, which arises from individuals and yet is larger collectively.
But this subtlety was apparently lost on many who appropriated Bultmann's
work. For decades, it was his modernist dismissal of the powers that set the
agenda for scholars and mainline church leaders.

Standing squarely on the shoulders of Bultmann (and others), Walter
Wink denies that the powers are "angelic or demonic beings fluttering about
in the sky."[82] Still, they are real. The powers are the very structures, institutions, and systems that order the world and keep it from falling into chaos.
The powers always have both an exterior aspect (such as the structure and
material assets of a corporation, or the machinery of government) and an
interior aspect (such as the personality of a corporation or the ethos of an
institution or epoch). The powers encompass social and cultural structures
of every kind, including the family unit, the church, the civic club, the university, the corporation, the labor union, the medical establishment, the
military, and the nation. Such structures uphold order and maintain the

boundaries essential for humans to flourish. Furthermore, every such social structure has an interior aspect or spirit. Apart from their incarnation in such systems, the powers have no existence. The powers can be redeemed, Wink says, because their evil is not intrinsic but the result of idolatry—a turn toward sin. The worst-case powers, Wink admits (and he names Nazism and sexism as examples) may need to be unmasked, abandoned, or destroyed, and replaced by structures more true to God's intent. But "the necessary social function they have idolatrously perverted will abide."[83]

How does Wink construe Christ's lordship over the powers? Wink rejects a worldview that sees heaven and earth as distinct realms and Jesus as divine. Jesus' chief accomplishment was that through his teaching and by his death he unmasked the powers—took away their semblance of respectability and revealed them for what they really are—and showed us how to call them back to their true vocation as given by God. That is how and why he exercised lordship over them.[84]

Wink has served as an important corrective to Bultmann, compelling us to see how the powers impinge on every aspect of our existence and how we ignore them at our own peril. But Wink is still married to Bultmann's project of demythologization. He still supposes that we can explain what happens in the world, including what we identify as evil, by referring only to what we already know to be in and of this world. In Wink's understanding, evil is finally subject to rational analysis, and therefore it is amenable to correction by means of enlightenment. If the powers know the good, Wink implies, they will pursue it (except, maybe, in those admitted worst-case scenarios). Consistent with his refusal to grant the powers any degree of world transcendence, Wink grants Christ no degree of transcendence. Christ was a master at unmasking—at discerning and revealing the idolatry into which the powers have fallen—but he neither possessed nor does he grant any extraworldly or more-than-mortal power to resist it. Christ offered not brute strength but insight, not power but perspicacity.

Now back to LaHaye and Jenkins. Sprawling across the twelve volumes of the Left Behind novels (not to mention the children's volumes and many spin-off products), we see the final war of good against evil, depicted in gory detail. Quite differently from Wink, LaHaye and Jenkins see no structural or systemic dimension to the powers. In the post-Rapture world of Left Behind, evil—like the Holy Spirit—invades from outside.[85] The powers are not to be redeemed or transformed, but expelled and cast into the abyss. As in the Crusades, those who refuse to convert die a most unpleasant—indeed, an eternal—death. The motto of these books seems to be, "We have met the enemy and he is *not* us, and we can get rid of him because our guy is stronger." [86] Jesus is Lord over the powers because, if and when he feels like it, he can nullify their miracles and do better ones. Like George W. Bush facing Saddam Hussein, Jesus has more firepower than the Enemy, and better troops at his disposal. This motif of Jesus' power as firepower climaxes in the twelfth book, *Glorious Appearing*.[87] When Jesus comes again to establish his millennial kingdom on earth, he first slays millions of non-Christian storm troopers by the sheer power of a spoken word, and then causes their bodies to be instantly decomposed. This is Jesus wielding, not the power of life, but the power of death.

One of the many dangers in this view of evil is the assumption that, once we are saved, all is right with us. We can safely pass the buck because the evil has been expelled from *our* individual souls. We need not worry about questions of systemic evil, such as, whether and how our own privilege depends on and reinforces the servitude and suffering of others, or how we who are in power regularly stereotype our enemies in ways that both provoke and rationalize our oppression of them.[88] Because LaHaye and Jenkins view evil powers as separable from people and institutions, they fail to see how the powers pervade *all* our institutions, including the church. They fail to see how spirits such as nationalism and racism can hold us captive even after we convert. They fail to see that churches—even fundamentalist churches—can and do function as places of domination and enmity and strife. Churches can function that way because the people and structures that incarnate the powers remain fallen—in the world and of the world. Even if forgiven, they are still prone to believe sin's twisted promises of well-being, and to heed its words of flattery and enticement. They are still susceptible to coercion by the powers that deal in death.

If we believe Wink, then evil (like a computer virus) may in some circumstances come to have a life of its own, but it is not actually a personal entity. Evil is not a *being;* it is always "in me" or "in us" and never "out there." We are all fallen but we can—at least theoretically—return to where we need to be. Jesus taught us how to do it; he showed us the way. On the other hand, if we believe Left Behind, then evil has not only a life of its own but also a mind of its own. Evil has entered into this world an unwelcome invader, with a power to corrupt that is greater than that of any mortal. It must be eliminated, but no amount of knowledge or good intent and planning on an individual's or society's part can do that: *Jesus* must evict the evil from the souls of the unrighteous and from the world.

Perhaps rather than having to choose between the conflicting views of LaHay/Jenkins and Bultmann/Wink, we can borrow elements from each and forge a more satisfying middle way. In any case, whether evil angels and evil powers are ontologically real or just our projections of complex this-worldly psychological, interpersonal, and intersocial forces may not matter in the end. The potential for damage—and, I will argue, the potential for victory in Christ—is just as great either way. I suggest that we refuse to forfeit the New Testament's personal language for the powers, but continue to use that language. We can use it with a metaphorical reserve that LaHaye and Jenkins lack—acknowledging, along with Wink, that the powers are always incarnated in people and structures and that we are complicit in them. With Wink, we can view our mission as one of naming the powers, unmasking their pretensions to being gods and their sinful domination of the weak, and redeeming them by calling them back to the Creator's purposes for them in this world. But with LaHaye and Jenkins (and the New Testament), we can also insist that the power to redeem is not actually ours but Christ's—and that it is *real* power, power beyond what we as mortals can muster, not merely human power to unmask but *divine power to create anew.*

According to our middle way, then, the present evil age continues. The rules and authorities and powers and dominions that structure our world persist in their fallen condition, evil mixed with good to varying degrees. But Jesus—God's agent in the creation of the world, the one who stands at God's right hand—is Lord over those powers. As Lord, Christ gives us authority over them when he calls us to confront them. The next question is, what does this authority look like?

"NO FEAR": COPING WITH EVIL AS DISCIPLES OF JESUS

Jesus promised the seventy-two disciples in Luke: "See, I have given you authority to tread on snakes and scorpions, and over all the power of the enemy; and nothing will hurt you" (Luke 10:19). But Luke understood that Jesus was not promising that disciples would be invulnerable to the world's evil. Quite the opposite: earlier in Luke's Gospel, Jesus taught that followers must daily take up their cross. They must be willing to forfeit life itself. In the remainder of Luke and in Acts (which is by the same author), Jesus will be crucified by the powers, believers will be bound and dragged to prison, and both Stephen and James, the brother of John, will be martyred. Luke must, therefore, assume that Jesus' lordship over evil powers—and hence our authority over those powers as his disciples—is manifested, not in supernatural protection of the saints, but in some other way. It is manifested, I suggest, in the divine strength we are given to persevere, indeed, to flourish and to help others flourish in the midst of this fallen world.

As Jesus contended against the principalities and powers, he showed himself as perfected, elevated, deified. He accomplished far more than could ever have been done solely by human power. The good news for us is that, as Jesus' disciples, we are united to Christ through the Spirit, who works in us to perfect and elevate us also (see pp. 98–99). The answer Christians are given to the problem of evil is not an explanation but a *charge* and a *benediction*. The charge is to resist evil and to watch with those who suffer. As Jesus said in Gethsemane, "Pray that you may not enter into temptation," and again, "Remain here [with me], and keep awake" (Mark 14:38).[89] The benediction is the promise of union with Christ through the Spirit and the consequent gift of divine empowerment to persevere in our resisting and our watching. As Paul wrote, "I can do all things through him who strengthens me" (Phil 4:13).

Among its other works on our behalf, the Spirit enables us to persevere in our grappling with the sinful and sorrowful conditions of human existence. We are not divine (the claims of many popular spiritual authors notwithstanding), but Jesus strengthens us to resist the powers of sin and death in ways that we never could alone:

- Jesus heals our blindness—gives us eyes to see when sin seduces us with its wily and deceptive promises. Sometimes such sight comes gradually. Sometimes it comes in an instant, with knee-buckling force, as understanding of our own elaborate duplicity and self-delusion overtakes us. Sometimes, the healing affects only individuals; sometimes, whole peoples have the scales lifted from their eyes.
- Jesus undergirds us when death buffets us and torments us. Throughout the ages, saints have faced down the powers that deal in death. They were, and are, able to conquer fear by trusting in the God who raises the dead. Few of us today have known martyrs, but most have seen Christians who witnessed to their faith by persevering in hope even in the midst of terrible affliction.
- Jesus forgives us when we fail morally. By accepting us, even running to meet and embrace us when we are dragged down with shame, he enables us to triumph over the forces that tempt us to despair.
- Jesus empowers us to love and serve ones whom we have wronged or hated, to forgive ones who have wronged us, and to call those wrongs to mind no more. In sum, Christ frees us from the dominion of the powers and *shows that he is their Lord.*

Though each could be elaborated, I will focus on the fourth empowerment: Jesus' gift to us of divine strength to return good for evil and to let love accede to the place where hatred once reigned.

One of the Satan figure's many aliases in ancient Jewish and Christian writings is Mastema.[90] The name means "enmity" or "hatred"—one of Satan's favorite tools. By means of hatred, he fosters blind obedience and even idolatrous worship—especially of those who claim the power to vanquish our enemies. Mastema delights in rousing our unrighteous anger. Anger can goad us to destroy the things, the people, the relationships that are most precious to us; anger can destroy even us. But Jesus is stronger than Mastema, for his power is that of love.

> You have heard that it was said, "You shall love your neighbor and hate your enemy." But I say to you, Love your enemies and pray for those who persecute you, so that you may be children of your Father in heaven; for he makes his sun rise on the evil and on the good, and sends rain on the righteous and on the unrighteous. For if you love those who love you, what reward do you have? Do not even the tax collectors do the same? And if you greet only your brothers and sisters, what more are you doing than others? Do not even the Gentiles do the same? Be perfect, therefore, as your heavenly Father is perfect. (Matt 5:43–48)

How dare Jesus command us—and how dare we aspire—to "be perfect?" He dared, and we do, because the power to love our enemies does not issue from our own hearts. The power to love our enemies comes from God, whose enemy we ourselves once were. Divine perfection is manifested in God's unconditional love for all. God freely gives the sun and the rain—the very means of life—to the righteous and the unrighteous alike. Jesus, too, loves with such reckless abandon, and he commands us to do likewise, trusting that the power to do so comes from above (see Jas 1:17). When we harbor hate, we walk in darkness. When we love, we have overcome the Evil One (see 1 John 2:9–14).

The power that Jesus grants us to vanquish hate is not a consolation prize, given in the absence of the vaporizing, annihilating sort of power depicted in the Left Behind series. Anyone who has ever been possessed by the demon of hate—what Miroslav Volf defines as "revulsion for the other that feeds on the sense of harm or wrong suffered"[91]—knows how completely and ruthlessly it exercises its rule. Hatred takes control of our deeds, our words, our very minds till we lose all recognition that something is awry. Moreover, hatred has the power to control us not only as individuals but as whole populations (as recent international events so grimly attest). Hatred is so potent because it is the power of death itself (see Matt 5:21–22; 1 John 3:15). But Jesus rebukes hatred, saying, "Come out, you unclean spirit!" (Mark 5:8).

Jesus' power to expel hatred and engender love is the most extraordinary power there is, for it is the power to overcome death with life.

CONCLUSION

How can we explain the bad things that happen to us and the bad things that people do? Over the centuries, philosophers and theologians have offered many answers to this question, but in Christian tradition Satan has usually played a role. In the New Testament, Satan is depicted as the ferocious archfiend of God and God's people. He is "the Evil One" and "Ruler of this World," keeping the peoples of the world in captivity and darkness, indwelling the wicked, deputizing the demons, deceiving the foolish, afflicting the righteous, and generally working to sabotage God's reign wherever he can. But, Jesus is Lord over him and all his servants, having put them to flight in his earthly ministry and triumphed over them on the cross.

Despite Satan's prominence in the New Testament—and despite his claim to be older than Adam ("Before he was made, I was already made" [*Life of Adam and Eve* 14:3])—Satan did not achieve his full identity and notoriety until rather late in the game. Although the *satan* is mentioned in Job, Zechariah, and 1 Chronicles, at the time those books were written the term probably designated a functionary ("the adversary") rather than a specific spiritual being ("Satan"). The point is easily missed because of our habit of reading the Satan known from subsequent depictions into earlier texts— a habit reinforced by published translations of the Old Testament, which invariably render *satan* in Job 1–2, Zechariah 3, and 1 Chronicles 21 as a proper name. But before the second century BCE (when the habit started), biblical authors gave other explanations for suffering. Typically affliction was interpreted as punishment for personal or corporate sin, although some early voices were raised in protest against such explanation. The author of Job rejected all theories that Job had brought his suffering upon himself.[92] The psalmist and others invoked mythic memories of God's earlier subjugating of cosmic opponents as they called on God to vanquish their enemy now, as in days gone by.

As national suffering increased, the mythic traditions about cosmic adversaries began to crystallize around the figure of the *satan*. These informing mythic traditions included stories of arrogant rulers cast down for insubordination (accounts already modeled on earlier myth), along with stories of rebellious angels, the sea dragon Leviathan, the serpent in the Garden of Eden, and others. The archfiend Satan who emerged from these coalescing stories was extraordinarily potent and possessed an immense range of talents for destruction, which he deployed in an ongoing battle to unseat the God of heaven and usurp the divine throne. Still, Jewish authors did not let go of the biblical insistence, seen in Job 1–2 and Zechariah 3, that Satan is *subordinate* to God.

Paul says of Satan, "We are not ignorant of his designs" (2 Cor 2:11). Satan's design or scheme is always to divide and conquer: here, to exploit a rupture in the fellowship of the Corinthian Christians so that he might take unwitting members captive. Paul presumed that Satan, like a vindictive employee, uses every opportunity to undermine God's work. Satan's designs for evil operate on several levels at once: psychological, social, and cosmic. He coerces humans psychologically by afflicting them and then offering relief (as with Job), or he seduces them by promising benefit or gain (as with Adam and Eve). He blinds people to keep them from seeing what he is up to. And he fosters hatred, anger, fear, lust, or grief—passions that split human psyches and prevent us from offering ourselves single-mindedly to God. At the social level, Satan breaks down the unity and peace that are God's design for the church and ultimately for the world. Isolation and disunity serve Satan, not God: those not reconciled to one another cannot spread God's message of reconciliation. Satan blinds whole peoples by promoting idolatry, and by orchestrating opposition to the gospel and its missionaries. Though acting locally, Satan is always thinking globally: his ultimate intent is nothing less than to be all-in-all. Indeed, he would have not just the earth and its inhabitants but the very cosmos with its stars and planets under his command.

Even though New Testament authors accorded a prominent role to Satan, they could parse out the problem of evil in different ways. Paul told that when Adam transgressed, powers called "sin" and "death" entered into the world and have reigned ever since. God is still sovereign but for the time has relinquished authority to "the powers"—all those seen and unseen forces that structure the world and preserve it, God's servants for good (Rom 13:4) and our guardians before faith came (Gal 3:23–24). But in keeping us from chaos the powers also keep us from God. Inevitably, though to greater and lesser extents, the powers exalt themselves, use threats and promises to blind us to their true nature, wrest allegiance from us and even subjugate us. In short, the powers replicate the behavioral pattern pioneered by Satan, who likewise is God's servant but uses deception and force to pursue his own subversive ends. Angels, too, may follow this pattern and so are not entirely to be trusted: some will try to lead us astray from the true Gospel (Gal 1:8), or to separate us from the love of God (Rom 8:38). But, Paul and other early Christians proclaimed that *Christ is superior to the powers.* For a time he was made lower than the angels, but now he is enthroned above them, and at the mention of his name their knees bow and tongues confess that he is Lord.

Today, much of conservative Christianity views the powers as evil personal beings who are wholly transcendent in origin. They come from beyond humans, indeed, from beyond this world. For example, in the Left Behind series, Tim LaHaye and Jerry B. Jenkins portray Satan and his demonic angels as beings who enter our world like infectious agents from the abyss and invade human hearts, taking people prisoner in Satan's ongoing war to control the earth and seize God's place of authority. LaHaye and Jenkins see Satan's agency as manifest wherever beliefs or social practices diverge from the fundamentalist party line. In their view, Christ is Lord because he banishes the evil powers from the individual whenever he is invited to dwell in a human heart.

Such a view of the powers—as transcendent beings who indwell the unconverted—has unfortunate consequences. Above all, it fosters an us-versus-them mentality: *we* are free from Satan's power; *they* are not. But if we define evil as always resident in someone else, then we are easily blinded to our own complicity in sin, especially our part in creating or maintaining sinful ideologies like sexism, racism, or nationalism. We assume that if we just get people saved, all will be well. And so we underestimate the tremendous force of the institutions and ideologies that shape our word and deed from cradle to grave. No one is *born* a racist, for example, but even a person saved by Jesus Christ may find it hard to escape the powers of a racist culture pressing one into its mold from infancy on. The power of the powers is the power of illusion: they convince us that the world we know is simply *the way things are.*[93]

The ancient traditions about Satan and the principalities and powers convey important convictions that are still relevant today. The first is the conviction that evil has been with us since the creation of humankind. No human except Christ has wholly overcome the human inclination to serve and protect self to the detriment of God and other human beings. As humans we long for God but inevitably go astray. The second such conviction is the belief that the powers of evil in our world are larger than we are, and are extraordinarily hard to resist. Forces—be they from beyond us or of our own making—work to disrupt the flourishing of the earth and all God's creatures in it. The powers draw us into sin and take us captive. This is what Berkhof calls the "tragic" dimension of sin. Because of it our guilt is lessened but not removed: the powers prevailed on us, but we gave our consent.[94]

The New Testament authors respond to these dire truths about evil by insisting that Jesus Christ is Lord over all the principalities and powers. Through his resurrection and ascension, Christ entered into a new and powerful mode of existence, into the very life of God. He is King of Angels, the one seated at God's right hand "in the heavenly places, far above all rule and authority and power and dominion, and above every name that is named, not only in this age but also in the age to come" (Eph 1:20b–21). In his life as the Risen One he is able to reach beyond the confines of his former physical body and be present in the minds and hearts of all through transforming knowledge, power, and love.[95] And, because he is exalted over the principalities and powers, no spiritual force in the cosmos can separate us from God's love as shown to us through him. This is not because humans will cling perfectly to God, but because Christ is at God's right hand, ready to intercede for us when the Accuser comes against us with his claims.

When we look around at the world it does not look as though Christ is enthroned over all. Satan and the other fallen angels appear to be alive and well. But in his dying Jesus unmasked the powers and showed them to be frauds, and because of his victory over death and his transforming presence in our lives, humans are no longer obliged to submit to the powers. In the preceding chapters I have suggested some of the ways that Christ enables us to oppose the forces of evil in our world: by healing our wounds, assuring us of his divine presence, reforming our errant desires, empowering us to face down the forces that deal in death, forgiving us when we stray, restoring us to fellowship, resolving our anger, and changing our hatred to love. In these and still other ways, Jesus both calls and empowers us to resist evil and to watch with those who suffer.

Many, many questions about evil must go unasked and unanswered. But I will take up at least one set of outstanding questions in the following chapter on guardian angels. In popular understanding, guardian angels are spirits assigned individually to each of God's faithful. As guardians their task is "to lead and guard, to light and guide"—especially to help us resist moral temptation and to rescue us from physical peril. Such a conception expresses our belief that God providentially cares for us, answering our prayers for deliverance from evil. But how does the conception of guardian angels square with our actual experience of this world—a world in which the faithful are so often *not* kept from sin or rescued from danger, a world in which Christ himself did not seek to escape from peril, but faced and endured it for our sake?

5

Guardian Angels

Imagine setting out on a long journey through the Amazon rain forest, a desert wasteland, or a foreign and hostile city, with only your bare wits for resources. Nearly every moment your life will be in peril. How would you survive? "I'd need a guide," you say. "I'd need a companion who knows the way." You recognize that this partner in travel should be someone familiar with the terrain and its pitfalls. He or she should know of any hostile forces in the region, and should have strength and savvy to assist you in confronting the dangers. This ideal guide should not be one to desert at the first sign of trouble, but must be utterly reliable, one of perfect integrity. Thirteenth-century theologian Thomas Aquinas, known as "Doctor Angelicus," envisioned life as a danger-fraught journey, and guardian angels as just such guides:

> Man in this present condition of life is, so to speak, on a road along which he must make his way to his homeland. On this road lurk many dangers, both internal and external. Thus, as the Psalm puts it, *On this road on which I walked they set up an ambush for me* [Psalm 142:2]. So, as guides are given to men walking along an unsafe road, guardian angels are also given to each man while he is a wayfarer in this life. (*Summa Theologiae* 1a.113, 4) [1]

As with Aquinas, so all ancient and medieval belief in guardian angels was rooted in a perception of the world as hostile and hazard-filled. Demons and other adversaries lurk at every turn in the road, ready to ambush. But,

139

graciously, God provides help. To each believer has been assigned a special angel to lead and guard, to light and guide.

Over nearly the entire first two millennia of the church's existence, the doctrine of guardian angels was used to answer pressing theological questions. How close is God? How close is heaven? How closely does God manage what happens in the material realm? How does God's managing of earthly events relate to human freedom? How does God protect us and care for us in the face of the many physical and spiritual threats to our well-being? When does such protection begin, and can it be taken away? How can we resist temptation, given our fallen and weak nature? What means does God offer so that we, though sinful and weighed down by fleshly desires, might approach the divine glory?

From the Reformation to Vatican II, strong belief in guardian angels was closely associated with Catholic piety. Many Catholics recall that as a child they prayed to their guardian angel each morning or night. This and many other such Catholic devotional practices reinforced the association of guardian angels with children, an association that lingers today. Who can count how many parents have taken comfort in thinking of special angels assigned to watch and guard their little ones when they are sent out each day into a perilous world? A famous painting depicts a small boy and girl crossing a rickety bridge, their guardian angel hovering protectively in the background. Judging from how widely the image is sold on the Internet (reproduced in various artistic media and without attribution), its power to ease parental anxiety must be very strong.[2]

Among today's angelphiles, however, the opinion has grown that guardian angels aren't just for Catholics or kids. Over the last decade or more, authors and teachers on the Web and the workshop circuit have informed spiritual seekers about their guardian angels. These angels are often (as in traditional Catholic piety) viewed as distinct angels assigned to individuals for life. Angel-experts—some Christian, some not—discuss such matters as the guardian angels' nature, the scope of their protective work, how to recognize their presence, how to discern their names, and how to tell them what we want and need. The angels offer miraculous protection: countless stories tell of burning buildings escaped, enemy fire avoided, ominous stalkers eluded. But, according to some current wisdom, angels offer much more than guardianship of the physical body. They also help with all kinds of emotional "stuff." They give comfort when one is depressed, strength when one is weak, affirmation when one is tyrannized by an inner voice that isolates and self-condemns. The angels help one to be one's own best self.

I begin this chapter with a brief overview of the history of belief in guardian angels. Here I can only sketch a few high points in the rich and variegated history of this doctrine as it evolved over two millennia. But the schematic character of my summary may allow certain patterns to emerge. We will see that, from the church's early days till the start of the Reformation, the spiritual realm was thought to impinge on the mundane world at infinitely many points. As Carlos Eire has written of the time just before the outbreak of the Reformation, "Heaven was never too far from earth. The sacred was diffused in the profane, the spiritual in the material."[3] From the New Testament era onward, Christians had viewed spirits, both demons and angels, as frequent actors in peoples' lives. Although guardian and other angels were often viewed as lower members of the presumed angelic hierarchy, for many, their actions—along with the actions of sainted humans—verified the intimate presence and agency of God in the world.

But with the rise of Protestantism, beliefs about divine immanence changed. The Protestants—particularly those in the Swiss Reformed (Calvinist) stream of tradition—argued that "the finite cannot contain the infinite." Their insistence on the separation of material and spiritual realities had its greatest impact on the Catholics' cult of the saints and understanding of the Eucharist. The Reformed Christians denied Catholics' contention that material objects, such as pictures or relics of the saints or the consecrated host of the Catholic Mass, could convey divine presence and power. This Calvinist emphasis on God's separateness from material objects had the incidental effect of undermining belief in angels' intimate presence among us.

And what did Catholics do in the face of views that so destabilized their accustomed reality? They did not remain silent, but shored up the traditional belief system. Still, they were not fully invulnerable to the Protestants' critique, but adjusted and compromised in various ways.

After sketching a history of belief in guardian angels, I will turn to examine present-day expressions of such belief. Here, knowing the alternate views of divine immanence versus transcendence that emerged in the Reformation will help us to make sense of the two major recent patterns of guardian-angel belief. Present-day stories about guardian angels as physical protectors reaffirm divine immanence and critique a view that God is largely removed from physical reality. Present-day stories about guardian angels as life coaches or spiritual counselors/comforters likewise critique a view that equates God's transcendence with divine indifference and distance from the world. Although those who tout angels' role as counselors/comforters often claim to be rejecting the Judeo-Christian view, it will become evident that they are reacting not against Christianity in general, but against a caricature of God as cold and remote that developed out of the Reformed Protestant stream of tradition. The angel advocates respond to this caricature by claiming the opposite, that God is not remote, but so thoroughly suffused through creation that the whole cosmos is essentially divine.

After considering present-day portraits of guardian angels, I will turn to Jesus, the "shepherd and guardian of your souls" (1 Pet 2:25). As we will see, Jesus does not so much protect us from evil as accompany us into the midst of it. Moreover, though Jesus brings peace "not as the world gives," this peace is not tranquillity of soul so much as a radical acceptance of us in our brokenness, an acceptance that frees us up to work in the world on Jesus' behalf.

GUARDIAN ANGELS: A SHORT HISTORY

BIBLICAL AND EARLY CHURCH VIEWS

There is no clear and certain knowledge about the origins of the notion of guardian angels. A few Old Testament passages refer to angelic guardianship over individuals or small groups, but these are too scattered and few to prove that there was widespread Israelite belief in specific angels assigned to protect individuals over an extended period of time.[4] Some scholars trace the idea back to biblical teaching about "the angels of the nations." In Deut 32:8 we read: "When the Most High gave to the nations their inheritance, when he separated the sons of men, he fixed the bounds of the peoples according to the number of the sons of God."[5] The text implies that every nation has been appointed its own angel ("god") except Israel, over whom YHWH rules. The author of *Jubilees* (second century BCE) affirms the teaching of Deuteronomy (*Jub.* 15:31–32), while others, including the author of Daniel, presumed not the LORD but Michael to be Israel's appointed guardian. Daniel 10 refers to "princes" (= guardian angels) of nations, whose actions bear on the military fate of their respective lands.[6]

It is not clear whether or how the idea of *national* guardian angels morphed into belief in *individual* guardians.[7] In *Jubilees,* Isaac tells Rebecca not to worry that Esau will succeed in harming Jacob, "because the protector of Jacob is greater and mightier and more honored and praised than the protector of Esau" (*Jub.* 35:17).[8] But it is uncertain whether the author is here thinking of Jacob and Esau as individuals or in their representative roles as the progenitors of nations.[9] A fragment of *1 Enoch* from the early first century BCE declares that God "will set a guard of holy angels over all the righteous and holy ones, and they shall keep them as the apple of the eye until all evil and all sin are brought to an end" (*1 En.* 100:5).[10] Here the author identifies a group of angels as having charge over a group of righteous humans, which is still not quite the same as a one-person-one-angel relationship. The angels' employment contract does, however, appear to be for the long haul rather than for isolated assignments.

Another pseudepigraphic book, *Biblical Antiquities* by Pseudo-Philo (first century CE), makes unambiguous reference to guardian angels in a few places. For example, in elaborating the commandment: "You shall not be a false witness against your neighbor," Pseudo-Philo adds: "Lest your guardians speak false testimony against you" (*Ps.-Philo* 11:12).[11] This looks like an early version of the idea that guardian angels police their charges and report any transgressions back to God. The second century CE document *3 Baruch* has an elaborate heavenly vision, in which angels overseeing the righteous report the work of those under their charge to the archangel, Michael. Meanwhile, other, distressed angels report that humans under their charge have performed so badly that the angels cannot bear to be with them anymore. So, the guardians implore Michael to "transfer us from them, for we are unable to remain with evil and foolish men" (*3 Bar.* 13:3).[12] We can conclude, then, that some Jews affirmed the existence of guardian angels at about the time of the birth of Christianity and that the notion was well established by the second century CE.

The view that personal spirits guided individuals had parallels in other cultures. Ancient Mesopotamians believed in personal deities who would advocate for a human before the divine council. Traces of this idea may be discerned in the book of Job, where Job appeals for a heavenly advocate, and perhaps also in the Johannine notion of the *paraklētos* (a word often translated as "Comforter," or "Advocate").[13] In the Greek world, Socrates was famous for claiming guidance by a *daimonion*, a personal genius or divine soul-double who guided or warned him when he was about to take a wrong course. For example, when Socrates was about to cross a river, his *daimonion* forbade him to leave the spot until he had atoned for an offense (words wrongly spoken) against heaven. The *daimonion*, he said, "which always checks me when on the point of doing something or other," came as something like a voice to his ear.[14] The *daimonion* of Socrates was one of a general class of intelligences or beings thought by Plato and his successors to emanate from and return to the supreme deity as mediators between the divine and human spheres. Plato explained that each of us has, in our pre-incarnate existence, received such a lower divinity to remain with us throughout life and after death.[15] Plutarch, the great biographer of the ancient world, echoed this teaching and explained that the reason why most people aren't aware of their *daimonion* is that its subtle guidance is overpowered by the force of their passions.[16]

Did these diverse ideas about personal deities influence emerging Jewish and then Christian beliefs about guardian angels? The likelihood seems great. Jews had long contact with Babylon, and appropriated various features of that culture's rich angelology.[17] With respect to possible Hellenistic philosophical influences, we know that Neoplatonic beliefs about spirit-beings as intermediaries between the ineffable God and the material world profoundly shaped early Christian notions on angelic hierarchy.[18] Still, it is hard to pin down the precise timing or extent of influence of these various teachings on the specific doctrine of guardian angels.

Two passages in the New Testament have commonly been taken as references to guardian angels. One passage is Matthew 18:10, in which Jesus says, "Take care that you do not despise one of these little ones; for, I tell you, in heaven their angels continually see the face of my Father in heaven." The statement certainly seems to imply some notion of guardian angels for each of the "little ones." Here Jesus is gesturing toward an actual child (see 18:2: "He called a child, whom he put among them"). But elsewhere Matthew uses the expression "little ones" as symbolic for the disciples, leaving open the possibility that the evangelist conceived of the angels mentioned in 18:10 as guardians not chiefly of children but of Jesus' followers.[19] The second possible New Testament reference to guardian angels is in Acts 12:15. Here disciples of Jesus are told by a maid named Rhoda that Peter (whom all believed to be in prison at the time) was standing at the gate. The incredulous disciples tell her she is out of her mind, but she insists on what she saw. They respond, "It is his angel." Their statement may reflect a notion that each person has a guardian angel who is his or her twin."[20]

The second-century Christian document *Shepherd of Hermas* depicts a world crowded with angels, whose identities meld together at many points. Of the many angels mentioned in the document, one is especially pertinent to the topic at hand: the author Hermas' shepherd-angel, who gives the ancient book its name. The Shepherd can fairly be termed a guardian angel: he has been sent to dwell with Hermas the rest of the days of his life, and Hermas has been "handed over" to him (*Visions* 5.2–3).[21] The Shepherd's purpose is to dwell with Hermas and interpret his visions to him, in order that Hermas might receive divine blessings and instruct others on important doctrine.

Several of the many other angels in *Shepherd of Hermas* are tied closely to, or even identified with, Christ or the Spirit. In one passage, for example, the "angel of the prophetic spirit" is identified with the Holy Spirit: "Then the angel of the prophetic spirit rests on [the true prophet] and fills the man, and the man, being filled with the Holy Spirit, speaks to the congregation as the

Lord wills. Thus, then, the spirit of the Godhead will be plain." [22] Throughout the *Shepherd of Hermas,* the author's variable way of referring to the divine makes the book very hard to follow. But, this variability has fascinating implications. Charles Gieschen suggests that the author thinks of one preexistent Holy Spirit, present in Jesus and continuing to manifest itself in angels. [23] Why isn't Hermas troubled that Christians might mistake lesser angels for God, or vice versa? Hermas apparently believed that the good angels are sent by God to perform the roles of Christ/the Spirit, and that all such angels reliably manifest God in the believer's life. In other words, the questions, "How do you know it was an angel, and not the Holy Spirit?" and conversely, "How do you know it was the Holy Spirit, and not an angel?" simply were not issues for Hermas.

The shepherd-angel serves as a guardian for Hermas, and indeed tells him that Hermas and all humans have not one but *two* guardian angels present throughout life, a righteous spirit and a wicked one:

> There are two angels for each man: one of justice and one of wickedness. . . . The spirit of justice is mild and reserved and meek and peaceful. When he enters into your heart, he speaks at once with you of justice and modesty and temperance and kindness and pardon and charity and paternal love. As often as these thoughts arise in your heart, know that the spirit of justice is with you. . . . Now learn the works of the spirit of wickedness too. First of all, he is irritable and bitter and rash, and his works are evil. . . . When you recognize his works, depart from him. (*Mandate* 6.2.2–5)

By portraying mortals as situated between opposing angels, Hermas accounts for the perplexing human tendency to oscillate between good and evil. The portrayal recalls the Dead Sea sectarians' doctrine of two governing spirits in the world, as well as widespread ancient teachings about the evil and good inclinations and about double-mindedness (see p. 119). Writing in the third century (that is, perhaps a hundred years after the author of the *Shepherd of Hermas*), Origen took the notion of paired opposite angels over from Hermas and made the tradition "an essential part of his spiritual teaching," which he in turn passed on "to a whole spiritual tradition." [24]

This tradition would prove to be extremely durable. For example, Gregory of Nyssa (fourth century) expounded on the idea, telling how God sent guardian angels to help fallen humanity. Unfortunately, as Gregory continues, "the destroyer of our nature" did likewise, sending "an evil, pernicious angel." So, now humans are caught in the middle and have to decide between the fruits of virtue offered by the good angel and the pleasures of earth offered by the wicked one.[25] Caesarius of Heisterbach (thirteenth century) also knows of this idea.[26] I do not know the number of great spiritual writers down through the centuries who expressed such a notion of paired opposite angels, but I suspect that many readers will recognize this idea's caricature in modern popular culture: the good and bad angels (or "shoulder people," as my daughter, at age six, identified them) who beset cartoon characters, including Fred Flintstone. Angel Fred and Devil Fred appear at moments of high temptation to wrestle for control of the Stone Age man's life.

Protecting charges from danger was long viewed as one of guardian angels' most important roles. Some dangers were physical. Thus Tobit prayed that an angel might travel with his son Tobias and his companion (ironically the Archangel Raphael, here incognito) and return them safe (see pp. 30–32). But guardian angels also protected their charges from spiritual dangers—an essential function because humans are weak, and beset on every side by powers that seek to lead them astray. The life of the believer was a life lived in spiritual combat, and the angels were helpers against the evil powers. As Hilary of Poitiers (fourth century) wrote, our weakness is such that

> If the guardian angels had not been given to us, we could not resist the many and powerful attacks of the evil spirits. To this end we had need of a higher nature. We know that this is so from the words with which the Lord strengthens Moses, trembling in his fear, "My angel will go before thee." That is why God has taken out these spirits from among his treasures, and has given through them an aid to human weakness, so that this divine assistance might help us against the powers of this world of darkness to attain the heritage of salvation.[27]

Others go beyond Hilary, arguing that the angels do not merely protect us from assault, but also offer peace and well-being to the believer's soul.[28] This angelic contribution is highlighted, for example, by Athanasius (fourth century) in his *Life of St. Anthony:* "The vision of the angels works softly and peaceably, awakening joy and exultation."[29]

The guardianship of the angels is preparatory, early Christians taught, for the guardianship of Christ. Origen wrote:

> So long as we are imperfect, and need one to assist us that we may be delivered from evils, we stand in need of an angel of whom Jacob said, "The angel who delivered me from all the evils;" but, when we have become perfected, and have passed through the stage of being subject to nursing-fathers and nursing-mothers and guardians and stewards, we are meet to be governed by the Lord himself.[30]

Until we reach maturity, like a foster father or like a nursing mother our guardian angel carries us on its shoulder, or in its bosom.[31] The angels shelter us from danger, they carry our prayers to God and God's answers back to us, and when we sin they induce us to repent and help to restore our souls to health.[32]

Origen also used the metaphor of the "friends of a bridegroom" to describe the angels. The friends of a bridegroom conduct him to the bride and then withdraw. So also the angels: they prepared the "Bride," the people of God, to meet the Bridegroom in the person of Jesus Christ, and rejoiced when Christ conducted her to the house of his Father at his Ascension.[33] In many ancient variations on this bridegroom metaphor, the angels retain a preparatory role: they prepare the way for the Bridegroom and then depart. Medieval writers would likewise insist on the centrality of Christ and on the angels' merely preparatory function. Proximity to the angels is never an end in itself but the means to the goal, which is union with Christ.[34]

Already in the patristic era there were anticipations of the notion of an angelic hierarchy that would come to govern much medieval angelology. The New Testament specified no rank structure among the various powers. By the beginning of the second century, however, Ignatius presumed that there must be such an ordering.[35] In the late fifth or early sixth century, an author falsely claiming (but long believed) to be the Dionysius of Acts 17:34 systematized earlier ideas, in *The Celestial Hierarchy,* a work that would profoundly influence later theologians.[36] Pseudo-Dionysius' scheme of nine orders of angels had itself been influenced by the Neoplatonic theory of emanations: a belief in intermediate intelligences or divinities that had emanated from the Godhead. In Neoplatonic thought, the theory of emanations served to distance the ineffable Godhead from all that perishes, by creating buffer gods between the supreme Deity and the material world. Likewise, in Pseudo-Dionysius' theory, only the uppermost tier of angels, the seraphim, interact with God, and only the bottom tier, the angels, interact with fleshly beings in the world. God never encounters the individual directly, according to this system of thought.[37]

MEDIEVAL OPINIONS

Though beliefs about guardian angels shifted throughout the medieval era, the shifts were gradual and so did not disrupt the overall continuity and stability of belief. Medieval views on guardian angels, like medieval angelology more generally, repeated many of the convictions first expressed by the church fathers.[38] Historian David Keck points out that the medieval church had inherited patristic traditions about guardian angels via the *Glossa Ordi-*

naria, a compilation of comments on the Bible by patristic authors, which included many remarks pertinent to a doctrine of angels. Keck reports that "Scripture, the *Glossa,* reason, the universal law, and basic piety all confirmed" the conviction of medieval theologians and clerics that humans are indeed guarded by particular angels, who protect their charges from demonic assault.[39]

Bernard of Clairvaux (1090–1153 CE) saw the desperate need of sinful humanity for divine forgiveness and protection, and took solace from the promise of Ps 90:10: "No evil shall befall you, no scourge come near your tent." In Bernard's view, God offers many guides and protectors, including angels, along the pathways of the Christian journey toward union in love with God.[40] Each of us has a guardian who sees all and who aids us in our trials. Sometimes, Bernard writes, men and women "are supported by the angels as if by two hands, so that, almost without consciously perceiving it, they are carried over those very things that terrify them the most. Afterward they are not a little in awe at the ease with which they overcame something that at first had seemed so difficult."[41]

The angels do more than protect us on our journey. They help us to take the first step on that journey by bringing us a sense of God's mercy, which fosters our own repentance and mercy toward ourselves. Bernard writes, "This divine mercy makes a person extricating himself from corruption compassionate toward the son of his mother [that is, toward himself], merciful to his soul, and thereby pleasing to God." There is ample reason, Bernard counseled, for us to love and honor our angels and cling to them. In doing so we love and honor God. "Have the angels as your familiars, my brothers, visit them with attentive consideration and devout prayer, for they are always present to guard and comfort you."[42]

Thomas Aquinas devoted substantial attention in his *Summa Theologiae* to the guardianship of the good angels. His style of argumentation throughout the *Summa* is to begin by posing yes-or-no questions, next to present (as devil's advocate) the negative position, and finally to counter the objections in the course of giving his own affirmative response.[43] So, for example, responding to the question as to whether a particular angel is deputed to guard each individual man, Aquinas begins by raising the objection (among others) that "each individual is not guarded by a particular angel. For angels are more powerful than men; but one man is adequate to guard a number of people, therefore all the more can one angel guard a number of men." To counter this objection, Aquinas cites the authority of Jerome (fourth century, in a comment on Matt 18:10) and remarks, "Particular angels are deputed to guard individual men, the reason being that the angelic guardianship is part of the carrying out of divine providence over men."[44] As Aquinas reasons out his position on this and related issues, he draws on Pseudo-Dionysius and concentrates heavily on matters to do with the hierarchy and rank of the angels assigned to guard individuals.

If Aquinas wrote dispassionately of guardian angels, his contemporary Umiltà of Faenza wrote of them adoringly and intimately. "Not only does she know the names of two guardian angels given especially to her by Christ, but one gets the feeling from reading her accounts of their presence in her life that she can, as well, touch, smell, and see them as if they were a part of her closest family."[45] Umiltà was born at Faenza, Italy in 1226, into a wealthy family, and named Rosanna de Negusanti. Of necessity she eventually married, but with her husband's agreement they each entered the monastic life after their children died. The name Umiltà (from *humilitas,* meaning "humility") was bestowed on her at that time. She lived first as a recluse and then as founding abbess of a nunnery of the Vallombrosan order (based on the Rule of Benedict). She composed and preached nine Latin sermons and poetic Lauds to the Virgin Mary. From her sermons one discerns that her guardian angels, named "Sapiel" and "Emmanuel," are only two of many divine figures (including the Virgin Mary, John the Evangelist, saints, other angels, and occasionally God) who surround her and speak to her. Umiltà knows and takes for granted the hierarchical ordering of all the angels, but she is most deeply interested in Sapiel and Emmanuel.

> I love all the angels of heaven, but two are the most cherished darlings of my joy who give me comfort day and night and offer me their gifts from the bountiful wealth of their riches. My Lord assigned them to me as guardians so that they might protect me from all harm. They have attended perfectly to this divine injunction as they have placed me, as it were, within the protection of their strong fortress. On my right and my left hand both angels hold me close, so that I cannot fall except through my own foolishness. While I hold myself firmly to them, my enemies are unable to harm me.[46]

Umiltà counsels her sisters to imitate her own attentiveness to divine speech and the angels' sweet song. Her paean is to her own two "darlings," but she presumes that all Christians have such guardians in this life. All the faithful should exhort their angels as she does hers, saying: "Rouse your guard to a fever pitch so that my enemies may not advance upon the door of my soul. Since you were given to me from the beginning, put your sword before me, guard me in every season from my enemies."[47]

Steven Chase suggests that in order to understand medieval beliefs about guardian angels, we have to set them in the larger context of what he calls "angelic spirituality," an aspect of medieval Christian mystical consciousness.[48] In their efforts to come close to God, medieval practitioners of angelic spirituality contemplated and imitated the angels, and also sought their guidance. Such mystics contemplated and imitated the angels because angels are, in the terms set by Augustine of Hippo (fourth to fifth centuries), true citizens of the Heavenly City. Hence angels function as models of life lived in communion with God.[49] Mystics sought the angels' guidance because (again following Augustine) angels participate as companions to the good citizens of the Earthly City. They are coworkers with Christ and the Holy Spirit in sanctifying humans' walk of faith.[50] Thus the angels, both by example and by direct assistance, lead the devoted "to the very heart and center of the transcendent." [51]

For medieval mystics, the angels are heavenly—from a world beyond or outside the individual soul and, indeed, from beyond the mortal realm. Inasmuch as they are beings from another sphere they signify God's transcendence or otherness. But, paradoxically, angels also signify God's immanence or nearness: as divine ambassadors they illuminate with divine light and draw the soul into a vision of God.[52] These poles of *transcendence* versus *immanence* correlate with *outer* versus *inner* dimensions of contemplation. Thus, when Gregory the Great (sixth century) counseled the faithful to study the ministries of various orders, or bands, of angels in the angelic hierarchy, ministries made manifest by their external effects in the world, he presumed that such study encompassed also a turn inward.

> But while I am speaking of these things, dear friends, lead yourself home into your innermost self, that is, into the core of your being. Examine the merits of your inner secrets and inmost understanding. Look inside yourself and see if what you are doing now is good; see if you are among the number of those bands of spirits whom we have briefly touched upon; see if you find your vocation among them.[53]

This outer versus inner dialectic is relevant for the study of guardian angels, who were viewed both as agents external to the human self and also as voices internal to the soul. As Gregory remarked, when the angels "come among us to implement their exterior ministry, they are nonetheless never absent interiorly through contemplation." [54] Similarly, today's accounts of guardian angels may emphasize either their external agency (as ones who rescue from physical danger) or their interior presence (as ones who are known through contemplation).

The medieval thinkers surveyed here were all learned religious professionals. What about less-educated medieval folk? Interest in angels at the popular level focused less on esoteric questions of angelic origin, nature, and rank, and more on the angels' practical benefit for the living of life. Umiltà's discourse may have been uncommonly articulate but, like Umiltà, average folk also inhabited a world where Mary, saints, and angels intervened in routine existence.[55] Caesarius of Heisterbach, a Cistercian monk in the German Rhineland in the early thirteenth century, offers us glimpses of popular belief. The stories in his *Dialogue on Miracles*[56] were allegedly narrated by a monk to a novice; the questions raised by the novice after each of the stories (a number of which involve angels) offer opportunity for further instruction by the monk. In Caesarius' world, angels, demons, and saints are always close at hand. Intervening in the lives of the faithful and unfaithful alike, they are able to influence behavior by appearing in visions and apparitions and by manipulating objects. Angels perform physical rescues (in one case physically supporting a young woman who is being hanged so that she will not be strangled by her own weight, then setting her down gently when the rope is finally cut). They are also described as strengthening the weak in times of moral temptation and offering them assurance of their future reward.

Members of religious orders were, in general, deeply interested in angels. Those entering the religious life took vows of poverty, chastity, and obedience, which they understood as warranted by the angels' own perfect poverty, chastity, and obedience.[57] According to David Keck, reflections on the angels were an integral part of the life of those belonging to the religious orders, and not only of the educated among them. Angels modeled approved behaviors for persons in religious orders, and also exercised surveillance and control over them. In a sermon on guardian angels, Bernard of Clairvaux wrote: "In every public place, in every hidden nook, respect thy angel. Would you dare to do in his presence what you would not if you saw me?" Indeed, the theme of angelic observation and perpetual surveillance had been present even in Benedict's rule (sixth century).[58] Although this deep interest in angels characterized all the medieval religious orders, the Franciscans revered and contemplated the angels with particular intensity. Keck writes, "Francis himself directed the friars' spiritual imaginations to the ranks of the heavenly hierarchy, and after his death, he was seen as an angel."[59] One event in particular linked Francis to the angels: in September 1224, Francis had been visited by a seraph (the highest-ranking of the angels, according to the Dionysian scheme), who marked him with the stigmata (the bloody wounds of Christ) and "imprinted on his heart a special burning love for God."[60]

Medieval people invoked their guardian angels in prayer. Even in biblical times, angels had been seen as ones who carry the prayers of the righteous to God.[61] Keck observes that the Winchester Cathedral (constructed in about 1230) features a chapel dedicated to guardian angels—an apt place, Keck suggests, to pray to one's protector. Such prayers date back at least to Carolingian times (eighth to eleventh centuries) and were formalized in the thirteenth century when a prayer to the guardian angels was added to the liturgy. In prayer, medieval Christians sometimes "sought to personalize their relationship to the supernatural world and to their guardians in particular." Like Umiltà, so also the author of a twelfth-century prayer to his guardian angel had addressed the guardian as *amicus,* "friend," and invited the angel "to speak to him frequently about God and the saints in heaven."[62] In the sixteenth century, Ignatius of Loyola, founder of the Jesuits, taught in his *Spiritual Exercises* that the faithful should contemplate the angels to gain insight into their own sin and recognize how the angels, with God, give true spiritual gladness and joy. Ignatius also offered instruction on how to tell whether one's good angel or one's bad angel is acting in the soul in a given instance.[63] An annual feast for the guardian angels was celebrated in many areas by the sixteenth century; in 1670 the feast, set for October 2, was extended by Pope Clement X to all areas of the Holy Roman Empire.[64]

Divine presence and power pervaded the late medieval world. The spiritual and material realms intersected everywhere. "The map of Europe bristled with holy places; life pulsated with the expectation of the miraculous."[65] The most miraculous event of all happened each time the Catholic Mass was celebrated, when the elements of bread and wine were changed into the very flesh and blood of Christ. The Eucharist was understood to be the decisive event in which God becomes present to humankind, thereby bridging the gulf between heaven and earth. Divine potency inhered in the consecrated host.[66] Images and relics of the saints likewise radiated numinous power, and could work all sorts of wonders. In such a world, angels bridged the material and spiritual spheres in an especially useful way. Like God they were transcendent beings, but closer. Their easy and ubiquitous involvement in the temporal realm—including their ability to alter natural laws and processes—attested to the radiation of God's power and presence downward from the heavenly sphere into the material world.[67]

But this sacramental view of reality, in which material things were suffused with the divine, routinely slipped over into the practice of magic and idolatry. Objects imbued with divine potency were, like gods, able to control nature and deliver humans from their mortal condition. Once divine power came to be seen as localized in material objects, that power was often turned into a commodity, manageable just as the things it imbued were manageable. Thus, Guillaume Farel, a leader of the Reformation in France and Switzerland, recounted how, as a child on a pilgrimage to the Shrine of the Holy Cross at Tallard, he witnessed a supposed fragment of the true cross of Jesus. The local priest claimed that it protected the whole countryside from devastating hailstorms sent by the devil. Carlos Eire elaborates:

> Farel and his family had no trouble believing that the elemental forces of the universe could be controlled by one small object, and the priests further reinforced this belief. Late medieval piety showed an almost irrepressible urge to localize the divine power, make it tangible, and bring it under control. The relic at Tallard fulfilled these expectations by making the divine commonplace.[68]

Angels, too, got caught up in the quest to control divine power. From late antiquity on, there were occasional condemnations of "excessive or suspect angelic practices," including the engraving of angels' names on amulets.[69]

THE PROTESTANT CRITIQUE

In the sixteenth century, the Protestant Reformers attacked both the Catholic doctrine of the Eucharist and the cult of the saints with its emphasis on images and relics. Especially in the Swiss Reformed (Calvinist) stream of tradition, the war cry became: *Finitum non est capax infiniti* (the finite cannot contain the infinite). In other words, neither the consecrated host, nor icons, nor statues, nor bones, nor the personal effects of the saints could contain or convey the power of God, who rules over the material world. To revere such objects ("idols" in the Protestant view) was to rob God of glory that God is due, and impugn God's majesty and freedom. This critique was influenced by the Reformers' reading of Scripture and by the metaphysical assumption (derived from Neoplatonism) that the material and the spiritual are strictly separated realms.[70]

As for angels, the Protestants did not dispute their existence. Luther, still a late medieval man, presumed the ubiquity of both angels and demons. His hymn "A Mighty Fortress" famously describes the world as "with devils filled," and the morning and evening prayers of his *Small Catechism* each includes the petition, "May your holy angel be with me, so that the evil enemy will not gain power over me."[71] Luther is also alleged to have hurled an inkwell at Satan, though the story was likely created by Luther hagiographers and tour guides to the Wartburg Castle, where the incident allegedly occurred and the stain on the wall was long visible.[72] John Calvin thought that the ancient Sadducees' rejection of belief in angels was ludicrous, given the biblical evidence for them. Unlike the saints (who were corporeal), the angels are pure spirits, and thus share wholly in the transcendence of God. Calvin called the angels ones "in whom the brightness of the divine glory" richly shines forth.[73]

Although they affirmed angels' existence, Luther, Calvin, and other Reformers assaulted the elaborate edifice of opinion about them that medieval thinkers had constructed. Luther rejected the Catholic notion that either saints or angels intercede for us in heaven.[74] He also challenged the authenticity of Pseudo-Dionysius' *Celestial Hierarchy*, a stance that contributed to the Sorbonne's condemnation of the Reformer on April 15, 1521.[75] For his part, Calvin called the *Celestial Hierarchy* subtle and skillful but, nonetheless, "nothing but talk." Calvin continued, "If you read that book, you would think a man fallen from heaven recounted, not what he had learned, but what he had seen with his own eyes. Yet Paul, who had been caught up beyond the third heaven [II Cor. 12:2], not only said nothing about it, but also testified that it is unlawful for any man to speak of the secret things that he has seen [II Cor 12:4]."[76] Questions addressed by Pseudo-Dionysius and the medieval thinkers who used his work—the day of the angels' creation, and their nature, order, and number—Calvin called matters of empty speculation and unworthy of Christians' attention.[77]

Calvin found little biblical warrant for the doctrine of guardian angels. He acknowledged evidence from Daniel for the notion of angels set over kingdoms and provinces (Dan 10:13, 20–21), and referred ambivalently to Matt 18:10: "Christ also, when he says that the children's angels always behold the Father's face [Matt. 18:10], hints that there are certain angels to whom their safety has been committed. But from this I do not know whether one ought to infer that each individual has the protection of his own angel."[78] Further, Calvin recognized that the passage in Acts about Peter's alleged twin angel (Acts 12:15) may have reflected "the common notion that each believer has been assigned his own guardian angel." Still, Calvin said, there was no reason to suppose that an angel to whom Peter (or any one else) had been entrusted for protection in a given moment would on that account be his *perpetual* guardian. Rather than affirming belief in guardian angels, Calvin preferred to "hold as a fact that the care of each one of us is not the task of one angel only, but all with one consent watch over our salvation." Otherwise why would Scripture teach that *all the angels together* rejoice over the turning of one sinner to repentance (Luke 15:7)?[79] Calvin observed that humans too easily drift toward belief "that angels are the ministers and dispensers of all good things to us." Such a view leads to our regarding angels too highly, even worshipping them. "Thus it happens that what belongs to God and Christ alone is transferred to them."[80]

In Calvin's opinion the appropriate disposition toward angels is one that does not engage in empty speculation about matters that Scripture does not give us to know—"those mysteries whose full revelation is delayed until the Last Day." We should not "probe too curiously or talk too confidently" of angels.[81] Yet, Calvin insisted that God chooses to use the angels as ministers to our need. For the angels raise our minds to hope, and confirm us in security.

> One thing, indeed, ought to be quite enough for us: that the Lord declares himself to be our protector. But when we see ourselves beset by so many perils, so many harmful things, so many kinds of enemies—such is our softness and frailty—we would sometimes be filled with trepidation or yield to despair if the Lord did not *make us realize the presence of his grace according to our capacity.* For this reason, he not only promises to take care of us, but tells us he has innumerable guardians whom he has bidden to look after our safety; that so long as we are hedged about by their defense and keeping, whatever perils may threaten, we have been placed beyond all chance of evil.[82]

So it happened that Elisha's servant, in despair, took strength and courage from the vision of a host of angels and thus "was able with undaunted courage to look down upon his enemies, at sight of whom he had almost expired."[83] God does not *need* angels to do his work, but in accommodation to our need sends them to shore up our confidence in God's protection, and for this we should rejoice.

Calvin's loss of conviction concerning guardian angels might not at first appear momentous. After all, he didn't deny angels altogether. But the net effect was to push *all* angels further out of the everyday world. They had now become something exceptional. Heaven is their "normal" sphere of operation. When angels do intervene, it is by giving us hope in God, rather than by swooping down and altering the course of actual events. One can see this changed worldview played out in the formal confessions of the Reformed tradition, which mention angels only briefly and only in connection with singular events before creation or at the end of time. The *Second Helvetic Confession,* written by Heinrich Bullinger (a contemporary of John Calvin) refers to the primordial fall of some angels.[84] The *Westminster Confession* and the *Larger Catechism* (both seventeenth century) discuss the fall of some angels and perseverance of others according to God's plan of election, the prohibition against worship of angels, and the certainty that angels (like humans) will one day be judged.[85] Nowhere in these documents is any mention made of the protective function of angels, or of the existence of guardian angels. Though angels were not banned from the cosmos, their realm of activity was sharply circumscribed and their intervention made something exceptional.

If Catholicism with its Mass and its cult of the saints had "fragmented" the divine, Calvin and those following in his steps "defragmented" it. No longer were little pockets of divine power to be found here and there—in this consecrated host or in that relic, at this hill or dale frequented by an angel or at that pilgrimage site. *Finitum non est capax infiniti,* the finite cannot contain the infinite. The Reformed leaders affirmed that there is but one God, source of all and sovereign over all. Moreover, they insisted, the divine is in no way subject to our control. Divine power cannot be managed, for God is transcendent—in the world but not of the world, present among us as Spirit but not resident in material things or the creation at large. Whereas Catholics had witnessed miracles everywhere and viewed them as proof positive of saintly or angelic intervention, Calvin argued "that the physical world is trustworthy and that divine revelation does not regularly or without reason contravene its laws."[86] The time of miracles is largely past and the Catholics' claims void. When a miracle does occur, Calvin said, it is something extraordinary: a sign or portent done to indicate God's providential ordering of events at the level of whole peoples and nations. Humans can still commune with divine Spirit, but they cannot and should not expect God, or angels, to alter the course of nature or the normal functioning of objects in the material world.[87]

Jonathan Edwards, the brilliant eighteenth-century evangelist and theologian, offers an interesting case study in how angels fared among Reformed thinkers in subsequent eras. Amy Plantinga Pauw observes, "While belief in angels and a personal devil was waning among some of his day, Jonathan Edwards retained a sturdy confidence in their existence."[88] Edwards could speak abstractly of angels as watching and perhaps intervening in the everyday world. He counseled children that the angels would rejoice when each of them came to love Christ: "They will be your angels; they will take care of you while you sleep, and God will give 'em charge to keep you in all your ways. And they will do it with delight, because they love you."[89] But often when Edwards wrote of angels, it was to reflect on their devotion to God (or lack thereof, in the case of the devil) and on their function in the spiritual realm. The angels were interested spectators of God's work of redemption. From such imaginative probings, Edwards drew analogies to illuminate "the faith struggles of earthly saints and their eschatological implications."[90] Thus, Edwards' construal of the good angels' humility and ministry underscored the love and humility in Christ's life, and in the life of faith; by contrast, Edwards' rendering of the devil's pride and hatred served as springboard to probe the character of human sin. As in the *Westminster Confession,* emphasis in Edwards' work is chiefly on what angels do (or have done) in a sphere wholly separate from the material world in which humans live and move and have their being.

But even if Edwards passed over the worldly activity of *angels,* he did not so downplay the worldly activity of *God.* By no means does Edwards view God as remote or unlikely to intervene in daily affairs. On the contrary, God was present and working powerfully among the people of New England! In the first Great Awakening, many worshippers—moved by the Spirit—fell into ecstatic raptures and emotional outbursts. Though skeptics (who were plentiful) sneered at such eruptions, Edwards argued that God could indeed move the heart and shape the emotions.[91] Edwards' position is significant because it indicates that in Reformed Protestantism a strong sense of God's *transcendence* could coincide with a strong sense of God's *immanence.* Later caricatures of Reformed piety (and of Edwards) notwithstanding, this eighteenth century heir to the Puritans saw God as intimately present in the world—acting not through relics, a consecrated host, patron saints, or even angels, but through the divine Spirit that speaks directly to the human heart.[92]

GUARDIAN ANGEL PIETY AMONG CATHOLICS IN THE UNITED STATES

Today, many Catholics who grew up in the United States in the mid-twentieth century recall the intimate place of their guardian angels in their childhood lives. Robert Orsi writes, "It is impossible to exaggerate the importance of the figure of the guardian angel to mid-twentieth-century Catholic children's imagination and spirituality."[93] In portraying the world to children, Catholic adults consistently depicted it as full of temptations and dangers, and assured children that their guardian angels were trustworthy companions, supervisors, and moral scrutinizers. For their part children knew that they could call upon their guardian angel for aid, and that their angel—like a hall monitor in a school corridor—watched over their actions and conveyed information about infractions of rules to the relevant authority.[94] Indeed, even children's thoughts were subject to angelic oversight. Children were taught that their angels "knew what they were thinking and feeling," and felt distress or joy at their charges' misbehavior or expressions of virtue. Angelic guardians were ever present, hovering on the edge of visibility: a child would even make room on her desk chair to accommodate her angel.[95] Some children named their angels; some did not. Many prayed to their protector nightly.

> Angel of God, my guardian dear,
> to whom God's love entrusts me here,
> ever this day be at my side,
> to lead and guard, to light and guide.

By nurturing children's sense of their guardian angels' intimate presence, Catholic adults ushered children into a world populated by many mystical beings. As the children grew to adulthood, they would increasingly call not just upon their angels but also on Mary, the saints, and Jesus. All of these beings helped to localize the divine presence—to bring the sense of God's presence and care into people's everyday lives.

But the Catholics whom I have interviewed (mostly third- or fourth-generation residents of the United States, of European descent) no longer live in this enchanted world. Intellectually these Catholics may still believe in angels and saints, but they no longer see themselves as living in such intimate proximity to the sacred. They report perceiving that "everything changed" sometime in the interval between World War II and the years just after Vatican II. The Catholic world shifted, both physically and psychologically: Catholics dispersed from their insulated parish neighborhoods into the suburbs and the mainstream culture, and many distinctive features of Catholic devotional life disappeared.

Why this shift in the Catholic world? And, prior to the shift, were guardian angels always a feature of Catholic piety in the United States? Questions are many, and answers are hard to come by. We can presume that various factors shaped the precise contours and affected the intensity of Catholics' concern with angels in any given time and place. Such factors would have included, for example, larger social and intellectual trends in society and in the Catholic church, the shifting intensity of pressure from the Protestant majority to conform to a mainstream view, and flux in the ethnic makeup and distribution of the Catholic population as wave after wave of Catholics from different nations immigrated to the United States. In the early decades of the nineteenth century, a Catholic revival swept across the world, profoundly affecting the lives of U.S. Catholics. The revival fostered the development of Catholic parishes, schools, colleges, universities, and religious orders. As historian Ann Taves comments: "This growing network of associations and institutions permitted and encouraged Catholics to remain within the confines of the group for all their primary relationships throughout the various stages of their lives." [96] Rhetoric from Catholic leaders (ranging from prominent bishops to the nuns teaching in local schools) often heightened Catholics' sense of separateness from the rest of society and their attention to their own distinctive beliefs and devotional practices, including devotion to Mary, saints, and angels. [97]

Accounts of miraculous healings or escapes from disaster are well attested in nineteenth-century Christianity in the United States, especially among Catholics. The graces and favors bestowed by angels or saints could be either spiritual (pertaining to salvation) or temporal (pertaining to fleshly well-being). The graces and favors were often reported in Catholic magazines of the era as responses to devotional acts or to the use of devotional objects. In one story, an old woman is healed when she makes a pilgrimage to the shrine of Our Lady of Loretto in Kentucky. In another, a Civil War commander is protected from injury by a scapular (a special devotional article draped over the shoulders) that shielded him from a bullet that just grazed his neck. [98]

Such stories of graces and favors served to reinforce the moral and spiritual identity and practices of the narrators and audience against those of outsiders. The most threatening outsiders of that day were the Protestants, known by Catholics for their skeptical insistence that the age of miracles had passed. [99] Hence, nineteenth-century Catholic stories frequently underscore the miraculous element, sometimes by describing how a skeptical (usually Catholic) observer was won over, and sometimes by emphasizing how laws of nature were violated. In the story of the woman's healing at the shrine of Loretto, a skeptical observer immediately underwent a change of heart and began to fear the judgment of God. [100] In the story of the scapular, the devotional garment was said to have "turned the bullet out of a straight line, to which it returned again, as if to make the power of God more manifest." [101] Thus the accounts made the case that in this impersonal world our God still attends and intervenes in a very personal way—and often in a very material way. So also today, stories of angelic rescue often stress the miraculous, either by showing how a helper appeared out of nowhere at just the right moment and against all odds, then disappeared without a trace; or by describing how laws of nature were violated.

In nineteenth-century Catholic devotional practice, the faithful often called upon Jesus, Mary, the saints, and their guardian angels in nearly the same breath. For example, John Neumann, Bishop of Philadelphia in the mid-nineteenth century, often addressed the members of the Trinity "as intimate companions of his spiritual journey," and "filled his journal with invocations to Mary, 'Mother of Grace,' his guardian angel, and the saints." [102] In one writing, Neumann addresses Mary, Queen of Angels and Heaven,

St. Francis Xavier, and (last but not least) his guardian angel: "My Guardian Angel, help me. Make me pay attention to what I say, do and think. My own inclination, my bad habits entice me to sin. O Lord, give me the grace I need to overcome the dangers that surround me." The angels and other spiritual beings assisted Neumann in his struggle to live a Christ-centered life in spite of what he perceived as a very strong propensity to sin.[103] To give a second example, when reflecting on all that children learn of Catholic piety and practice at their mother's knee, William Henry (Bishop of Natchez, writing in 1865) mentions her teaching them "to invoke the sweet names of Jesus and Mary, to make the sign of the cross, to love and fear their Guardian Angels, to cherish their medal, to recite the first lessons of the Catechism, to love and imitate the Infant Jesus at Bethlehem and Nazareth."[104] An 1866 discussion of the history of sodalities (voluntary Catholic associations) mentions many such unions devoted to "the Holy Angels."[105] And the Baltimore Catechism, first published in 1891 and used by countless Catholic school children for seven decades, taught that guardian angels help us by praying for us, protecting us from harm, and inspiring us to do good.[106]

A massive cultural shift in U.S. Catholicism began around the time of World War II. Historian John McGreevy identifies various mid-twentieth-century social changes that pulled Catholics out of the insulated Catholic neighborhoods and infrastructure, where angels and other heavenly intercessors could be taken for granted. He writes, "Following the war, while a world of parallel [Catholic] societies remained, and even flourished, much of what made the Catholic experience of the early twentieth century distinctive faded into the larger American kaleidoscope." Developments such as the movement of more Catholics into the middle class, migration of city dwellers to suburbs, and the blurring of different national traditions "were already creating a different American Catholicism before the twin shocks of the Second Vatican Council and the cultural upheavals of the 1960s." McGreevy suggests that the decline of belief in guardian angels may not be a phenomenon limited to the United States: rather, it may reflect a collapse of the world created and sustained by the international Catholic revival begun more than a century before.[107]

Whatever the causes, in the latter half of the twentieth century many U.S. Catholics moved away from a focus on the invisible presence of guardian angels, Mary, and the saints. Further, after Vatican II (although the trend had begun earlier), emphasis in the training of the young and of new converts shifted to Scripture. The shift "moved the fulcrum of Catholic belief away from guardian angels, who although present in the biblical narrative, take a secondary role."[108] After the Vatican Council, many Catholics zealously

committed themselves to ridding the Church of all the old devotional practices, which had for so long served to carry them into the invisible presence
of sacred beings. Orsi writes, "The past to be grown up and moved away
from came to be represented by many things . . . but above all it came to be
represented by the saints and the Blessed Mother, and denying and forget-
ting the saints, putting them out of memory and out of history, became the
way of closing off the past from the present."[109] In the new Catholic culture that emerged in the 1970s and 1980s, insofar as the sacred figures per-
sisted they were reinterpreted. For example, they were reimagined as moral
exemplars—as ones whose lives illustrated particular virtues or sound spiritual disciplines. No longer, however, did they arouse in humans the previous
emotional excesses or claims to the miraculous.[110]

But, as Orsi points out, the past is not so easily abolished. Some U.S.
Catholics have continued their old devotion to saints, shrines, and angels.[111]
Others look wistfully back to the days before Vatican II as a kind of golden
era and seek to recapture its sense of the sacred. Some dedicate themselves
to old-style veneration of the saints and angels. Surely the nostalgia felt by
many Catholics for a remembered sense of sacred presence contributed to
the wave of popular interest in angels that washed over the United States in
the 1990s.

Finally, it must be noted that many Hispanic, Filipino, and Vietnamese
immigrants have been added to the Catholic population in the United States
since the 1960s. This development complicates any effort to summarize the
present state of Catholic belief in guardian angels in this country, because
such immigrants have brought with them a different cosmology than that
of Catholics already assimilated into the wider U.S. culture.[112] The picture I
have sketched here would be much more complex if I were able to give adequate account of current views among various ethnic groups, in the United
States and elsewhere. The size and diversity of the Catholic communion
worldwide renders any generalization on the status of a given doctrine at the
grassroots level subject to endless exceptions and qualifications.

GUARDIAN ANGELS TODAY

Many were shocked when the flood of angelic encounter stories hit television, bookstores, and the Internet in the early 1990s. And it was not only the
avowed secularists who marveled. Since so many mainline Christians share
the mind-set of scientific modernism—assuming with Bultmann that "their
own inner life and their practical life is nowhere interrupted by the intervention of supernatural powers"—they, too, were taken by surprise. I spoke

to a Lutheran pastor intimidated by the guardian angel lapel pin that his secretary wore every day. He worried that she might ask him if *he* believed in guardian angels. He told me he supposed he did believe in angels in a general sense—and yet he scoffed at the accounts he had heard of angels saving stranded travelers, shielding vulnerable missionaries, and the like.

Despite the skepticism of many, stories of encounters with angels have proliferated. The angels who manifest themselves in these accounts fall mostly into two categories: search-and-rescue angels, and therapist angels. In the first category are the accounts of angelic protection or assistance in a moment of dire need, usually physical need. Sometimes such protection or assistance comes by way of warning: an internal voice gives notice of an impending car theft and possible assault, and directions on how to avoid it. Sometimes the help comes by direct physical intervention: an invisible arm stops a mother from accidentally slamming the basement door on her toddler, who would have been pushed off balance and down the stairs. Sometimes a person appears, out of nowhere, at just the needed time: a tow truck rescues motorists stranded on a country road on a bitterly cold night and no one in the car saw the truck coming; a man dressed in white carries a boy, bitten by a rattlesnake, one hundred and fifty yards to the boy's home, then disappears. Sometimes a person appears who is visible to would-be assailants but not to the one protected: gang members do not follow through on threats to harm a female evangelist because they see her seven-foot boyfriend with her, though no such man is present. Sometimes these and other such protections and rescues are ascribed to guardian angels specifically, and sometimes they are ascribed to more generic angels. Persons raised as Catholics are more likely to name their guardian angel as the rescuer.[113] Either way, the genre as a whole traces back to notions of guardian angels as divine agents assigned to protect us from harm. Skeptics notwithstanding, the audience for such stories is broad and crosses denominational lines.

Stories of encounters with therapist angels, the second category of angels, describe spirit beings that intervene in a person's inner life to foster happiness, alleviate anxiety, or answer other psychological needs. Gnostic-type thinking—often mingled with notions from Eastern or New Age spirituality—has influenced many such accounts. Popular author and workshop leader Doreen Virtue remarks on the presence of the divine spark in each of us.

> The voice of your Creator has never left you, and, in fact, can never leave you. The spark of Divine light created when God first thought of you remains tucked away within you. This light is one with God,

which means that *you* are one with God. Through the Divine light, which is your true essence, you are privy to every thought that comes from God's mind. In truth, then, your mind is eternally connected to the Divine wisdom of God's mind.[114]

The help that God sends our way comes through various means, Virtue teaches, including guardian angels. She explains that, like all angels, guardian angels are "thoughts of love sent from God," but also "very real messengers." Every person has two or more guardian angels.[115] Through these and other means God guides us, protects us, and heals our physical, emotional, and relational illnesses. "Whenever we ask heaven to help, we receive assistance. Sometimes the help is direct, as when an angel intervenes in a lifesaving incident. More often, though, God answers our prayers by giving practical advice."[116] Another author, Denny Sargent, calls guardian angels "the emanation that God has given to you." Sargent describes how forming a relationship with them can help us to overcome the dislike of self that, he claims, is at the root of so many people's unhappiness. "Strengthen your bond with your angel and you will become more like it every day. You will also become more and more aware of what a miracle you are and all you are capable of being. Then you can begin to love that new self more and more."[117] The audience for this second category of angelic encounter story includes many who are disaffected with traditional religion and with images of God as tyrant, as well as some self-professed Christians.[118]

Both the search-and-rescue angels and the therapist angels show continuity with guardian angels as known from ancient and medieval traditions. Indeed, it is remarkable how much of what people are saying about angels today has been said for centuries or millennia! Yet, there are also important discontinuities.

Both current types of guardian angel accounts raise pressing theological questions. Questions regarding stories of angelic rescue include whether and how God exercises divine providence, and how we should understand God's involvement in the material realm. Questions regarding stories of angelic therapy include how we can identify our true needs, and what it is that God actually offers us. Does God affirm us unconditionally, as many report angels as saying? Or does God shine a light upon our innermost selves with all their weaknesses and failings? For both sorts of encounter story, the most pressing question of all is this: Is there any escape from suffering while in this earthly life?

ANGELIC RESCUE

The Old and New Testaments include many stories of angelic rescue from danger or death. Angels protected Elijah in a dispute with the king of Samaria, protected Elisha and his servant from the Arameans, shut the lions' mouths for Daniel, guided Joseph to flee with Mary and Jesus to Egypt, and rescued Peter from prison. Moreover, angels comforted and strengthened Jesus during his testing in the wilderness and in his moment of extreme trial in the Garden of Gethsemane.[119] Although none of these and other such biblical accounts identifies the angel in question as a guardian angel, the biblical stories have long influenced popular notions of the sorts of things that guardian angels might do for those under their charge.

In modern stories, the angelic identity of the helper is not always stated explicitly but is sometimes left ambiguous. For example, in one story a young woman visiting the Grand Canyon inadvertently slips on loose gravel and skids under the guardrail. She is bumping and sliding down the canyon wall when a tall old man in impeccable, old-fashioned, Sunday-best clothes reaches out and grabs her hand. He is accompanied by a comparably dressed old woman. They direct the young woman and her husband, who is waiting in a car above and is unaware of the near-catastrophe, to a nearby hospital. The young man and woman ponder the anomalies of this sequence of events, but never explicitly name the rescuers as angels.[120]

In other accounts the supernatural aspect (and hence the angelic identity of the helper) is stressed.[121] For example, an old story reported on a Catholic Web site dedicated to angels tells of a Marine wounded on a Korean battlefield in 1950. The soldier, who was in the habit of praying to St. Michael every day, was accidentally separated from the others in his patrol. But then a big, strong soldier he didn't know appeared beside him and introduced himself as Michael. When seven enemy soldiers began firing on them at close range a few minutes later, Michael never even hit the ground to protect himself, yet he was not struck. The soldier narrating the story, however, was hit in the shoulder, whereupon Michael—his face suddenly shining "with a terrible splendor"—softly laid the wounded soldier on the snow.[122]

The same Web site offers another account in which the angelic visitor is explicitly named as a guardian angel—the question is, whose? A woman named Edith, in her farmhouse alone, was protected from a hostile caller. When the stranger at the door asked her if she were by herself, she bluffed, calling out the name of her husband, who was not home. To her amazement she heard what sounded like her husband's voice answering her from upstairs, and the voice scared off the intruder. In concluding, the narrator speculates on whose voice had been heard. Was it that of Edith's guardian angel? Could it have been the voice of her husband's angel? Or was it, perhaps, the voice of the intruder's guardian angel, "keeping him out of trouble?" [123] This story is one of the few modern accounts I have seen alluding to the *moral* as well as *physical* protection potentially offered by guardian angels. (This story dates from the early twentieth century.) As seen above, in earlier centuries guardian angels were frequently or even chiefly seen as moral protectors.

The foregoing handful of stories is but a tiny sample from a boundless supply in books and magazines and on the Internet. When authors Sophy Burnam and Joan Wester Anderson began asking people to tell them their angel stories in the early 1990s, their mail boxes were inundated. A number of people have shared their own stories with me as I have worked on this book. Always the stories are told in a way intended to inspire hope, faithfulness, and prayer. As the aforementioned Catholic Web site explains, the point is not so much to offer "an apodictic demonstration that an Angel was absolutely involved in this or that case," as to illustrate "how the Angels take interest in our personal lives and not infrequently do intervene tangibly on behalf of their wards." [124]

The trouble comes when we press angelic rescue stories and try to make them answer our philosophical questions about divine providence as it relates to the problem of unjust suffering. Whenever we speak of angelic rescue, we are deliberately affirming God's omniscient and sovereign directing of human destiny. We are also hinting, perhaps unintentionally, at those times when God seems not to direct human destiny in such a favorable way. If I say that God sent an angel to rescue me when in dire straits, then I am implying that God did *not* send an angel to rescue someone else when in equally dire straits. Indeed, the nonrescues are what make the rescues so marvelous, so worthy of telling. If no one ever suffered harm undeservedly, what would be the point or pleasure in telling of those who were saved from calamity? We expect our audience to let their imaginations run on ahead to the disaster that might have happened—but did not.

Some angelic rescue stories do not leave the what-ifs to the imagination but instead describe how others were not saved. For example, Joan Wester Anderson relates a woman's story about passing a menacing stranger in an alleyway on a dark night. Later she learns that, twenty minutes after she had passed the alleyway, another woman was raped by that very man. The rapist, when asked why he let the first woman go by, said he saw a large male companion with her, although she had been walking alone at the time. [125] To be fair, the woman is not gloating but trying to demonstrate that the danger had been real and not imagined: "See, that stranger really *was* dead set on harming me." But when storytellers make explicit what is usually kept implicit, that is, by describing the nonrescue of another, their stories backfire and expose the weakness inherent in all angelic rescue stories. When I have told this protection/rape story to others, someone in the audience inevitably asks, "Where was the guardian angel of the woman who was *not* protected? Taking a coffee break?" The added scene has made it hard to use the story as it was intended, as a vehicle for praising God's providence and care. Instead, audiences hear the story as *indicting* God for distributing care unequally, or at the very least, they hear it as evidence against the doctrine of guardian angels. Often a defender of angels will step in to save the story: "The person who wasn't rescued probably ignored her angel's advice." But carrying this counterargument to its logical conclusion reveals its flaw. Can we really believe that, if only all people everywhere listened to their guardian angels, all accidents or crimes would cease?

Thomas Aquinas recognized that the question comes down to a matter of God's providence. When humans suffer ills, he explained, such suffering is not evidence for withdrawal of the sufferer from divine providence, for all are subject to God's "general providence over all existent things." Still, "God's providence is said to forsake men" insofar as God "allows them to suffer some ills, *either from being punished or from moral faults*" (emphasis added). Thus, according to Aquinas, even the divine "forsaking" is in its way an exercise in divine providence. God refrains from rescuing, so as to punish. Similarly, Aquinas argued, guardian angels "never *completely* forsake men, but sometimes they do partially forsake them, for example, by not saving them from suffering some particular tribulation or even from falling into sin, *in accordance with the disposition of the divine decrees*" (emphasis added). The last clause is critical: Aquinas is saying that, when guardian angels seem to fall down on the job, they are not *really* failing but are acting in accordance with God's providential plan. Thus "it is clear that angelic guardianship is a kind of carrying out of God's providence over men" (*Summa Theologiae* 1a. 113, 6).

I agree with Aquinas' contention that God's providence never fails. Even when bad things happen, God sees and knows. God's creative power upholds the universe; nothing happens that is outside God's permissive will. But I disagree with Aquinas' implication that human ills are always to be explained as divine *punishment*. By saying that God consistently chooses to save or not save in accordance with the merits of the individual involved (a view supported also by Caesarius), Aquinas construes the world as a perfectly ordered, moral system. Any failures are not the angels' but ours: we always get what we deserve. New Testament authors see suffering, rather, as evidence for the grip of fallen powers on the cosmos during this broken age, before God's full and final redemption. In this early Christian perspective, a human's experience of affliction does not automatically prove that God is displeased.[126] Neither, when someone is *not* rescued, can we conclude that he or she ignored angelic guidance. Sometimes, for reasons we cannot know, the angel does not save.

I cannot begin to solve the paradox of divine sovereignty and providence in the face of human suffering. I can only affirm with the psalmist that God is always present: "If I take the wings of the morning and settle at the farthest limits of the sea, even there your hand shall lead me" (Ps 139:9–10a). And I affirm that God sees all: "You know when I sit down and when I rise up; you discern my thoughts from far away" (Ps 139:2); "even the hairs of your head are all counted" (Matt 10:30). Moreover I am convinced that God is *able* to do all for those who ask of him in faith, as Jesus promised: "Truly I tell you, if you say to this mountain, 'Be taken up and thrown into the sea,' and if you do not doubt in your heart, but believe that what you say will come to pass, it will be done for you" (Mark 11:23). Yet, despite these givens, the fallen powers and principalities often have their way. The God who hears the voice of the suffering and who loves us unfailingly does not always rescue. Jesus—himself unrescued at Golgotha—is exhibit A.[127]

Lacking, then, the ability to comprehend divine providence, the best I can do is to say once again how I understand God's redemption in the midst of this pain-filled world. *The redemption God offers is not an escape from present suffering, but a promise of victory over the suffering that is the unmistakable hallmark of life in the present, fallen order.* In Chapter 4, I suggested four ways that the Spirit of Christ enables us to resist the powers of sin and death: by healing our blindness, by undergirding us in terrible affliction, by forgiving us when we fail, and by empowering us to give and receive love and forgiveness where hatred or hostility has reigned. To be sure, there is always the possibility of actual *rescue* from trial. After all, Jesus taught his disciples to pray the petition, "deliver us from evil." When danger threatens, it is always right to pray for God's angel or other, nonangelic agent to rescue; when rescue comes, it is always right to offer thanks and praise. But if and when the hoped-for deliverance does not come, it does not mean that God is inflicting punishment on us, was not present, or does not care; or that our angel fell down on the job; or that we failed to tune in to some angelic prompt.

Jesus prayed for deliverance from death: "Father, if you are willing, remove this cup from me" (Luke 22:42). For him, deliverance was not to be. But Luke tells something that the other evangelists do not: when Jesus was praying just before his arrest, "an angel from heaven appeared to him and gave him strength" (Luke 22:44). In other words, according to Luke Jesus didn't succeed on his own. The angel of God was there right beside him, strengthening him, as an answer to his earnest prayer and a source of help for him to persevere. The angel who accompanied Jesus as he prayed was nothing less than the very presence of God. In prayer Jesus called to God and God answered him through the angel, who was the visible face of God's invisible being. That was how and why Jesus could persevere. And when we call upon God in the midst of our trials, God answers us, too, with God's very own presence.

How one perceives and understands this divine presence—as God's Holy Spirit, or as an angel (and if the latter, in what *form* or *guise* one perceives it)—has much to do with one's own theological presuppositions and cultural background. As I argued in the Introduction, expectations about angels tend to predetermine experience. But does it matter? In other words, are people who sense an angelic presence in time of need somehow short-changing themselves—or shortchanging the Spirit, by ascribing to an angel what is really of God? Generally, I believe, the answer is that they are not shortchanging themselves or God's Spirit. As we have seen, there is plenty of warrant in the Bible and in Christian tradition for seeing God's angels as true manifestations of the presence of God. The angel is a form or extension of God's very self.

But error can sneak into the picture. It would be an error if one were to suppose that the angel is merely an intermediary acting for a God who is unable or unwilling to get involved in the material realm. For God is both creator of the material realm and intimately involved in it; God "gives to all mortals life and breath and all things" (Acts 17:25). God is indeed transcendent, but this assertion does not mean that God is distant or removed, but rather that God is not bound by the rules of time and space. Angels are not go-betweens who bridge a gap between us and God, but markers or symbols of God's own presence.[128] A second potential error is related to the first. It would be an error if one were to infer from the occurrence of angelic visitation that God is absent at other times. The Christian affirmation is that God is with us always—not only when we experience miraculous rescue, or an unusual sense of God's intimate presence, but also when, because of our nature as beings of mortal flesh, we fall into suffering and pain. God does not sit in a far-distant heaven, deigning to intrude only occasionally, and our suffering does not mean that God has departed. Even when God's face is hidden from us, God is still present. God will never leave us or forsake us.[129]

GUARDIAN ANGELS AS PSYCHOLOGICAL HELPERS

I have already described the phenomenon of the angel as therapist in Chapters 1 and 2. In many recent books and across the workshop circuit, angels are described as benign presences who reassure us of our own goodness—even divinity—and help us to actualize our best selves. Sometimes the angelic presence is specifically conceived as that of a *guardian* angel. In *Your Guardian Angel and You,* author Denny Sargent[130] teaches that each person has a guardian angel, who is both an emanation of the divine (the "inner spark of God that is within you") and the individual's own Higher Self. According to Sargent, the guardian angel is not actually God, whose presence is so large that our small and inadequate human minds can scarcely conceive of it; rather, the angel is a link to God. Sargent writes, "But God has given you a personal connection to the divine, a being who will always answer your prayers and questions. This is your Guardian Angel."[131] The guardian angel offers various kinds of emotional support, nurture, and solace. Above all, the role of one's guardian angel is to help one find the path that he or she was born to take in this life, a path that Sargent calls "True Will." He writes,

> Remember the classic picture of a Guardian Angel hovering over a child, protecting it and keeping it on the safe path through the dangerous woods? This path is the way you are supposed to go through life; it is your True Will. As it unfolds, you will accomplish those things you were meant to do, help those you were meant to help, and evolve mentally, physically, and spiritually in ways that you are meant to evolve.[132]

Sargent describes a number of exotic rituals by which one may communicate with one's guardian angel and, ultimately, unite with it. There is a paradoxical quality to such union as Sargent describes it, since in his view the guardian angel is not only "a glowing divine energy light, a ray of God connecting the divine to Earth," but also part and parcel of one's very self. Thus the journey to union with the divine is a journey inward, to self-knowledge: "By looking at yourself, you will begin to see your angel, but only if you see yourself as you really are!"[133]

Sargent's work will be readily dismissed by Christian readers as New Age, or just flaky. (Presumably Sargent is indifferent to such reaction, since he surely approved the description of himself on the back of the book as a "practicing eclectic ritualist" who has written for "pagan and magickal magazines" and who, with his wife, "holds workshops and festivals out of the Forest Yurt set in the woods behind their house in Seattle, Washington."

Sargent is not trying to appeal to a traditional Christian crowd.) And yet, his presentation is continuous with Christian tradition in many ways. To give a few examples:

- Sargent's conviction that angels offer us not only protection from physical harm but also psychological benefit is quite ancient, as we have seen. Already in the fourth century Athanasius proclaimed, "The vision of the angels works softly and peaceably, awakening joy and exultation."[134]
- In Sargent's telling, as in more ancient ones, the guardian angel's function is *not* one of unconditional affirmation: Sargent uses the venerable doctrine of paired good-and-evil angels—shoulder people—as a way of personifying "the human choice of flesh and self-interest over spirit and love."[135]
- Sargent's interest in personalizing the relationship with one's guardian angel is attested from medieval times: recall Umiltà of Faenza's intimate relationship with her two guardians.
- Sargent's insistence that the journey outward to God is also a journey inward to the depths of the self is prefigured as early as the sixth century, when Gregory the Great counseled the faithful, saying, "Lead yourself home into your innermost self, that is, into the core of your being. Examine the merits of your inner secrets and inmost understanding."[136] Doing so, Gregory taught, was a way to discover one's angelic vocation—not unlike Sargent's counsel to discover one's "True Will."

There are also profound differences between current views of the guardian angel as companion/psychological aide and ancient and medieval Christian beliefs. I see the following losses in the present-day accounts:

- A loss of a sense of the transcendence or *otherness* of God. In traditional Christian theology, creatures are not the Creator. Even if indwelt by divine power or Spirit, as humans we remain in an irreducible way distinct from God. For their part, angels illumine the soul with divine light and draw the soul into a vision of God, but paradoxically, angels also reflect or veil the divine ray, thereby concealing the face of God. By contrast, some current angel accounts stress, not God's otherness, but our divinity: we aren't really separate from God at all, because our guardian angels or Higher Selves are emanations from (and so, still part of) God.
- A loss of any notion of a "fall": of a conviction, in other words, that the world (and each human in it) has always tended toward rebellion against the creator and a usurping of God's role. Up until the modern

period, Christians held that, because the world and they themselves were fallen, they must engage in unrelenting spiritual warfare against forces (both external and internal to the human self) that were working to lead them into idolatry. In the midst of such struggle, the guardian angel's role was to watch over one continually and keep one from giving in to temptation. Because authors of the new spirituality insist that humans are part and parcel of the divine, their works have lost any sense of the world's rebellion and of the consequent difficulties for our own perseverance in God's way. The loss finds mythological expression as a denial or downplaying of fallen angels, or even as an insistence that all evil is merely illusion.

- A loss of Christ at the center. In the early development of angel piety, this centrality of Christ was often expressed through the bridegroom metaphor: angels are *friends* of Christ as bridegroom, and their function is to lead the faithful soul to him, then depart. The believer experiences union, not with the angel, but with Christ.[137] In some recent works, by contrast, there is no sense that the angels prepare one for guardianship by Christ. Some authors, such as Sargent, are explicitly post-Christian; other authors, who seek to hold onto Christian readers, insist that their teachings are at least compatible with Christian life. Either way, Christ has been moved from center stage to the wings, or out of the theater entirely.

The new worldview represents a pendulum swing away from old stereotypes of God. Christians, especially Protestants, have sometimes misconstrued God's radical transcendence as distance and dispassion, thus fostering an image of God as tyrannical, judgmental, and eager to punish. In Chapter 1, I described the way that many New Age authors rail against such a picture of God and react by veering to the other extreme. They contend that God is radically immanent and scarcely transcendent, and indeed, that all of creation, including humanity, is divine. In such a view, God and humans have been maligned; God is our benevolent cocreator and we are by nature both good and wise. Any failures that we exhibit are due to the corrupting influences of our world and may not be failures at all.

The extent to which our Judeo-Christian heritage is held to blame for our wrong view of divine and human natures is laid out very clearly in a book by Tara Brach, *Radical Acceptance*.[138] This is not an angel book, but an intelligent and articulate statement of much of today's popular psychological wisdom, and incidentally, of key presuppositions that underlie some recent angel books. Brach is a clinical psychologist as well as a Buddhist lay priest and popular teacher of mindfulness (*vipassana*) meditation. From her work as therapist she concludes that our society is overrun with hyperactive consciences.

> Over the past twenty years, as a psychologist and Buddhist teacher, I've worked with thousands of clients and students who have revealed how painfully burdened they feel by a sense of not being good enough. Whether our conversation takes place in the middle of a ten-day meditation retreat or during a weekly therapy session, the suffering—the fear of being flawed and unworthy—is basically the same.
>
> As a friend of mine put it, "Feeling that something is wrong with me is the invisible and toxic gas I am always breathing." When we experience our lives through this lens of personal insufficiency, we are imprisoned in what I call the trance of unworthiness. Trapped in this trance, we are unable to perceive the truth of who we really are.[139]

Brach sees Western culture as a "breeding ground for the kind of shame and self-hatred" that traps people in this "trance of unworthiness." The culture's poisonous guiding myth, Brach contends, is the story of Adam and Eve's exile from the Garden of Eden. The myth "shapes and reflects the deep psyche of the West," teaching us that because of original sin we are intrinsically flawed and undeserving. Brach strives to undo the myth by teaching its opposite, the story of our inherent worth. She quotes the Dalai Lama, who was astonished when informed that many Westerners experience self-hatred. "How could they feel that way about themselves, he wondered, when 'everybody has Buddha nature.'" Buddhism challenges the Western worldview by teaching us to recognize "our essential goodness, our natural wisdom and compassion."[140]

In her book, Brach teaches how to retrain our own inner voice so that it offers comfort and encouragement rather than constant judgment. She does not turn to angels, but in one meditation she encourages readers to imagine the voice of comfort as that of "a spiritual figure or deity you associate with compassion." We should imagine this being as present, and as embracing one with unconditional love.[141] The imagined spiritual figure is not real, but a kind of psychological device: in Buddhist thought no single, separate entity can actually encompass the universal consciousness and compassion that Brach calls "the Beloved." Denny Sargent makes a similar acknowledgment (after an entire book about guardian angels as "real"). In an appendix entitled "Buddha and the Holy Guardian Angel," Sargent explains that Buddhists, with few exceptions, focus their prayers and visualizations on "an exteriorized image of the Total Self or Being who is transcendent, the Buddha."

The fastest way to union with the infinite is to "focus on an external image of the divine and then merge with it." Similarly, in Western occult mysticism, the idealized guardian angel is "a handy or useful fiction, a 'vehicle' if you will, that carries us over the rough seas of spiritual evolution (Dharma) and facilitates our complete awareness of All as All, that is, as Void."[142] In other words, the "Holy Guardian Angel" that Sargent has been describing is not external to us at all, but a psychological projection of our own (and the world's) divinity.

Brach, Sargent, and others stress the disparity between Western notions of the self as flawed and undeserving, and the view (promulgated in adaptations of Buddhism, and in New Age thought more generally) of the self as essentially good and compassionate. But the worldviews are not entirely dissimilar: according to both, we are presently living an inauthentic existence. The difference of opinion does not center on our present neediness, since both sides agree that we are much less than we ought to be. It centers, rather, on whether this condition is due to our flawed ("fallen") human nature, or to destructive socialization within a toxic culture that breeds separation and shame.[143]

Christianity teaches that humans are caught in contradiction: they desire to praise God, but because they are prone to sin, they also want to have their own way in the world. The doctrine of Adam's fall expresses in narrative form the belief that this condition has prevailed from the outset of human life in the world, and that it applies to everyone (with the single exception of Jesus Christ) as well as to social and corporate structures. In this perspective, there is no way to pull ourselves up by our own bootstraps. We are saved from the prison of our many wants only by God's grace, which is manifested to Christians in and through the person of Jesus Christ.[144]

By contrast, the new spirituality teaches that we can, in effect, save ourselves. Humans are born innocent and good, but their pure consciousness is corrupted by life in the world. The good news is that what has been damaged can be repaired through our own effort, by using certain rituals or meditative techniques. We can awaken from our trance (perhaps aided by angels, who are psychological projections of our Higher Self). We can become aware of our essential goodness and inborn unity with the divine.

So, the debate crystallizes around this question: What is our human nature? A second question, related to the first is: What do we really need? For if we are by nature good, then we need a method to help us recover our true, good selves and to transform our misguided inner critic into a voice of affirmation and solace. But if we are by nature prone to sin—and prone to shield ourselves at all costs from ever having to acknowledge our own sin—then we need a light to shine on us, that we might see ourselves as we really are and repent. We need to know that we are forgiven, and we need a source of strength to help us in the future to overcome the forces that would pull us astray.[145]

How one chooses between these two starting points will not be based on scientific evidence but on the texture of life as lived and observed by a given individual. Defenders of each position see their opinion verified daily in the news and in their own and others' lives. Nor is it the case that accepting the truth of one position necessitates denying all wisdom or insight of its opposite. We can assume that as humans we are prone to sin and prone to hide our sin (the traditional Christian stance) and still see insights and benefits derived from the other point of view. Many Westerners *do* suffer from a hyperactive and misguided conscience, and *can* benefit from methods that retrain their inner critic to be more reasonable, compassionate, and forgiving. But we choose the Christian point of view when the Holy Spirit, like Dr. Phil, moves us to see how consistently we have been deceiving ourselves, how diligently we have worked to defend and justify what we have done or left undone. We choose the Christian point of view when recognition dawns that our lives are not our own to secure (whether through meditation, self-affirmation, or other means) but are given to us, moment by moment, by God. We choose the Christian point of view when we perceive how badly we need someone to show us where we have erred and give us strength to follow another way.

JESUS: THE SHEPHERD AND GUARDIAN OF OUR SOULS

During Jesus' earthly life as depicted in the Gospels, angels aided him in time of need and strengthened him in time of trial. Angels ministered to him during his temptation in the wilderness, and again in the dark hour just before his arrest. But angels did not intervene or come to rescue him from the consequences of his mortal existence in a world run by fallen principalities and powers. Despite the angels, Jesus experienced hunger, grief, and death. According to one evangelist, he rejected angelic intervention at his crucifixion (Matt 26:53) so that the Scriptures might be fulfilled. His identification with us in our fragile mortal state was complete. He died as any other man would die when nailed to a cross.

After death, Jesus manifested himself with the marks of his wounds still present on his resurrected body—as if to signify the permanent effect on him of the suffering he had endured. The author of Hebrews remarks on this effect:

In the days of his flesh, Jesus offered up prayers and supplications, with loud cries and tears, to the one who was able to save him from death, and he was heard because of his reverent submission. Although he was a Son, he learned obedience through what he suffered; and having been made perfect, he became the source of eternal salvation for all who obey him. (Heb 5:7–9)

The author is not implying that Jesus was sinful before he suffered and "perfect" only afterward, but is insisting that, sinless though he had been, nonetheless Jesus learned from his ordeal and was changed by it. His suffering was what made him fit to intervene for us before God in *our* times of trial: Jesus is not an advocate without empathy but *one who has been there*. He knows what it means to suffer temptation. He understands pain.

The New Testament witness is that Jesus continues to manifest himself in and through those who are suffering. Jesus taught that when we minister to the thirsty, naked, sick, strangers, and prisoners, we are ministering to Jesus himself (see Matt 25:37–40). And Paul writes to the Galatians: "You know that it was because of a physical infirmity that I first announced the gospel to you; though my condition put you to the test, you did not scorn or despise me, but welcomed me as an angel of God, as Christ Jesus" (Gal 4:13–14). Paul is recalling the Galatians' offer of hospitality to him when he first evangelized them. He was suffering a bodily weakness (he does not say of what kind), but instead of snubbing him, they received him "as an angel." Indeed, they received Paul as an angel extraordinaire—as Jesus Christ himself. Usually interpreters assume that Paul is here making a metaphorical or hypothetical assertion: "You received me as warmly as you would have *if I had been* an angel—indeed, as warmly as *if I had been* Jesus Christ himself." But Paul is not being metaphorical. Rather, he is saying that the Galatians saw in him none other than Jesus Christ, God's chief angel or messenger. A little earlier in the letter Paul wrote, "It is no longer I who live, but it is Christ who lives in me" (2:20). When Paul first worked among the Galatians, it was *Christ himself working through the suffering Paul for their benefit.*

In identifying himself with an angel and that angel with Jesus, Paul was picking up on ideas current in Judaism of his day, about a chief angelic mediator. Some of Paul's contemporaries identified this chief angel with the glory of God known from Ezekiel 1, or with the word of God, or with divine wisdom. As I have argued in foregoing chapters, early Christians insisted that in Jesus these aspects of God had taken flesh. The glory, word, and wisdom of God were manifest in the human Jesus—even as he was being crucified. After his death and resurrection, the "angel" Jesus had shown himself again, in resurrection appearances recorded in the Gospels and in 1 Corinthians. Now, amazingly, Paul is suggesting that Jesus had manifested himself through Paul as well. But Jesus did not do so by miraculously healing Paul's affliction; instead, Jesus showed himself through Paul *even as Paul suffered.* Thus it came about that the Galatians, in receiving the suffering Paul, entertained an angel unaware.

When we ourselves suffer, or when we are threatened, it is right for us to pray for divine deliverance. In the garden, Jesus asked for deliverance, and he urged his disciples, saying, "Pray that you may not come into the time of trial" (Mark 14:38). And, three times Paul besought Jesus concerning the "thorn" in his flesh (see 2 Cor 12:8). Furthermore, if and when the deliverance for which we have prayed comes, it is right for us to offer praise. Perhaps we discern an angel, a messenger of God, to have been at work. But when petitioning for such deliverance, we can never assume that release from our trial is inevitable. Being human means being of flesh, and so being subject to the tribulations of our mortal condition, as Jesus was subject to the tribulations of his mortal condition, and as Paul was subject to the tribulations of his. For the duration of "the present evil age" (Gal 1:4) humans still suffer.

When we ourselves suffer, we should also ask and expect to be given the bittersweet fruits of suffering. These include a heightened sense of our own dependence on God, and of the grace that can sustain us (see 2 Cor 12:9). They also include an ability to understand and be in solidarity with others who suffer. As Jesus learned through his suffering and gained empathy through it, so do we. Thus we may become a vehicle of God's grace and Jesus' presence to others.

When others suffer, we should pray for their deliverance, even as we would pray for our own. If able, we should also offer hospitality, as the Galatians did to Paul. In Chapter 2, I argued that love is the means by which we may sustain a sense of God's presence. Living in the love of God as shown through Jesus Christ is the way for us to move from experiencing sacred moments to living a sanctified life. Acting in solidarity with the suffering is perhaps the highest form of Christian love. But there is no denying that it can be a hard thing to offer hospitality to the suffering. Who wants to get close to someone who is in wrenching physical pain or emotional anguish? Drawing near to those who suffer compels us to face our own mortality, and to discover how fragile is our own emotional scaffolding. The sufferer has fallen into an abyss, and we who draw close stand on the very brink of that abyss. Giving love—always a risky proposition—is here all the more so. It is risky because there is no guarantee of protection. There is only the promise that the face of God will shine on us, illuminating us with divine light.

So, for the duration of this age, humans still suffer. But even if we cannot count on physical protection or deliverance, is there not a guarantee of comfort in our troubled emotional lives? Can we not trust that Jesus, the "shepherd and guardian of our souls" (1 Pet 2:25) will bring us peace? The answer is both yes and no. On the one hand, Jesus and New Testament authors do promise peace:

- Peace I leave with you; my peace I give to you. I do not give to you as the world gives. Do not let your hearts be troubled, and do not let them be afraid. (John 14:27)
- For the kingdom of God is not food and drink but righteousness and peace and joy in the Holy Spirit. (Rom 14:17)
- The peace of God, which surpasses all understanding, will guard your hearts and your minds in Christ. (Phil 4:7)

Additional passages could be cited. Even the standard greeting of early Christian letters, "Grace to you and peace," suggests that peace with God, one another, and self is an expected outcome of devotion to Jesus Christ.

On the other hand, the peace that Jesus brings does not come automatically or without cost. One such cost is our submission to searching, searing judgment. John's Gospel teaches that the judgment Jesus effects is not strictly reserved for the end time, but happens now: Jesus is "the true light, which enlightens everyone" (John 1:9). This divine light illuminates the good but also exposes the evil (see John 3:18–21). The author of Hebrews describes judgment through the Word as a searching of each one's heart: "Indeed, the word of God is living and active, sharper than any two-edged sword, piercing until it divides soul from spirit, joints from marrow; it is able to judge the thoughts and intentions of the heart. And before him no creature is hidden, but all are naked and laid bare to the eyes of the one to whom we must render an account" (Heb 4:12–13). We can hide the secrets of our hearts from others. We can even hide them from ourselves: we can split the self, keeping one part walled off so that it might not see and judge what the other part is doing (see pp. 117–18). But we cannot hide from the Word of God. When we come to Jesus, he sees us as we are. He shows us where we have failed. He insists that we let him take down the partition in our hearts, that we might see for ourselves what we have wrought.

Moreover, this divine act of exposing the thoughts and intentions of our hearts does not happen only once. We never get it over with, because as we live the Christian life we continue to sin and continue to deny our sin. And the Light of the World continues to shine on us, illuminating the good that we have done but also disclosing all our idolatries and lusts and hardnesses of heart. The way to peace is not automatic or without cost, because facing what we would rather hide causes pain.

Paradoxically, submitting to divine disclosure of our innermost selves need not culminate in despair—in a "trance of unworthiness" such as Brach describes. Instead, the true end of such submission is the glorious freedom of the children of God (see Rom 8:21). It is a freedom from the powers that blind us and so keeps us in bondage, a freedom that comes from being wholly known and accepted just as we are. My own face is imperfect, I am usually self-conscious, but I can hold a beloved child's gaze and allow her to study my face (in a way that would make me quite uneasy with other people) because I trust in her love. I know that she sees my flaws, but I also know that they do not matter to her. Likewise we willingly submit to Christ's light upon us and allow him to look upon our flawed selves, because we trust in his love and in his being for us in an unqualified way.

Here is the cause for our gratitude, and ultimately, for our peace: Jesus Christ accepts us, radically, as we are. His radical acceptance of us is not contingent on our making amends for ways we have erred. He accepts us *first,* then forgives us our failures. Above all, this acceptance has been demonstrated through his willing death on our behalf:

> Hope does not disappoint us, because God's love has been poured into our hearts through the Holy Spirit that has been given to us. For while we were still weak, at the right time Christ died for the ungodly. Indeed, rarely will anyone die for a righteous person—though perhaps for a good person someone might actually dare to die. But God proves his love for us in that while we still were sinners Christ died for us. (Rom 5:5–8)

David Fredrickson notes that in this passage, Paul used imagery that his readers would have associated with *love* and *friendship.* When Paul wrote of divine love "poured into our hearts," his depiction of love as a liquid would have suggested love's *mutuality* (as the image did in some ancient love poetry). Paul is saying that we have hope even in our trials because of the mutuality of our relationship with God: God shares in our sufferings. When Paul wrote that "Christ died for the ungodly," the apostle echoed the commonplace philosophic idea that true friends are willing to undergo hardships or even death for one another. But whereas the philosophers put strict limits on friendship, contending that it was possible only between equals in rank and in virtue, Paul taught that "Jesus dies for the weak, sinners, and enemies." By dying for us *while we were yet sinners* Christ showed the radical nature of his friendship with us. Through his death he has reconciled us to God and brought us peace (see Rom 5:1).[146]

It is one thing to *know* of Jesus' friendship and God's love; it is another thing to *feel* those realities in a direct and personal way. Though God loves us always, the "peace that passes understanding" comes irregularly and as a gift; its advent in our hearts is not subject to our control. Bernard of Clairvaux captured the mystery of its coming when he wrote of angels as the ones who bring us a sense of God's mercy. "This divine mercy makes a person extricating himself from corruption compassionate toward the son of his mother [that is, toward himself], merciful to his soul, and thereby pleasing to God."[147] On the one hand, describing angels as "bringers of the knowledge of mercy" seems out of keeping with the Bible, where angels more often provoke awe and trembling. On the other hand, what do the angels typically say to those who have fallen prostrate before them? "Do not fear, greatly beloved, you are safe. Be strong and courageous!" (Dan 10:19; cf. Luke 5:8–10). When we first understand that we are indeed safe before God, we are moved to repent *and to practice mercy toward ourselves.* Our awareness of divine grace—like the gift of an angel—gives us courage to expose the innermost recesses of our hearts to Christ's healing light, to confess our sins, to forgive ourselves and others, and to live free.

There is another cost to the freedom that Christ brings, however. Christ delivers us from our old bondage, not that we might be free of *all* control, but that we might willingly submit to the rule of his Spirit in our lives. To the Corinthians Paul wrote: "For if we are beside ourselves, it is for God; if we are in our right mind, it is for you. For the love of Christ controls us, because we are convinced that one has died for all; therefore all have died. And he died for all, that those who live might live no longer for themselves but for him who for their sake died and was raised" (2 Cor 5:13–15). Here Paul is in the midst of defending himself and his ministry, which have come under attack. He concedes his own weakness, admits even a certain mania or madness about his own actions. But this divine mania is the work of another power controlling Paul: the power of Christ. The Greek word here translated "control" (*sunechei*) could be used to talk about someone being in the grip of a fever, or being held prisoner. Paul is saying that he is possessed by the love of Christ, the way a person might be possessed by a fever. Think of someone with a very high fever speaking deliriously. "It's the fever talking," we might say. Likewise, Paul does not control his own words or actions: the love of Christ controls him. "Maybe I *am* crazy," he is saying—"Certainly I am no longer in full control of what I say or do." By his radical act of friendship Jesus frees us from our old bondage but also requires that we make room at the center for his possessing, transforming love. He requires that we allow him to live as the guiding Spirit in our lives.[148]

This Spirit brings peace, but it does not tranquilize. It did not tranquilize Paul, but drove him to love fiercely, madly, even in the face of great opposition. Preaching on Mark's Gospel, Brian Blount describes how the Spirit drove Jesus at his baptism and now drives us:

> Want to know what happens when you get too close to God, when you get touched by the power of God's Spirit? You don't sit still and enjoy the view, you don't lay down and take a nap, you don't bask in the glory of what great thing has just happened to you. You go immediately to wild work. To work for God is to be thrown directly into the path of those who would oppose God. And so Mark tells us that Jesus was immediately *driven* into the wilderness by the Spirit of God. He didn't get lost. He didn't just happen to wander across the wilderness by mistake because his compass was broken. He didn't take a campfire holiday. He was *driven* by the Spirit into the wilderness for the specific purpose of engaging Satan in hand-to-hand spiritual and physical combat.[149]

Living with Jesus' Spirit as our guardian and guide, we are not shielded from evil but driven to confront evil, and to overcome it with good. Living with Jesus' Spirit as our guardian and guide, we are possessed by a love that controls us, by a power that drives us to "wild work" for God.

CONCLUSION

We want to believe that God watches out for us as we and our loved ones move through our risk-filled days, months, and years. We want to trust that, in moments of danger, God will protect us. And, if we should narrowly escape a disaster of some sort, we naturally want to affirm the wisdom and providence of God in keeping us safe. For centuries—nearly since the birth of Christianity—the doctrine of guardian angels has addressed these desires. Moreover, historically guardian angels have been viewed as filling other roles besides protection or rescue from external danger. They have been comforters and companions, instructors in divine truth, moral guides and watchdogs, bearers of prayer to the heavenly throne, and aides in spiritual warfare. Today, much of the popular lore about guardian angels traces back to such earlier views.

Although there is minimal biblical foundation for the belief that each person has a lifelong guardian angel, such ideas were known in both pagan and Jewish circles before the rise of Christianity. The ancient Mesopotamian idea of a personal deity and the Platonic notion of a personal and eternal *daimon*, or soul-double, bear some resemblance to later ideas about guardian angels, and several Jewish writings from the late Second Temple era clearly attest to belief in such guardians. New Testament references are just two in number: a possible reference to Peter's angelic double in Acts 12:15, and a reference to guardian angels of "little ones" who "continually see the face of the Father in heaven" in Matthew 18:10.

The idea that each person has a guardian angel seems to have been well-established in Christianity by the mid-second century, and was taken for granted and elaborated on by many patristic writers. Their teachings were adopted by medieval authors and passed down to subsequent generations. Although the medieval authors did make innovations as centuries passed, in general their references to angels (and to guardian angels specifically) over nearly a millennium were stable, and continuous with what patristic authors had written. Medieval reverence for guardian angels was part of a larger cultural pattern of "angelic spirituality," in which angels both model and assist those who strive for deeper union with God. If God seemed distant, guardian angels helped by modeling devotion to God, conveying God's mercy and love, and protecting their charges both from physical hazards and from the relentless assaults of the devil and his allies. It was taken for granted that guardian angels are both external to us and able to inhabit our innermost selves. It was assumed that, in the cosmic battle between forces of darkness and light—a battle raging both out there and in here in our souls—guardian angels will neither stray from goodness nor abandon us to our enemies. Their constancy can be trusted, medieval authors affirmed, because back when the wicked angels fell, the good angels had persevered in goodness, and they will continue to do so eternally. They are perfectly reliable to show us humans—weak and vulnerable to testing as we are—how we might likewise persevere. Thus we endangered travelers can hope one day to arrive at our homeland safe and sound.

Though patristic and medieval authors insisted that angels serve a preparatory function on the spiritual journey—like friends of the bridegroom, leading the soul as bride to Christ—still, the Protestant Reformers worried. Luther rejected the notion that angels or saints can intercede for us in heaven. Calvin noted the slim biblical warrant for Catholic elaborations on the angelic hierarchy and for teachings about guardian angels, and condemned the propensity by some to esteem the angels too highly. "Thus it happens that what belongs to God and Christ alone is transferred to them." Calvin effectively consigned *all* angels to the heavenly sphere. From that location they could edify people's spirits—offering encouragement and bolstering confidence in God's providential care—but they could not contaminate the material realm, and certainly would not alter the course of natural events. Seventeenth- and eighteenth-century Protestants, following along on the Reformers' trail, adopted their reserve toward the angels, and especially toward guardian angels. In the nineteenth and twentieth centuries, the trend continued: many Protestant theologians denied all mediating powers—angelic or demonic—any meaningful activity within the mundane sphere. To be sure, one might still sing of angels in hymns, or affirm their partnership in the liturgy, but the world of everyday life remained untouched by their presence. *Finitum non est capax infiniti,* the finite cannot contain the infinite.

In Catholicism, meanwhile, interest and belief in angels as intimate spiritual companions continued uninterrupted. Angels, together with the saints and the Virgin Mary, herself "Queen of angels," were accessible through prayer, and were felt to be intimately, almost tangibly present. They often granted graces and favors. These included both spiritual blessings and material favors. In the United States, Catholics' devotion to guardian angels escalated in the mid-nineteenth century, during the Catholic revival that swept the world. Thereafter, and for a hundred years, guardian angels were welcomed hospitably and invoked for assistance in Catholic churches, hospitals, schools, homes, and individual hearts. The Baltimore Catechism taught generations of Catholic children that our guardian angels "pray for us, protect us from harm, and inspire us to do good." Children, especially, were encouraged to think of their angels often and to trust that their guardians would protect them from physical harm and from temptation—as well as report their misdoings to God.

But the post-World War II years brought changes that, if not universal, were nonetheless widespread. Many Catholics left the old neighborhoods and old cosmology behind. The days when a Catholic child could grow up in the United States knowing not a single Protestant disappeared. The new, more culturally diverse environment rendered the existence of guardian angels less obvious, less able to be taken for granted. In the early 1960s, when Vatican II led Catholics to reassert the priesthood of all believers and to place new emphasis on the centrality of Christ, the mediation of higher powers such as saints and angels seemed less urgently needed. Some Catholic leaders actively discouraged the invocation of such beings, viewing them as relics of a bygone cosmology and obsolete spirituality. But the denial by some did not eradicate these higher powers from all Catholics' piety. Many, even in the

United States, have continued to believe. Moreover, new immigrant populations are changing the landscape of Catholic piety in the United States in ways that can scarcely be measured at present.

The huge surge of popular interest in angels in the 1990s was in part a reaction against the sterility of the Reformed Protestant cosmos—against its insistence on strict separation of the material and spiritual, the earthly and heavenly spheres. The surge also encompassed a reaction by some Catholics against the new, Protestant-influenced worldview encouraged after Vatican II. And so, for the decade of the 1990s and beyond, the public exhibited an insatiable thirst for stories of angelic intervention in the material realm. In these popular accounts, search-and-rescue angels intervene by heading disasters off at the pass, much like the Angel of the LORD blocking Balaam's ass: thus the rapist never rapes, the bullets miss their mark, the tow truck arrives before frostbite and death. Often, though not always, search-and-rescue stories emphasize God's ability to affect physical reality. Meanwhile, therapist angels show that God cares about our healing. Such angels are seen as a spark of God present in each of us, calling us to ascend to a higher plane of existence.

By reflecting on guardian angels, Christians down through the ages have struggled with extraordinarily difficult questions about God's relationship to the physical world. On the one hand Catholic belief in God's power as suffused throughout creation and manifested in miracles, and on the other hand the Reformed Protestants' hyperemphasis on God's transcendence can be traced to the influence of Neoplatonism as mediated by Pseudo-Dionysius. This highly influential theologian had postulated nine classes of angels who served as buffers between the celestial and material realms, which according to Neoplatonist theory cannot intersect. The angels who actually intervene in human life, including guardian angels (about whom Pseudo-Dionysius had no explicit teachings) were presumed to be the most distant from God. Nonetheless, countless Catholics have *experienced* the angels—guardian and otherwise—not as lesser beings in the angelic hierarchy, but as ones who effectively convey an awareness of God's presence, illumination, guidance, judgment, comfort, and love. The Reformers were likewise influenced by Neoplatonism's postulated chasm between the spiritual and the material or perishing worlds, but they allowed no spirits to bridge that yawning gap. God, according to their understanding, is pure Spirit, who lets the material world run according to its laws. Being Spirit, God only intervenes in a spiritual way: by turning the heart to repentance, for example. But there is no intervention by God or angels that contravenes the normal functioning of the physical world.

I have not tried to defend one of these views or the other, but to insist that God is both radically transcendent *and* radically immanent. When I say that God is transcendent, I do not mean that God is remote, but that God transcends the usual rules of time and space, of causality and change. As Luke Timothy Johnson puts it, God has "the capacity to be interior to all existence simultaneously, and present to all that is created without ever being defined by creation, without ever ceasing to be Other to all the sensible round of being."[150] God is neither absent from our world nor just a force bridging the gap between the power we have and the power we wish we had. Rather, God undergirds everything that is; God is the one in whom we live and move and have our being. God is present always: in good times and in hard times, in rescue and when there is no rescue. God governs the world and our individual lives providentially, but in ways that we cannot begin to understand. God is not a Creator who set the world to working and then stepped aside, but one whose work of creation is continual and unending.

This transcendent yet immanent God accommodates to our needs in many ways. For some Christians, God may self-manifest as an angel, possibly a guardian angel. Such an angel is not an intermediary who is separate from and lesser than God. Such an angel is not an underling who takes on the job because God is too busy. Rather, such an angel manifests the very presence of God. It is a bearer of the divine Spirit, of Christ's spirit—much like the angel of the LORD in the days of the patriarchs and matriarchs, like the shepherd-angel of Hermas, or like the angel who comforted and strengthened Christ on the night of his arrest. Those Christians who never know the presence of an angel are not worse off, however, because for all Christians God has become manifest in the person of Jesus Christ, who at his ascension entered into God's power and now continues to show himself to us, above all in the bonds of love and community and in the persons of those who suffer.

On the subject of miracles: even those of us who by natural disposition and upbringing are skeptical about miracles cannot deny the possibility of miraculous working by God or God's agents in the world. We cannot section off the human mind as a safe haven for God's spiritual intervention, as if the brain were not part of the material world. To affirm the incarnation of Jesus Christ is to insist that God operates in and through physical, material reality. God entered human history, taking the form of a slave, being born as a human. God, who calls all reality into being and sustains it moment by moment, is neither defined nor bound by natural law or by any assumed separation between worlds. Miracles are possible.[151]

God does not stay isolated from the earthly realm but enters wholly into mortality. In the person of Jesus, God "humbled himself and became obedient to the point of death—even death on a cross" (Phil 2:8). In keeping with that humbled condition, Jesus was not promised protection from suffering, and neither are we: instead we are called to minister to a suffering world. Nor does God promise us peace—if by "peace" we mean anesthetization to our own sin or the suffering of the world. The peace that Jesus brings us, rather, is the calmness and purposefulness that come to us when our better angels prevail over any who would lead us astray. This peace is a curtailing of our own duplicity and self-deception. We come to dwell in light, which illuminates our path so that we may step surely. The light also illuminates our frailties and failures—yet we do not fear. Christ befriends us and accepts us radically, just as we are, filling us with his own spirit and driving us into the world to work on his behalf.

6

Angels and Death

THE MANY FACES OF DEATH

Death has many faces, and as ideas about death change so do the faces. Several of death's visages can be seen on a stroll through old New England graveyards. On gravestones from the late seventeenth and early eighteenth centuries, a winged skull or death's head accompanies an admonition to the viewer to consider her own mortality, as in this inscription:

> My youthful mates both small and great
> Come here and you may see
> An awful sight, which is a type of which
> you soon must be.[1]

The death's head images became simpler and more stylized over time, but the skull-like features were always in evidence. The carved pictures seem intended to evoke thoughts of death's unwelcome visitation—not to celebrate the macabre, but to perform a service by reminding viewers of their own coming demise, and hence the brevity of time to repent.[2] By the middle of the eighteenth century, the death's heads had ceased to appear, and winged cherub-faces had taken their place as tombstone icons of choice. Did these cherubic faces represent the souls of the deceased taking flight? Or the angels who guided them to heaven? Either way, the accompanying inscriptions were more upbeat, rejoicing in the immortality of the deceased and pointing out that what lay below were but remains—the immortal part having departed for above.[3]

For millennia, the faces of death have often been represented by angels.

186

As on the tombstones, the angels may be portrayed as grim or pleasant, depending on how death and afterlife are understood. Does anything follow this mortal existence? If so, then where do we go and how do we get there? Do we arrive unaided, or does someone or something take us to our destination? Is that destination contingent on the life we have lived? Or perhaps there is no afterlife at all; life simply ceases when each of us breathes our last. If so, does the cessation last forever—nonbeing into the far reaches of eternity? Or is the cessation of life and of awareness more like sleep that will end with a wake-up call to resurrection? The assumed answers to such questions shape portrayals of the various angels associated with death and life after death.

In the seventeenth century, it took years or decades for tombstone fashions to reach American shores from England and then to fan out into the countryside. Today, accessing an entire smorgasbord of ideas about (or visual representations of) death is as easy as turning on the television or radio or logging onto the Internet. Even a casual survey will quickly locate (along with the more traditional scenarios of death and afterlife) such varied fare as books and television appearances by people who talk to the dead, or who died momentarily and then came back to life; movies and television shows about vampires, zombies, and other undead; and movies and television shows about love relationships between the living and the dead. This variety reflects the overall richness of our religious culture, which is heir to the Western orthodoxies of earlier generations but influenced also by Eastern religions, occult mysticism, and nineteenth-century romanticism and spiritualism. All these diverse ideas and images pertaining to death arose at particular points in history and originally reflected distinct worldviews, but today they mingle indiscriminately in our media- and Internet-saturated psyches.

In colonial New England it was difficult to deny death because death was all around. Infant mortality rates were high, and common illnesses were often fatal. Moreover, people regularly died in homes, where family, church, and community were near to witness and to prepare the body for burial. Today, by contrast, death has been largely removed from our routine intimate experience. Hence we can more readily deny the inevitability—or at least the imminence—of our own deaths.[4] We expect to live seventy or perhaps eighty years, and feel that anyone who gets less has been cheated. The physical changes that used to mark a person's progression toward death—declining muscle tone, graying or thinning hair, and so forth—are now declared unacceptable and largely unnecessary. As a society we reverence youthful bodies, youthful hairlines and hair color, youthful faces. We entertain ourselves by watching movies and reading romance novels about vampires, who prevent real death from occurring and who look perpetually young and beautiful.[5]

Remarkably, we deny death even as the world dies around us. The twentieth century was the most violent in human history, with countless millions killed in wars, murders, and various atrocities. We deny death even though we in the United States execute prisoners, and send thousands of our young overseas to wage war and cow our enemies into submission by wielding the threat of death. We deny death even as our own factories, automobiles, and air-conditioned homes destroy the ozone layer and our life-supporting ecosphere. We deny death even though the threat of nuclear annihilation hangs over the globe. We deny death even as our society feasts on more vivid, graphic, and horror-inducing images of the deaths of strangers than ever before.[6] In other words, we are in the habit of denying that death will come, even though—or is it because?—death rules our world. The tyrannical power of death is much larger than the biological certainty of our own individual demise. The power of death encompasses all the forces that oppress, bind, corrupt, alienate, segregate, divide, and destroy humans in their relationships with God, each other, and the rest of creation.[7]

As the author of Hebrews observed, it is not death itself but the *fear of death* that enslaves us (see Heb 2:14–15). Decades ago Ernest Becker brilliantly described the elaborate mechanisms of repression and transference that humans develop in order to cope with the fear of death. He acknowledged that we cannot avoid such mechanisms altogether, and indeed *must* develop coping strategies if we are to live well. "The great boon of repression is that it makes it possible to live decisively in an overwhelmingly miraculous and incomprehensible world, a world so full of beauty, majesty, and terror that if animals perceived it all they would be paralyzed to act."[8] But repression has its limits, and our habit of repressing the fear of death has a high cost. Our denial only makes death's insidious control over our lives grow, robbing us of vitality. At some point each of us must face our own finitude in order to see beyond it—in order to live authentically, and with faith in a grander purpose for our lives. As I review ancient beliefs about death and its associated angels a persistent question will be, do these ideas serve to deny death or to acknowledge it, and with what consequences for the living of life?

As we will see, the Bible does not look away from death, even when it promises life eternal. For example, the psalms often refer to the brevity of human life and the threatening power of death: "Remember how short my time is—for what vanity you have created all mortals! Who can live and never see death? Who can escape the power of Sheol?" (Ps 89:47–48; see also Ps 103:15–16). Jesus knew that facing death took enormous courage and the strengthening power of God, but insisted that facing it was essential. He taught his disciples that each must "take up his cross" in order to follow him, pledging his or her very life for the realm of God that Jesus proclaimed.[9] But willingness to face death did not make it easy to do so, as Jesus' own example testified: he grieved over the loss of a friend, and over his own impending death (see John 11:35; Mark 14:33–35). The Apostle Paul taught that for the duration of this age death remains a potent ruler under whom all creation groans, and to whom Paul and the other apostles are subjected daily (see Rom 8:22; 2 Cor 4:11). He worried about how the members of his churches would cope with the death of loved ones in Christ (see 1 Thess 4:13). In these passages and others, the sting of death is felt acutely.

In this chapter, I will trace changes in beliefs about death and afterlife in the biblical era and beyond, focusing especially on personifications of death and of the angels associated with death.[10] We will see that in the Hebrew Bible, the dead are often said to exist in a shadowy and miry realm called Sheol. Sheol was not viewed as a place of punishment or blessing, but simply as the location where the dead reside—especially those who had died a violent or untimely death, or whose lives were marred by wickedness.[11] Views shifted over the centuries, and during the second century BCE some Jews began to anticipate a day when God would resurrect the just and the unjust, judge them, and reward or punish them. The righteous would participate in a redeemed and restored Israel. Further, nearly from its inception this notion of "sleep in the dust" followed by resurrection (Dan 12:2) was interpreted by some in ways that made it more compatible with Hellenistic notions of immortality of soul. Eventually, the idea of end-time resurrection and judgment gave way to a view that all souls would be judged *at the very hour of death*—no waiting required. Angels play many roles in these assorted scenarios, including:

- Guides on tours of heaven and hell
- Escorts for the dying to what lies beyond
- Agents or assistants in the divine judgment (for example, as ones who record or recite the good or evil deeds of the one being judged, or as the heavenly accuser)
- Agents who punish or reward
- Fellow denizens of heaven, offering continual praise to God, or priests in the heavenly temple of God

As I explore these various angelic roles, I will reflect also on their continuity with what people believe about angels and about death and afterlife today.

Early Christians held that in his resurrection Jesus was victorious over death. He is now exalted to a place of great authority, a place above the angels. Moreover, his followers are destined to share his glory—certainly in the afterlife, but perhaps beginning even now, in the context of Christian community.[12] In the final section of this chapter, I will consider New Testament portrayals of such transformation to the angelic life—of what Alan Segal has called *angelification*. What do such claims mean for Christians' hope for life after death, and for full and abundant living of life on earth?

FACES OF DEATH IN THE BIBLICAL WORLD

FEARSOME ADVERSARIES: DEATH FIGURES IN THE OLD TESTAMENT

Personified Death. Throughout history, death has often been personified as an angel, spirit, or specter whose approach cannot be deflected, and whose arrival on the scene initiates a terrifying sequence of events. In a plaintive Appalachian folksong, Death informs its victim:

> I'll fix your feet so you can't walk.
> I'll lock your jaw so you can't talk.
> I'll close your eyes so you can't see.
> This very hour, come and go with me.
> I'm Death; I come to take the soul,
> Leave the body and leave it cold,
> To drop the flesh off of the frame;
> The earth and worm both have a claim.[13]

Such practice of referring to death in personified terms is very old. Among ancient Greek authors, for example, Homer and Euripides both portrayed *thanatos* (death) as a deity.[14] In the ancient Near East, the Ugaritic (Canaanite) god of the underworld was named Mot; he was a ravenous and cruel monster, and an adversary of Baal, another Canaanite god. Biblical authors show their familiarity with the ancient Near Eastern traditions about Mot by occasionally referring to death or to Sheol as a person, or by mentioning his hands, feet, and mouth.[15] The mouth image was significant because in Canaanite mythology, Mot killed the god Baal by swallowing him. The book of Isaiah plays ironically on this image when the author prophesies that the LORD will host a great banquet, at which time death itself will be swallowed: "And he will destroy on this mountain the shroud that is cast over all peoples, the sheet that is spread over all nations; he will swallow up death forever" (25:7). Death is also personified in Job, in a vivid description of the fate of the wicked person that alludes to the tortures of the underworld.[16] The passage reads:

> His skin is gnawed by disease;
> Death's firstborn feeds on his limbs.
> He is snatched away from his comfortable tent
> And haled before the King of Terrors.
>
> (Job 18:13–14)

The epithet the "King of Terrors" is especially provocative. Marvin H. Pope observes that the title "may be taken to imply that Mot is ruler over a host of infernal spirits who seize the victim and hustle him into the presence of their king."[17]

Despite such vestigial allusions to underworld deities in the Old Testament, more often it is Yhwh ("the Lord") who is declared to be the one God, sovereign over both life and death. Occasionally biblical authors speak of having already descended to the underworld; it is the Lord who brings them back to the land of the living (see Pss 9:13; 30:3; 86:13; Isa 38:16–18; Sir 51:5–12). Such references are figurative, but as Richard Bauckham notes they are more than just poetic fancy. These speakers understand themselves *actually to have been already in death's power*—like Jonah in the belly of the whale (see Jon 2:2–9). Their insistence that it is the Lord who has redeemed them prepares the way for eventual development of a doctrine of resurrection.[18]

The Destroyer. In addition to scattered images of personified death, the Old Testament occasionally refers to a "destroyer" or "destroying angel." Through plague or other such means, this figure slays large numbers of the unrighteous (rather than isolated individuals). The destroyer is viewed by Old Testament authors as an agent not of the underworld but of the Lord. In Exodus 12:23, for example, the destroyer accompanies the Lord through Egypt and kills the firstborn in each household.[19] In 2 Samuel 24:11–16, when the Lord grows angry at King David for conducting a census in Israel, a destroying pestilence (later identified with "the angel of the Lord") is set upon the people.[20] In the New Testament, Paul refers to the destroyer's slaying of Israelites who complained in the wilderness (1 Cor 10:10, probably alluding to Num 16:41–50).[21] The author of Revelation refers to the destroyer (Gk. *apollyon*), identified as the "angel of the abyss," who slays people who do not have the seal of God on their foreheads (Rev. 9:22). So, Matt Damon's gruesome yet comical portrayal of a destroying angel in the film *Dogma* is in continuity with a literalistic reading of the biblical accounts. In one scene, the angel shoots the board members of a corporation for promulgating images of a modern-day golden calf named "Mooby." [22]

The absurdity of the film's scenario gives us pause to reflect on this theological model for explaining wide scale destruction. If God, through an angel, caused a pestilence or plague, then why not the destruction of the Twin Towers? The worldwide AIDS epidemic? The tsunami of 2004? Hurricanes? Earthquakes? Should we interpret these events as the work of God or God's agents, sent with intent to kill? Certainly some observers, including some prominent right-wing Christian evangelists, have done so. But there are other ways—ways deeply consonant with biblical witnesses—to view the operation of the world and the destructive events that happen in it. Especially in the Pauline tradition, the world is shown to be broken, or fallen, and, hence, subject to powers and principalities that oppose God's intent for all of creation to flourish. That is why creation "groans in travail" as it awaits its full redemption (see Rom 8:18–23; 1 Cor 15:24–28). Paul does occasionally speak of death in personified terms, but not as an agent doing God's express will. "Death" for Paul symbolizes forces that entered into the cosmos at the beginning, that inflict suffering on the world in the present, and that will be put "under Christ's feet" at the end. Moreover, the death-dealing forces do not operate by God's express manipulation. Rather, God *permits* them to operate—for now—but promises one day to bring them into line with God's good purposes for the world.

In considering biblical language about the destroyer, we also may be helped by Eugene Boring's reflection on the "slaughter of the innocents" in Matthew. Boring ponders Matthew's implication that God instigated this mass murder while sending a rescuing angel to save Jesus alone (see Matt 2:16–18; the account alludes to the destroyer's murder of the firstborn at the Exodus). Matthew's account, Boring contends, must be understood as confession rather than as objective reporting. In it, the believer proclaims his or her conviction of faith that God was active in the deliverance and protection of the Christ-child. (So likewise, I might proclaim that an angel intervened to save my child from serious harm when she fell down the stairs.) Such confessions are misinterpreted whenever we treat them as objective reporting of fact, and draw implications about causes and effects from them. So it is false to infer that God actively destroyed the other male babies in Jerusalem (just as it would be false to infer that God killed other toddlers who did not survive a fall down the stairs). Even Matthew seems to shy away from so horrific an interpretation of Herod's action; as Boring points out, in 2:17–18 Matthew uses the passive voice to remark on the fulfillment of prophecy, which is different from his usual infinitival construction to express divine purpose. The evangelist thus minimizes the implication that the murders happened for the purpose of fulfilling Scripture.[23]

Satan and the Power of Death. In the Old Testament, the *satan* (accuser or adversary) is a member of the heavenly court, and *not* a personified death figure. Yet apparently the *satan* was viewed as able to orchestrate deaths: he brings on the calamities that kill Job's livestock, servants, and children (see Job 1:12–19; 2:6). Moreover, as centuries passed and the anonymous *satan* developed into the full-fledged character, Satan, he continued to be associated with the realm of death. Some Jews and Christians saw the archfiend Satan as the agent behind death-dealing human adversaries, including those who persecuted the prophet Isaiah, the evil tyrant Antiochus Epiphanes, the enemies of Jesus, and the enemies of the Christian faithful. The author of Hebrews names the devil as the one who holds the power of death (Heb 2:14), and the author of Wisdom blames an envious devil for death's entry into the world (Wis 2:24). The Apostle Paul (echoing Wisdom?) also remarks on death's entry into the world, and ties that momentous event to Adam's transgression; the devil is not mentioned but he lurks between the lines (Rom 5:12).

The various early associations of the devil with death reflect the influence of ancient Near Eastern combat myths on developing beliefs about Satan. These myths included stories about Mot, a god of the underworld and death. In the earliest biblical portrayals, Satan had been conceived as a servant of God. But, over time there was an interpretive shift, and Satan came to be viewed as "archfiend" and the "chief adversary of God."[24] Probably under the influence of Satan traditions, Paul makes an analogous interpretive shift with respect to death: he personifies it and refers to it as "the last enemy" to be destroyed by Christ at the end (1 Cor 15:26). In another place Paul refers to Satan as Beliar, a Greek rendition of the Hebrew term *belial,* which is linked in some traditions to Sheol and death.[25] "Satan/Beliar" and personified "Death" were alternate (yet mythologically related) ways that Paul and contemporary Jews and Christians named the forces working to undermine God's intentions for the world.[26] Because of the linkages among the terms in the mythic tradition and because of the characters' similar functions, there was often overlap in portrayals of them.

Despite this partial merging of the characters of Satan and Death, depictions of Satan from the turn of the Era did not yet portray him as master of the fires of hell. That came later, as a further development of the long-standing conceptual connections.[27]

ANGELS IN THE AFTERLIFE

For almost the entire Old Testament period, the Hebrews had no notion of a beatific afterlife. The general tenor of Israelite religion, as Alan Segal observes, was an emphasis on life on this earth and behavior in the world.[28] When Israelites did speak of postmortem existence, they spoke of Sheol, or alternately of being "gathered to one's ancestors."[29] Darkness and gloom characterized the existence of the shades or ghosts in Sheol. In much of today's lore, angel-guides lead people to "the other side," but in the Old Testament, angels are never spoken of as leading people to Sheol. People "go down" to Sheol, but they seem to do so on their own power, without angelic aid (see, for example, Gen 37:35; Job 7:9; Isa 5:14). In the second century BCE, however, new ideas about the afterlife began to spread.

Early Beliefs about the Resurrection. Daniel (written ca. 164 BCE) is the first biblical book to make unequivocal reference to the doctrine of bodily resurrection.[30] The relevant passage, which profoundly influenced subsequent Jewish and Christian doctrines of the afterlife, is Daniel 12:2–3:

> Many of those who sleep in the dust of the earth shall awake, some to everlasting life, and some to shame and everlasting contempt. Those who are wise shall shine like the brightness of the sky, and those who lead many to righteousness, like the stars forever and ever.

The exceptionally righteous and the exceptionally wicked will be raised from the dust of the earth so that they may receive deserved punishment or reward.[31] Segal argues that the expression "those who make others wise" (Heb. *hammaskilim*) probably designated martyrs for the political cause of the Maccabean revolt, an event that lies behind the book of Daniel. The promise of resurrection was intended to show that God would vindicate these righteous ones, who had persevered until death. Thus, the promise expressed belief in God's commitment to justice.[32]

To what sort of existence would the martyrs be raised? Segal argues that Daniel's promise—that the righteous would shine "like the brightness of the sky" and "like the stars forever and ever"—is not to be understand only as figurative. Rather, the wisdom givers will literally become luminous beings, shining stars—a promise that "can only mean to the Jews that they shall become angels."[33] Stars and angels had long been closely identified in Hebrew thought (see, for example, Judg 5:20; Job 38:7).[34] In the Greek world, Plato had suggested that souls go to live among the stars, and the Romans claimed that stars and souls are of the same substance. First-century Jewish philosopher Philo of Alexandria described the soul as made of the same stuff as stars, and identified the righteous dead with the stars/angels.[35]

An Intermediate Existence? Jewish Views. The promise of a resurrection that will take place in the future raised the question of the status of the dead in the present. Indeed, this crucial discrepancy between the possibilities of eschatological versus immediate postmortem recompense has given rise to many of the variations down through the centuries in Jewish and Christian expectations for the end time and depictions of the fate of the dead. A key question has been, when people die do they simply cease to exist for a time, or is there some sort of continuing life as they await the resurrection, judgment, and the restoration of God's people?

During the last two centuries before the Common Era, some Jews began to think of Sheol (or Hades, as it was often rendered in Greek texts or translations) as a temporary holding cell for the spirits of the dead, rather than as the permanent destination it had always been. Here people would await the resurrection and judgment, either to eternal life or to eternal punishment. When visionaries were taken on otherworldly tours, they might be shown the temporary lodgings for the shades. For example, in *1 Enoch* 22 (which likely predates Daniel 12), Enoch is shown a great mountain in the west, where four different categories of the dead await judgment in four deep, hollowed-out places:

> Then I went to another place, and he showed me on the west side a great and high mountain of hard rock and inside it four beautiful corners; . . . and it (the place) was deep and dark to look at. At that moment, Rufael, one of the holy angels, who was with me, responded to me; and he said to me, "These beautiful [or "hollow," according to one manuscript] corners (are here) in order that the spirits of the souls of the dead should assemble into them—they are created so that the souls of the children of the people should gather here. They prepared these places in order to put them (i.e., the souls of the people) there until the day of their judgment and the appointed time of the great judgment upon them. I saw the spirits of the children of the people who were dead, and their voices were reaching unto heaven until this very moment. (*1 En.* 22:1–5)[36]

Rufael goes on to explain that the people are separated according to whether they lived as righteous or as sinners, and according to whether or not they had received recompense in their earthly lives. So, although the actual judgment of the dead will not take place until some future date, immediately after death their experience anticipates their eventual, permanent outcome. Other texts also refer to the delay that the righteous dead must endure, and to the differential treatment of the bad and the good during the wait. In *4 Ezra* (late first century CE), the angel Uriel gives the seer Ezra an elaborate account of the intermediate existence of the unrighteous and the righteous dead as they await the judgment in the last days. As soon as they die, the unrighteous will wander in confusion, and be tormented by their shame and fear of judgment. The righteous, meanwhile, will experience joy and rest in their chambers, "guarded by angels in profound quiet" as they anticipate "the glory waiting for them in the last days" (7:75–101).

These Jewish apocalyptic texts portray souls who await end-time redemption. But the word "soul" is ambiguous because of changes in how it was used during this era. In the more ancient Hebrew context, "soul" (Heb. *nefesh*) referred chiefly to the personality or personhood of a living person, viewed as unified with the body. The word *refa* ("ghost" or "spirit") designated the aspect of the person that survives death. Alan Segal sees no evidence that the ancient Hebrews conceived of "an immortal soul, which is deathless by nature and capable of attaining bodiless felicity." That idea came from Greek philosophers, notably Plato.[37] But during the Hellenistic Era (when *1 Enoch* and *4 Ezra* were written), the idea that the soul is immortal and that it separates from the body at death became widely known. Hebrew writers began to use the word *nefesh* to designate either an eternal "soul" (much like the "soul" of Hellenistic anthropology) or an intermediate state before resurrection. The emergence of these new linguistic possibilities make references to "soul" in Jewish, or Jewish-Christian, texts from the Hellenistic period "ambiguous and difficult for us to parse because the same word can stand for either the Greek immortal soul, the intermediary state of the Hebrew tradition, or both alternately, or even at once, in the same document."[38] Further, Segal doubts that the references in *1 Enoch* 22 and *4 Ezra* to "souls" awaiting final recompense were influenced by Platonist notions of immortality. Rather, the souls in these accounts are more like the shades that went down to Sheol in older Hebrew thinking. They serve as placeholders, maintaining the moral identity and continuity of people until the final judgment.[39]

An Intermediate Existence? Jesus and New Testament Authors. The beliefs of the historical Jesus about the afterlife (and more specifically, about a possible intermediate existence between death and resurrection) are hard to discern, because all of Jesus' words come to us filtered through later authors who had their own views. Most of the pertinent sayings point to belief in an eventual resurrection and day of judgment, without telling us anything about the interim status of the dead. For example, in Matthew 25 Jesus tells of the Son of Man coming "in his glory, and all the angels with him"; he will sit on the throne of his glory with the nations gathered before him. On the basis of their deeds the righteous will be sent to "the kingdom prepared for you from the foundation of the world," but the wicked will go to "the eternal fire prepared for the devil and his angels" (see Matt 25:31–46).[40] Elsewhere in Matthew Jesus speaks of angels as reapers at the end of the age; the wicked will be cast into a furnace of fire and the righteous "will shine like the sun in the kingdom of their Father" (see Matt 13:36–43). Disputing with the skeptical Sadducees, Jesus says that in life after the resurrection humans will live without marital relations, "like angels in heaven" (see Matt 22:23–33), but this tells us nothing regarding the interim condition of the dead.[41] John's Gospel often has Jesus speak of "eternal life" (see, for example, John 6:40). But, the phrase does not necessarily imply an immediate transition to blessedness, since elsewhere in the Fourth Gospel, Jesus proclaims a coming day of judgment, "when all who are in their graves will hear his voice and will come out—those who have done good, to the resurrection of life, and those who have done evil, to the resurrection of condemnation" (John 5:28–29).

Jesus refers to immediate postmortem requital for the dead in Luke 16:19–31, the parable of Lazarus and the rich man. When Lazarus dies, he is "carried away by the angels to be with Abraham," but when the rich man dies, he goes to Hades, where he is tormented in flames. Abraham tells the rich man that a chasm separates the two places of the dead. Nothing is said here about an end-time judgment; it is assumed that the dead receive reward or punishment as soon as they die. The story is found only in Luke, and fits closely with distinctive Lucan concerns; moreover, it somewhat resembles an Egyptian folktale about a reversal of fortunes of a rich man and a poor man in the realm of the dead.[42] These factors complicate our assessment of how accurately the story transmits the historical Jesus' views about what happens when we die. It is possible that the story is not an authentic teaching of Jesus, but was adapted by Luke from cultural tradition to advance his narrative. If Jesus did speak the parable, he may have been adapting a popular motif to rebuke his adversaries for their disordered priorities, rather than to provide primary instruction about the afterlife. So the story ought not to be weighed too heavily in formulating doctrine about the postmortem state. But what of Jesus' words (again in Luke) to the repentant thief on the cross? When the thief asks Jesus to "remember me when you come into your kingdom" (23:42), Jesus replies, "Today you will be with me in paradise" (v. 43). Jesus here seems to suggest that the righteous dead go immediately to their reward: his word "today" contrasts pointedly with the thief's "when" or "whenever."[43] But again, we cannot be sure whether Jesus actually spoke these words or whether Luke penned them and ascribed them to Jesus.

Paul, who is actually the earliest New Testament witness, apparently thinks in terms of two stages of afterlife for those who die as Christians. The first stage, at death, takes the believer "away from the body" to be "with the Lord," who is "in heaven."[44] Paul keeps silent on such questions as the nature of that which survives (as spirit or soul), whether there are angels or others present there, and generally what it is like to exist in this intermediate state. At times he uses the widely-employed metaphor of "sleep," which goes back to Daniel 12:2, to describe the intermediate existence. Elsewhere he tells us that we can continue to "please the Lord" while in this existence (perhaps suggesting ongoing consciousness and agency), and that being "with the Lord" is preferable to being in the fleshly body.

> So we are always confident; even though we know that while we are at home in the body we are away from the Lord—for we walk by faith, not by sight. Yes, we do have confidence, and we would rather be away from the body and at home with the Lord. So whether we are at home or away, we make it our aim to please him. For all of us must appear before the judgment seat of Christ, so that each may receive recompense for what has been done in the body, whether good or evil. (2 Cor 5:6–10)

Paul is arguing that we aim to please Christ both in our mortal life and while in the intermediate state, so that we may be prepared to appear before his judgment seat when the resurrection and judgment at last occur.[45]

Finally, the book of Revelation refers to the souls of martyrs under the altar in the heavenly temple, awaiting their end-time vindication (6:9–11). John later sees how the souls of those martyred for Jesus (perhaps the same martyrs as in 6:9–11) will "come to life" and "reign with Christ a thousand years" (20:4). The rest of the dead do not participate in this first resurrection, but remain dead until the thousand years are ended, at which point they will be raised and judged (20:11–13). Overall it is difficult to extract from Revelation a clear doctrine concerning the experience of all people (or even all believers, or all martyrs) immediately after death or after the resurrection. The timing and sequence of events in Revelation is too complex: there is often ambiguity as to whether depicted events are happening as John writes, or are destined to happen at the end of days (which John regards as imminent, in any case). It is also unclear whether John thinks all these events certainly *will* happen or may yet be altered by the course of current events on earth. All that said, it is still worth noting that the drama depicted in Revelation features many angels, who serve as priests, givers of praise, interpreters of revealed visions, agents of judgment, and warriors fighting on behalf of God. The angel Satan is a key player, and Death and Hades appear twice (6:8; 20:13–14). Besides the martyred souls who plead for vindication, John sees a throng of the sanctified dead who join with the angels in praise of God (7:4–17).

In summary, Jesus and the New Testament authors surveyed here say little about the intermediate existence of humans between death and the general resurrection, and even less about angels' roles vis-à-vis the dead during the interim period. Insofar as they speak of the fate of the righteous and the wicked, they mostly refer to what will happen on and after the day of resurrection and judgment. In his letters Paul does imply a state of blessed union "with the Lord" between death and resurrection, but he remains tantalizingly vague about the details. Luke alone gives clear evidence for belief that the dead go immediately to their punishment or reward. In Luke's account of Jesus' word from the cross, Jesus declares that "today" he will be with the repentant thief in paradise. In the Lukan parable of Lazarus and the rich man, the dead go straightaway to their places of recompense; moreover, angels escort the righteous man to his place of reward.

Later Accounts of Travel to the Beyond. Certain later documents give much more elaborate depictions of the afterlife, and of angels' roles in it. Broadly speaking, such accounts continue a very long tradition of journeys to the underworld, a tradition that goes back to the ancient Sumerian version of the story of Gilgamesh. In *Gilgamesh, Enkidu, and the Netherworld*, Enkidu descends via a chasm in the ground to the netherworld. His ghost returns and tells Gilgamesh about what it is like there: how Enkidu's own corpse is decaying, and how the different categories of the dead are treated. Moreover, Akkadian, Egyptian, Syrian, Iranian, and classical Greek and Hellenistic cultures all likewise tell stories of people who visited the underworld.[46]

It was, however, certain Old Testament passages together with the journeys of Enoch in *1 Enoch* that most directly influenced important Jewish and early Christian tales of travel to the world of the dead.[47] *First Enoch* recounts Enoch's visit to the place of the punishment of the watchers, to the chambers of the dead who are awaiting judgment, and to the valley of Gehenna where the wicked would one day be punished.[48] On his travels Enoch is accompanied by an angel who acts as tour guide. All of these motifs are repeated in the later Jewish and Christian reports of travel to (or visions of) the beyond. These later travelogues present various scenarios for the course of the soul immediately after death and for the roles that angels play in the afterlife. Here, I will discuss two of the earliest: the *Apocalypse of Peter* and the *Apocalypse of Zephaniah*. Later in the chapter, I will discuss two more: the *Testament of Abraham,* which includes an extended portrait of the "angel of death," and the *Acts of Thomas,* which features what may be the earliest extant account of a Christian near-death experience. These and other Jewish and early Christian apocalyptic accounts of the afterlife influenced medieval Christian and Muslim accounts, which in turn influenced Dante's *Divine Comedy* and the entire western worldview.[49]

The *Apocalypse of Peter* is the earliest extant Christian account of a tour of hell; it likely dates from the first part of the second century CE but draws on earlier such traditions, which are no longer extant.[50] In this account Jesus tells Peter that the souls of the dead wait in Hades until the day of resurrection and judgment. At the resurrection, Jesus explains, not only those whose bodily remains lie moldering in the earth but even those who have been devoured by beasts and fowl will be given back for judgment, "for nothing perishes for God" (*Apoc. of Pet.* 4).[51] The ensuing predictions of the judgment and the tortures of the damned are explicit and extravagant. The author does not think of these punishments as happening immediately after death; rather, they are reserved for the end time. When the end comes, all will first be judged by fire: those who have done good will pass through unharmed and come to Jesus, whereas "the evil creatures, the sinners and the hypocrites will stand in the depths of the darkness that passes not away, and their punishment is the fire, and angels bring forward their sins and prepare for them a place wherein they shall be punished for ever, each according to his offence" (*Apoc. of Pet.* 6). The angel Uriel and several other named angels play significant roles in the judgment.[52] After judgment, various sorts of requital will be meted out: not only unquenchable fire, but also crime-specific punishments, such as hanging by the tongue for blasphemers, hanging by the hair for women who beautified their hair in order to commit fornication, and the souring and congealing of breast milk for women who exposed infants born of illicit sex.[53] There will also be venomous beasts and unsleeping worms in great quantity. Meanwhile, the elect will be borne by angels and clothed with the garments of eternal life, and will witness the punishment of their former persecutors.

Another document from this era, the *Apocalypse of Zephaniah,* combines belief in resurrection with belief in immortality of the soul. This intriguing account of the fate of the soul of an ordinary person, that is, one who is neither exceedingly sinful nor exceedingly righteous, is likely Jewish in origin.[54]

The seer (possibly the prophet Zephaniah, though his identity is not entirely clear) is taken on a tour of Hades. He sees that hideous angels, with faces like leopards, tusks likes wild boars, wild hair, and bloodshot eyes, deliver the souls of the ungodly to Hades for punishment immediately after their deaths. Later Zephaniah sees this place of punishment again, and learns that the damned actually have opportunity for repentance "until the day when the Lord will judge" (10:11). The righteous patriarchs Abraham, Isaac, and Jacob intercede on behalf of the tormented souls once a day. So the punishment of the wicked in Hades begins at death, lasts until Judgment Day, and will continue after it—but can be ended now if the sinners repent. Hades is not only the designated site for the eternal damnation that will run from judgment day onward but, in the meantime, a kind of purgatory for the wicked dead. Besides the places of punishment, Zephaniah also sees the place of reward, where the righteous and the saints are.

Angels play many roles in the *Apocalypse of Zephaniah*. There is the "angel of the Lord" who leads Zephaniah on his tour (2:1). There are "angels of the Lord Almighty" who record all the deeds of the righteous (3:6), and "angels of the accuser" who write down all the sins of humans and tell them to the accuser "so that he might accuse them when they come out of the world (and) down there" (3:8–9). There are the hideous angels who "come to the souls of ungodly men" and "spend three days going around with them in the air before they bring them and cast them into their eternal punishment" (4:1–7). There are myriads of praising and praying angels, whom Zephaniah eventually joins, putting on an angelic garment and discovering that he can speak their language (8:1–5). There are "great angels," including both "the accuser" (who has wild hair, bear-like teeth, and a serpent-like body, and who "accuses men in the presence of the Lord" [6:8, 17]); and also Eremiel, who has charge over the abyss and Hades (6:15).[55]

In these and other such apocryphal tours and visions, angels are the supporting actors who make the mechanisms of recompense work properly. They are also the extras who fill out the casts of heaven and hell and so enhance the grandeur and awe-inspiring (or fear-inducing) scope of those realms. Although the accounts vary in details as to the timing and sequence of afterlife/end-time events and the precise appearance and duties of angels, still there are common patterns. In such accounts the angels regularly serve as escorts and guides, advocates and accusers, agents or assistants in judgment,[56] agents of punishment or reward, and functionaries or givers of praise in the heavenly temple.

As the early centuries of the Common Era passed, the apocalyptic visions of hell depicted ever greater and more horrific punishments of the wicked, often with angels administering the sentences. The notion that angels punish the unrighteous in the afterlife developed out of a motif present already in the Hebrew Scriptures, in which angels sometimes carry out divine justice against humans still living (including in the passages about the "destroyer," discussed earlier). Earlier apocalyptic works had expanded upon this motif. For example, in *1 Enoch,* the angels Raphael, Michael, and Gabriel served as jail keepers of the errant angels who mated with human women, and other angels prepared punishments for wicked "kings and potentates of this earth." [57] The *War Scroll* from Qumran depicted angels as soldiers fighting alongside humans to destroy Belial and his hordes in the final battle of good against evil (see, for example, 1QM 1.10–11). [58] And Revelation depicted an angel binding Satan and throwing him into the pit for the duration of Christ's millennial reign (see Rev 20:1–3; 12:7–9). Given such precedents, it was not a big leap to the idea that angels administer the punishments of hell. Greek influence may also have pushed the tradition in this direction. [59]

As with the portrayal of the bloodthirsty death-angel in the movie *Dogma,* the excessiveness of these renditions exposes their indecency. The more hell begins to look like a medieval torture chamber or a Holocaust death camp and the angels like the sadistic operators of such depraved human institutions, the more urgent the impulse we may feel to jettison the whole doctrine of eternal punishment in hell. Mythological language about hell and its angelic torturers may originally have served the somewhat positive purposes of underscoring God's commitment to justice and intolerance for evil and of persuading people to repent. But, as Dale Allison points out, divine justice is obtained here at the unacceptably high price of the rest of God's attributes. When raised to the level of "sober doctrine," the mythological notion of "a god who does things to human beings that we would never dream of doing to a dog" becomes impossibly inconsistent with theological commitment to a God of love. It is appropriate, Allison notes, that the later depictions of hell show demons, not angels, in charge. "Their deity has morphed into his adversary, the devil." [60]

REAPERS OF SOULS

Ask someone today to describe the "angel of death" and you will likely get one of two answers. He or she will describe either a frightening, faceless being in a hooded cloak, come to cut life short—the Grim Reaper—or a beautiful angel who appears at the time of death to serve as a gentle escort to heaven. Although the Grim Reaper's hooded cloak appears to be a nineteenth-century innovation, in other respects both the grim and the pleasant angels lay claim to ancient ancestry. Broadly speaking, many ancient mythologies featured psychopomps (from the Gk. *psychopompos;* beings who guide the souls of the deceased to the afterlife). For example, Greek mythology included Hermes, who guided the dead to the underworld, and Charon, who ferried souls of the dead (those who could pay the toll) across the river Styx. In the cult of the Roman emperor, the god Helios conducted the emperor's soul away in a four-horse chariot.[61] Early Hebrew tradition—lacking belief in any significant kind of afterlife—did not know of a being who escorted souls to the beyond. But once the idea of immediate postmortem judgment and afterlife took hold, the psychopomps began to make their appearance.[62] The psychopomps in ancient Jewish testimonies fall into two categories: glorious—or at least benign—angels; and ferocious, terrible angels.

As for the glorious angels, consider again Luke's account of the beggar Lazarus and the rich man who ignored him. When poor Lazarus dies, he is "carried away by the angels to be with Abraham" (16:22). No account is given of how the rich man arrived at his fiery destination. Less well-known is the story of Job as retold in the *Testament of Job,* a document that may have originated at about the same time as the Gospel of Luke (first century CE). Here Job, having already proved himself utterly righteous by his patient endurance of trial, is spared all further suffering at his death. An angel comes in a chariot (or chariots; the manuscripts differ) to take away his soul. Upon seeing the arriving escort, Job's three virtuous daughters bless and glorify God. Then comes Job's departure.

> After these things the one who sat in the great chariot got off and greeted Job as the three daughters and their father himself looked on, though certain others did not see. And taking the soul he flew up, embracing it, and mounted the chariot and set off for the east. But his body, prepared for burial, was borne to the tomb as his three daughters went ahead girded about and singing hymns to God. (*T. Job* 52:8–12).[63]

The chariot heads off toward the east, where Job will presumably join the deceased wife and children of his first marriage, who were already "crowned with the splendor of the heavenly one" (40:3; cf. 33:3–9).

In contrast to this happy account of a friendly angel and heavenly reward, the *Apocalypse of Zephaniah* (discussed above) portrays fearsome angels of death. The terrifying angels that Zephaniah sees on his heavenly tour collect souls in order to ferry them to their place of punishment. When Zephaniah asks his angelic guide who the hideous angels are, the guide says: "These are the servants of all creation who come to the souls of ungodly men and bring them and leave them in this place. They spend three days going around with them in the air before they bring them and cast them into their eternal punishment" (4:6). In other words, these angels—or demons—visit the ungodly at the time of death, reap their souls, punish them for three days, and then deliver their souls to Hades.

Both pleasant and unpleasant angels of death play key roles in another document from this era, the *Testament of Abraham*. This engaging, humorous story likely originated in Egypt.[64] It is very relevant to the origin of the angel of death, and so is worth recounting in detail. The story tells of Abraham's several visitations at the time of his demise. The old man has to be visited repeatedly because the first few times he flatly refuses to cooperate.

At the outset of the story, God dispatches the "Commander-in-chief," Michael, telling him to announce Abraham's death to him and to comfort the patriarch by saying, "At this time you are about to leave this vain world and depart from the body, and you will come to your own Master among the good" (*T. Ab.* 1:7).[65] At first, Abraham does not recognize that this being is an angel, despite the various miracles that occur in Michael's presence, but Sarah does, and when she has informed Abraham they conclude "that a revelation of something is among us, whether it be evil or good" (6:8).

Michael is reluctant to take Abraham's soul because of Abraham's great righteousness. So the Lord arranges for a more oblique announcement: God's holy spirit will be sent to Isaac, and in a dream the mention of Abraham's death will be thrust into Isaac's heart. This happens, and when Isaac tearfully reports his dream, Michael interprets it, concluding, "And now know, most honored Abraham, that at this time you are about to leave the earthly life and journey to God" (*T. Ab.* 7:9). Abraham responds, "Now I do know that you are an angel of the Lord, and you were sent to take my soul. Nevertheless, I will not by any means follow you, but you do whatever he commands" (v. 12).

At Abraham's refusal Michael dutifully goes back to God for further instructions. God gives Michael a new message to convey to Abraham, including these chiding words:

> Do you not know that all those who (spring) from Adam and Eve die? And not one of the prophets escaped death, and not one of those who reign has been immortal. Not one of the forefathers has escaped the mystery of death. All have died, all have departed into Hades, all have been gathered by the sickle of Death. But to you I did not send Death. I did not allow a fatal disease to befall you. I did not permit the

sickle of Death to come upon you. I did not allow the nets of Hades to entwine you. I did not ever want any evil to come upon you. But for (your) good comfort I sent my Commander-in-chief Michael to you. . . . And so why do you say to my Commander-in-chief, 'I will not by any means follow you'? Why did you say these things? Do you not know that if I give permission to Death, and he should come to you, then I would see whether you would come or not come? (*T. Ab.* 8:9–12)

The remarks imply that everyone must die, but that God is able to make the end of bodily life painless by sending Michael as soul-reaper. God could as easily have sent Death, who cannot be resisted.

When Abraham hears God's message via the angel, he stalls for time by asking Michael to take him on a tour of the world. After obtaining authorization from God, Michael escorts Abraham on a cloud of light, pulled by cherubim. Abraham tours not only the realm where mortals live, but also the places of postmortem reward and punishment. He sees souls being judged and led to eternal life or destruction.[66] (The judgment and punishment/ reward happen immediately after death; there is no expectation of resurrection in the *Testament of Abraham*.) When the tour is completed, Abraham (predictably by now) again refuses to go with Michael. As Dale Allison wryly observes, Abraham is "denial [of death] incarnate. . . . He never comes to terms with the fact that his death is at hand."[67]

Finally, God pulls out the big gun: Death, a being "who is called the (one of) abominable countenance and merciless look" (*T. Ab.* 16:1). The narrator never explicitly identifies Death as an angel, but such identity is implied.[68] God instructs Death on how to take Abraham:

"Come, bitter and fierce name of the world, hide your ferocity, cover your decay, and cast off from yourself your bitterness, and put on your youthful beauty and all your glory, and go down to my friend Abraham and take him and conduct him to me. But I also tell you now that you may not terrify him; but rather you are to take him with soft speech, because he is my true friend." When Death heard these things he left the presence of the Most High and donned a most radiant robe and made his appearance sunlike and became more comely and beautiful than the sons of men, assuming the form of an archangel, his cheeks flashing with fire; and he went away to Abraham. (vv. 4–6)

When approaching Abraham, the disguised figure of Death looks so lovely that at first the patriarch thinks that he is Michael. But Death says straightforwardly, "I am the bitter cup of death" (v. 12). When he tells Abraham that he has come for Abraham's soul, the patriarch says "I will by no means follow you" (v. 16). Death falls silent, but instead of leaving when Abraham asks him to, he follows Abraham around. Allison writes, "Death, unlike Michael, does not go anywhere; he cannot be driven away—a circumstance that symbolizes his character for all people." [69]

Abraham then says, "I beg you, since you are Death, tell me, do you also come to all thus, in pleasing shape and glory and such youthful beauty?" (*T. Ab.* 17:6). Death explains that he has come in this form only because of Abraham's righteousness and boundless hospitality. "In youthful beauty and very quietly and with soft speech I come to the righteous, but to the sinners I come in much decay and ferocity and the greatest bitterness and with a fierce and merciless look" (vv. 7–8). Abraham begs Death to show him his ferocity and decay and bitterness; Death protests but finally puts on his "robe of tyranny, and he made his appearance gloomy and more ferocious than any kind of wild beast and more unclean than any uncleanness" (v. 13). Death shows Abraham seven fiery dragon heads and fourteen terrible faces. The seven heads represent the seven ages in which Death has led all humans down to Hades, and the fourteen faces correspond to all sorts of unpleasant deaths (for example, there is a "face of a most horrible precipice," and "a sword-bearing face and a face of lightning flashing frighteningly and a noise of frightening thunder" [vv. 14–17]).[70] The sight of these faces is so awful that seven thousand of Abraham's servants are struck dead (though they are later restored on account of the joint intercession by Abraham and Death). Even stubborn Abraham seems to realize that the end is near: he enters "the depression of death, so that his spirit failed" (v. 19).

Yet, Abraham is not quite over his denial. Halfheartedly he asks Death to leave and poses a few more questions about the terrible faces. Death obligingly answers but then says to Abraham, "Now I tell you, most righteous Abraham, set aside every wish and leave off questioning once and for all, and come, follow me as the God and judge of all commanded me" (*T. Ab.* 20:3). Abraham's family and servants encircle his couch, wailing. "And Abraham entered the depression of death" (v. 7). Then Death deceives Abraham, saying "Come, kiss my right hand, and may cheerfulness and life and strength come to you" (v. 8). But when Abraham does so, his soul cleaves to Death's hand. "And immediately Michael the archangel stood beside him with multitudes of angels, and they bore his precious soul in their hands in divinely woven linen" (v. 10).[71] The body is buried, and angels escort Abraham's soul and ascend into heaven, singing a hymn to God. After a short stop to worship God, Abraham is taken into Paradise, "where there are the tents of my righteous ones and (where) the mansions of my holy ones, Isaac and Jacob, are in his bosom, where there is no toil, no grief, no moaning, but peace and exultation and endless life" (v. 14).

The story is humorous yet poignant. Even pious and beloved Abraham resisted death! So much so, that, ironically, he never got around to putting his affairs in order and delivering his deathbed testament as God had invited him to do (and as the work's genre would seem to require).[72] No one—not even the worthiest friend of God—escapes death. Stubborn human efforts to delay death may work for a time, but they will fail in the end because death is more stubborn still.

The *Testament of Abraham* uses the figures of Michael and Death to express several ideas that are important in the development of angelic roles and imagery. The first such notion is that at the hour of death a visiting angel will escort the soul to immediate judgment. Immortality of soul is assumed; there is no mention of an end-time resurrection. A second notion is that the beings who are dispatched by God to fetch the soul will differ, depending in part on what an individual merits by the life he or she has lived. For most people the angel is Death, showing one of its many terrible faces, though for some righteous individuals God will soften the blow by dispatching Michael instead.[73] A third notion is that Death is a spirit-being or angel of terrible appearance: not skeletal, as in medieval and later depictions, but nonetheless exhibiting decay, bitterness, and ferocity. To look upon him is to die. The narrator of the *Testament of Abraham* presumes the readers' familiarity with these and other such ideas, which suggests that they were already well-established folkloristic motifs (though the author's own creativity in using traditional materials is noteworthy).[74] Each of these motifs has survived and evolved down to the present day.

What should we make of the *Testament of Abraham*'s idea that different angels are available to reap the soul at life's end? The motif reflects the reality that people experience death in very different ways. The possibility of a good death is represented by the image of Michael (or even Death in his beautiful guise) appearing to lead the soul gently away. Bad death is symbolized by Death's seven dragon heads and fourteen ghastly faces. The motif of good versus bad death-angels correlates with a worldview in which righteous behavior is rewarded and unrighteousness behavior punished. As Jewish beliefs about postmortem recompense developed, desire for divine justice was an influential factor: if justice did not prevail before death, the thinking went, then the scales would be balanced afterward. Here, the variance of death-angels in accordance with one's morality (good or bad) extends this principle of the moral coherence of the cosmos. God's measure-for-measure payback begins already as death draws nigh.

Today, we may still discern existential truth behind the notion that people see a different death-angel depending on the life they have lived. The point is not that each one gets the sort of death that he or she deserves, but that the type of life one lives does influence whether one approaches death peacefully and with gratitude, or with denial and terrible dread. Yet, there are limits to this modified interpretation. The *Testament of Abraham* uses humor to show that even the most obedient and faithful servant of God may flatly refuse to accept that the end is near. And the Gospels show that even the Son of God may grieve in the hour of death or at the death of a friend, because mortal life is so precious.

Each of the angelic reapers in the *Testament of Abraham*—beautiful Michael and hideous Death—has descendants in the culture today. The old correlation between track record and the sort of reaper one sees is not usually assumed, though it does make occasional appearances in popular culture. In the movie *Ghost*, for example, whenever an evil person dies, cartoonish black creatures suck its soul away (differently than when a good person dies). And in Howard Storm's near-death experience (see Chapter 2), demonic beings lead his soul down into torment until the moment he calls upon Jesus to help.[75] But most often those who portray any sort of angel of death (especially in films and on television) depict one or the other: either a Grim-Reaper-type figure or a benevolent and gentle angel. Each of these figures deserves further consideration.

THE ICONOGRAPHY OF GRIM DEATH

For the modern reader, the *Testament of Abraham* evokes the many images of the person or angel of death offered to us in art and by the film and entertainment industries. These range from the robed, romantic figure of Death in the 1934 film *Death Takes a Holiday;* to Ingmar Bergman's classic 1957 portrayal of Death in *The Seventh Seal* with its many takeoffs, including *Bill and Ted's Bogus Journey* (in which Bill and Ted play Twister and Battleship with the Grim Reaper); to the Grim Reaper in *Monty Python's The Meaning of Life* (in which, when the Reaper appears at the dinner party, the host sees the enormous scythe and says, "Is it about the hedge?"); to a Halloween episode of *The Simpsons* (in which Homer Simpson kills Death and then must step into the Reaper's role).[76] The serious portrayals depict Death as dark and sinister. Even the comic portrayals depend on our knowledge of a cultural idiom in which the robed figure of Death strikes fear and depression into the hearts of those who encounter him.

There are many surviving images of personified Death from the mid-fourteenth century onward. Some historians attribute this new fascination with Death to the decimation of Europe's population from the Black Death, an epidemic that began in the fourteenth century but included new outbreaks for centuries after. Fifteenth-century books called *artes moriendi* (arts of dying) were designed to help the sick prepare for death. They illustrate deathbed scenes in which angels and devils vie for the dying person's soul.[77] But by the sixteenth century, the figure of Death began to appear, either instead of the other spirit-beings or in addition to them. Art historian Philippe Ariès observes that this personified figure of Death is "less an allegorical character than a supernatural agent that has taken the place of the angels and devils to execute the decrees of God."[78] Styles for the portrayal of the figure of Death changed over the decades and centuries, from a shadowy or vaguely outlined human form in some early depictions, to a *transi* or decomposing corpse, to a clean and dry skeletal figure (sometimes draped with the remnants of a burial shroud, and very occasionally robed but seldom hooded).[79]

The methods that Death used to kill his victims varied. In the *Testament of Abraham*, as we have seen, simply to look upon one of Death's faces was fatal. When Death finally took Abraham's soul, it was by enticing Abraham to kiss his hand; when Abraham did so, his soul cleaved to Death. Elsewhere the document made reference to the "sickle of death," thereby alluding to Death's role as a reaper.[80] A rabbinic account tells that the angel of death wields a sword from which hangs a drop of gall; the dying person opens his mouth in terror at the sight of the angel, who drops in the fatal gall.[81] Medieval and later iconography depicts Death wielding a sword, a bow and arrows, a sickle, or a scythe (a tool that first appeared in Europe in the twelfth and thirteenth centuries, and that became the tool of choice for reaping grain in the sixteenth century). The sickle or scythe could readily symbolize Death's harvesting of souls for eternal punishment or reward, as well as its indiscriminate mowing down of its victims like stalks of grain. Instead of (or in addition to) a weapon, Death was often pictured carrying an hourglass, to symbolize the passage of time and, hence, his inevitable approach (a detail replicated on some of the old New England tombstones).

The image of the robed Grim Reaper is attested in artwork as early as the fourteenth century, but does not appear with any regularity until the nineteenth century.[82] Published in 1843, Charles Dickens' *A Christmas Carol*—with its unforgettable portrait of the Spirit of Christmas Future—has left its mark on many subsequent depictions of Death.

> The Phantom slowly, gravely, silently approached. When it came, Scrooge bent down upon his knee; for in the very air through which this Spirit moved it seemed to scatter gloom and mystery.

It was shrouded in a deep black garment, which concealed its head, its face, its form, and left nothing of it visible save one outstretched hand. But for this it would have been difficult to detach its figure from the night, and separate it from the darkness by which it was surrounded.

He felt that it was tall and stately when it came beside him, and that its mysterious presence filled him with a solemn dread. He knew no more, for the Spirit neither spoke nor moved.[83]

This Spirit is at least a close associate of Death: though he does not take Scrooge's soul, he shows him his tombstone. A few decades after the publication of *A Christmas Carol,* illustrator Gustave Doré produced a striking woodcut illustration for Edgar Allan Poe's "The Raven," depicting a hooded, skeletal Reaper sitting atop a sphere (presumably the world that he rules).[84] In decades following, Death was sometimes portrayed wearing a dark cloak (with or without hood), and often with his tool for reaping at his side. Today the image of the hooded reaper with his scythe is everywhere, and has been parodied so often that it may be more a cause for laughter than for fear.

Dark and grim images of death are used for so many ends that it is hard to say anything meaningful about the subject in a short space. But perhaps it will be helpful to highlight three such uses.

First, grim images of death sometimes serve to remind us of our own mortality. Death cares not how beautiful, youthful, or powerful one is, or how far from death one's thoughts are. The "dance macabre" theme that became popular in the fifteenth century illustrates this usage: Death comes to dance even with those who are yet young and vital. In Hans Holbein the Younger's woodcuts of the skeletal figure of Death (published in 1538), no one escapes—not the judge, not the emperor, not even the Pope, for Death comes to all.[85] The New England death's head tombstones also function in this way: no matter how far from death you may feel, those whose graves you behold inform you that you will soon be as they are. So repent! A modern variant occurs in the film *Dead Poets Society,* in which Robin Williams' character instructs his high school students to study the pictures of their counterparts from decades before, now dead. Those former students, like the current ones, were once full of life and dreams—but now they are fertilizing daffodils. The lesson from this evocation of decaying corpses? "Carpe diem!"[86]

Second, grim images of death are used for leverage by those who seek to instill fear to assert their own mastery or wield power over others. Pirates hoisted a flag with skull and crossbones to strike fear into the hearts of those who viewed it; the Death Eaters in the Harry Potter novels use a magical equivalent toward the same end. Tormenters ranging from Ku Klux Klan members to gang leaders to mafia members have devised death-related symbols to strike fear and despair into those whom they would dominate. Some Christians, too, resort to this technique: in recent years, Halloween hell houses have threatened those whom their organizers define as unsaved with eternal death and horrific punishment in hell.

Third, grim images of death are used to shock and critique those in mainstream culture and assert alternative values, as well as to offer a particular kind of aesthetic pleasure. So, for example, rock star Marilyn Manson, whose makeup is suggestive of the undead, proclaims, "I'm here to call Christian America on their bluff," and speaks freely of hanging out in cemeteries and robbing graves.[87] In presenting himself this way, Manson picks up on cultural images of the macabre that are rooted in the nineteenth-century Romantic revival and the Gothic novel, and seen also in all the variations of the current Gothic culture. Today, some Goths claim that immersion in the darker imagery of death enables them to transcend the vacuity of mainstream popular culture and to connect with the sublime.[88] Here there is a reversal of widely accepted values: the macabre is held to be beautiful and empowering, whereas the mainstream models for life (suburbia, consumerism, etc.) are anesthetizing, moribund. In the film *My First Mister*,[89] Leelee Sobieski plays a seventeen-year-old who finds beauty in death. J, as she likes to be called, dresses in black, pierces and cuts herself, reads Anne Rice's vampire novels, hangs out in cemeteries, and writes multiple eulogies for herself. She feels at peace in the cemetery, where she can commune with the spirits of the dead, including her recently deceased grandmother—the one person who understood her. J's thoughts of death give her welcome refuge from her pervasive fear of *life*, especially its loss and loneliness. The problem with this course (in real life as in the film) is that Death does not make a charitable friend. J suffers from depression—the stereotypical mood of the Gothic subculture.[90]

In the Christian story, the power of death is not something to which one reconciles oneself, or that one dismisses as inconsequential, and it is no friend. Death is "the last enemy," who opposes God's desire that all should flourish. It is the chief principality governing the present evil age. Since the time of Adam, death has held humanity in bondage by instilling a paralyzing fear of estrangement, separation, alienation, lost identity, and meaninglessness. But Jesus unmasked the death-wielding powers and principalities by showing that their claims to deity and offers of salvation were hollow and idolatrous. By his martyr's death Jesus exposed the powers' sham, and by his resurrection he offered freedom to those who are held in slavery by the fear of death (see Heb 2:14–15). Because of Jesus' victory, death is not to be feared. But, neither is it to be befriended. Death is the mark of the old order of things, the order that is passing away—but for now it still rages, and taunts us with its continuing hostile power. So, along with all of creation, we sigh, we groan under the weight of our loss and our grief, we protest that we have to suffer this way, that the earth has to suffer this way.

Images of death's dark angel convey the message that no one escapes death. The spirit points its outstretched hand to the grave marker under which each of us will lie. Confronting our own mortality need not lead us to denial or despair, however; instead it may impel us, as it did Ebenezer Scrooge or the boys in *Dead Poets Society,* to refocus life energies and live more fully in the present. Despair over death may prove to be a stage on the way to fuller and more abundant earthly life. But in the Christian story there is hope for more than just a fuller earthly life: there is the promise of *resurrection life.* The one who drinks the earthly cup to the dregs will also be raised with Christ. The old iconography of personified Death often included some reminder that even though death now triumphs over mortal life, one day life will triumph over death. For example, some medieval paintings of the triumph of death also pointed to the final judgment, when death will be undone. And some of the old New England tombstones depicted not only the death's head but also various symbols of the transformation to new life.[91] We should not too quickly dismiss the dark angel of death, or concede it to the trivializations of popular culture, for it reminds us that death and life each has its place in the Christian story.

DEATH AND THE LIGHT

The figure of the Grim Reaper has proven tremendously useful to movie producers, Halloween costume designers, and political cartoonists, because it reduces the abstract notion of death and all the complicated attitudes and fears associated with it and presents them in a simple and instantly recognizable form. Yet, in today's world of popular spirituality, discussions of death give relatively little attention to this dark angel.[92] By contrast, images of attractive, benevolent angels abound in such discussions. Betty Eadie, for example, was met by three beings dressed as monks, who informed her that they had been her friends and helpers since before her incarnate existence as a human being. They guided her to the arms of Jesus (see Chapter 2, pp. 42–43). Films and television also incorporate the upbeat angel imagery. In the opening scene of *City of Angels,* Nicholas Cage (dressed in black, but hardly grim) leads a pajama-clad child to the beyond, speaking to her gently about her favorite things and assuring her that her distraught mother will understand her departure someday. And in the CBS series, *Touched by an Angel,* actor John Dye portrayed the kindly and attractive angel Andrew. Andrew and his colleagues (a caseworker angel named Monica and her supervisor, Tess) routinely helped their human charges to overcome spiritual, psychological, and interpersonal problems. But Andrew's chief function was as an angel of death. Whenever it was time for a character to die, Andrew arrived to lead the person's soul away. In the story world of *Touched by an Angel,* no one ever dies alone.

As we have already seen, the notion that benevolent angels may escort one at death is well attested in ancient Jewish and early Christian writings. Moreover, this belief has parallels in various other religious traditions down through the centuries.[93] The idea has become extraordinarily popular in recent decades, fueled in part by the thriving of interest in near-death experiences, which often feature such benevolent beings. The popular interest in near-death experiences burgeoned in 1975, when Raymond Moody published *Life After Life*—a work presenting over one hundred case studies of people who had been revived after clinical death. This study of near-death experiences (a term that Moody coined) "started a revolution in popular attitudes about the afterlife and established Dr. Moody as the world's leading authority in the field of near-death experiences" (from Moody's Web site). *Life After Life* has sold over thirteen million copies worldwide, and has generated a small industry connected with such experiences.[94]

Near-death experiences are each unique in details, but recent accounts often follow a basic pattern. There is frequently an out-of-body experience; travel through a dark space or tunnel; perception of a golden or white light; a meeting with angels, deceased relatives, or other benevolent beings ("beings of light," in Moody's description); a message from those beings (or from an unidentified source) that one's time has not yet come; experience of a "life review" (the proverbial I-saw-my-life-flash-before-my-eyes experience); and the granting of knowledge of heavenly or earthly mysteries. Those who have had such experiences typically report that their lives have been dramatically changed. For example, Howard Storm (see Chapter 2, pp. 62–63) narrates his transition from a hedonistic but meaningless existence to life as a zealous, mainline Protestant (if somewhat unorthodox) pastor. Many others report an intensified interest in spiritual matters, a loss of the fear of death, and an evangelical fervor regarding the need for and availability of unconditional love. As Kevin Williams (webmaster of the popular Web site www.near-death.com) observes, "Those who experience a NDE [near-death experience] learn that loving others is the way to heaven within, heaven on

Earth, and heaven after death." Love, in Williams' estimation, is the means to overcome the illusion of "separation" that plagues our world.[95]

Historian Carol Zaleski has helpfully compared recent accounts of near-death experiences to medieval accounts. She finds strong evidence that both the medieval and the modern experiences are culturally shaped. In medieval accounts the guide is usually "a guardian angel or patron saint, who for the sake of the visionary's eventual salvation is not above dangling his charge over the pit of hell," whereas in recent accounts the angelic guide is typically a friendly and comforting family member or generic spiritual presence. Whereas medieval reports of near-death experiences often refer to judgment, purgatory, or hell, recent reports almost uniformly lack those elements. The more recent accounts do typically have the "life review," a narrative element that Zaleski finds to be comparable in some ways to traditional portrayals of judgment, but with important differences: the life review is nearly always "a reassuring experience, modeled on contemporary methods of education and psychotherapy," with no real possibility of failure or loss. Finally, Zaleski notes that because the contexts for medieval and modern stories of near-death experiences differ, so do the normative responses. Medieval people were more likely to express their transformation in institutionally sanctioned ways (for example, by embarking on a pilgrimage to a holy site). In today's highly individualistic culture, by contrast, near-death experiences move their subjects to love more, to seize the day, and to stop fearing death.[96]

Certain ancillary beliefs are widely shared among today's near-death enthusiasts. First, many such enthusiasts think it is possible to communicate with the dead, who are not truly gone, but merely "on the other side of the veil." George Ritchie, whose near-death experience inspired Raymond Moody, commented that "death is nothing more than a doorway, something you walk through."[97] Modern-day mediums such as James van Praagh tap into widespread readiness to believe that the dead are not really away, but simply present in a different form. Van Praagh conducts sessions in which he contacts the deceased significant others of audience members and conveys or receives messages on the members' behalf. Concerning his unusual abilities Van Praagh comments, "Often people think of me as some sort of miracle worker, but there is nothing superhuman about speaking with the dead. The only difference between me and you is that I have learned to use my sixth sense incredibly well."[98]

Second, many near-death enthusiasts share the notion that nothing truly evil ever happens in the world, because all events occur according to the divine plan. Even an event as seemingly terrible as the Holocaust is supposedly governed by this plan. When, during the course of her near-death experience, Beverly Brodsky asked the divine presence about the sufferings of the Jewish people, it was explained to her that "there was a reason for *everything* that happened, no matter how awful it appeared in the physical realm."[99] Variations on this theme occur. Betty Eadie, for example, admits to the reality of evil, which "by its opposing nature, is rising up" to challenge the great spiritual awakening that is sweeping across the globe. But Eadie still insists that all happens according to plan and for our good. Before our births each of us freely chose the suffering that we would undergo in life. In response to the terrorism of September 11, Eadie comments: "We knew before coming to earth that some trials would be very traumatic. . . . But we volunteered for them anyway, seeking all things that might refine us, humble us, and empower us to use our divine gifts to overcome and grow beyond these adversities."[100]

The consistency of many recent accounts of near-death experiences with regard to both the content and sequence of reported events and the content of ancillary beliefs may be due in part to the work of a small group of near-death researchers and their highly influential accounts in the early phase of the current near-death movement.[101] Though not possible here, it would be fascinating to trace these researchers' influence, as well as to discern how their accounts were themselves rooted in previous spiritual movements. Such movements would surely include the American spiritualist movement and the theosophical movement, both of the nineteenth century.[102] Whatever their origin, many motifs of the recent near-death accounts have dispersed throughout the wider culture—or perhaps they were already in the wider culture, and the near-death movement merely tapped into them.

The history of near-death experiences extends back much earlier than the nineteenth century or even the medieval period. Zaleski finds antecedents in the pervasive ancient belief in Mediterranean culture of "a free soul that ventures abroad during sleep, trance, death, and ecstasy." In the ancient Greco-Roman mystery religions, such folk beliefs were given greater narrative and ritual structure, setting in motion "a complex process by which the adventures of the free soul came to be linked to the personal experience of salvation, transformative knowledge, and victory over death."[103] The mystery religions offered an opportunity for a kind of rehearsal of the passage from life to death to life. Plutarch, the second-century biographer, compared initiation into the mysteries to the soul's experience with death. Both experiences begin with "wandering, and wearisome roaming, and fearful traveling through darkness with no end to be found." But then a marvelous light appears, and the soul is transported to a delightful place where there are "pure and pious people." One looks back on the uninitiated and unpurified, who are trampling each other "in deep mud and murk, but who hold onto their evil things on account of their fear of death, because they do not believe in the good things that are in the other world." [104]

In early Judaism, the reported heavenly journeys of Abraham, Moses, Enoch, Isaiah, Zephaniah, and others offer analogies to the more recent envisioning of otherworldly regions after death. Among early Christians, Paul claimed to have visited Paradise—"whether in the body or out of the body I do not know; God knows" (see 2 Cor 12:3–4). In the *Acts of Thomas,* a Christian work dating to the first half of the third century, a young woman's vision is recounted as a near-death experience. She had been murdered and was restored to life by the Apostle Thomas, who instructed her to "relate to us where thou hast been." [105] The woman recounted how she was met by a man "hateful of countenance, entirely black, and his clothing exceedingly dirty." He led her to a place with many chasms, which gave off a terrible stench and in which souls were being tortured in ways appropriate to their various sins.[106] Unspecified beings (angels? demons?) served as torturers and guards. The guards in a central holding-cave demanded that the woman's escort hand her over to them, but he refused, saying that he did not have the appropriate orders to do so. Then a spirit-being (apparently Jesus) said that the woman was "one of the sheep that have gone astray," at which point she awoke from death. Upon hearing her account, Thomas immediately used the opportunity to admonish the audience of bystanders and urge them to repentance, lest they suffer such punishments as the woman had observed (again, Halloween hell houses come to mind).

Many questions about today's near-death experiences remain unresolved. Probably the chief unanswered question is whether the subjects only came *near* death, or actually died—as many of those who have undergone such an experience assert. The answer partly hangs on complicated medical questions about the process of dying: the meaning of brain death versus clinical death, and so on. It also hangs on differences of opinion at the popular level: some would say that dead is dead—in other words, by definition, "dead" indicates that there is no coming back. Zaleski conceives of the near-death experience as a "border crossing," which is "at once imaginative and real": "It is a real experience mediated by the religious imagination. It is an imaginative encounter with death and a symbolic crossing of the threshold of death. Across that threshold lies the other world, which for our present purposes can be understood as the realm of the imagination, a realm in which the ideals that animate this life are encountered in their fullest, most embodied form." [107] In such mystical experiences, people see flashing before their eyes not only the events of their lives, but also symbolic expressions of the values and commitments that give their lives meaning. The near-death event functions as a conversion experience, "in which the subject undergoes a symbolic death and rebirth." The person awakes as a different being. Such an imaginative-yet-real encounter with death clarifies how one will think about death and—more importantly—how one will think about life.[108] Near-death experiences are valuable, not because they give objective information about the hereafter, but because they crystallize the beliefs of a person or a people about the shape and meaning of the good life.

What may we infer about our own culture's values and commitments, given its pervasive imagery of death-angels as attractive and benevolent? Such imagery conveys belief that the universe is fundamentally a loving and kind place. To those left behind in mortal life, the death of a loved one may seem to tear at the fabric of existence. But God has so arranged the world that the dying themselves experience their end as but a gentle transition, with a comforting presence at hand to guide and ease the way. (One sometimes hears the corollary assertion that angels take the souls of those fated for a violent or agonizing death a moment or two before expiration, so that they feel no pain.) Earlier I suggested that imagery of the Grim Reaper, or Death, can serve the constructive end of reminding us of our mortality—but some people may find such dark symbolism nihilistic and depressing. I also suggested that imagery of hellfire like that in *Apocalypse of Zephaniah* or the *Acts of Thomas* can function positively to remind us of God's commitment to justice and intolerance for evil, and of our own need for self-examination— but such depictions do run into conflict with our commitment to a God of forgiveness and love. The benevolent angels about whom we have heard so much in recent years conjure none of these dilemmas. They serve the quite noble end of reminding us that love, connection (not separation), and hope for a blessed eternal future are the means to the good life here and now.

Some have objected that such depictions of kindly death-angels and gentle crossings eliminate the sting of death and conflict with the biblical worldview, according to which those who die really and truly are dead. But this objection oversimplifies the complex historical data. There never was a unitary biblical view to which all early Jews and then Christians subscribed; as we have seen, views of the afterlife among biblical and contemporaneous authors were varied; and Hellenistic beliefs about immortality left their mark even in very early texts expressing hope in a resurrection of the dead. Critics of the immortality language often ignore this complex and early development of the doctrine, and, as Zaleski observes, fail to appreciate the varieties of the eschatological imagination. "What they gain in consistency, they lose by cutting Christian eschatology off from its imaginative roots, from its links to the past, and from its relevance to popular religious longings." [109]

A particular episode of *Touched by an Angel* illustrates how belief in immortality and pleasant death-angels can coexist with awareness of the sting of death. "Psalm 151" was voted viewers' all-time-favorite episode in the series. [110] It tells the story of Petey, a boy dying of cystic fibrosis. His mother Audrey, played by Wynonna Judd, is a songwriter who began a song entitled "Psalm 151" on the occasion of Petey's birth but has been unable to bring herself to finish writing it because the song is so tied together with Petey's life; to finish the song would be to concede that his life is over. But Petey knows that his time is short, and getting his mother to finish the song is the last item on his list of things to accomplish before he dies. He, his friends, and the angels all struggle to help Audrey face the reality of Petey's coming death and do what he needs her to do. In order to let her son go she must be able to imagine her life without him. The gist of the angels' message to her is not that death is nothing, but that strengthened by love she will survive, and that love requires her to say goodbye. At last she is able to complete the song—the long-missing line is "I will testify to love"—and a chorus from a nearby church (with angels intermingled) serenades Petey as he dies. Andrew, the angel of death, is at his side. Maudlin though it may sound in the telling, it is hard not to be moved to tears by this episode. (I once watched it in a classroom full of students among whom none had a dry eye.) The tears flow because the show compels one to look straight at death and consider its cost, both to the dying and to those left behind.

On the other hand, some expressions of belief in immortality *do* seem designed to obscure the harsh reality of death. Zaleski comments on the "saccharine optimism about death" in many contemporary accounts of near-death experiences. [111] In my estimation this charge applies especially to portrayals of immortality that downplay the importance of human embodiment. "Humans are spiritual beings presently having a bodily experience," one often reads in such accounts—as if our physicality were only a temporary guise that can be readily discarded without impairing our essential identities. [112] In such a worldview, bodily death does not mean the end of human interaction but only a change in its mode. Indeed, if the dead are only "beyond the veil," then the great divorce between the living and the dead is illusory. Not only can we foreshorten grief or forgo it altogether, we can even take care of unfinished business with our deceased loved ones who are still, essentially, here. By contrast, Christian hope for the afterlife is a "complex, even bittersweet" affair. [113] The sweetness derives from our confidence that the dead are "at home with the Lord" (2 Cor 5:8); the bitterness, from our keen awareness that for now death still reigns on earth, and we who live must agonize on account of "the breaking of the bonds of love" that death entails.[114]

The near-death movement, in general, exhibits too narrow a conception of death, regarding it as merely the termination of biological life. In this view, since living as an immortal spirit trumps living as a biological entity, death doesn't matter so very much: it is effectively neutralized by each individual's immortality. But death's domain in our world is much more vast than this conception allows. The rule of the power of death is exhibited not only (nor even chiefly) in the terminating of biological lives, but also in the oppressive grip of *all* the idolatrous powers on the world. These principalities and powers are incarnated in the icons, ideologies, and institutions that structure our day-to-day existence. Many serve good purposes, but all such entities function as emissaries of death insofar as they demand that humans regard them as ultimate and give homage to them instead of to the God of life. They make this demand even though they, too, are fallen, and consigned to death.[115] One can see evidence of the reign of death in a hundred or a thousand places: not only where age, disease, accident, or famine wrest away lives, but anywhere that stronger powers exploit the weak by dint of physical threat or denial of their essential humanity and worth, or anywhere that some lesser power has gained the status of a god in people's lives. From this perspective, biological death is only the most obvious symptom of the forces in our world that contend with God for sovereignty over the cosmos and its creatures. Survival of individual souls cannot by itself bring an end to this reign of death and all its allies, for such survival does not loosen death's grip on the world of the living. That is why the Christian hope for liberation is a hope not only for life beyond physical death, but for *divine deliverance of creation from the ruling idolatrous powers.*

When will the deliverance occur? Traditional Christian faith has the second coming and final judgment as its horizon. On that day Christ will subject all powers to himself and turn the kingdom over to God (see 1 Cor 15:25–28). Exactly how the expected end-time events will fit together with the redemption of individual believers (both those who died earlier and those who remain alive until the end) is never clearly spelled out in the Bible. As we have seen, theories about the status of individual souls in the interim period began to spring up at nearly the same time as the earliest Jewish expressions of belief in resurrection. Down through the millennia, various theologians and church bodies have worked out their own sequences and scenarios. But the eschatological, or end-time, dimension has nearly always been crucial. It has been crucial because, even if individual believers have died and gone to be "at home in the Lord," the continuing evidence of the power of death in our world tells us that the plot has not yet run its course. Death itself must be put under Christ's feet.

To be sure, the near-death movement does have an eschatological aspect. Many published near-death visions have a dire apocalyptic element: earthquakes, famine, and global war loom on the horizon. These ominous prophecies are often conditional, stating that the predicted calamitous events may be averted if society (especially in the United States) changes in drastic ways. And such authors find plenty of reason for hope, for they contend that at this very moment spiritual awareness is spreading, good forces are aligning, and the angels are awakening people to the need for universal love. So there is reason to think that the disasters may not come to pass. Betty Eadie acknowledges that evil is rising up in the world, then comments: "But truth is also expanding in the world, surging with new light and new ideas and generating exciting opportunities and challenges. For many this is a frightening time as old orders change and new values seep in. Time is speeding up, and many of us were among the strong ones, ready and determined to come and bless this world in these chaotic times. Now is our chance."[116] Other near-death authors do not think the disasters will be avoided, but do anticipate a golden age on the far side of the catastrophes. Kevin Williams summarizes the apocalyptic predictions of many near-death authors, then offers his own opinion that the coming disasters will purify civilization of its sins and "force people to get back to nature as these disasters will remove the artificial barriers between people." People will come to need, love, and rely on one another, and spirituality will grow. All this will happen soon.[117]

Such near-death apocalyptic revelations resound with critiques of Western (especially U.S.) culture for its national hubris and military expansionism, rampant individualism, racism, consumerism, violence, pornography, destruction of the natural world, and other sins. These scenarios express deep and pervasive anxiety about the state of the world—an anxiety that many others in our society also feel. But the recipients of these near-death visions of the end time are unable to move from generalized anxiety to the sorts of concerted social action that might actually improve the world's dire situation, *because they fail to recognize and to analyze systemically the reign of the power of death and its lesser allies over the living.* Their vague identification of our collective sins and their mystical gnosis about a spiritual awakening are by themselves insufficient to make a difference. The offer of gnosis must be complemented by tough-minded, this-worldly instruction in the concrete ways and means of the icons, ideologies, and institutions that promise life but instead rob us of it.

It is possible to engage in systemic analysis of any of the powers that be, ranging from the U.S. military or Exxon Mobil Corporation to a local school board or church governing body, from images of feminine beauty to ideals of the perfect Christian family.[118] Variables include the locus of the principality's institutional power and continuity, its characteristic culture or spirit, its intended purpose as well as how it has diverged from that purpose, the promises that it makes and the sacrifices that it demands, how it is allied with or rivaled by other principalities, and how it may be renewed and restored to an original good vocation from which it has fallen.[119] Analyzing a principality in this way demystifies it and enables its subjects to discern and resist its encroachments on the sovereignty of God in their lives. I have routinely had my students engage in such analysis of an icon, ideology, or institution that they have experienced closely; subjects have included the Soviet military, a local police force, a Native Canadian tribe, the NCAA, and a pharmaceutical corporation. The students are typically impressed by the insight that such analysis brings.

In the Christian account of the world, Jesus has unmasked the principalities and powers, including the last and greatest enemy, the power of death. Jesus' confrontations with the powers happened throughout his ministry, and are symbolized in the Gospel accounts of his stilling the storm, healing the sick and freeing the demon-possessed, demonstrating lordship over the Sabbath, cleansing the Temple, and raising the dead. In the wilderness at the start of his ministry, Jesus met the powers at their most deceptive and enticing; in his passion and death he faced them at their most "militant, pervasive, ruthless, and undisguised."[120] His refusal to be duped or cowed by the powers is captured in different ways by the four evangelists, but finds quintessential expression in his encounter with Pilate, according to John's account: "Pilate therefore said to him, 'Do you refuse to speak to me? Do you not know that I have authority to release you, and authority to crucify you?' Jesus answered him, 'You would have no authority over me unless it had been given you from above'" (19:10–11). Pilate's claim to lordship is inherently misleading, as is the claim of every idolatrous power in the world. Such claims constitute demands for allegiance, obedience, and veneration that are due God alone. God alone can give life, whereas the powers confronted by Christ—and wreaking so much havoc in our world today—are themselves subject to the reign of death and functioning as its agents.

Repeatedly in Jesus' ministry, but above all in his resurrection, we see the reality and grace of God triumphing over the fallen powers.[121] We who are in Christ share in the victory—but that sharing comes at the price of our own death. As Jesus taught: "For those who want to save their life will lose it, and those who lose their life for my sake will save it" (Luke 9:24). Or as Paul wrote: "For the love of Christ controls us, because we are convinced that one has died for all; therefore all have died. And he died for all, so that those who live might live no longer for themselves, but for him who died and was raised for them" (2 Cor 5:14–15). I interpret Paul's declaration to mean that when we let the love of Christ control us, we die to all the idolatrous powers that controlled us before. We can name these false gods in different ways. For example, we may identify specific institutions or ideologies that have ruled our lives: nation, corporation, university, economic system, political party, racial or gender hierarchy, class consciousness, marriage, and so forth. Or we may name the rudimentary weapons that the powers have wielded to achieve their ends with us: enticements to money, control, beauty, privilege, prolonged youth; the promise of insensibility to pain; the arousal of lust, fear, anger, hatred, jealousy, loneliness, despair. However we name these demonic powers, when we die to them we disavow their claims to our absolute allegiance. The consequence is a genuine diminishment of death's rule in the world. As Oscar Cullman wrote, wherever the Holy Spirit is at work "we have what amounts to a momentary retreat of the power of death, a certain foretaste of the end." [122]

William Stringfellow commented on that death which is an essential part of conversion to life in Christ. "The event of becoming a Christian," Stringfellow wrote, is "the event in which one utterly and unequivocally confronts the presence and power of death in and over his own existence, and, in the same event, is exposed to the presence and power of God overwhelming death in his own existence. Conversion is the personal experience, within the course of one's present life, of one's own death and of one's own resurrection." [123] (The power of near-death experiences resides in a similar sense of having died and been made alive again.) Conversion to life in Christ is not a one-time event, however, but recurs in any faithful life of some duration. There are multiple confrontations with death in such a life, and multiple resurrections. Concerning a difficult time in Asia, Paul wrote, "We were so utterly, unbearably crushed that we despaired of life itself. Indeed, we felt that we had received the sentence of death so that we would rely not on ourselves but on God who raises the dead. He who rescued us from so deadly a peril will continue to rescue us; on him we have set our hope that he will rescue us again" (2 Cor 1:8b–10). So too, in our walk of faith there are times when we despair of life, and must rely on God who raises the dead. Thus, the moment of our own physical death will be the seal on those stretches of our lives lived in the barren wilderness. None of us can know whether we will experience an angel's presence in the hour of our physical death. But we do know that *God* will be present, overwhelming death in God's own existence.

What does a human life look like when it has been freed from the power of death? Can a neutral observer see any difference? The lyrics to an old Shaker song tell us:

> Come little children, come to Zion
> Come little children, march along
> And your clothing and your dress
> Shall be robes of righteousness.

The Shakers believed they could don the "robes of righteousness" here and now, by living their lives in a way that reflected their current participation in glory. Their celibacy was one expression of their present angelic existence, for hadn't Jesus said that the angels neither marry nor are they given in marriage? So also, Paul and other early Christians thought that the *heavenly* or *angelic life* begins already during this mortal existence. In examining this notion, we will have opportunity to explore some of the practical consequences of the central Christian claim that Christ has overcome death with life.

TRANSFORMATION TO THE ANGELIC LIFE

The idea that people become angels when they die is widely known and often assumed in tales of the angelic realm or angelic intervention. For example, in Charles Tazewell's story, *The Littlest Angel* (made into a television movie starring Johnny Whitaker), a little shepherd boy becomes an angel and wonders what to give the baby Jesus, who is about to be born. He decides on the gift of a crude box filled with earthly treasures that he had loved as a mortal child: a butterfly, a robin's egg, two white stones, and the tattered collar from his devoted dog. God favors this gift above those from all the other angels and elevates the box to a position in the sky; it gives off a brilliant light that shines over the stable where Jesus is born.[124] Or, consider *It's a Wonderful Life*, in which guardian angel Clarence Oddbody is revealed to be a man who lived two centuries earlier; he must help George Bailey (Jimmy Stewart) in order to earn his wings. No doubt the reader will think of other illustrations, whether from popular culture or the beliefs of personal acquaintances. The usual learned response is to dismiss such ideas. People do not become angels! The Bible clearly teaches that angels are angels, members of a species unto itself, created by God and completely separate from humanity. Or so the wisdom goes.

But some Jews from the late Second Temple era apparently *did* believe that life after death and the angelic life are similar, if not identical.[125] The belief seems to have been connected with Dan 12:2–3, which had promised the wisdom givers a shining existence "like the stars" after the resurrection, and also with tales of especially righteous individuals who were transfigured into the appearance of angels during earthly life. Enoch was the most well-known figure to have undergone transformation to angelic form; his experiences were a topic of discussion over the span of centuries. In *1 Enoch* 39 (probably first century CE), as Enoch ascends to heaven, his face is transformed.[126] In *2 Enoch,* Enoch is commanded to put on fresh garments, and after he has done so he looks at himself and sees that he "had become like one of his glorious ones, and there was no observable difference" (*2 En.* 22:6–10).[127] Some Jews supposed that angelic transformation would happen only to such highly exceptional individuals, but others assumed that all the righteous would be elevated to a place among the angels after death. For example, in *2 Baruch* (early second century CE) it is said that the righteous "will live in the heights of that world and they will be like the angels and be equal to the stars" (*2 Bar.* 51:10).[128]

Ideas about the afterlife were very fluid in the first few centuries of the Common Era, as we have seen, and beliefs as to just when such a glorified existence would begin varied. Some supposed that angelic life would commence immediately at death, while others expected the transformation to occur at the time of the resurrection and judgment.[129] Remarkably, some Jews and Christians appear to have believed that the angelic existence of the righteous begins even while mortal life continues.

Qumran—the community that produced the Dead Sea Scrolls—offers especially suggestive evidence for belief in an angelic here-and-now. The inhabitants of the Dead Sea Community lived a celibate lifestyle and engaged in ritual purification so that they would be fit to worship with the angels and, eventually, to fight with them in the final war of the forces of light against the forces of darkness. Alan Segal observes that the elite at Qumran were attempting to live "in a permanent state of Temple purity, which they understood as tantamount to and anticipatory to full angelic existence."[130] Scholars debate about whether the sectarians thought that they actually became angels during this earthly life or only interacted with angels.[131] For our purposes here, it is unnecessary to try to resolve this debate. Our twenty-first century notions of "being" and "becoming" are radically different from those of the Qumran inhabitants; we would be unlikely to affirm that they actually became angels, even if we concurred that *they* thought so. I believe that we may speak meaningfully (as Segal does) of the Qumran sectarians' "angelification," whether they supposed that they became angels or just that they became partners with angels. Either way, they appropriated the symbolism of the angelic world and used it to fashion a new world for themselves, a world in which they experienced transcendence of the normal limitations that tie humans to earth and to mortal existence.

Likewise some early Christians fashioned an angelic world for themselves. Crispin Fletcher-Louis has argued that Luke and Acts depict the early Christian community using language and imagery that are "angelomorphic" (that is, suggesting the form, if not the being, of angels). In Luke's view, according to Fletcher-Louis, the one who enters the sphere of Jesus' activity through conversion experiences death and immediate resurrection to the angelic life. Indeed, the risen Jesus is himself portrayed by Luke as having the form of an angel.[132] Moreover, when Luke takes over Mark's account of Jesus' dispute with the Sadducees about the woman who was married seven times, Luke edits the material to support an ascetic lifestyle among Jesus' followers—a lifestyle that mimicked or realized a widely held vision of the angelic life.[133] And in Acts, when the council members gather to put Stephen on trial, they see that "his face was like the face of an angel" (Acts 6:15). In his ensuing speech, Stephen makes reference to the Torah having been given *so that its recipients might establish an angelic order* (see Acts 7:53; the passage is usually translated to refer to angels' mediation of the law, but the traditional rendering has difficulties). The Jewish leaders have failed to live such a life, according to Stephen. Meanwhile, he and the community of Christians living harmoniously in Jerusalem have succeeded.[134]

The Apostle Paul assumes that Christians live and worship in proximity to angels, and alludes to the Corinthians' worship practice of glossolalia as speaking in the "tongues of angels." Further, according to Paul's doctrine of resurrection, Christians will one day be transformed into "spiritual bodies," which he compares to stars; Segal interprets Paul's language as a reference to Christians' end-time transformation into angels.[135] But, like the author of Luke and Acts, Paul believes that believers' *eventual* angelic life is presaged *in this present existence.* While still mortals, Christians have undergone a kind of "death" through baptism into Jesus Christ, and a "resurrection" to new existence as members of a "body." And that "body" is already being transformed into Christ's image, which is the image of the glory of God (see 2 Cor 3:18; cf. Col 3:10). Already during their earthly existence Christians experience angelification—a kind of transformation to glory that will be completed on the day of resurrection.

In his allusions to Christian angelification, Paul makes a number of important assumptions (several of which were discussed in Chapter 2). First, he implicitly identifies the risen Jesus with the "likeness of the glory of the

LORD" seen by Ezekiel, and identified by other Jews of Paul's day with the chief angelic mediator of God. Jesus is the glorious alter ego of God—like the angels, but above them (cf. Heb 1:3–4). Paul counts himself among those rare visionaries (Moses, Enoch, and Ezekiel) privileged to enter into the presence of God and witness the glory.

Second, Paul assumes that beholding the glory changes or transfigures one, much as beholding the glory transfigured Moses, and much as what Enoch saw on his heavenly journey changed him to a glorified, angelic form. The divine glory isn't simply a sight to see; *it is a force that transforms.* It affects all that it touches. It transforms believers so that they share in the image of the glory of God. Paul likely tied his own transformation to his individual vision of the risen Lord Jesus, but for Christians more generally the process of transformation begins at baptism. This transformation will then be completed at the end time, when Jesus will change our bodies to be like his glorious body (Phil 3:10).[136]

Third, Paul assumes that the context in which such change occurs is not chiefly the private space occupied by God and a believer (Paul's own experience notwithstanding), but *the gathered church.* In the assembled body of Christ, Christians witness the glory, and the body is thereby changed into Christ's image (see 2 Cor 3:17–18).[137] Moreover, there is a cosmic dimension to the transformation: "If anyone is in Christ," Paul writes in 2 Cor 5:17, "there is a new creation: everything old has passed away; see, everything has become new!" This notion of a communal and even cosmic transformation is foreign in much of the church today. Salvation is most often understood as the result of a once-and-for-all exchange between the individual and Jesus. "He touched me, and made me whole," as the hymn lyric proclaims. But in Paul's view the church is quintessentially the place where Jesus is present to the people, and Jesus' work of making us whole does not end at conversion but continues until the day when Jesus turns the Kingdom over to God. As Paul writes to the Philippians: "I am confident of this, that the one who began a good work among you will bring it to completion by the day of Jesus Christ" (Phil 1:6).[138]

Fourth, the glory witnessed in the gathered people of God is intimately and paradoxically *tied to suffering.* That is why the glory can be so hard to see. The rulers of this age did not see it; if they had, they would have known that it was the Lord of glory whom they held in their hands and would not have crucified him (1 Cor 2:8). In Paul's ministry, too, the glory is hard to discern. To some of his detractors, Paul looks weak and pitiable; to them his ministry exudes the stench of death. Paul says that the god of this world has blinded their minds, "to keep them from seeing the light of the gospel of the glory of Christ, who is the image of God" (2 Cor 4:4).[139] They can't see the glory of Christ manifest in Paul's ministry, because the devil has them looking for glory and power in the usual worldly packaging and in the usual places. They don't understand that human frailty and even death are not an obstacle to God, but an opportunity to offer healing sustenance, and, indeed, life itself.

It is important to note that Paul is not merely fiddling with semantics. He is not simply renaming suffering as glory. Rather, he is insisting that God chooses to manifest divine glory and power precisely in those contexts where Christians are suffering and weak. This pattern is in keeping with God's character as one who "gives life to the dead and calls into existence the things that do not exist" (Rom 4:17). This pattern of God's self-manifestation also ensures that all will know that the power bestowed comes from God (see 2 Cor 4:7). Even though many cannot see the glory, those whose eyes have been opened by encounter with the risen Lord can see it (see 2 Cor 3:14–16; cf. Gal 4:13–14). One day, moreover, the glory will be beyond all measure and fully manifest (see Rom 8:18; 2 Cor 4:17).

The term "angelification" is appropriate and useful in describing the transformation "from one degree of glory to another" (2 Cor 3:18) that Christians experience beginning at conversion, as long as one employs the term with a certain metaphorical reserve. It is a useful term (alongside more conventional words like "sanctification," and less common but still traditional words like "deification") because it reminds us that *we are being given a heavenly stature and a new capacity to reflect divine glory—a capacity like that of the angels.* But metaphorical reserve is important. As with language about Satan and demons, we should avoid interpreting this notion of angelification in a crassly literalist or positivist way. In a published sermon, I referred to the angelification of the Christian saints, and was reminded by an irate reader of Paul's assertion that humans will judge angels. The reader felt I was demeaning the gift of salvation by saying that we will "only" become angels. In one respect I grant the objection: our present and future lives are bound up with the death and life of Jesus Christ, who is no ordinary angel but far above them. But if interpreted more symbolically, claims to our "angelic" status remind us powerfully that in Christ there is a new creation: a world in which we are enabled to transcend our human finitude and moral weakness, and—with the angels, and with Christ—to reflect the glory of God.

This transcendence is not obvious because it is not of a form that counts in the eyes of the world. It is too tied up with suffering and death. It involves renunciation of the idols. It involves paying the price that the powers and principalities exact from those who refuse to give them homage. It involves death to the self—or, in the reformulation of Miroslav Volf, the "de-centering" and "re-centering" of the self in the "self-giving love made possible by and patterned on the suffering Messiah."[140] This recentering is what enables the self to work for peace, reconciliation, and justice in a world that places so little premium on these. It is what enables the self to escape its imprisoning web of personal anxieties and the fear of death to reach out to others in love.

An example may help to clarify. When Rosa Parks died, she was accorded high honor and glory by the powers that be. Her body lay in state in the Capitol Rotunda, and she was lauded by dignitaries. But it took decades for the world to come around to this position. Initially the principalities reacted to Rosa Parks quite differently. In the aftermath of her action in Montgomery she lost her job and suffered slander and abuse—as she must have known she would. It was in those days that Rosa Parks first manifested *angelic* glory. She manifested glory when she did not regard her security and anonymity as something she must hang on to, but suffered their loss voluntarily, submitting herself to the powers and principalities. She acted without seeing the future but trusting, nonetheless, that a new day would come, that a new creation would be born. Whenever the world offers laurel wreaths to someone like Rosa Parks there is always room for suspicion about the purity of the world's motives. But the glory that God bestows is beyond reproach. That divine glory is reflected in the face and in the lifelong actions of Rosa Parks, and of others like her who give of themselves in love, not counting the cost. Such persons are angels because they are genuinely *messengers of God*. And people who see them are changed by them.

Paul assumed that transformation to glory happens within the context of Christian community. When he wrote about such transformation (see 2 Cor 3:17–18), he was addressing a dysfunctional body of persons who were estranged from one another and from him. The entire first half of 2 Corinthians is a plea for their mutual reconciliation. "In Christ God was reconciling the world to himself" (2 Cor 5:19)—but for God's act to become effective in their lives the Corinthians had first to become reconciled to one another. If and when they did so, a new creation would come into existence in their midst, a creation in which the alienating forces would be subject to the power of love.

The communal context is essential for a new creation to emerge because only in solidarity with others can we confront the errant powers and principalities and call them back to their intended purposes. These forces are not only "out there," separate and distinct from us. They are also "in here," in our individual minds and in the rules and norms we collectively agree to let govern our relationships to one another and the world. Individuals are part of systems, and the systems are big enough to overwhelm our isolated efforts and infect our very beings with their ideologies. No one person can change a whole system without concerted help from others. The Montgomery bus boycott succeeded because not only Rosa Parks but also many, many others stood up to walk rather than take the bus, thereby unmasking the system and bringing it to repentance. Today, to continue the illustration, any person in U.S. society who wants to live in a nonracist way needs others: to reveal the unsuspected places where thinking has been infected by the principality of racism, and to partner in working for social and cultural reforms so that all may enjoy the privileges that only some have thus far been able to take for granted. One could make a similar argument that resistance of other powers, too, must be carried out in the context of community in order to be effective.

Certainly it is easier to bear the high cost of such resistance when one is joined to others who share a vision of the glory of God manifested in community. Timothy Tyson tells of ugly events that transpired in Oxford, North Carolina in 1970: a black man was murdered in cold blood and his white murderers, known to many, were acquitted.[141] Protests and riots and the destruction of businesses ensued. The full cost of the damage caused by the series of events will never be known—damage to property, but even more, damage to families and to psyches on both sides of the racial divide. For Tyson, who is white, there was personal damage: his father was forced out of his pastorate for siding with the victim, and Tyson himself, a ten-year-old boy at the time, suffered debilitating anger that lasted for years. But he completes the story with a vision of community restored: an account of a trip taken with an interracial group of college students to see the sites where racism had been so viciously enacted, to lament what had been lost, and to find healing balm in fellowship along the way. For the duration of the trip, the students and their chaperones were an *angelic* community, united by their common vision and common grief, and reflecting divine glory. Tyson and his father (who was also on the journey) had shared in the sacrifices that made such a trip thinkable; the young people were the beneficiaries of many who had gone before them and paid a price.

Angelic communities emerge wherever and whenever love and mutual care, rather than enmity and egoism, govern the way the members of a body of people relate to one another. The transient nature of the little community in the foregoing example—its members gathered on a bus pilgrimage of short duration—suggests the ephemeral nature of the times and places in history where such community has been realized. Or, consider Luke's portrait of the first Christians in Jerusalem, offered in Acts.

All who believed were together and had all things in common; they would sell their possessions and goods and distribute the proceeds to all, as any had need. Day by day, as they spent much time together in the Temple, they broke bread at home and ate their food with glad and generous hearts, praising God and having the goodwill of all the people. And day by day the Lord added to their number those who were being saved. (Acts 2:44–47)

But this angelic body, brightly as it shone, dissipated in short order.[142] Self-interested hypocrites sullied the communal ethic (Acts 5:1–10), members disputed over offices and roles (6:1–5), and persecution arose to drive them away (8:1). Depravity within and enemies without: here in a nutshell we see some of the major reasons why an angelic community is so difficult to achieve and sustain.

Indeed, the very notion of such a community may seem hopelessly naïve. The world is a hard place and, hardened by it, most of us become not more but less angelic as time passes. Garrison Keillor comments, "As we get older, we accumulate certain griefs that never go away. They're simply a part of our lives."[143] Grief, anger, cynicism, and fear edge out the vision of flourishing that we may once have cherished. We have seen too much arrogance, deception, and self-deception to believe in the sanctifying, angelifying power of the Lord. Indeed, our cynicism, or is it realism, runs so deep that we fear for the very survival of the planet. All our experience tells us that, from the living room to the board room to the war room, narrow self-interest and shortsightedness brook no higher authority and know no bounds. How could we be so foolish as to trust in a divine power to transform us, a power to make us look and act like angels?

Such cynicism has its place, even in the community of faith. The cynicism is an implicit acknowledgment that there will be no utopia achieved in this fallen world. As Volf writes, "Before the dawn of God's new world, we cannot remove evil so as to dispense with the cross. None of the grand recipes that promise to mend all the fissures can be trusted." Modernity "has set its high hopes in the twin strategies of *social control* and *rational thought*," but the "wisdom of the cross" teaches that neither the right design nor the final argument can save us.[144] They cannot save us because, for the duration of the present age, the powers of sin and death still exercise dominion in the world. Our cynicism and grief are a kind of gut-level acknowledgment of this continuing ascendancy of all the powers that are set against God and God's ways.

Our cynicism and grief are an acknowledgment, too, of our own mortality: as individuals, as a nation, as a world. After all the wars of the last two centuries, after the bombs and the Cold War and the doctrine of mutual assured destruction, it is a miracle that we are still here. But the threat is not over: we still seem to be set on a course to ruin our planet, whether through nuclear annihilation or global warming. Day-by-day, moment-by-moment, the world continues to be sustained by God's grace. Yet one day the earth as we know it *will* die—perhaps when the sun burns up the fuel at its core in five billion years or so, or perhaps much, much sooner. Paradoxically, accepting the fact of our world's eventual death, even the possibility of its imminent death, offers liberation. Once we have accepted death, whether our own or the earth's, we are freed from the fears that have imprisoned and paralyzed us. We are able to recognize, and then to moderate or abandon, the myriad of strategies we have developed to cope with our terror of death. The strategies promise to soothe our anxiety but never wholly succeed, because no design, argument, demagogue, or diverting obsession can take away our knowledge of the fragility of our well-being and certainty of our death.

When the false hopes that rest on human strategies die, however, then "a new hope in self-giving love can be born."[145] The cross is the symbol of both the cost of resisting the powers and the love that frees us to do so. Set free, we are liberated to work for the health and salvation of the planet. Enabled to see death's deception and warmongering for what they are, we may labor—uncowed—at turning the principalities back to their God-given purposes in the world. In the *Testament of Job*, when Job's wife tells her suffering husband to "curse God and die," Job shouts at Satan to come forth and stop hiding himself. Job recognizes her admonition to give up on his work of persevering in faith and devotion as a satanic demand for obeisance to the powers. The powers want us to think that their violence and coercion are irresistible. But Job refuses to quit and instead embraces what remains of the gift of life. Might we not enhance and prolong the life of our precious world if we do likewise? If by "cynicism" we mean a clear-eyed awareness of the means and methods and intentions of the fallen powers, and a realistic assessment of the dangers that they pose to every sort of human flourishing, then this sort of cynicism is essential. "Be wise as serpents," Jesus said.

Yet, Jesus also said, "Be innocent as doves." The word "innocent" here means something like pure, untainted, or undiluted. The cross of Jesus Christ symbolizes the cost of resisting the powers, but it also symbolizes the undiluted love that frees us to resist and to reform them. It symbolizes uncompromising idealism: idealism that refuses to be stymied by belief that the obstacles are too great, stubbornly repudiates death's claims to full sovereignty, and steadfastly resists the fear of death. With such idealism comes an intoxicating sense of the power of the Holy Spirit in us: power to see our

⌄wn sins at last, power to forgive old and sometimes terrible wounds and also to accept God's forgiveness of us, power to reconcile enemies, power to endure in the face of terrible adversity, power to love where once we had hated. Innocence, purity, and idealism are often associated with youth, but youth doesn't have a monopoly on these attributes: the Spirit can refresh even a wizened and toughened old soul. We need both cynicism and idealism in the body of Christ. "See, I am sending you out like sheep into the midst of wolves; so be wise as serpents and innocent as doves" (Matt 10:16).

I may seem to have wandered far from our topic of angels and death. Let me retrace the connections. The New Testament witness is that transformation—angelification—happens. As Christians we look forward to our full transformation on the coming day of resurrection, when "in a moment, in the twinkling of an eye . . . the dead will be raised imperishable, and we will be changed" (1 Cor 15:52). At that time we will put on imperishability and take our place in the heavenly body of Christ—a place among the angels, but above them, for Christ is no ordinary angel but above every principality and power. But angelification begins here and now. It begins wherever the Spirit of the Lord is, in the church and outside it, for "where the Spirit of the Lord is, there is freedom." This freedom, bestowed by the Spirit, includes freedom from the fear of death that has held us captive. It includes freedom to love the world and to turn the fallen powers back to their creator. It includes the freedom of the glory of the children of God.

CONCLUSION

There is a deep and long-standing human urge to give death a face: to see it not merely as something that happens to each of us but as a presence, a being, an agent of larger, hostile forces. The ancient Canaanite deity Mot, the biblical figure of the destroyer, and biblical and other ancient personifications of Death all illustrate this human impulse to control and comprehend death by picturing it or giving it a name. In the early Christian world, Death and Hades came to signify not only the necessity of physical death but also (like the figure of Satan, with whom Death and Hades were sometimes seen as allied) the chaotic forces that strive to undermine God's intentions for the cosmos.

Angels have been associated with death throughout the previous two millennia, in different capacities. One fascinating work, the *Testament of Abraham* (from around the turn of the Era) offers a full and lengthy portrait of personified Death. In the Bible, however, there is no explicit depiction of a single angel of death. The closest we come to finding such a depiction is in Luke 16:22, where there is passing reference to multiple angels who carried the poor man Lazarus to Abraham's bosom. Other Jewish and Christian texts from early in the Common Era portray angels as guides for those rare living individuals privileged to tour heaven/hell, escorts to take the souls of the deceased to their eternal recompense, agents of punishment and reward in the afterlife, participants in divine judgment, and denizens of heaven who offer God continual praise. The multiplicity of death-related angels reflects the lively speculative interest in heavenly realms and their inhabitants which has always been a constituent element of apocalyptic thought. This multiplicity also reflects the wide variation and flux in ideas about death during and since biblical times: variation, for example, in understandings of how the redemption of God's people at the end time relates to the redemption of individuals at the hour of death.

The great range of these portrayals of death, afterlife, and associated angels is a lesson in itself. It reminds us that all such portrayals are imaginary border crossings, which reflect the immeasurable variety across the centuries of human imaginations shaped by diverse cultures. The range of the portrayals should also caution us against ever claiming to know much about what lies beyond the border of death. I once led a youth retreat on the subject of heaven and hell—a subject given to me, and one I would never myself have chosen for such an event because of the topic's huge complexity and the absence of a single and transparent biblical message. A few present at the retreat, including some leaders, were frustrated by my unwillingness simply to state the bottom line, that is, what we should believe about heaven and hell. Indeed, throughout contemporary western culture the desire for a simple and consistent message about the afterlife and the end time is widespread and strong; this desire is reflected in the popularity of scenarios for the future posited by groups ranging from dispensationalists (on which see Chapter 4) to near-death enthusiasts. But on this topic a simple message can be derived from the Bible only by dishonest measures: by screening out some voices in the varied biblical witness, and by elevating to literal and firm doctrine the authors' tentative and poetic imaginings.

In today's popular mythology, there are both angels of light and angels of darkness associated with death. Both sorts of imagery have ancient pedigrees, tracing back to ancient Near Eastern and biblical traditions and to Hellenistic portraits of Thanatos and other underworld deities. In medieval art, Death was often portrayed as a gruesome, skeletal figure who comes to all, regardless of age or social station. By the middle of the nineteenth century, the figure of Death had morphed into the Grim Reaper widely known and portrayed today. On the other hand, today's bright angels of death—exemplified by the figure of Andrew on *Touched by an Angel,* and by the shining figures who appear in so many accounts of near-death experiences—also date back millennia. In the ancient sources these benevolent angels are sometimes generic and sometimes identified with a specific angel, usually Michael. Those who tell of encounters with death-angels sometimes correlate the type of angel one sees (pleasant or fearsome) with the type of life one has lived. As more detached observers, we may find correlations between the type of angel a person reports and his or her cultural context, expectations for the afterlife, and deepest beliefs concerning the nature of human existence and relationship to God.

Today's popular culture is so saturated with pictures of death and gore that it is very easy for us to become inured to the shock effect that grim icons of death must once have held. Moreover, the humorous portrayal of certain death figures (such as the Grim Reaper) in film and on television reduces our sensitivity still further. We may cease to take such images seriously at all. In such a cultural context it is useful to recall that images of a dark angel of death have historically served to contain or limit the human propensity to deny the power of death in the world. This pervasive and destructive power of death is manifest in our individual deaths, but its reach extends far beyond the capacity to stop a beating heart. The power of death is operative wherever persons or institutions use deception and coercion (the threat of death) to oppress or to exact obeisance from those who are weaker. The power of death is operative wherever demonic social and cultural forces—or persons shaped by them—infect others with the message that their lives are futile, meaningless, without worth, and destined to end in oblivion. William Stringfellow's decades-old exhortation is still pertinent and wise: "Do not laugh or scoff at the venerable images of the power of death named the Devil or the Angel of Death," for they are the symbols that humans have used to convey the truth that "death is a living, active, decisive reality." [146]

Death is distinctly *not* taken as "a living, active, decisive reality" in sectors of the culture that disseminate hope of exemption from the sting of death. These death-denying social/cultural sectors include the Christian dispensationalist movement, which promises that the faithful will be raptured away before the world descends into the utter chaos and confusion expected to be brought by the Antichrist. They include also the producers/consumers of a modern gnostic mythology that often features angels of light, and that is rife in the near-death literature. According to this mythology, death is no more than a painless transition from a lesser physical state to a superior spiritual one. Both the dispensationalists and the near-death enthusiasts exhibit insufficient regard for the precious worth of *bodies*—our own human bodies, the bodies of the rest of God's creatures, and the "body" of earth itself. The dispensationalists teach that the damned on the one hand and the earth (together with its non-human creatures) do not matter to God, who will eternally punish the former and replace the latter. The gnostics teach that even the bodies of the "saved" do not matter, since bodies are but temporary containers for authentic and eternal spiritual selves. In different ways, both movements treat bodies and spirits as separable, and exalt the latter at the expense of the former.[147]

Such assumptions result in failure to cherish that which God cherishes: "Are not two sparrows sold for a penny? Yet not one of them will fall to the ground apart from your Father. And even the hairs of your head are all counted" (Matt 10:29–30). They result also in a failure to take seriously the ways that the death-dealing spiritual powers are themselves embodied or incarnated in humans and in their icons, ideologies, and institutions. Only when we take the incarnation of the fallen powers seriously may we discern their workings and know how to resist or reform them.

The New Testament witness is that Christ unmasked the powers and principalities, and won his battle against death. The consequence of his victory is that Christians need no longer be enslaved by their fear of death. Yet, the power of death has not yet been wholly conquered: it remains as "the last enemy," to be defeated once and for all by Christ at the end. Until then, the sting of death continues. Hence the Christian life elicits a certain kind of *cynicism:* a cynicism that recognizes this incompleteness of the victory over death and the lesser fallen powers. So we accept that leaders may become corrupted, that beloved institutions (including churches) may fall into disunity and hypocrisy, that relationships may crumble, that health and well-being may fail. We accept that loved ones and, yes, we ourselves, will die. We accept that God has given the world over to rulers and powers who do not fully uphold God's good intentions for the world. We accept that in this fallen world *all is not the way God would have it be.* But Christian discipleship elicits also *idealism,* because Christ has set us free from the fear of death. We do not deny death's present power, but neither do we submit our spirits to its rule. Freed from bondage to the fear of death, we have room in our lives for the Spirit to move and work. And the flame of the Spirit kindles—or re-kindles—hope, which "does not disappoint us, because God's love has been poured into our hearts through the Holy Spirit that has been given to us" (Rom 5:5). This hope is not a saccharine optimism, a false expectation that things will inevitably get better, or that we will personally escape the sting of death. Rather, in Henri Nouwen's words, it is the "trust that God will fulfill God's promises to us in a way that leads us to true freedom."[148]

Jews and Christians at the turn of the Common Era employed various models or metaphors to describe their expectation of divine redemption from the suffering and injustice of this fallen world. A number of their images circled around the conviction that God would elevate the righteous to be like the angels. For many, transcendence of the human condition and transformation to the angelic state would begin after death or on the Day of Resurrection, but some believed that such transformation begins already in this present life. Early Christians tied such belief in angelification to their conviction that Jesus had *already* experienced death and exaltation—to a place, not just among, but *above* the angels. By virtue of their own death and rebirth into Christ's body, already during their earthly lives such Christians experienced a foretaste of their eventual full transformation. They expressed this identity with the crucified and glorified Christ and their consequent victory over the powers in various ways. Some lived "as the angels" by remaining celibate—thus defying the power of death, which required propagation of the species through sexual intercourse. To choose the celibate life was to declare one's status as a child of the resurrection, and to scorn death. Others exhibited their victory over the powers (and especially the power of death) in other ways, including endurance of suffering, and the choice of love and reconciliation over hatred and estrangement. None of these ways of angelic living denied that physical death will come, but all of them denied that death would have the last word.

What does it mean for Christians to live as angels today? I suggest that the present moment calls for a holistic and incarnational approach—an approach that sees God's Spirit as made manifest in and through human bodies and (like all the lesser powers) in and through humanly created images and symbols, institutions, and cultural forms. To live like the angels is to live a life according to the pattern of self-giving love made possible by the suffering Messiah. It is to live in solidarity with those who suffer. It is to rise above paralyzing fear of and obedience to the power of death and the other idolatrous powers. It is to strive for peace, love, and justice by working to reform the fallen icons, ideologies, and institutions in the world. It is to accede to the astonishing power of the Spirit of Life in our lives.

The Spirit's work of transformation begins here and now, by enabling fellowship in which all are brothers and sisters, joined to one another in solidarity and love. Such a fellowship reflects the image of Christ (who gave up his godly status and bound himself to us in solidarity and love), and serves as an island or outpost of heaven here on earth. Such a fellowship is a place where the sacred meets and invades the everyday. It is a place where people can behold the divine glory—manifested in human flesh and transformed relationships—and can move beyond despair over the power of death to embrace faith, hope, and love. It is a place where people may, indeed, live like angels—shining like lights in the world.

Conclusion

Attending to talk about angels—talk in the Bible, and talk today—opens a way into serious reflection on important theological questions. Is God present in the world, and if so, how? Can we enter into that presence? Does God govern or guide what happens to us, in world events and in our social and psychic lives? What role does God play in causing and responding to evil? What future does God hold for us and for the world beyond the limits of mortal life? It might seem surprising that attention to talk about angels could lead us so deep into such central questions about God—surprising because angels seem to be relatively minor characters in most of the biblical story. Across the expanse of Scripture, angels are supporting players and bit characters, who seldom steal the limelight. Yet, they are often essential to the unfolding story. Because angels can appear in visible guise and converse with human beings, they assist in the portrayal of an invisible, ineffable deity. Hence, paying attention to what is said about angels enables us to gain a fresh perspective on the larger story and its more central players.

As we have seen, portraits of angels are influenced by the cultures in which the portraits take shape. Interactions with angels are depicted in ways that reflect and reinforce the values of those who encounter them (or those who tell of such encounters). So, for example, the incognito Raphael aids in the healing not of just any blind man but of Tobit, almsgiver par excellence, and facilitates the (culturally approved) marriage of Tobit's son, Tobias, to his kinswoman, Sarah. Or, to give a second example, the beings who appear in medieval near-death experiences customarily warn their charges of the dangers of eternal punishment; today, by contrast, angelic guides typically embrace their charges with love, comfort them, and offer therapeutic knowledge that will aid them when they return to mortal life. What sense ought we to make of this culturally governed variability in the portrayal of angels across the centuries? If we are people of faith, we may conclude that *God uses our imaginations.* By this I do not mean that angels are imaginary, but that, of necessity, we gain access to intangible realities through the images, words, and concepts given to us by our culture. Carol Zaleski finds nothing embarrassing or offensive about this necessity, comparing it to the divine incarnation in the person of Jesus. She writes, "If God, the unknowable, wishes to be known, what other recourse does God have but to avail himself of our images and symbols, just as he has availed himself of our flesh?" God, who was "willing to descend into our human condition" may also "descend into our cultural forms and become mediated to us in and through them."[1]

In the Old Testament, angels—especially the angel of the Lord—are portrayed as a means by which God takes up contact with the creaturely world. As Michael Welker argues, in biblical representations of angels we see the infinite God becoming "finite" and "concrete" for humans' benefit.[2] Biblical and subsequent Jewish authors reflect on divine power, presence, and agency not only by depicting *angels,* but also by referring to God's *word, glory, wisdom, power, spirit,* and *name.* Sometimes their comments on these various divine attributes hint that the attributes are themselves distinct angelic beings separate from God. Thus, for example, Ezekiel beholds in a vision the "appearance of the likeness of the glory of the Lord"—an astonishing figure, somewhat resembling a human being but clad in gleaming amber and encircled with fire and the brilliance of the rainbow (see Ezek 1:26–28). Or, consider the portrayal in Wisdom of God's "word" as a warrior who leaps "from heaven, from the royal throne," like a destroying angel (see Wis 18:14–16).

By the late Second Temple era, the various traditions about angels and about personified divine attributes had coalesced for some Jews into the figure of a chief heavenly mediator. This figure is depicted by the author of Daniel as "one like a son of man," by the author Philo as "the divine logos," and by other writers in still other ways. Early Christians used these interpretive conventions to make sense of the person and work of Jesus. They identify him with the chief heavenly mediator: Jesus *is* the Son of Man, the angel of the Lord, the divine *logos,* the one through whom the world was created, the exact imprint of God's very being, the likeness of the glory of the Lord. Jesus is never called an angel in the New Testament, and indeed he is distinguished from them in quite important ways. For example, the author of Luke's Gospel tells that the risen Lord ate a piece of fish—something an angel would never do, and a clear marker of Jesus' humanity (Luke 24:41–43). As a second example, the author of Hebrews insists that Jesus is "as much superior to angels as the name he has inherited is more excellent than theirs," for he (unlike the angels) is God's son, God's firstborn (see Heb 1:4–5). Yet, angelomorphic language—that is, the set of terms and images customarily used to talk about angels—is regularly applied also to Jesus. If angels are a means of divine accommodation, Jesus is supremely so. He is God's ultimate stooping down to humans, who, as finite creatures, cannot look directly upon God's face and live.

Ancient Jews told tales of humans privileged to enter into heaven, where they beheld the angels or even God and were changed into angelic likeness. Early Christians, looking upon Jesus, insisted that they were likewise changed. God has "shone in our hearts to give the light of the knowledge of the glory of God in the face of Jesus Christ" (2 Cor 4:6; see also 3:17–18). God shines in our individual hearts, and, above all, in the heart of the community gathered to worship and work for God. The Spirit of Jesus in our midst effects a transfiguration. It heals our spiritual blindness and helps us to see where we are in need of change; it persuades us of God's grace toward us; it strengthens us in times of trial. But above all the presence of Christ transfigures human relationships. It is love, the Apostle Paul teaches, and not angelic speech that is the best evidence of divine charisma, giftedness. Love is made manifest wherever the strong humbly accommodate to the weak, wherever we share one another's burdens and joys, wherever we forgive those who have wronged us and repent of our own wrongdoing, wherever we reconcile with those from whom we are estranged. Wherever the love of Christ is expressed, there is a New Creation, and a ministry of reconciliation. There is a glimpse or a foretaste of heaven, itself a "world of love." [3]

Today, much of the talk about angels is a reaction against the alleged distance of God from the world, and against the related tendency in Western culture toward separation of creator from creature. Popular spiritual authors often tell of childhoods lived under the pall of a deity portrayed to them as removed, detached, and coldly indifferent to the suffering his judgments imposed. Over against this caricature, talk about angels has served to assert God's indwelling of creation, and the unity of spirit and flesh. The angels teach receptive humans that the divine is suffused throughout creation, and therefore that all things, including humans, are in some measure divine. God is utterly accessible, as accessible as one's own breath, one's Higher Self. In the mind-set of separation, we the strong are at the center and all other creatures and things are given to our disposal. Such separation is held to be the root of much of what plagues us, including rampant consumerism and human exploitation of weaker peoples and nature. By asserting the unity of all created things with the divine, the angels of the new spirituality refuse to allow us to objectify and abuse creation.

An alternative view, which I see as more coherent with the biblical narratives, insists that creation is precious to God, yet indeed separate from God. God is radically immanent, but also radically transcendent. There is a boundary separating us as finite beings from the divine. To affirm God's transcendence is not to say that God is removed or inaccessible, however. God reaches across to us in the person of the Holy Spirit, the Spirit of Jesus, who transforms us and fosters in us love and empathy for God's world, enabling us to reach across the boundaries separating us from one another and from the nonhuman world. The Spirit reshapes our desires, taking us out of the center and fostering in us a desire that all of God's creatures should flourish. We live in a perishing world, a mortal world—yet it is a precious world, to be cherished and nurtured. Authentic Christian spiritual life begins when we recognize, not our divinity, but our finitude. We recognize that, left to our own devices, we err—above all by setting up false gods and following them instead of the way of love exemplified by Jesus. We are not divine, yet the Spirit of Jesus elevates us, deifies us—*angelifies* us—and so empowers us to accomplish what we could not accomplish alone. The Spirit helps us to tame our unruly and clamorous desires and put God at the center of our lives.

Some accounts of angels, intending to assert God's involvement in the world, actually fail to assert that involvement radically enough. Stories about search-and-rescue angels, in particular, sometimes suggest that God's agency is one saving factor, on the same causal plane as others. An analogy derives from the theater world, where an "angel" may step up with funds or influence to support a production that would otherwise fold. Here the "angel" is like other investors, but with a deeper pocket. So also, in some accounts of angelic rescue, God, via an angel, simply fills in a gap that humans cannot fill. Such a model may be taken to suggest that God is present *only* when and where an angel intervenes. So, if one woman passes safely down a dangerous thoroughfare and another is raped on the very same path on the very same night, the apparent implication is that the angel/God was present to the one but not to the other. But God does not intervene only on occasion. Rather, God is radically immanent, the one in whom we live and move and have our being. God is present in good times and in hard times, when the angel comes to rescue and when the angel does not. God governs the world and our individual lives providentially, but in ways that we cannot begin to understand.

By no means do I think it wrong to talk about angelic encounters, or angelic rescue. Such talk may eloquently express the deepest convictions of faith and the deepest sense of gratitude for help received in desperate times. But it is important that we recognize the limits of our perceptions and our speech. When we discern and declare that an angel has intervened in our life, we are making a confessional statement, from the perspective of a believer. Another observer may well interpret the event in another way. When we discern and declare that an angel has intervened in our life, we are striving to characterize the ineffable God's presence with us by using finite imagery and symbols—symbols given to us by our cultural forebears and so thoroughly wired into our brains that they control our very perception. Therefore, such encounters must always be described with a sense of humility and awe; with recognition of the sharp limits of our perception, understanding, and capacity for expression; and with empathy for those not given to interpret the event in the same way. Conversely, humility is also appropriate for those persons not inclined to see angels in our midst: their perception also is limited.

In the Bible there are other ways besides talk about angels to parse out the problem of divine agency, including language about the principalities and powers. These are the structures and forces that organize our world and preserve it. Broadly speaking, interpreters today make sense of the Bible's language about principalities and powers in two ways. Some emphasize the *fleshly* or material face of such rules and rulers. In their view, the principalities and powers are the human leaders, the social and political institutions, the cultural norms and structures by which we govern our daily existence, but which we ourselves have created or whom we ourselves have boosted to power. Others emphasize the powers' *spiritual* dimension. In their view, the principalities and powers are not human-created entities but unseen spirit-beings, including angels, demons, and Satan. The New Testament authors share elements of each perspective, and I have suggested that we try to find a middle way. According to this middle way, we acknowledge that the powers are always incarnate in people and structures, and that we are complicit in them. It is incumbent on us to own up to our involvement as well as our capacity to work for change. But we also acknowledge that the capacity truly to redeem those in bondage to the principalities—a capacity that is nothing less than the power to give life—comes not from us but from God, through Jesus Christ.

The greatest of the principalities and powers is the power of death. Jesus was personally victorious over this power at the resurrection, but for the duration of the present age, death remains active in the world. The power of death has often been symbolized as an angel, but it is so much more than a being who appears at the end of mortal life. Death is a force with vast influence over the living—a force that many try to domesticate for their own benefit or protection, in nearly every sphere of human activity. In the sphere of warfare, for example: as I write these remarks, Iran and North Korea are both in the news for their emergence or possible emergence as nuclear threats to the world. They are wielding *the power of death,* and other world leaders have been quick to feel the sting. Meanwhile, the United States and the insurgents in Iraq each marshal their own forces of death against each other, trying to wrest influence and ground. But Christ's way of humility and love unmasks the powers, including the power of death, and shows them for the idols that they are. The radical claim of Christian discipleship is that it is Christ's way of humility and love (and not death marshaled against death) that will lead to the ultimate redemption of the powers.

Christ has been raised above the angels. He has been victorious over the powers. Still, "we do not yet see everything in subjection to him" (Heb 2:8). We see the world still mired in the Fall and it is hard to fend off cynicism or even despair. But let our cynicism be a virtue: disabused of our delicate sensibilities, let us stop shielding our eyes from the brokenness of the world. When we place ourselves in solidarity with those who suffer—watching with them, and acting in their interest—we will find that the Spirit has room to move and work in our lives. The flame of that Spirit will kindle love, and hope for a New Creation—across the world, or in our tiny corner of it.

Jesus is no ordinary angel, but rather, the peerless example of God's stooping down to be present with us in our brokenness. Through Jesus we are enabled to enter into God's presence, trusting that the one who sees all faults will neither mock nor condemn but offer us mercy and grace to help in time of need. By accepting us as we are, Jesus in turn enables us to give of ourselves in love—to come to know God by serving God. And we ourselves become the balm for all wounds, the angel to others' needs. We reflect God's glory to one another and to the world, and even as our ministering changes others, we are ourselves transformed. We harbor no illusions that God's realm has arrived in power, and yet we do not lose hope, for, with the angels, we have glimpsed the face of the glory of God.

NOTES

INTRODUCTION

1. For an insightful study of recent trends in American spirituality, including angel piety, see Robert Wuthnow, *After Heaven: Spirituality in America since the 1950s* (Berkeley: University of California Press, 1998).

2. Peter L. Berger, *A Rumor of Angels: Modern Society and the Rediscovery of the Supernatural* (Garden City, N.Y.: Doubleday, 1970), 5.

3. According to research conducted by the National Study of Youth and Religion from July 2002 to March 2003, 69 percent of American teens who were asked if they believed in the existence of angels answered "definitely"; 29 percent answered "maybe." These results are based on a national, random-digit-dial telephone survey of U.S. households containing at least one teenager aged 13–17 years. In total, 3,370 interviews were completed (Christian Smith and Melinda Lundquist Denton, *Soul Searching: The Religious and Spiritual Lives of American Teenagers* [New York: Oxford University Press, 2005], 43). See also Lynn Schofield Clark, *From Angels to Aliens: Teenagers, the Media, and the Supernatural* (New York: Oxford University Press, 2003).

4. Quoted by Karl Barth, *Church Dogmatics,* vol. 3, part 3 of The Doctrine of Creation (trans. G. W. Bromiley and R. J. Ehrlich; Edinburgh: T. & T. Clark, 1960), 377.

5. Billy Graham writes, "I believe in angels because the Bible says there are angels; and I believe the Bible to be the true Word of God" (*Angels: God's Secret Agents* [Dallas: Word, 1994], 15).

6. The dismissal of all notions of mythological interventionist powers came with the transition to modern forms of discourse in the Enlightenment. Theologians of the modern era typically sought to explain what exists and what transpires in creation by referring, not to transcendent realities, but only "to what is also in and of the world according to principles manifested by the visible intra-worldly connections of proximate and particular causes" (Kathryn Tanner, *God and Creation in Christian Theology: Tyranny or Empowerment?* [Oxford: Basil Blackwell, 1988], 125). Thus, in the twentieth century,

the works of modernist theologians such as Rudolf Bultmann and Paul Tillich reflected their efforts to construe God's presence and care in a nonmythological way, in keeping with the truths of the scientific age. Bultmann wrote, "Modern men take it for granted that the course of nature and of history, like their own inner life and their practical life, is nowhere interrupted by the intervention of supernatural powers" (*Jesus Christ and Mythology* [New York: Charles Scribner's Sons, 1958], 16; see also 20–21). But Bultmann and Tillich endeavored to construe *all* supernatural powers (including God/the Holy Spirit) nonmythologically, and therefore did not fall into the kind of self-contradiction referred to above. In today's (postmodern) era, many theologians reject the modernist conviction that it is even possible to speak nonmythologically, holding instead that we never escape the grip of our own mythological constructs, though we may substitute one set of conceptual models for another. Kathryn Tanner *(God and Creation),* argues compellingly against the modernist framework, insofar as it forces us to choose between construals of divine powers as transcendent to the created order and as emphasizing God's immanent presence. Such a framework is responsible, Tanner argues, for the incoherence of much modern theological discourse about God's ongoing role vis-à-vis creation: For the modernists, God's radical transcendence excludes God's creative operation within the world. Rather, Tanner argues, God must be described "non-contrastively," as both radically transcendent and radically immanent.

7. See, for example, Ambika Wauters, *The Angel Oracle: Working with the Angels for Guidance, Inspiration, and Love* (New York: St. Martin's, 1995); Alma Daniel, Timothy Wyllie, and Andrew Ramer, *Ask Your Angels* (New York: Ballantine, 1992); Barbara Mark and Trudy Griswold, *Angelspeake: How to Talk with Your Angels* (New York: Simon & Schuster, 1995); Eileen Elias Freeman, *Touched by Angels: True Cases of Close Encounters of the Celestial Kind* (New York: Warner Books, 1993); Denny Sargent, *Your Guardian Angel and You* (Boston: Weiser Books, 2004).

8. A good example of a best-selling book emphasizing the "plan" for each of our lives (but without reference to the Judaeo-Christian God, or indeed to any omnipotent deity) is James Redfield, *The Celestine Prophecies: An Adventure* (New York: Warner Books, 1993).

9. Jeffrey Burton Russell, *A History of Heaven: The Singing Silence* (Princeton: Princeton University Press, 1997), 7.

10. Ibid., 9.

11. Many modern English translations of the Old Testament use Lord (written in small caps) to translate the Hebrew Yhwh. Called the "tetragrammaton," Yhwh is the proper name of the God of Israel, used by most writers of the Hebrew Scriptures. Translating Yhwh as Lord respects the ancient tradition of discouraging readers from pronouncing the divine name out loud. Indeed, vocalization of the divine name is still avoided by many Jews today. The term Lord is itself problematic, inasmuch as it seems to imply that God is male. I recognize this limitation, yet to preserve clarity of reference while avoiding overuse of the tetragrammaton, I do regularly use Lord when quoting or citing Old Testament passages that mention Yhwh or Yhwh's angel.

12. John J. Collins (*Daniel* [Minneapolis: Fortress, 1993], 331) observes that in the ancient Near Eastern world stars were not viewed as inanimate objects but were "the visible manifestation of the heavenly beings." Cf. Theodore H. Gaster, "Host of Heaven," *Encyclopaedia Judaica* (22 vols.; 2nd ed.; Detroit: Macmillan Reference USA), 9:566–67; Patrick D. Miller, Jr., *The Divine Warrior in Early Israel* (Cambridge, Mass.: Harvard Uni-

versity Press, 1973), 123–28 (on conceptions of the celestial bodies as members of the divine council and warring heavenly host in Josh 10:12–13; Judg 5:20; and Hab 3:11).

13. Miller (ibid., 139–40) notes the military connotations of several of the terms in this passage. Here the LORD is portrayed not as "shepherd of the stars," but as "captain of the host."

14. It is now very widely recognized among critical biblical scholars that Isa 1–39 and 40–66 were written by different authors, working centuries apart. The audience of chaps. 1–39 consists of Judeans under Assyrian threat in the eight century BCE; that of chaps. 40–66 consists of a group of Babylonian exiles in the sixth century BCE (for a brief discussion of the history of the authorship question, see Richard J. Clifford, "Isaiah, Book of [Second Isaiah]," *ABD* 3:490–91). But even within chaps. 1–39 there are materials that seem to date from a later era, including the so-called "Little Apocalypse" (Isa 24–27). On the difficulty of dating this unit of text, see William R. Millar, "Isaiah 24–27 [Little Apocalypse]," *ABD* 3:488–90). On the use of an ancient Near Eastern myth in Isa 24:21–23, see Gaster, "Host," *Encyclopaedia Judaica,* 2nd ed., 9:567.

15. The term "angelomorphic" has been used by scholars in recent years to signify the influence of angel traditions on a given ancient portrayal of Jesus or other human or divine entities. The term, which means literally "having angelic form," is useful because it stops short of saying that the portrayed being actually *is* an angel. So, for example, in Rev 1 the author describes the risen Jesus in angelomorphic terms—using images culled from portrayals of angels in Ezekiel and Daniel—but does not explicitly claim that Jesus is an angel.

16. The discussion of Gal 4:14 is based on Charles A. Gieschen, *Angelomorphic Christology: Antecedents and Early Evidence* [Leiden: Brill, 1998]), 315–25.

17. See works cited in n. 7 above. Collections of testimonies include Sophy Burnham, *A Book of Angels: Reflections on Angels Past and Present and True Stories of How They Touch Our Lives* (New York: Ballantine, 1990); Joan Wester Anderson, *Where Angels Walk: True Stories of Heavenly Visitors* (New York: Ballantine, 1993); J. Anderson, *In the Arms of Angels: True Stories of Heavenly Guardians* (Chicago: Loyola, 2004).

18. David F. Ford, *The Shape of Living: Spiritual Directions for Everyday Life* (Grand Rapids: Baker Book House, 1998), 34.

19. Frank Peretti's novels include *This Present Darkness* (Westchester, Ill.: Crossway Books, 1986), and *Piercing the Darkness* (Westchester, Ill.: Crossway Books, 1989). The reader reviews of Peretti's works at the Amazon Web site are revealing of the power and influence the works have had for many readers.

20. Robert Wuthnow (*After Heaven,* 115) writes of the "legacy of spirituality within congregations and families that supplies the underlying models for these experiences." Wuthnow's chapter "Angel Awakenings" (in ibid., 114–41) gives an insightful overview and sociological analysis of the recent boom of popular interest in angels, and shows how this interest relates to larger trends in American spirituality.

21. For Peretti's works, see n. 19 above. LaHaye and Jenkins have co-authored the phenomenally popular Left Behind series, published by Tyndale House.

22. The First (Solomon's) Temple in Jerusalem was destroyed by the Babylonians in 586 BCE. The Second Temple was rededicated around in 515 BCE, substantially remodeled by Herod the Great beginning around 19 BCE, and destroyed by the Romans in 70 CE. So, in this book, references to the period of the Second Temple designate the interval from 515 BCE to 70 CE.

CHAPTER 1: AGENTS OF HEALING, MESSENGERS OF TRUTH

1. Martha Beck, *Expecting Adam* (New York: Times Books, 1999). I classify this book with what I term the "angelic self-help" books. These books, which flooded the marketplace in the 1990s, advocate that readers tune in to the angels alleged to be present on every side to make use of the angels' therapeutic power and, generally, to improve the quality of readers' lives. For several other titles that fall into this category, see Introduction, n. 7. Beck's book differs insofar as she couches her remarks in the form of an extended first-person narrative, and does not lay out steps or procedures for tapping into angel power. But with its therapeutic emphasis, its use of the conversion paradigm to characterize her shift from ignorance of spiritual presences to awareness of them, and its descriptions of the sort of things those spiritual beings do, the book resembles the self-help books. Today Beck works as a life coach and contributes a monthly column to *O: The Oprah Magazine*.

2. Richard Paul Evans, *The Christmas Box* (New York: Simon & Schuster, 1993).

3. A plaster inscription dating to the eighth century BCE, discovered at Tell Deir Alla in Jordan, "relates that Balaam, son of Beor, a 'seer of the gods,' receives an upsetting night visit from the gods and then reports to his people that he has seen a divine council meeting where impending disaster is apparently planned for the earth" (Jo Ann Hackett, critical notes to the book of Numbers, in *HCSB*, 245 [note to Num 22:2–24:25]). The Balaam story in Num 22–24 combines elements from various sources, resulting in some tension and apparent contradictions. For example, in Num 22 the LORD seems repeatedly to change his mind about whether or not Balaam should answer the call from the king of Moab (22:12–19: no, Balaam should not answer; v. 20: yes, he should answer, but do only what the Lord tells him; v. 22: he should not have answered). Negative traditions that accused Balaam of inciting apostasy are reflected at Num 31:8, 16, and additional references and allusions to Balaam and also to the incident at Peor are made in several other scriptural passages (see Jo Ann Hackett, "Balaam," *ABD* 1:569–72). Hackett points out that Philo, Josephus, Pseudo-Philo, and several New Testament authors all appraise Balaam negatively.

4. The Hebrew word for "adversary" is *satan;* it is the same word that will eventually be read as a proper name for the archfiend and adversary of God, Satan; see Chapter 4. On the term LORD (written in small caps), see Introduction, n. 11.

5. Michael S. Moore makes the suggestion that Balaam's rod may have been a divining rod; the word has magical connotations in some other biblical passages, such as Exod 4:2–4 (*Balaam Traditions: Their Character and Development* [Atlanta: Scholars, 1990], 102–3). On Balaam's shift from seeing to knowing, see George Savran, "Beastly Speech: Intertextuality, Balaam's Ass and the Garden of Eden," *Journal for the Study of the Old Testament* 64 (1994): 47–48.

6. The angel of the LORD appears to Hagar (Gen 16:7–11; 21:17), Abraham (Gen 22:11–15), Jacob (Gen 32:24–30), Moses and the people of Israel (Exod 3:2; 14:19; 23:23; 32:34), Balaam (Num 22:23–35), Joshua (Judg 2:1–4), Deborah (Judg 5:23), Gideon (Judg 6:11–12), Manoah and his wife (Judg 13:3–21), David (1 Chr 21:15–29), Elijah (1 Kgs 19:7; 2 Kgs 1:3, 15), Hezekiah (2 Kgs 19:35), Haggai (Hag 1:13), Zechariah (Zech 1–6), and Daniel (Dan 3:28). This list is taken from Stephen F. Noll, *Angels of Light, Powers of Darkness: Thinking Biblically about Angels, Satan, and Principalities* (Downers Grove, Ill.: InterVarsity, 1998), 40; Noll includes in the list passages referring to the "angel of God"

and passages where YHWH refers to "my angel," as well as the story of Jacob's wrestling with the "man" (never called an "angel" in the text). Charles A. Gieschen (*Angelomorphic Christology: Antecedents and Early Evidence* [Leiden: Brill, 1998]) recognizes, with many scholars, the variability of the traditions about the angel of the LORD in the Hebrew Scriptures: in some passages this angel seems nearly identical to the LORD, but in others, the angel is portrayed as a mediator distinct from God. But Gieschen makes the further important point that Jews around the turn of the Common Era (and likewise early Christians) did not recognize this variability, but, instead, tended to read all traditions about the angel of the LORD as referring to an angel who was distinct from God but who possessed full divine authority and power. Gieschen sees Exod 23:20–21 as an important influence in the shaping of this interpretive convention (ibid., 56–57).

7. See Timothy R. Ashley *The Book of Numbers* (Grand Rapids: Eerdmans, 1993), 456. Ashley suggests that the angel was there, not to prevent Balaam from going, but to make sure that he understood that without the LORD's inspiration he could not "see" anything (ibid., 459).

8. On what can be inferred from the biblical texts about the supposed appearance of the angel of the LORD, see Gieschen, *Angelomorphic Christology,* 58–61.

9. Note the use of first-person speech, and the promise of offspring. Compare Gen 15:4–5, where it is not an angel but the LORD who makes a similar promise to Abraham, there called Abram.

10. This position, held by Hermann Gunkel and a number of scholars since, is described in Claus Westermann, *Genesis 12–36* (Minneapolis: Augsburg, 1985), 243.

11. Gerhard von Rad, *"angelos," TDNT* 1:77. For a brief overview of types of explanatory theories, see Gieschen, *Angelomorphic Christology,* 53–57.

12. Carol A. Newsom, "Angels: Old Testament," *ABD* 1:250. Newsom cautions that the perspective was not "a dogmatic belief of ancient Israelite religion": in other narratives God does converse with humans (as in Gen 15; Exod 24:9–11), and in still others the LORD and his angel are consistently distinguished (as in 1 Kgs 19).

13. James L. Kugel, *The God of Old: Inside the Lost World of the Bible* (New York: The Free Press, 2003), 34. Kugel also comments, "One almost has the impression that these biblical narratives attest to an awareness that the 'angel' they speak of is really a construct, one might even say a literary device. What an 'angel' really *is,* these texts are saying, is a way of reporting that God Himself appeared to someone in human form, or more precisely, in what *at first looked like human form*" (ibid., 31; cf. 34–35).

14. Brevard S. Childs (*The Book of Exodus* [Philadelphia: Westminster, 1974], 76) writes, "God announces that his intentions will be revealed in his future acts, which he now refuses to explain." Hendrikus Berkhof (*Christian Faith: An Introduction to the Study of the Faith* [Grand Rapids: Eerdmans, 1979], 107) remarks that, on the one hand, God's answer to Moses is "an evasive tautology of one who himself wants to remain subject and lord and refuses to be manipulated"; on the other hand, "this name also contains a promise: 'I shall be with you,' and you will experience my saving presence."

15. According to Exod 33:11, the LORD did speak to Moses "face to face," but David Noel Freedman and B. E. Willoughby remark that "the context clearly indicates that the manifestation of the divine presence here was the function of the 'pillar of cloud' (vv. 9, 10). The entire narrative emphasizes as forcefully as possible that any direct experience of God is fatal for a human being, even for Moses, and that this experience must be mediated by a mitigation of such immediacy" (*"mal'āk," TDOT* 8:321).

16. Berkhof (*Christian Faith,* 52; cf. 107) cites Calvin's *Institutes* I.x.2; I.xi; I.xiii.1 and passim for Calvin's point that God engages in divine accommodation to our human nature; God uses pedagogical means analogous to a mother's lisping (talking baby talk) to her child (I,xiii,1).

17. Michael Welker, "Angels in the Biblical Tradition," *Theology Today* 51 (1994): 369–70.

18. Newsom, "Angels," *ABD* 1:250.

19. See also Exod 23:20; 32:34; 33:2; Num 20:16; Isa 63:9; Mal 3:1.

20. Mary Farrell Bednarowski, *The Religious Imagination of American Women* (Bloomington: Indiana University Press, 1999), 47.

21. Terry Lynn Taylor, *Guardians of Hope: The Angels' Guide to Personal Growth* (Tiburon, Calif.: H J Kramer, 1992).

22. Neale Donald Walsch, *Friendship with God: An Uncommon Dialogue* (New York: G. P. Putnam's Sons, 1999), 5–13.

23. Here, I am influenced especially by Kathryn Tanner, *God and Creation in Christian Theology: Tyranny or Empowerment?* (Oxford: Basil Blackwell, 1988). For a brief description of Tanner's argument see Introduction, n. 6.

24. For helpful introductions to prophecy in the ancient Near East, the preexilic and postexilic Hebrew tradition, and early Christianity, see the several articles included under "prophecy" in *ABD* 5:477–502. Passages referring to a "spirit" possessed by leaders and prophets include Num 24:2–3; Judg 3:10; Isa 11:2; 42:1; 61:1; Ezek 2:2; Joel 2:28–29; Hag 1:14; 2:5; Zech 4:6; 7:12; for the transmission of such "spirit" to others, see Num 11:24–29; 1 Sam 10:5–10; 19:18–24; 2 Kgs 2:9–15.

25. Conversely, false prophets were those who had *not* stood in the divine council. For prophets (or false prophets) and the divine council, see especially Isa 6:1–8; Jer 23:18, 22; Dan 7:9–14; Zech 3. Other passages making reference to the divine council include Pss 29:1; 82; 89:6–9 (ET 5–8); Job 1:6–12; 2:1–7; 15:8; Dan 7:9–14. For general background see E. T. Mullen, "Divine Assembly," *ABD* 2:214–17. On how beliefs about the divine council served as backdrop to beliefs about angels, see Darrell D. Hannah, *Michael and Christ: Michael Traditions and Angel Christology in Early Christianity* (Tübingen: Mohr [Siebeck], 1999), 17–19. Hannah shows how, according to the depiction in the Hebrew Scriptures, the angels' service to God "in many ways parallels the humans servants of an ancient oriental potentate." Thus, angels form the armies of the LORD, occasionally act as intercessors and mediators on behalf of humanity, and serve as delegates in administration of the nations—all roles paralleling roles of the servants of ancient kings. On the portrayal of some prophets with angelic traits in the Second Temple era, see Crispin H. T. Fletcher-Louis, *Luke-Acts: Angels, Christology, and Soteriology* (Tübingen: Mohr [Siebeck], 1997), 129–37.

26. Dreams or visions interpreted by revealing angels occur, for example, at Ezek 40:3–4; Zech 1–6; *4 Ezra;* Rev 17; 21:9–22:6, 8, 16. The word "apocalyptic" comes from the Greek word *apokalypsis,* meaning "revelation," and is used to characterize a type of writing (and a corresponding worldview) in which heavenly secrets are specially revealed to persons of God's choosing.

27. For an introduction to the Hellenistic philosophical background and Jewish and early Christian usage of the term *logos* or "word," see Thomas H. Tobin, "Logos," *ABD* 4:348–56.

28. Justin Martyr identified the angel of the LORD with the pre-incarnate Christ; see

Gieschen, *Angelomorphic Christology,* 187–200; Hannah, *Michael and Christ,* 111–13; more generally on early angelomorphic Christology, see Richard N. Longenecker, "Some Distinctive Early Christological Motifs," *New Testament Studies* 14 (1967–68): 526–45; Christopher Rowland, *Christian Origins: An Account of the Setting and Character of the Most Important Messianic Sect of Judaism* (2nd ed.; London: SPCK, 2002), 32–36. David Keck (*Angels and Angelology in the Middle Ages* [New York: Oxford University Press, 1998], 35) notes that in the early church, identification of the Angel of the LORD with Christ "became an essential ingredient of anti-Jewish polemics."

29. On the prevalence in early Jewish thinking of ideas about a chief angelic mediator, see Larry W. Hurtado, *One God, One Lord: Early Christian Devotion and Ancient Jewish Monotheism* (Philadelphia: Fortress, 1988), especially 71–92; Gieschen, *Angelomorphic Christology;* Alan F. Segal, *Paul the Convert: The Apostolate and Apostasy of Saul the Pharisee* (New Haven: Yale University Press, 1990), 40–52. On the influence of angelomorphic traditions on early Jewish and Christian ideas about the "word," see Gieschen, *Angelomorphic Christology,* 103–14; for example, Gieschen argues, the portrayal of the word as eschatological judge in Rev 19:11–16 (cf. Heb 4:12–13) seems to build on or to parallel Wis 18:14–16, in which the word is named as the destroyer who carried out the tenth plague against the Egyptians in the Exodus. Wisdom's portrayal of this sword-bearing word echoes scriptural traditions about the angel of the LORD as warrior or destroyer (see especially 1 Chr 21:15–16 [ibid., 105–6]). See also Hannah, *Michael and Christ,* 187–200. On angelomorphic Christology in the writings of Justin and other patristic authors, see n. 28 above.

30. See Welker, "Angels in the Biblical Tradition," 372–74.

31. Beck, *Expecting Adam,* 288–89.

32. Robert N. Bellah et al., *Habits of the Heart: Individualism and Commitment in American Life* (Berkeley: University of California Press, 1985), especially chap. 3. Quotation taken from p. 84.

33. Ibid., 84.

34. On the "legacy of spirituality within congregations and families that supplies the underlying models" for angel experiences, see Robert Wuthnow, *After Heaven: Spirituality in America since the 1950s* (Berkeley: University of California Press, 1998), 115.

35. Representative titles are given in Introduction, n. 7.

36. Alma Daniel, Timothy Wyllie, and Andrew Ramer, *Ask Your Angels* (New York: Ballantine, 1992), 252.

37. To say that the focus in such works is on the self-actualization of individuals is not to say that such individuals necessarily act in a self-centered way: Beck, for example, was led by her experiences to pursue a career in which she helps others to achieve self-actualization. Rather, the point is that the angels in the self-help literature generally deal directly with individuals to help them achieve their personal, self-defined aims, rather than dealing with whole communities and leading people to see how their very existence and destiny depend on meaningful relationships with others past and present.

38. Kugel (*God of Old,* 37–46) points out that the figures to whom the angel of the LORD appears in the older parts of the Hebrew Bible are portrayed neither as seeking a divine epiphany nor as especially deserving of one, though later Jewish authors tried to make them out as such. The earlier biblical authors portray God as one who "simply buttonholes people and starts speaking" (ibid., 44). But it is a mistake to infer, as Kugel seems to do, that the lack of moral desert or active seeking by these figures means that the biblical authors

thought God appeared to "just anyone" (ibid., 45). Deserving or not, the figures in question are all still *representative* figures, larger than life for the authors and their earliest readers.

39. Significantly, the two named angels, Michael and Gabriel, first appear in the book of Daniel (Dan 8:16; 9:21; 10:13, 21; and 12:1), which, according to many scholars, was not written until late in the Second Temple period (see the discussion in Chapter 2, n. 43). Additionally, the angel Raphael appears in the book of Tobit, which belongs to the collection of Jewish writings known to Protestants as the Apocrypha of the Old Testament. (These fourteen books of the Septuagint [an ancient Greek version of the Jewish Scriptures] are included in the Vulgate [a standard early Latin translation] but not in the Jewish canon of Scripture. They are considered deuterocanonical Scripture by the Roman Catholic and the Greek and Russian Orthodox churches but noncanonical by the Protestant churches.) Michael and Gabriel are mentioned in the New Testament: see Luke 1:11, 19, 26; Jude 9; and Rev 12:7. Regarding possible influence from Zoroastrianism on developing Jewish angelology, see D. S. Russell, *The Method and Message of Jewish Apocalyptic* (Philadelphia: Westminster, 1964), 258–62. Jews came into contact with Persian culture beginning at the time of the deportation of the North Israelite tribes by Sargon II, when some of the exiled were placed in the cities of Media (2 Kgs 17:6). In 550 BCE, the Babylonian kingdom fell to Cyrus, founder of the Achaemenian (first Persian) empire, and from 538 BCE until the conquest of Alexander in 330 BCE, the Jews were subjects of the Persians. Although direct Persian influence in Palestine ceased with the conquest of Alexander the Great, after about 150 BCE (when the Parthians occupied Mesopotamia) Jews in some cities of that region were living side by side with Persians. Influence could have been mediated to Palestine by Jews returning from such diaspora communities. For further discussion of when and how Persian influence on Judaism may have occurred, see Geo Widengren, "Iran and Israel in Parthian Times with Special Regard to the Ethiopic Book of Enoch," *Religious Syncretism in Antiquity* (ed. Birger A. Pearson; Missoula, Mont.: Scholars, 1975), 85–129.

40. Newsom, "Angels," *ABD* 1:249, citing John J. Collins, *The Apocalyptic Vision of the Book of Daniel* (Missoula, Mont.: Scholars, 1977), 101–4. Martin Hengel (*Judaism and Hellenism: Studies in Their Encounter in Palestine during the Early Hellenistic Period* [2 vols.; Philadelphia: Fortress, 1974], 1:231–34) does not find arguments about Zoroastrian influence to be helpful or persuasive, and appeals instead to conceptions from Canaanite popular religion that were "adopted, transformed and systematized" (ibid., 232). Kugel (*God of Old*, 193–195) contends that "the appearance of a wholly new sort of angel" (namely, "real divine humanoids with specific names and functions") was a consequence of the increasing emphasis in the closing centuries of the biblical period on the remoteness of God. Angels filled in the gap.

41. See the helpful introduction and notes to Tobit by George W. E. Nickelsburg, in *HCSB*, 1293–1312.

42. Raphael reveals his identity privately before Tobit and Tobias, but not before any of the female characters. No contact is depicted between the angel and the women in the story (from the note by George Nickelsburg to Tob 12:6–10, *HCSB*). This careful delimitation of Raphael's appearances solely to men shows how cultural expectations of that era influenced the portrayal of angels.

43. On notions of angelic hierarchy, see especially pp. 124, 147, 154.

44. For the book's view of the righteous life, see Tob 1:3–22 and 4:3–21. Almsgiving or charity is mentioned at 1:3, 7, 16–17; 2:2; 4:7–11, 16; 12:8–10; 14:2, 8–9, 10–11.

45. Sarah's piety is not as celebrated as that of her future father-in-law, but she is, in any case, sexually pure and undeserving of her disgrace (Tob 3:14–15). The portrayal of Sarah's marriages to seven relatives "seems to be derived from the case of the daughters of Zelophehad in which there was no male heir to guarantee the retention of ancestral property (Num 27:5–11; 36:2–12)" (Irene Nowell, "Tobit," *New Jerome Biblical Commentary* [Englewood Cliffs, N.J.: Prentice-Hall, 1990], 570). Sarah is her father's only child, his only heir (3:15); if she were to marry an outsider the family property would presumably be merged with that of her new family.

46. See Tob 4:12–13, where Tobit exhorts Tobias to "marry a woman from among the descendants of your ancestors; do not marry a foreign woman, who is not of your father's tribe" (see also 1:9; 6:12–13, 16; 7:10, and the preceding note).

47. On the motif of blindness and sight in Mark see Susan R. Garrett, *The Temptations of Jesus in Mark's Gospel* (Grand Rapids: Eerdmans, 1998), 63–66 and passim.

48. Fletcher-Louis, *Luke-Acts,* 34–38.

49. Ibid., 38–50.

50. John E. Alsup, *The Post-Resurrection Appearance Stories of the Gospel Tradition: A History-of-Tradition Analysis with Text-Synopsis* (Stuttgart: Calwer-Verlag, 1975), 265. Quoted in Fletcher-Louis, *Luke-Acts,* 62.

51. Ibid., 63.

52. On the ways in which the Damascus Road story resembles an angelophany, see ibid., 55–56.

53. The NRSV has "rubbish" where I have translated "dung." The Greek *skybalon* regularly means excrement or filth; "rubbish" is a euphemism.

54. David F. Ford, *The Shape of Living: Spiritual Directions for Everyday Life* (Grand Rapids: Baker Book House, 1998), 36. Ford uses the metaphor repeatedly; he has drawn it from a poem entitled "Out of the Blue," by Micheal O'Siadhail.

55. Fletcher-Louis, *Luke-Acts,* 63–70.

56. See Barbara Mark and Trudy Griswold, *Angelspeake: How to Talk with Your Angels* (New York: Simon & Schuster, 1995), 36. Mark and Griswold identify "asking" as one of the "Four Fundamentals for Living Successfully" (i.e., in partnership with one's angels). The other three Fundamentals are "Believe," "Keep Your Mouth Shut," and "Say Thank You" (ibid., 34).

57. Henri J. M. Nouwen, *Bread for the Journey: A Daybook of Wisdom and Faith* (San Francisco: HarperSanFrancisco, 1997), entry for April 20.

58. Ford, *Shape of Living,* 169.

59. Ibid., 170.

CHAPTER 2: ANGELS AT THE THRONE

1. Robert Wuthnow, "To Dwell or To Seek: Where and How Do We Find Spirituality in Our Lives?" *In Trust* (New Year 1999): 14. The article draws from Wuthnow, *After Heaven: Spirituality in America since the 1950s* (Berkeley: University of California Press, 1998). In both book and article, Wuthnow contrasts the model of spirituality as "seeking"—so popular today—with the model dominant in America through the 1950s, of spirituality as "habitation." Where the habitation model dominates, God is more likely to be sought and found in established religious communities. See also Wuthnow's discussion of religious "shoppers," who affirm that truth may be found in many religions, in his book

America and the Challenges of Religious Diversity (Princeton: Princeton University Press, 2005), especially 106–29. On the antipathy toward established religion exhibited by many practitioners of channeling and other alternative forms of spirituality, see the astute comments of Michael F. Brown in *The Channeling Zone: American Spirituality in an Anxious Age* (Cambridge: Harvard University Press, 1997), 115–41.

2. Eugene Taylor, "Desperately Seeking Spirituality," *Psychology Today* (November/ December, 1994): 58; see also Marci McDonald, "The New Spirituality," *McLeans* (October 10, 1994): 44–48.

3. Eileen Elias Freeman, *Touched by Angels: True Cases of Close Encounters of the Celestial Kind* (New York: Warner Books, 1993), 5–10.

4. Ibid., 18–19.

5. Ibid., 23.

6. Betty J. Eadie, *Embraced by the Light* (reprint ed.; New York: Bantam, 1994), 41.

7. Ibid., 45.

8. Ibid., 68.

9. Ibid., 147.

10. Alma Daniel, Timothy Wyllie, and Andrew Ramer, *Ask Your Angels* (New York: Ballantine, 1992), 101–209. Other books that offer ways to communicate with angels include Launa Huffines, *Healing Yourself with Light: How to Connect with the Angelic Healers* (Tiburon, Calif.: H J Kramer, 1995); Kim O'Neill, *How to Talk with Your Angels* (New York: Avon Books, 1995); Barbara Mark and Trudy Griswold, *Angelspeake: How to Talk with Your Angels* (New York: Simon & Schuster, 1995); Doreen Virtue, *Divine Guidance: How to Have a Dialogue with God and Your Guardian Angels* (Los Angeles: Renaissance Books, 1998); Ambika Wauters, *The Angel Oracle: Working with the Angels for Guidance, Inspiration and Love* (New York: St. Martin's, 1995); Denny Sargent, *Your Guardian Angel and You* (Boston: Weiser Books, 2004).

11. Daniel et al., *Ask Your Angels,* 69; cf. Eadie, *Embraced by the Light,* 44, 97; Neale Donald Walsch, *Friendship with God: An Uncommon Dialogue* (New York: G. P. Putnam's Sons, 1999), 47.

12. Daniel et al., *Ask Your Angels,* 168. On the notion of the Higher Self as presupposed in various forms of New Age and occult thinking, see online: http://en.wikipedia .org/wiki/Higher_Self.

13. The goals and presuppositions about communicating with angels made in Daniel et al., *Ask Your Angels* (and in other self-help books about angels) are closely related to those associated with the phenomenon of channeling. It is impossible to say just how many people across the United States and around the world are involved in channeling, either as practitioners or as consumers, though the numbers are probably higher than one might suppose and may be growing. Figures supplied by Amazon.com indicate brisk sales for books about channeling or communicating with angels and other spirit-entities, as well as for books claiming to convey the message of channeled entitities (such as *A Course in Miracles* [Tiburon, Calif.: Foundation for Inner Peace, 1995], by Helen Schucman, who claimed to be channeling Jesus Christ). In general on channeling, see Brown, *Channeling Zone;* on the ambiguous identity of channeled entities (angel? Higher Self? Ascended Master? collective unconscious? etc.), see ibid., 21, 36, 72, 87.

14. David Spangler, "The Movement toward the Divine," in *New Age Spirituality: An Assessment* (ed. Duncan S. Ferguson; Louisville: Westminster John Knox, 1993), 94. Spangler, who is himself a noted New Age philosopher, offers a incisive critique of the

"undiscerning borrowing" by many popular New Age authors of the concept of God found in the Eastern mystical traditions. In the Eastern context, Spangler observes, "God is beyond all phenomena: the No-Thing or nothingness about which nothing can be said. In this context, to attain God-consciousness in a mystical sense is to disappear as a phenomenal, isolated, individuated self separate from all the rest of creation, whereas in the West we would tend to see this state as a universal self, the ultimate individuation, the cosmos as person and the person as cosmos" (93). On the dialectic or tension between angels as interior and exterior to the self, see p. 150.

15. Walsch, *Friendship with God*, 23, 75. The divinity of the self is a fundamental premise in much popular spiritual writing. Michael F. Brown writes, "The first and most important theological postulate of channeling is that human beings are in essence gods" (*Channeling Zone*, 47; cf. 176).

16. Spangler, "Movement," 94.

17. Kurt Rudolph, "Gnosticism," *ABD* 2:1033. For introductions to gnostic writings and to ancient gnosticism, see ibid., 1033–40; see also Bentley Layton, *The Gnostic Scriptures: A New Translation with Annotations and Introduction* (Garden City, N.Y.: Doubleday, 1987), 5–22.

18. According to noted theosophist-writer-lecturer Stephan A. Hoeller, "Most of the New Age and 'alternative' religious movements have roots in gnostic ideas, whether their participants know it or not" (quoted in an interview by Brendan Mullen, "To Know God: A post-New Age dialogue with Dr. Stephan Hoeller," *LA Weekly*, May 7–13, 1999; online: http://www.laweekly.com/general/features/to-know-god/11959/). Two informative treatments of the transmission of ancient gnostic ideas to New Age thinking are Stephan A. Hoeller, "Angels, Holy and Unholy: The Gnostic Alternative to Mainstream Angelology," in *Angels and Mortals: Their Co-Creative Power* (ed. Maria Parise; Wheaten, Ill.: Quest Books, 1990), 97–105; and Harold Bloom, *Omens of Millennium: The Gnosis of Angels, Dreams, and Resurrection* (New York: Riverhead Books, 1996), especially 173–215.

19. Eadie, *Embraced by the Light*, 113, 115.

20. On the possible allusion to a ziggurat, see Terence E. Fretheim, "Genesis," *NIB* 1:541.

21. *Frg. Targum Neophyti* (MS P), Gen 28:12, quoted from James L. Kugel, *Traditions of the Bible: A Guide to the Bible as It Was at the Start of the Common Era* (Cambridge, Mass.: Harvard University Press, 1998), 364. On the likely origin of the tradition that Jacob's bust was carved on the divine throne, see ibid., 374–75. The tradition about angels ascending from and descending to Jacob is likely reflected in John 1:50–51, where Jesus says to Nathanael, "Very truly, I tell you, you will see heaven opened and the angels of God ascending and descending upon the Son of man."

22. James L. Kugel (*The God of Old: Inside the Lost World of the Bible* [New York: The Free Press, 2003]) argues that the close proximity of the mundane and spiritual realms (and the permeability of the boundary separating them) is a significant theme in the oldest characterizations of God in the Hebrew Bible: "The spiritual is not something tidy and distinct, another order of being. Instead it is perfectly capable of intruding into everyday reality, as if part of this world. It is not just 'in here'; it is also out there, a presence, looming" (ibid., 36).

23. The Hebrew of Gen 28:13 leaves the LORD's precise location vis-à-vis Jacob ambiguous; the NIV translates "There above it [i.e. above the stairway or ladder] stood the LORD," whereas the NRSV translates "And the LORD stood beside him." Fretheim observes

that "the immediacy of the deity's communication to Jacob" supports the NRSV's rendering (*NIB* 1:541).

24. See Gen 28:13–15; cf. 13:16; 15:5.

25. Kugel, *The God of Old,* 44.

26. The last two lines allude to Gen 35:9–5, in which "God appeared to Jacob again when he came from Paddan-aram, and he blessed him."

27. See the interesting discussion of Ps 139 in Kugel, *The God of Old,* 64–70. Kugel argues that the psalm falls short of presenting God as omnipresent: "Instead, it seems to present a deity who is, in some inexplicable way, both here and there (or able to zip around the universe so fast that the speaker cannot outrun Him): 'If I could go to the sky, there You would be, or down to Sheol, there You are too'" (ibid., 65).

28. *Prayer of Joseph* (trans. Jonathan Z. Smith, *OTP* 2:713), which survives only in fragments, "maintains that the patriarch Jacob was the earthly incarnation of the angel Israel," and "concerns a conflict between the angels Israel and Uriel over their relative rank in heaven" (idem, "Introduction to *Prayer of Joseph*," *OTP* 2:699). The document may have been written in the first century CE, but is certainly no later than early third century CE (ibid., 700). Smith suggests that, in making such grandiose assertions about Jacob/Israel, the author of the *Prayer of Joseph* (and other ancient authors who made similar claims about Jacob, including Philo) built on Gen 32:28, where God confers the name "Israel" on Jacob, and on texts such as Exod 4:22, where "Israel" is referred to collectively in a way that might suggest existence in heaven from time immemorial (ibid., 701–3; see also Charles A. Gieschen, *Angelomorphic Christology: Antecedents and Early Evidence* [Leiden: Brill, 1998], 137–42; Christopher Rowland, *Christian Origins: An Account of the Setting and Character of the Most Important Messianic Sect of Judaism* [2nd ed.; London: SPCK, 2002], 34–36).

29. The roots of merkabah mysticism go back at least to Paul's day. See Alan F. Segal's discussion, "Merkabah and Its Predecessors," in *Paul the Convert: The Apostolate and Apostasy of Saul the Pharisee* (New Haven: Yale University Press, 1990), 40–52; also Gershom Scholem, "Merkabah Mysticism," *Encyclopaedia Judaica* (22 vols; 2nd edition; Detroit: Macmillan Reference USA), 14:66–67. An important treatment of merkabah interpretation is David J. Halperin, *The Faces of the Chariot: Early Jewish Responses to Ezekiel's Vision* (Tübingen: Mohr), 1988.

30. Ibid., 3.

31. Jon D. Levenson, *Resurrection and the Restoration of Israel: The Ultimate Victory of the God of Life* (New Haven: Yale University Press, 2006), 85. The quotation refers to Ezekiel's oracle in 28:11–19, about the fall of the Phoenician city-state of Tyre: here Ezekiel identifies the Temple on "God's holy mountain" with "Eden the garden of God." In ibid., 82–107, Levenson traces the strong associations of the Temple with paradise in Ezekiel and the Psalms, arguing that the theme would have had resonance throughout the cultures of the ancient Near East.

32. For a brief discussion of these and other such theological questions raised by the first phase of the Exile, see Robert R. Wilson, "Ezekiel," *HBC,* 583–86.

33. See Ezek 3:22; 8:1; 37:1; 40:1; 1 Kgs 18:46.

34. Wilson, "Ezekiel," *HBC,* 592.

35. Cover of the Ark of the Covenant: Exod 25:18–22; 37:7–9; 1 Sam 4:4; 2 Sam 6:2. Solomon's Temple: 1 Kgs 6:23–28; 8:6–7. It is surprising that Ezekiel identifies the living creatures as cherubim, because ancient sources indicate that cherubim looked different.

Cherubim take the sphinxlike shape of winged monsters with *animal* bodies and *human* faces, whereas according to Ezek 1, the living creatures have *human* bodies and *animal* faces. See the discussion in Halperin, *Faces of the Chariot*, 39–44. Halperin holds to a theory of the composite authorship of Ezekiel, and sees the identification of the living creatures (*hayyot*) and cherubim as deriving from a secondary author. He writes, "Given that so much of chapter 10 was written to interpret chapter 1, it seems to me . . . likely that the *hayyot* = cherubim equation was made by someone who was baffled by the *hayyot* and needed a context in which he could make sense of them. He found this context in the Jerusalem Temple" (ibid., 43).

36. The narrative in the first part of Ezek 10 is difficult to follow. The author seems to distinguish between the pair of statues standing in the Holy of Holies (9:3a; 10:4a) and the "real" cherubim of 10:1–2, 5–22, and to suggest that "as God's glory abandons its position above the replica, the real thing arrives—its appearance signaled by the sound of the cherubim's wings (v. 5)—ready to transport the glory as needed" (Katheryn Pfisterer Darr, "Ezekiel," *NIB* 6:1183 [citing D. I. Block and Moshe Greenberg]).

37. For a helpful discussion of the ancient Semitic notion that the earthly sanctuary follows a heavenly pattern or replicates a heavenly temple, see Harold W. Attridge, *Hebrews* (Philadelphia: Fortress, 1989), 222–24. In the New Testament, the books of Hebrews and Revelation build heavily on such a notion of correspondence between the earthly and heavenly sanctuaries.

38. David Halperin explains that the extant Hebrew (Masoretic) text of Ezek 3:12–13 preserves a very ancient textual alteration that enhances the impression of the living creatures and cherubim as antiphonal angelic choirs. Modern translations tend to obscure this impression, by correcting the text back to what many commentators agree must have been the original form (*Faces of the Chariot*, 44–45). Halperin explains further that the author of Ezek 10:9–17 (whom he holds to be distinct from the author of Ezek 1) expands the role and identity of the *ofannim*, wheels, depicting them as separate angelic beings (ibid., 45–46). Later, in the New Testament book of Revelation, the seer John will compare the voice of multitudes that sing hymns before God to the sound made by the wings of the *ofannim* (see Rev 14:1–3; 19:6).

39. Other attributes of God sometimes described in ways that make them sound like angelic beings are *wisdom, word, spirit, power,* and *name.* Charles Gieschen uses the word "hypostasis" (defined as "an aspect of the deity that is depicted with independent personhood of varying degrees") for the ancient sources' angel-like portrayals of divine attributes. An hypostasis "shares the nature, authority, and will of the deity since it remains an aspect of deity" (*Angelomorphic Christology*, 45). Gieschen's discussion of the hypostases in ancient sources is extensive and helpful (ibid., 70–123).

40. See also Exod 16:10; 33:18–23; 40:34; Num 20:6; Pss 24:7–10; 78:60–61.

41. See also Ezek 10:4; 28:22; 43:2–5.

42. Segal, *Paul the Convert*, 42; cf. Gieschen, *Angelomorphic Christology*, 80–84.

43. The Hebrew/Aramaic book of Daniel had probably reached its present form around 164 BCE, though some of the materials in it are older. This dating, widely accepted by critical commentators, is based on the observation that the book recounts events of the reign of Antiochus Epiphanes correctly up to a point, but in chap. 11 gives a mistaken prophecy of his death (John J. Collins, "Daniel, Book of," *ABD* 2:30–31).

44. It is common to capitalize the designation "son of man" when it is being used as a Christological title; hence the NRSV usually capitalizes it in the New Testament but not

in the Old. In Daniel, the absence of the definite article and the use of the word "like" before "son of man" suggest that the designation is here descriptive rather than titular. Regarding the enthronement of this figure in Daniel, see John J. Collins, *Daniel* (Minneapolis: Fortress, 1993), 300–301; also Christopher Rowland, "The Vision of the Risen Christ in Rev. i.13ff.: The Debt of Early Christology to an Aspect of Jewish Angelology," *Journal of Theological Studies* 31 (1980): 2. Regarding the identification of the "one like a son of man" in Dan 7 with an angel, or specifically with Michael, see Collins, *Daniel*, 304–10 (especially p. 310); see also Darrell D. Hannah, *Michael and Christ: Michael Traditions and Angel Christology in Early Christianity* (Tübingen: Mohr [Siebeck], 1999), 34–35. In Dan 10, there appears a glorious angel who resembles Ezekiel's "likeness of the glory of the Lord"; concerning the influence of Ezek 1 on this portrayal, see Collins, *Daniel*, 306; Rowland, "Vision," 3.

45. Segal, *Paul the Convert*, 41–43.

46. Ibid. On Philo's depiction of the "word" or "spirit" as an angel-like being, see Gieschen, *Angelomorphic Christology*, 107–12; Hannah, *Michael and Christ*, 77–90; John R. Levison, "The Prophetic Spirit as an Angel According to Philo," *Harvard Theological Review* 88 (1995): 189–207.

47. Segal, *Paul the Convert*, 47. See also the important work by Carey C. Newman, *Paul's Glory-Christology: Tradition and Rhetoric* (Leiden: Brill, 1992); for a summary of Paul's views on "the Glory," see especially pp. 241–47. In the course of his analysis, Newman provides thorough discussion of the term "glory" as "part of the characteristic field of signifiers used to describe the heavens" in Jewish apocalypses. He observes that "when a seer peers into the heavens, he sees Glory—be it associated with God, a throne, or angels" (ibid., 91). He argues that Ezek 1 strongly influenced the importance of the "glory" as signifier in such discussions (ibid., 92–104).

48. See the discussion in ibid., 229–35; also Gieschen, *Angelomorphic Christology*, 333–37.

49. Ibid., 248; see also Rowland, "Vision"; Loren T. Stuckenbruck, *Angel Veneration and Christology: A Study in Early Judaism and in the Christology of the Apocalypse of John* (Tübingen: Mohr, 1995).

50. Here the name given to Jesus—the "name that is above every name"—is surely to be understood not as "Jesus" but as "Yhwh," the very name of God. Segal (*Paul the Convert*, 62) writes, "We have seen that sharing in the divine name is a recurring motif of early Jewish apocalypticism, where the principal angelic mediator of God is or carries the name Yahweh, as Exod 23 describes the angel of God" (cf. Gieschen, *Angelomorphic Christology*, 339).

51. Gieschen, *Angelomorphic Christology*, 273–75; Gieschen argues that such identification of Jesus with the glory of God also underlies John 5:19–47 (note especially v. 44). See also Hannah, *Michael and Christ*, 149, 172.

52. Words of the hymn "Let All Mortal Flesh Keep Silence" quoted from *The Presbyterian Hymnal: Hymns, Psalms, and Spiritual Songs* (Louisville: Westminster John Knox, 1990), #5.

53. Regarding this consistent pattern in New Testament portrayals of Jesus (spanning the Gospels, epistles, and other writings), see Luke Timothy Johnson, *The Real Jesus: The Misguided Quest for the Historical Jesus and the Truth of the Traditional Gospels* (San Francisco: HarperSanFrancisco, 1996), 141–66; also Johnson, *Living Jesus: Learning the Heart of the Gospel* (San Francisco: HarperSanFrancisco, 1999), 199–201. Johnson's analysis is used

effectively by Miroslav Volf, *Exclusion and Embrace: A Theological Exploration of Identity, Otherness, and Reconciliation* (Nashville: Abingdon, 1996), especially pp. 24 and 30.

54. Jürgen Moltmann, "In the End Is My Beginning: A Hope for Life—A Life for Hope" (address given at Louisville Presbyterian Theological Seminary, April, 2000), 6. Cf. Michael Welker's comments on God's "withdrawal" and "finitization of self" in the person of Yhwh's angel, in "Angels in the Biblical Traditions," *Theology Today* 51 (1994): 369–70.

55. Ralph Harper, *On Presence: Variations and Reflections* (Philadelphia: Trinity Press International, 1991), 108.

56. Barbara Mark and Trudy Griswold, *The Angelspeake Book of Prayer and Healing* (New York: Simon & Schuster, 1997), 47.

57. *The Dead Sea Scrolls in English* (trans. G. Vermes; 3rd edition; London: Penguin, 1987), 192. The Dead Sea Scrolls are a collection of Hebrew, Aramaic, and Greek manuscripts discovered between 1947 and 1956 along the northwestern coast of the Dead Sea in Israel. Most of the scholars who study the Scrolls associate them with an ancient sectarian community that lived at Khirbet Qumran, which was destroyed by the Romans in 68 ce, though some dispute this theory. Whatever their origin, the Scrolls offer evidence of many important aspects of Jewish thought around the turn of the Common Era.

58. The theme that life inevitably unfolds according to a master plan is widely attested in recent popular writings on the topic of spirituality, including works such as James Redfield's best-selling *The Celestine Prophecy: An Adventure* (New York: Warner Books, 1993), which makes no claim or pretense of allegiance to Christian doctrine. And yet this idea of the "master plan" seems to be drawn directly from Christian theology, with its most important source being Paul's remark at Rom 8:28, taken out of context.

59. Moltmann, "In the End," 11–12.

60. Howard Storm, *My Descent into Death: A Second Chance at Life* (New York: Doubleday, 2005), 112.

61. Victor C. Pfitzner, "Worshipping with the Angels," *Lutheran Theological Journal* 29 (1995): 50. Space limitations prevent me from discussing the role of angels in Christian worship of the patristic and medieval periods; on this, see Jean Daniélou, *The Angels and Their Mission* (reprint ed.; trans. David Heimann; Westminster, Md.: Christian Classics, 1991), 55–67; David Keck, *Angels and Angelology in the Middle Ages* (New York: Oxford University Press, 1998), 37, 54.

62. Clark Carlton, *The Faith: Understanding Orthodox Christianity: An Orthodox Catechism* (Salisbury, Mass.: Regina Orthodox Press, 1997), 211.

63. Ibid., 211–12.

64. George A. Maloney, *Gold, Frankincense, and Myrrh: An Introduction to Eastern Christian Spirituality* (New York: Crossroad, 1997), 140.

65. 1QH 3.21–22, quoted from *The Dead Sea Scrolls in English* (3rd ed.; trans. Geza Vermes; London: Penguin, 1987), 64–65.

66. Martha Himmelfarb, *Ascent to Heaven in Jewish and Christian Apocalypses* (New York: Oxford University Press, 1993), 48–49. On the Dead Sea Sectarians' beliefs about earthly fellowship with angels, see Maxwell J. Davidson, *Angels at Qumran: A Comparative Study of 1 Enoch 1–36, 72–108 and Sectarian Writings from Qumran* (Sheffield: JSOT, 1992), esp. 316–19; also Crispin H. T. Fletcher-Louis, *All the Glory of Adam: Liturgical Anthropology in the Dead Sea Scrolls* (Leiden: Brill, 2002). See pp. 223–32 for further discussion on this topic.

67. Carol A. Newsom, "Job," *NIB* 4:347.

68. For further background on ancient notions of the divine council, see Chapter 1, n. 25, and the works cited there. The Canaanite (Ugaritic) myths are known to us from texts preserved on clay tablets in the Ugaritic language. On the possible origin of angels in Canaanite mythology, see Lowell K. Handy, "Dissenting Deities or Obedient Angels: Divine Hierarchies in Ugarit and the Bible," *Biblical Research* 35 (1990): 18–35. Handy argues that the angels of the biblical tradition are not demoted deities from the middle tiers of the Canaanite hierarchy of gods; rather, biblical angels correspond directly to the Canaanite messenger-deities (the lowest tier in the Canaanite pantheon).

69. Himmelfarb, *Ascent to Heaven,* 11–13. According to Ezekiel, God's "return to a fixed dwelling awaits the temple of the eschatological future" (ibid., 12; see Ezek 40–48).

70. *Testament of Levi,* trans. H. C. Kee, *OTP* 1:1789. For more on this passage, see Himmelfarb, *Ascent to Heaven,* 34–35. She thinks that the "pleasing odor" or "sweet savor" is intended to suggest that the heavenly sacrifices are both like and unlike earthly ones: "The sweet savor is the most ethereal product of the sacrifices performed on earth; in heaven it becomes the sacrifice itself" (35).

71. The translation is by James R. Davila, *Liturgical Works* (Grand Rapids: Eerdmans, 2000), 97. Square brackets indicate places in the original manuscript where characters are missing or illegible.

72. Some have suggested that Paul fears something like angelic sexual attack upon the women, along the lines laid down in Gen 6:1–4. The Genesis passage tells of "sons of God" who came to earth and mated with human women (for further discussion of the Genesis text, see Chapter 3). But Antoinette Clark Wire (*The Corinthian Women Prophets: A Reconstruction through Paul's Rhetoric* [Minneapolis: Fortress, 1990], 121–22) argues that Paul is concerned, rather, with the deflecting of glory away from God. She cites the notion, evident in some ancient rabbinic texts, that when the angels tried to worship Adam, God stopped them from doing so because worship is due God alone. Paul may fear that if women remain uncovered, the angels will be tempted to worship man, whose glory (in Paul's understanding) woman reflects (see 1 Cor 11:7). Wire writes, "The danger is not only that human males will be drawn away from the praise of God's glory toward their own glory reflected in women but even the angels will be enticed to defect."

73. *Testament of Job* 48:2–3, trans. R. P. Spittler, *OTP* 1:866.

74. Wire, *Corinthian Women Prophets,* 127. On the portrayal of women in the *Testament of Job,* see Susan R. Garrett, "The Weaker Sex in the *Testament of Job*," *Journal of Biblical Literature* 112 (1993): 55–70.

75. In some ancient Jewish accounts of the ascension of biblical heroes to heaven, they are transformed into angels. For example, *2 Enoch* contains a striking account of Enoch's transformation, which Himmelfarb sees as a heavenly version of priestly investiture: after Michael anoints him and clothes him in glorious garments, Enoch reports "I looked at myself, and I was like one of the glorious ones, and there was no apparent difference" (*2 En.* 9:19; quoted from Himmelfarb, *Ascent to Heaven,* 40; see further her discussion of "transformation and the righteous dead," ibid., 47–71; see also James H. Charlesworth, "The Portrayal of the Righteous as an Angel," *Ideal Figures in Ancient Judaism: Profiles and Paradigms* [ed. John J. Collins and George W. E. Nickelsburg; Chico, Calif.: Scholars, 1980], 135–51; Alan F. Segal, *Life After Death: A History of the Afterlife in the Religions of the West* [New York: Doubleday, 2004], 356–59 and passim). The idea of human transfor-

mation to angelic existence as it developed in Judaism in the Second Temple era and in early Christianity will be discussed more fully in Chapter 6.

76. In *1 Enoch*, also, the prayers (as well as the blood) of the righteous ascend to heaven, "where they are joined by the prayers of the angels in heaven" (Himmelfarb, *Ascent to Heaven*, 60, referring to *1 En.* 47, a part of the document that probably dates from the first century CE).

77. Here I follow Robert M. Royalty, Jr., "Dwelling on Visions: On the Nature of the So-Called 'Colossians Heresy,'" *Biblica* 83 (2002): 329–57. Royalty reviews various theories about the identity of the heretics of Col 2:18. The passage has long been controversial; the ambiguous Greek (*thrēskeia tōn aggelōn*) could refer either to believers' worship of angels or to the believers' participation with angels in the heavenly worship of God. My own inclination is to assume that the heretics are claiming access to view or participate in the angelic liturgy in heaven.

78. Marta Vogel, "Looking for Reverence in All the Wrong Pews," *Washington Post*, May 11, 1997.

79. Laurie Zoloth-Dorfman, "Traveling with Children: Mothering and the Ethics of the Ordinary World," *Tikkun* 10:4 (1995): 26 (quoted in Mary Farrell Bednarowski, *The Religious Imagination of American Women* [Bloomington: Indiana University Press, 1999], 103).

80. Brown (*Channeling Zone*, 58–59) traces the distrust of rules and established systems of morality back to nineteenth-century Spiritualists. On the ambivalence of channelers (and by extension practitioners of other alternate forms of spirituality) toward established community and communal worship, see ibid., 115–41. The preference of many seekers for individualism over community is also a prominent theme in Wuthnow, *After Heaven*.

81. Medieval authors viewed the cherubim and seraphim—the two highest tiers of the presumed angelic hierarchy—as representing respectively the roles of knowledge and love in assisting the believer on the mystic path toward union with God. In his helpful review of this long discussion within the medieval tradition of "angelic spirituality," Stephen Chase (*Angelic Spirituality: Medieval Perspectives on the Ways of Angels* [New York: Paulist, 2002], 48–56) notes that the tendency was to assign priority to the path of the heart: the seraphim (representing love) are closer to God than the cherubim (representing knowledge). But love, it was noted, must be tempered by various kinds of knowledge and discernment. For more about the medieval tradition of "angelic spirituality," see pp. 149–53.

82. The appearance of Jesus to Paul is recounted in Acts 9, 22, and 26 in ways that recall angelic epiphanies; see Crispin H. T. Fletcher-Louis, *Luke-Acts: Angels, Christology, and Soteriology* (Tübingen: Mohr [Siebeck], 1997), 50–57. On Paul as mystic, and on connections between his experiences and early merkabah mysticism, see Segal, *Paul the Convert*, 34–71; Gieschen, *Angelomorphic Christology*, 321–22; Christopher R. A. Morray-Jones, "Paradise Revisited (2 Cor 12:1–12): The Jewish Mystical Background of Paul's Apostolate," *Harvard Theological Review* 86 (1993): 177–217, 265–92. Morray-Jones argues that the vision recounted in Acts 22:17–22 is the same one recounted in 2 Cor 12:2–4. Some ancient texts presume that heaven has seven levels, others that it has three. Morray-Jones argues that when Paul mentions his ascension to the "third heaven," he means it as the highest level.

83. See N. T. Wright, "Reflected Glory: 2 Corinthians 3.18," in *The Climax of the Covenant: Christ and the Law in Pauline Theology* (Minneapolis: Fortress, 1991), 175–92. Col

3:9–15, likewise, connects the taking on of God's image to the transformation of human relationships in community. On "new creation," see Susan R. Garrett, "New Creation," *Dictionary of Feminist Theologies* (ed. Letty M. Russell and J. Shannon Clarkson; Louisville: Westminster John Knox, 1996), 192–93.

84. Harper, *On Presence,* 74.

85. Volf, *Exclusion and Embrace,* 26.

86. Ibid., 26.

87. See Susan R. Garrett, "The Patience of Job and the Patience of Jesus," *Interpretation* 53 (1999): 254–64; also S. Garrett, *The Temptation of Jesus in Mark's Gospel* (Grand Rapids: Eerdmans, 1998), 89–99, 130–33.

88. On the noncanonical apocalypses ascribed to these and other ancient worthies, see Himmelfarb, *Ascent to Heaven.* For more about apocalyptic visions of the afterlife, see pp. 199–202, 205. Note that the Psalms portray persons as entering into God's presence in the *earthly* Temple (on this theme, see n. 31).

89. For the metaphor, see Harper, *On Presence,* 18–19.

CHAPTER 3: FALLING ANGELS

1. David F. Ford, *The Shape of Living: Spiritual Directions for Everyday Life* (Grand Rapids: Baker Books, 1997), 52.

2. Regarding the angelic advice to "BE SPECIFIC AND ASK BIG," see Chapter 1, n. 56.

3. Neale Donald Walsch, *Friendship with God: An Uncommon Dialogue* (New York: G. P. Putnam's Sons, 1999), 25–35.

4. *Wings of Desire,* produced by Wim Wenders and Anatole Dauman, directed by Wim Wenders, 128 minutes, 1987; *City of Angels,* produced by Charles Roven and Dawn Steel, directed by Brad Silberling, 115 minutes, 1998; *Michael,* produced by Ethan Coen, directed by Nora Ephron, 106 minutes, 1996; *The Preacher's Wife,* produced by Debra Martin Chase, directed by Penny Marshall, 124 minutes, 1996. Two other angel films are worthy of mention here: *In The Prophecy* (produced by Joel Soisson, directed by Gregory Widen, 1995), the angel Gabriel, played by Christopher Walken, envies and hates human beings because of their preferred status with God. In *Dogma* (produced by Scott Mosier, directed by Kevin Smith, 130 minutes, 1999), angels played by Matt Damon and Ben Affleck do not exhibit a desire for human pleasures, rather, they are conniving to get back into heaven, from which they have been expelled.

5. *The Bishop's Wife,* produced by Samuel Goldwyn and directed by Henry Koster, 109 minutes, 1948.

6. *1 Enoch* 5:9; cf. *Jubilees* 10:1–6.

7. *Testament of Reuben* 5:1–6.

8. Note that the 120-year limit that God here imposes on human life is not observed in the rest of the story; Noah lived to be 950 years old (see Gen 9:29).

9. Gerhard von Rad, *Genesis: A Commentary* (trans. John H. Marks; Philadelphia: Westminster, 1961), 110.

10. Dale B. Martin, *The Corinthian Body* (New Haven: Yale University Press, 1995), 21. Where ancients did argue for a body/soul dualism (in the various forms of Platonism, for example), what they meant by the key terms in such discussions "differed considerably from what we moderns mean by such terms" (ibid., 3). Martin traces the physical/spiritual (or body/soul) dualism in its modern sense to the work of René Descartes (ibid.,

3–6). Descartes entertained but rejected the notion (ironically the premise of many ancient theorists) "that the soul may be 'something extremely rare and subtile, like wind, or flame, or ether, spread through my grosser parts.' " In Descartes' view, the soul or "I" "is not corporeal and can have no participation in the physical, material, or natural realm" (ibid., 5). On medieval discussions of angels' nature (whether they are composed of form and matter, or of form alone), see David Keck, *Angels and Angelology in the Middle Ages* (New York: Oxford University Press, 1998), 93–99.

11. *1 En.* 15:6, trans. E. Isaac, *OTP* 1:21. His translation of *1 Enoch* is used throughout this chapter.

12. Conversely, spiritual teachers may identify the chief symptom of separation as an obsessive quest for bodily pleasures to the exclusion of all interest in spiritual matters. In general on separation, Michael F. Brown (*The Channeling Zone: American Spirituality in An Anxious Age* [Cambridge, Mass.: Harvard University Press, 1997], 58) writes, "Among channels [persons who channel spirits], separation carries the emotional resonance that sin holds for evangelical Christians. Separation causes us to lose sight of our oneness with the divine, thus furthering a destructive internal alienation." Wouter J. Hanegraaff (*New Age Religion and Western Culture: Esotericism in the Mirror of Secular Thought* [Albany: State University of New York Press, 1998], 119–20) describes the quest for holism in New Age thought as "among the most central concerns of the New Age movement." The nonholistic views that are opposed boil down to two categories, according to Hanegraaff: *dualism* (especially between Creator and creation; man and nature; and spirit and matter) and *reductionism* ("associated with the scientific revolution and the spirit of modern rationalism").

13. Divine knowledge was at stake already in the Garden of Eden. There Adam and Eve defied God's ban on the fruit of the tree of the knowledge of good and evil. If they ate of it, God feared, their new knowledge would make them too much like God.

14. The theme of revelation is complicated in *1 En.* 6–11 by the fact that this section of the text incorporates two or more originally distinct traditions. The name of the leader of the rebellious angels is sometimes given as Semihazah, and sometimes as Azazel; the content of their respective revelations and the extent to which humans are said to have collaborated with them varies in the two traditions. See Carol A. Newsom, "The Development of *1 Enoch* 6–19: Cosmology and Judgment," *Catholic Biblical Quarterly* 42 (1980): 313–14.

15. George W. E. Nickelsburg, *1 Enoch 1: A Commentary on the Book of 1 Enoch*, Chapters 1–36; 81–108 (ed. Klaus Baltzer; Minneapolis: Fortress, 2001), 42.

16. Stephan A. Hoeller, "Angels, Holy and Unholy: The Gnostic Alternative to Mainstream Angelology," in *Angels and Mortals: Their Co-Creative Power* (ed. Maria Parisen; Wheaton, Ill.: Quest Books, 1990), 100.

17. Betty J. Eadie, *Embraced by the Light* (Reprint ed.; New York: Bantam, 1994); Howard Storm, *My Descent into Death: A Second Chance at Life* (New York: Doubleday, 2005). Both books are discussed in Chapter 2.

18. Dr. Michael Abrams, *The Evolution Angel: An Emergency Physician's Lessons with Death and the Divine* (Boulder: Abundance Media, 2000), 7.

19. Ibid., 19.

20. Ibid., 14.

21. Ibid., 20.

22. Ibid., 38.

23. These chapters in *1 Enoch* are unmistakably a combination of separate, still-earlier traditions; see Newsom, "Development," 310–29. For helpful scholarly analysis of ancient retellings of the angelic fall in *1 Enoch* and other texts, see Henry Ansgar Kelly, *The Devil, Demonology, and Witchcraft: The Development of Christian Beliefs in Evil Spirits* (rev. ed.; Garden City, N.Y.: Doubleday, 1974), 26–31, 36–38, 47–48, 128; James L. Kugel, *The Bible As It Was* (Cambridge, Mass.: Belknap/Harvard University Press, 1997), 107–16; D. S. Russell, *The Method and Message of Jewish Apocalyptic* (Philadelphia: Westminster, 1964), 249–54; James C. VanderKam, "1 Enoch, Enochic Motifs, and Enoch in Early Christian Literature," in *The Jewish Apocalyptic Heritage in Early Christianity* (ed. James C. VanderKam and William Adler; Assen: Van Gorcum; Minneapolis: Fortress, 1996), 60–88.

24. On the link in ancient Canaanite culture between the stars and the pantheon of gods, see Introduction, n. 12. On *1 En.* 18:14–19:1, see Newsom, "Development," 323.

25. The verse echoes *1 En.* 10:4–6, 12–14; 12:4; 14:5; 15:2–10 (VanderKam, "1 Enoch," 63; VanderKam also analyzes use of the angel story in 1 and 2 Peter).

26. Cf. Newsom, "Development," 315.

27. Gary A. Anderson, *The Genesis of Perfection: Adam and Eve in Jewish and Christian Imagination* (Louisville: Westminster John Knox, 2001), 30.

28. The pictures in Isa 14 and Ezek 28–32 of "the royal mount of dominion and the dry pit at its base where are hurled the rebels against God's authority" has apparently influenced *1 En.* 17–19, in which Enoch witnesses the dry pit where errant stars and angels are punished (Newsom, "Development," 327). Paul D. Hanson ("Rebellion in Heaven, Azazel, and Euhemeristic Heroes in *1 Enoch* 6–11," *Journal of Biblical Literature* 96 [1977]: 195–233), argues for a close connection between the rebellion and punishment of the angels in *1 En.* 6–11 and the rebellion and punishment of rebellious rulers (compared to celestial beings) in Isa 14 and Ezek 28–32. Hanson points out that the description of the netherworld in Ezek 32:27 as populated by "the fallen mighty heroes of antiquity" directs one explicitly to the primeval heroes of Gen 6:4, part of the text being interpreted by *1 En.* 6–11.

29. In the text of Job 1–2 in the Hebrew Bible, the term *satan* has the definite article and likely refers to a particular role ("the adversary") rather than being a proper name. But in the century or so before the turn of the Common Era, this figure began to be viewed by many Jews as a distinct individual with the name "Satan." The term "devil" is a translation of the Greek *diabolos,* which means "slanderer." *Diabolos* was used in the Septuagint (the ancient Greek translation of the Hebrew Scriptures) as a rendering of *satan.* In the New Testament both terms are used for the one character without any apparent nuance of distinction. On the evolution of the character Satan, see the works cited in n. 30.

30. For Satan's effort to entice Jesus to worship him, see Matt 4:8–9; Luke 4:6–7. For fuller discussion of developing ideas about the fall of the angels and of Satan, see Kelly, *Devil, Demonology, and Witchcraft,* 26–31, 34–38, 47–48; Kelly, "The Devil in the Desert," *Catholic Biblical Quarterly* 26 [1964]: 190–220, esp. 202–13; Neil Forsyth, *The Old Enemy: Satan and the Combat Myth* (Princeton: Princeton University Press, 1987).

31. See G. Anderson, *Genesis of Perfection,* 21–41. For patristic variations on the theme of the angels' envy of humans, see Jean Daniélou, *The Angels and Their Mission* (trans. David Heimann; Westminster, Md.: Christian Classics [reprint ed.], 1991), 45–51. Daniélou notes that for patristic authors, the Ascension appears as the counterpart of the

fall: "The jealousy of the angels had caused the expulsion of man from Paradise; their rejoicing greets the restoration of humanity in Paradise" (47).

32. *Life of Adam and Eve,* trans. M. D. Johnson, *OTP* 2:262.

33. G. Anderson, *Genesis of Perfection,* 32–35.

34. Newsom, "Development," 324–25; cf. Martha Himmelfarb, *Ascent to Heaven in Jewish and Christian Apocalypses* (New York: Oxford University Press, 1993), 72–94.

35. The Book of the Heavenly Luminaries is constituted by *1 En.* 72–82, and is dated ca. 110 BCE according to "the consensus of critical scholars" (Isaac, "Introduction to *1 Enoch,*" *OTP* 1:7).

36. More specifically, for some early readers of *1 Enoch* the portrayal of the fallen angels pointed to what was wrong with the Jerusalem priesthood, perceived as corrupt and defiled. See Himmelfarb, *Ascent to Heaven,* 20–22; Nickelsburg, *1 Enoch 1:* "A myth of heavenly rebellion has become, in part, an indictment of human sin, specifically, the defilement of the Jerusalem priesthood and its cult" (46–47). This defilement consisted partly in the practice of exogamy: Jewish priests marrying Gentiles are like the angels marrying human women. See further Crispin H. T. Fletcher-Louis, *Luke-Acts: Angels, Christology, and Soteriology* (Tübingen: Mohr [Siebeck], 1997), 169.

37. Philo writes at length about desire in his treatment of the tenth commandment, "Thou shalt not covet" (*On the Special Laws* 4.79–94; in the Greek translation of the Scriptures used by Philo, the word "covet" [*epithymeo*] is the verbal form of the word for "desire" [*epithymia*]).

38. For a brief but helpful treatment of ancient views of desire or lust (Gk. *epithymia*) see Luke T. Johnson, *The Letter of James* (New York: Doubleday, 1995), 193–94. On the role of desire in temptation, see ibid.; see also Susan R. Garrett, *The Temptations of Jesus in Mark's Gospel* (Grand Rapids: Eerdmans, 1998), esp. 96–99. An important and very full discussion of ancient views of desire and other passions is Martha C. Nussbaum, *The Therapy of Desire: Theory and Practice in Hellenistic Ethics* (Princeton: Princeton University Press, 1994). Shorter but illuminating discussions regarding ancient beliefs about the danger of desire and the need for self-mastery include Martin, *Corinthian Body,* 198–228; Stanley K. Stowers, *A Rereading of Romans: Justice, Jews, and Gentiles* (New Haven: Yale University, 1994), 42–82.

39. Dio Chrysostom, *Discourses,* trans. J. W. Cohoon, LCL.

40. Martin, *Corinthian Body,* 213.

41. Ibid., 212.

42. Ibid., 214 (citing Soranus, *Gynecology* 1.9.35).

43. On the testing of Abraham by Mastema (a Satan-figure), see *Jub.* 17:15–18:19; for a lengthy retelling of the trials of Job (elaborating on Satan's role), see the *Testament of Job,* especially 27:1–7.

44. Seth has learned that if he literally falls to the earth, he will become human. So, standing at the edge of a tall building, arms outstretched, he leans forward and allows himself to fall to the ground. At impact he cuts his lip and *bleeds*—the first indication that his effort to incarnate has succeeded.

45. Augustine, *The Confessions* 1.1 (ed. John E. Rotelle; trans., introduction, and notes by Maria Boulding; Hyde Park, N.Y.: New City Press, 1997), 39.

46. For an interesting discussion of this contradiction described by Augustine and his interpreter Blaise Pascal, see David Dawson, "Why Are We So Indifferent about Our Spiritual Lives?" in *Why Are We Here? Everyday Questions and the Spiritual Life* (ed. Ronald F.

Thieman and William C. Placher; Harrisburg: Trinity Press International, 1998), 17–39. Following Pascal, Dawson suggests that indifference about one's spiritual life and the endless search for diversions are actually a form of desire: "To be spiritually indifferent is not to care one way or another about our own lives, but instead *to care* about everything else. We turn outward to the things around us and away from ourselves as we are; paradoxically, we become careless by multiplying our cares (I originally typed in the phrase 'multiplying our cars,' which, for the upper-middle-class suburb I live in, may drive the point home especially well)" (23–24; italics original). See also the interesting work by Wendy Farley, *The Wounding and Healing of Desire: Weaving Heaven and Earth* (Louisville: Westminster John Knox, 2005). Influenced by the great Christian women writers of medieval Europe and also by Buddhist philosophy and practice, Farley downplays individual sin, and stresses, instead, the ways that our lack of self-knowledge and ignorance of our true situation lead us into bondage and suffering.

47. Here I am paraphrasing a comment made by Brad Silberling in reference to *City of Angels*, which Silberling directed. He made the remark in an interview included on the special edition DVD of the film; he says that he himself borrowed the phrase from painter Andrew Wyeth.

48. Sallie McFague, *Life Abundant: Rethinking Theology and Economy for a Planet in Peril* (Minneapolis: Fortress, 2001), 10.

49. Ibid., 10.

50. Ibid., 12; cf. Farley, *Wounding and Healing of Desire*, 31–34.

51. McFague, *Life Abundant*, 21.

52. Ibid., 21–22.

53. *The Last Temptation of Christ*, produced by Barbara DaFina, directed by Martin Scorsese, 164 minutes, 1988; based on a novel by Nikos Kazantzakis.

54. Throughout this paragraph I am indebted to Kathryn Tanner, *Jesus, Humanity, and the Trinity: A Brief Systematic Theology* (Minneapolis: Fortress, 2001), especially 1–32. Tanner writes, "Jesus is both the Word incarnate and deified or exalted humanity because these are just different descriptions of the same process from different points of view—the one highlighting the agency of the Word in uniting itself with humanity; the other coming at the same process from the flipside of its effect, humanity assumed and thereby perfected" (17).

55. Augustine, *Confessions* 10.6, 8; quoted from Jürgen Moltmann, The *Source of Life: The Holy Spirit and the Theology of Life* (trans. Margaret Kohl; Minneapolis: Fortress, 1997), 87.

56. Moltmann, *The Source of Life*, 71. Cf. McFague, *Life Abundant*, 13. McFague goes further than Moltmann in stressing the incarnation of God throughout creation.

57. Moltmann, *The Source of Life*, 87–88.

58. Ford, *Shape of Living*, 54.

59. For a fuller treatment of how Jesus empowers us to resist temptation, see S. Garrett, *Temptations of Jesus*, especially 159–69.

60. Henri J. M. Nouwen, *Bread for the Journey: A Daybook of Wisdom and Faith* (San Francisco: HarperSanFrancisco, 1997), entry for April 20.

61. McFague, *Life Abundant*, 10.

CHAPTER 4: SATAN AND THE POWERS

1. Cornelius Plantinga, *Engaging God's World: A Reformed Vision of Faith, Learning, and Living* (Grand Rapids: Eerdmans, 2002), 48–49. Plantinga alludes, in part, to Arthur Shopenhauer's description of the human condition. Parts of this chapter follow closely my article "Christ and the Present Evil Age," *Interpretation* 57 (2003): 370–83. The material is used here with permission.

2. The Left Behind series is written by Tim LaHaye and Jerry B. Jenkins and published by Tyndale House. The figure of sixty-two million was taken from David Gates, "The New Prophets of Revelation," *Newsweek* (May 24, 2004): 46. The series has been translated into over twenty languages.

3. Frank Peretti's most influential novels are *This Present Darkness* (Westchester, Ill.: Crossway Books, 1986), and *Piercing the Darkness* (Westchester, Ill.: Crossway Books, 1989). Clinton E. Arnold (*3 Crucial Questions about Spiritual Warfare* [Grand Rapids: Baker, 1997], 31) observes that many Christians take Peretti's works as detailed manuals on demonology.

4. The quotation of LaHaye is from Steve Rabey, "Apocalyptic Sales out of this World," *Christianity Today* 43 (March 1, 1999): 19.

5. Tim LaHaye and Jerry B. Jenkins, *Are We Living in the End Times? Current Events Foretold in Scripture . . . and What They Mean* (Wheaton, Ill.: Tyndale House), 264. The book is an exposition of the theology and defense of the end-times scenario underlying the Left Behind series.

6. Tim LaHaye and Jerry B. Jenkins, *Left Behind: A Novel of the Earth's Last Days* (Wheaton, Ill.: Tyndale House, 1995).

7. Tim LaHaye and Jerry B. Jenkins, *The Indwelling: The Beast Takes Possession* (Wheaton, Ill.: Tyndale House Publishers Inc., 2000), 90.

8. LaHaye and Jenkins, *End Times*, 103.

9. For an exposition of the views of LaHaye and Jenkins on angels, see ibid., 355–62.

10. LaHaye and Jenkins, *The Indwelling*, 244–45.

11. Gershom Gorenberg, "Intolerance: The Bestseller" (Review of the Left Behind series), *The American Prospect* 13:17 (September 23, 2002). Online: http://www.prospect.org/print/V13/17/gorenberg-g.html.

12. The Dallas Theological Seminary Web site includes a full doctrinal statement, which defines "dispensations" as "stewardships by which God administers His purpose on the earth through man under varying responsibilities. . . . We believe that different administrative responsibilities of this character are manifest in the biblical record, that they span the entire history of mankind, and that each ends in the failure of man under the respective test and in an ensuing judgment from God. We believe that three of these dispensations or rules of life are the subject of extended revelation in the Scriptures, viz., the dispensation of the Mosaic law, the present dispensation of grace, and the future dispensation of the millennial kingdom. We believe that these are distinct and are not to be intermingled or confused, as they are chronologically successive." Online: http://www.dts.edu/about/doctrinalstatement/.

13. On Darby's use of the term "Rapture," see Raymond F. Bulman, *The Lure of the Millennium: The Year 2000 and Beyond* (Maryknoll, N.Y.: Orbis Books, 1999), 106. For an explanation of how dispensationalists come up with a figure of seven years for the duration of the Tribulation, see LaHaye and Jenkins, *End Times*, 152–53. The calculation

depends on a presumption that Daniel was written in the sixth century BCE. Many critical scholars today reject the traditional dating and ascription of authorship, concluding, instead, that Daniel was written under a pseudonym ca. 164 BCE (though some of the material in Dan 1–6 may have originated earlier; see Chapter 2, n. 43).

14. For a short biographical treatment of Cyrus Scofield and an assessment of his influence, see John H. Gerstner, *Wrongly Dividing the Word of Truth: A Critique of Dispensationalism* (2nd ed.; Morgan, Pa.: Soli Deo Gloria Publishers, 2000), 40–45. Gerstner offers a brief but helpful discussion of the life and work of John Nelson Darby and the history of dispensationalism, along with trenchant critiques (written from the perspective of conservative, inerrantist Calvinism). For a more irenic critique of dispensationalism (written from the perspective of covenant theology, and taking into account recent variations and modifications of dispensationalism), see Vern S. Poythress, *Understanding Dispensationalists* (2nd ed.; Phillipsburg, N.J.: P. & R. Publishing, 1993). Critiques of the Left Behind books have multiplied in recent years; two excellent treatments are Craig C. Hill, *In God's Time: The Bible and the Future* (Grand Rapids: Eerdmans, 2002); and Barbara Rossing, *The Rapture Exposed: The Message of Hope in the Book of Revelation* (Boulder: Westview, 2004).

15. Bulman, *Lure of the Millennium*, 109–10.

16. On the predicted desecration, see LaHaye and Jenkins, *End Times*, 194. On the history of and reasoning behind conservative (especially dispensationalist) Christian support for Israel and the political ramifications of that support today, see Timothy P. Weber, *On the Road to Armageddon: How Evangelicals Became Israel's Best Friend* (Grand Rapids: Baker Academic, 2004); for a shorter treatment, see Donald E. Wagner, "Short Fuse to Apocalypse?" *Sojourners* 32 (July/August 2003): 20ff.

17. Gorenberg, "Intolerance." Dispensationalism works with a very distinctive (and to the outsider, bewildering) set of hermeneutical principles on the fulfillment of prophecy; for review and critique, see Poythress, *Understanding Dispensationalists;* Gerstner, *Wrongly Dividing the Word of Truth,* 89–111. Gerstner shows that dispensationalists' claim to literal interpretation is problematic, because the literalist hermeneutic is inconsistently applied, and applied where genre considerations make literalism inappropriate. He also shows how dispensationalists' prior presumptions about what will happen in the end times determine their reading of the text (rather than vice versa).

18. Gorenberg, "Intolerance"; cf. Wagner, "Short Fuse to Apocalypse," 47. The book referred to is Tim LaHaye and Jerry B. Jenkins, *The Remnant: On the Brink of Armageddon* (Wheaton, Ill.: Tyndale House, 2002).

19. For a brief theological analysis of the spiritual warfare movement, see Thomas H. McAlpine, *Facing the Powers: What Are the Options?* (Monrovia, Calif.: MARC, 1991), 43–56. Works considered authoritative by insiders in the spiritual warfare movement include Arnold, *3 Crucial Questions;* Ed Murphy, *The Handbook for Spiritual Warfare* (rev. ed.; Nashville: Thomas Nelson Publishers, 1996); Francis Frangipane, *The Three Battlegrounds* (Cedar Rapids, Iowa: Arrow Publications, 1989).

20. Arnold, *3 Crucial Questions,* 19, 27.

21. Consider, for example, the character Bobby in Frank Peretti's novel *This Present Darkness.* Bobby is a drug-addicted rapist whose vices and violent nature are a direct consequence of the many demons who inhabit his body. Once the demons have been expelled, Bobby is miraculously and immediately transformed into an upstanding and trustworthy young man. Peretti's depiction of Bobby disregards any notion of the his-

torical conditioning of behavior by systemic factors such as family and upbringing or the social and cultural environment, and fosters unrealistic expectations concerning the potential ease and speed of recovery. The depiction oversimplifies the causes and cure of human affliction and human evil.

22. So, for example, Frangipane, *Three Battlegrounds,* and Arnold, *3 Crucial Questions.* See Duane A. Garrett, *Angels and the New Spirituality* (Nashville: Broadman & Holman, 1995), chaps. 12 and 13 for astute critiques from an evangelical Christian perspective of the depictions of angels in evangelical novels, the spiritual warfare movement in evangelism, and the writings of Walter Wink.

23. Bernhard W. Anderson, "Sin and the Powers of Chaos," in *Sin, Salvation, and the Spirit* (ed. Daniel Durken; Collegeville, Minn.: Liturgical Press, 1979), 71–72.

24. Ibid., 75–76.

25. Ibid., 77.

26. Ibid., 74.

27. Ibid., 77–78.

28. Habakkuk was probably written sometime between 609 and 597 BCE, when Judah was a vassal state of the Chaldean or Neo-Babylonian Empire. In the year 598, "Nebuchadnezzar deported the new king, Jehoiachin, and leading members of Judean society to Babylon" (Marvin A. Sweeney, "Habakkuk," *HBC,* 668).

29. On the dating of Daniel, see Chapter 2, n. 43.

30. B. Anderson, "Sin and the Powers of Chaos," 80.

31. Ibid., 81.

32. So also, prophets before and after the Exile had drawn on this ancient mythic material. The suggestion in Daniel that the cosmos harbors forces of chaos—pockets of resistance to God's sovereignty—was not a new one. The idea was common in the mythologies of the ancient Near Eastern world, and as Jon D. Levenson has shown, it surfaces with remarkable frequency throughout the Hebrew Scriptures. See his book, *Creation and the Persistence of Evil: The Jewish Drama of Divine Omnipotence* (San Francisco: Harper & Row, 1988).

33. See the discussion in John J. Collins, "The Mythology of Holy War in Daniel and the Qumran War Scroll: A Point of Transition in Jewish Apocalyptic," *Vetus Testamentum* 25:3 (1975): 601.

34. Collins, "Holy War," 601. As Collins observes, the authority of the heavenly figures mentioned in Dan 10:13, 20–21 is strictly coterminous with the boundaries of their respective nations. On the "one like a son of man" as an angel, see Collins, *Daniel* (Minneapolis: Fortress, 1993), 304–10.

35. For a brief discussion of the ancient myths of divine combat as they relate to the development of ideas about Satan, see Susan R. Garrett, *The Temptations of Jesus in Mark's Gospel* (Grand Rapids: Eerdmans, 1998), 32–49. A much longer treatment is by Neil Forsyth, *The Old Enemy: Satan and the Combat Myth* (Princeton: Princeton University Press, 1987), especially 44–66 and 126–30. On elements of combat myths preserved in the Hebrew Scriptures, see Patrick D. Miller, *The Divine Warrior in Early Israel* (Cambridge: Harvard University Press, 1973).

36. David Noel Freedman pointed out to me, in personal correspondence, that in Job 1:22 it is said that Job "did not sin or charge God with wrongdoing"; in chap. 2, however, the declaration is qualified: "Job did not sin with his lips" (2:10). Why the qualification? Moreover, at the end of the book, Job repents in dust and ashes. The implication is that

Job believes he has sinned against God "in his heart," a possibility that concerned him greatly in chap. 1, where he offered penitential sacrifices on his children's behalf, in case they "have sinned, and cursed God in their hearts" (1:5). Job's tirade against God in chap. 3 includes thinly disguised curses aimed at God. Despite these implications that Job did, in fact, sin in his heart, the ancient reading was that Job remained steadfast in his uprightness. For example, in the *Testament of Job* (from around the turn of the Common Era), Job is presented as the model of "patient endurance" (Gk. *hypomonē*).

37. Peggy L. Day (*An Adversary in Heaven:* Śaṭān *in the Hebrew Bible* [Atlanta: Scholars, 1988], 15) has argued that at the time of the composition of these passages, the term *satan* did not refer to a *single* such being, nor to a celestial office. As used in the Scriptures, "the noun *śaṭān* could mean both 'adversary' in general and 'legal accuser' in particular, and it was used to refer to various beings both terrestrial and heavenly when they played either of these adversarial roles." But apparently there was no designated office of "accuser" or "district attorney" in ancient Israel; anyone could assume this role (ibid., 39–40).

38. *Jubilees* 17:16, trans. O. S. Wintermute, *OTP* 2:90 (all quotations of *Jubilees* in this chapter are from Wintermute's translation).

39. See further S. Garrett, *Temptations of Jesus,* 41–42; S. Garrett, "The Patience of Job and the Patience of Jesus," *Interpretation* 53:3 (1999): 254–64; S. Garrett, "Paul's Thorn and Cultural Models of Affliction," in *The Social World of the First Christians: Essays in Honor of Wayne A. Meeks* (ed. L. Michael White and O. Larry Yarbrough; Minneapolis: Fortress, 1995), 82–99; S. Garrett, "The God of This World and the Affliction of Paul: 2 Cor 4:1–12," in *Greeks, Romans, and Christians* (ed. David Balch et al.; Minneapolis: Fortress, 1990), 99–117.

40. On the mythological antecedents of the serpent as portrayed in Gen 3, see K. R. Joines, "The Serpent in Genesis 3," *Zeitschrift für die Alttestamentliche Wissenschaft* 87 (1975): 1–11.

41. In about the first century BCE, the author of Wisdom wrote that "God created us for incorruption, and made us in the image of his own eternity, but through the devil's envy death entered the world" (2:23–24a). Here the reference to creation in God's image points to Adam, and the mention of death's entry into the world alludes to God's pronouncement in Gen 3:19 of the curse that (by common understanding) ended human immortality (see Michael E. Stone, *Fourth Ezra* [Minneapolis: Fortress, 1990], 64–65; for citations of Jewish sources expressing this interpretation of Gen 3:19; see also ibid., 65 n. 26). Some scholars think the allusion to the devil's envy in Wis 2:23–24 refers to the incident with Cain and Abel, but the accompanying reference to creation in God's image more strongly evokes the temptation in the Garden of Eden. In 2 Cor 4:3–4 (cf. 4:6) Paul asserts that the "god of this age" prevents "the perishing" from seeing the light of the good news of the glory of Christ—Christ, "who is the image of God." Paul, like the author of Wisdom, is probably thinking of the story of the devil's envy at God's creation of Adam/ Christ in God's image. Paul may even have known the story (recounted in *Life of Adam and Eve*) about how Satan deceived Eve a second time by appearing to her as an angel of light (see 2 Cor 11:14).

42. The phrase "beautiful presentation" is taken from Ron Rosenbaum, "Staring into the Heart of the Heart of Darkness," *New York Times Magazine* (June 4, 1995), 39. The phrase was used by the Reverend Mark Long, pastor to Susan Smith, who infamously drowned her two young children in a South Carolina lake in 1994. Affirming the reality of free choice between good and evil, Long postulated that on the night when she killed

her children, Susan Smith was witness to two presentations: " 'God made her a presentation and Satan made her a beautiful presentation.' She evaluated them, the pastor believes, and chose Satan's."

43. Dietrich Bonhoeffer, *Creation and Fall, and Temptation: Two Biblical Studies* (New York: Macmillan, 1959), 113.

44. *Fourth Ezra* has been preserved as part of another document, entitled *2 Esdras* (included in the Slavonic Bible as *3 Esdras,* but not found in the Greek; included in the appendix to the Latin Vulgate Bible as *4 Esdras*). See also Stone's commentary, *Fourth Ezra.* In the NRSV, *4 Ezra* = 2 Esdras 3–14.

45. The Greek of this verse is ambiguous at one crucial point: the phrase translated as "because all have sinned" may alternately be translated as "in whom [that is, in Adam] all sinned." Interpreted in the latter fashion, the phrase became a key argument for the doctrine of original or hereditary sin.

46. Hendrikus Berkhof, *Christian Faith: An Introduction to the Study of the Faith* (Grand Rapids: Eerdmans, 1979), 207; cf. 189. Berkhof's two-part discussion of anthropology ("Man: Love and Freedom" and "Man: Guilt and Fate," ibid., 178–210) has influenced my discussion here.

47. F. C. Porter, "The Yeçer Hara," in *Biblical and Semitic Studies: Yale Bicentennial Publications* (New York: Scribner's, 1902), 151–52. Michael Stone stresses *4 Ezra*'s refusal to blame God for the evil heart (Stone, *Fourth Ezra,* 63–64; within *4 Ezra,* see, for example, 3:21; 4:3–4, 30; 7:72; 8:59–60; 9:17–22). See also the insightful discussion of the evil inclination and cosmic adversaries in Levenson, *Creation and the Persistence of Evil,* 38–46.

48. Berkhof, *Christian Faith,* 201. He writes also of the "tragic" dimension of human sin: "That [the human] sin is his own fault; yet there is also something in it of being overpowered, which in the Bible is variously designated as 'God,' 'our being "dust," ' 'slavery,' 'the powers,' or 'the devil' " (ibid., 200; cf. 202). Cf. William C. Placher, *Jesus the Savior: The Meaning of Jesus Christ for Christian Faith* (Louisville: Westminster John Knox, 2001), 145–47.

49. Berkhof, *Christian Faith,* 201.

50. Michael Stone does not think there is any doubt that the "evil heart" of *4 Ezra* is to be identified with the "evil inclination" of the rabbis (*Fourth Ezra,* 63 n. 18; 64 n. 19).

51. The text is from the Community Rule (1QS 3.13–4.14). Pertinent here is John J. Collins' comment on the dualism of the Dead Sea Scrolls: "The single dualism of Light and Darkness is found then on a series of distinct levels—the individual heart, the political and social order, and the cosmic level embracing earth and heaven" ("Patterns of Eschatology at Qumran," in *Traditions in Transformation: Turning Points in Biblical Faith* [ed. Baruch Halpern and Jon D. Levenson; Winona Lake, Indiana: Eisenbrauns, 1981], 365).

52. *Testament of the Twelve Patriarchs,* trans. H. C. Kee, *OTP* 1:817.

53. *Tanḥ, šĕlaḥ-lĕkā* 15 (quoting Ezek 36:27). Quotation taken from Levenson, *Creation and the Persistence of Evil,* 39.

54. See further the discussion of how Jesus resisted the force of desire (and empowers us to do likewise), pp. 97–100.

55. See pp. 86–88; see also the discussion of the relevant traditions from the Hebrew Scriptures, the pseudepigrapha, and the New Testament in Susan R. Garrett, "Exodus from Bondage: Luke 9:31 and Acts 12:1–24," *Catholic Biblical Quarterly* 52 (1990): 666–67, 676–77. On whether this pattern was applied to Satan already in the first century CE, see ibid., 667 n. 42.

56. On early Jewish explanations for the origin and existence of demons, see n. 68. In Zoroastrianism, the evil or Destructive Spirit (Angra Mainyu, or Ahriman) was linked to a host of maleficent powers (Avestan: *daevas*), said to be worshipped by those who choose the Lie rather than Truth. R. C. Zaehner (*The Dawn and Twilight of Zoroastrianism* [New York: G. P. Putnam's Sons, 1961], 39, 154–72 and passim) contends that the *daevas* were pre-Zoroastrian deities who had been demoted to the status of demons. Zoroaster tried to eradicate the cult of the *daevas,* but the cult continued to exist alongside the evolving Zoroastrian movement, which reabsorbed some aspects of it. On the historical circumstances that would have facilitated Zoroastrian influence on developing Jewish thought, see Chapter 1, n. 39.

57. In discussions of possible Zoroastrian influence on Jewish beliefs, a key point of contention has been the date and reliability of the sources. The Pahlavi books, an important source for knowledge of certain Zoroastrian beliefs, were not compiled until the ninth century CE. Inasmuch as Zoroastrianism evolved considerably during the centuries after its founding, it is hard to know from such late sources which doctrines would have been available to the Jews who came in contact with Persians at any given point. But parts of the Avesta (the sacred book of Zoroastrianism) are generally thought to date from Achaemenid times (530–330 BCE). Persian influence, in the form of loanwords and specific doctrines, can be detected already in the later writings of the Hebrew Scriptures. Moreover, for several important doctrinal points, Plutarch's description of Zoroastrianism in *Moralia* 369B–370C (= *Isis and Osiris* 45–47) serves as a check on other, later sources. See David Winston, "The Iranian Component in the Bible, Apocrypha, and Qumran: A Review of the Evidence," *History of Religions* 5:2 [1966]: 186–87); on Plutarch's depiction of Zoroastrianism (from which I have borrowed here) see Collins, "Holy War," 605.

58. For further exposition of this passage, see S. Garrett, "Paul's Thorn."

59. The unresolved tension in the biblical tradition between Satan's roles as servant of God and adversary of God is disturbing to many persons today. Many fundamentalist and evangelical Christians eliminate the tension by emphasizing Satan's identity as archfiend and ignoring the Bible's insistence on his subservience to God. Certainly this is true of the Left Behind series and much of the spiritual warfare literature. As Old Testament scholar Duane Garrett [no relation to the present author] observes, "How quickly we forget that in the Bible, the devil is always under God's authority. It seems that many Christians would rather have a nearly omnipotent Satan than a truly sovereign God." But the Bible insists that nothing—not even Satan—lies outside God's jurisdiction (D. Garrett, *Angels and the New Spirituality,* 232). For further discussion of the tension between Satan as servant and as adversary of God in New Testament portrayals, see S. Garrett, *Temptations of Jesus,* 44–48.

60. For Walter Wink's detailed exegetical study of the relevant terms, see especially the first volume in his trilogy on the powers (*Naming the Powers: The Language of Power in the New Testament* [Philadelphia: Fortress, 1984]).

61. Ibid., 9–10.

62. Ibid., 11–12; see 40–45 for Wink's discussion of 1 Cor 2:6–8.

63. Ibid., 28.

64. Ibid., 12.

65. Though Pseudo-Dionysius' scheme heavily influenced later medieval thinkers, he was not the only or even the first to group the angels hierarchically. Ambrose (fourth

century) had done so, and Gregory the Great (an approximate contemporary of Pseudo-Dionysius) did also, though he may have been dependent on Pseudo-Dionysius. See Steven Chase, *Angelic Spirituality: Medieval Perspectives on the Ways of Angels* (New York: Paulist, 2002), 18–24, 93.

66. For a fuller exposition of this view of Satan's role in the passion account in Luke's Gospel, see Susan R. Garrett, *The Demise of the Devil: Magic and the Demonic in Luke's Writings* (Minneapolis: Fortress, 1989), 46–57.

67. Hendrikus Berkhof (*Christ and the Powers* [trans. John H. Yoder; Scottdale, Pa.: Herald, 1977], 16, 23–26) recognizes that Jewish apocalyptic writings of Paul's time conceive of the powers as "classes of angels located on higher or lower levels in the heavens," who exercise influence on terrestrial events. Berkhof argues that Paul has partly "demythologized" these powers, viewing them not as heavenly angels but as "structures of earthly existence."

68. In *1 En.* 15:8–9, the giants who were the offspring of the union between angels and human women die, and evil spirits come forth from their bodies. In some later versions of the story, the giants are forgotten and the evil spirits are presumed to be the direct offspring of the sons of God and the daughters of men—or are even presumed to be the angels themselves (*Jub.* 10:1–6, but cf. 5:1; Justin Martyr *2 Apology* 5). Centuries later, in John Milton's *Paradise Lost,* the fallen angels take on a twisted appearance, which is a demonic perversion of their former glory. Even today, many Christians refer to demons as "fallen angels." The Dead Sea Scrolls make mention of "evil angels"; their wickedness is explained by reference not to Gen 6:1–4 but to a Zoroastrian-influenced myth relating how, at the beginning of creation, God created two chief spirits—the prince of lights and the angel of darkness—and allotted to the angel of darkness a number of evil spirits who "seek the overthrow of the sons of light" (1QS 3.13–4.14). On Zoroastrian influence on this passage see Collins, "Holy War," 610–11; Michael A. Knibb, *The Qumran Community* (Cambridge: Cambridge University Press, 1987), 96; on Zoroastrian demonology more generally see n. 56 above. For scholarly discussion of the origin of ideas about demons (including discussion of Zoroastrian influence), see Greg J. Riley, "Demon," *DDD,* 235–40. Specifically on ancient traditions about the offspring of the fallen angels, see James C. VanderKam, "1 Enoch, Enochic Motifs, and Enoch in Early Christian Literature," in *The Jewish Apocalyptic Heritage in Early Christianity* (ed. James C. VanderKam and William Adler; Assen: Van Gorcum; Minneapolis: Fortress, 1996), 62–63.

69. For a popular treatment of this view, influenced by process theology, see Gregory Knox Jones, *Play the Ball Where the Monkey Drops It: Why We Suffer and How We Can Hope* (San Francisco: HarperSanFrancisco, 2001), 35–61. For Paul, there was no distinction between natural and moral evil; all could be understood as the work of the powers in the world.

70. With other commentators, I read Rom 8:20 ("For the creation was subjected to futility, not of its own will but by the will of the one who subjected it, in hope") as alluding to the curse that God pronounced after Adam and Eve ate the forbidden fruit (Gen 3:17–19), which was understood by ancient readers to have initiated the onset of death and decay in the world.

71. See Samuel E. Balentine, "For No Reason," *Interpretation* 57 (2003): 349–69.

72. God sends suffering to chastise; see 1 Cor 11:29–30; 2 Cor 12:7; Luke 13:2–5; Rev 3:19. Satan as God's archenemy; see 1 Thess 3:5; Luke 8:12; 2 Cor 6:15; 11:14–15. Satan as God's servant for good; see 1 Cor 5:5; 2 Cor 12:7.

73. In S. Garrett, "Paul's Thorn," the notion of "cultural models" from cognitive anthropology is used to analyze Paul's ad hoc explanations of affliction.

74. See pp. 54–58. Identification of Christ with God's glory is not explicit in the Gospels, but emerges in such places as the Johannine prologue and the Synoptic accounts of the Transfiguration. Although there are scholars who disagree, I believe such ideas were prevalent enough by the time the Gospels were written that all four evangelists must have been aware of them or even taken them for granted.

75. Jesus as firstborn: Rom 8:29; Col 1:15, 18; Heb 1:6; Rev 1:5. As agent in creation: John 1:3; Col 1:16; Heb 1:2, 10. As seated or standing at God's right hand: Matt 26:64; Mark 14:62; 16:19; Luke 22:69; Acts 2:25, 33, 34; 5:31; 7:55–56; Rom 8:34; Eph 1:20; Col 3:1; Heb 1:3, 13; 8:1; 10:12; 12:2; 1 Pet 3:22.

76. Philo, *Questions in Genesis* 4.97. Quotation taken from James L. Kugel, *The Bible As It Was* (Cambridge: Belknap/Harvard University Press, 1999), 54. In ibid., 58–61, Kugel discusses ancient Jewish traditions about which day saw the creation of the angels.

77. On Satan's claim to have preceded Adam in creation, see pp. 87–88.

78. Robert M. Royalty ("Dwelling on Visions: On the Nature of the So-Called 'Colossians Heresy,' " *Biblica* 83 [2002]: 329–57) argues that the emphasis in Colossians on the powers as *already* subject to Christ correlates with the realized eschatology throughout that document, and reflects an ideological struggle going on between the author of that letter and the author of Revelation, who sees the powers' subjugation as still in the future. On the New Testament's expressions regarding Christ's preeminence, see also Richard N. Longenecker, "Some Distinctive Early Christological Motifs," *New Testament Studies* 14 (1967–68): 536–41.

79. See McAlpine, *Facing the Powers,* for a useful survey of how different theological traditions interpret the powers.

80. Bultmann, *Jesus Christ and Mythology* (New York: Charles Scribner's Sons, 1958), 16.

81. Ibid., 20–21.

82. Walter Wink, *The Powers That Be: Theology for a New Millennium* (New York: Galilee, 1999), 3. This book is largely a digest of the third volume of Wink's trilogy on the powers: *Engaging the Powers: Discernment and Resistance in a World of Domination* (Minneapolis: Fortress, 1992). The first book was *Naming the Powers* (see n. 60 above); the second was *Unmasking the Powers: The Invisible Forces That Determine Human Existence* (Philadelphia: Fortress, 1986).

83. Wink, *The Powers That Be,* 31, 34. In his exposition of Christ's unmasking of the powers, Wink draws on Hendrikus Berkhof, who wrote profoundly on this theme. See Berkhof, *Christ and the Powers,* 47–52, especially p. 49. In his work on the theme of the powers, Wink has also been influenced by the writings of William Stringfellow.

84. Wink, *The Powers That Be,* 83.

85. Many spiritual warfare writers refer to "the heavenly places" (or simply "the heavenlies") as the place where Satan and his minions reside and from which they launch their assaults. This assumption derives from a reading of Eph 6:12, which refers to the "the spiritual forces of evil in the heavenly places." Frangipane (*The Three Battlegrounds*) argues that this abode of the powers is not the same as the high heaven, which is "the eternal abode of God, angels, and the redeemed." Rather, the powers' base of operations is a different, second realm, the "spirit world that immediately surrounds and blankets the consciousness of mankind" (ibid., 99). Frangipane is driven to make this distinction by a

theological conviction that the God "in whom there is no darkness" would never "countenance the devil intruding upon the eternal worship, accusing the very church for whom his Son had died" (ibid., 88). For a scholarly discussion of the cosmology of Ephesians, see Nils Alstrup Dahl, "Ephesians," *HBC,* 1215–16. Interestingly, Dahl's reading of the popularized science of Hellenistic culture also suggests that "heavenly places" in these passages (along with the reference to "air" in Eph 2:2) may be designating a presumed lower heavenly sphere. Dahl points out, "The same poetic circumlocution 'in (the) heaven(s)' can, however, also be used about the heavenly throne of God and Christ outside the world of space and time" (ibid., 1215).

86. McAlpine uses the Pogo quote in reference to Wink: "We have met the enemy, and he is us." See his useful summary of Wink's work (*Facing the Powers,* 17–25).

87. Tim LaHaye and Jerry B. Jenkins, *Glorious Appearing: The End of Days* (Wheaton, Ill.: Tyndale House, 2004).

88. See Stephen G. Ray, *Do No Harm: Social Sin and Christian Responsibility* (Minneapolis: Fortress, 2002), 66.

89. This verse (Mark 14:38 [cf. v. 34]) evokes the petition of the Lord's prayer, "Do not bring us into temptation" (Matt 6:13; Luke 11:4). On resisting evil: see also Rom 12:9, 17, 21; Eph 6:16; 1 Pet 3:9–12; 3 John 11. On watching with those who suffer: see also Rom 12:15; 1 Cor 12:26.

90. Mastema appears in the pseudepigraphic book *Jubilees.*

91. Miroslav Volf, *Exclusion and Embrace: A Theological Exploration of Identity, Otherness, and Reconciliation* (Nashville: Abingdon, 1996), 77. On how Christian discipleship de-centers the self and re-centers or remakes it "in the image of 'the Son of God who loved me and gave himself for me,' " see ibid., 69–71. Volf's stunning work has many insights into the workings of the powers (in societies and in psyches), the dynamics of evil, and the Spirit's freeing and re-creative power.

92. But see above, n. 36.

93. Berkhof, *Christ and the Powers,* 39. Berkhof writes that at the cross Christ disarmed the powers by depriving them of their weapon of "the power of illusion, their ability to convince men that they were the divine regents of the world, ultimate certainty and ultimate direction, ultimate happiness and the ultimate duty for small, dependent humanity. Since Christ, we know that this is illusion. We are called to a higher destiny; we have higher orders to follow and we stand under a greater Protector."

94. Berkhof, *Christian Faith,* 202–3; cf. Wendy Farley, *The Wounding and Healing of Desire: Weaving Heaven and Earth* (Louisville: Westminster John Knox, 2005), 73–76 for insightful treatment of the mechanics of seduction and of our consent.

95. Here, the language is borrowed from Luke Timothy Johnson, *Living Jesus: Learning the Heart of the Gospel* (San Francisco: Harper SanFrancisco, 2000), 16.

CHAPTER 5: GUARDIAN ANGELS

1. St. Thomas Aquinas, *Summa Theologiae* (61 vols.; Cambridge: Blackfriars; New York: McGraw-Hill; London: Eyre & Spottiswoode, 1964), 15:59. Subsequent quotations of Thomas are also from this volume.

2. Robert Orsi (*Between Heaven and Earth: The Religious Worlds People Make and the Scholars Who Study Them* [Princeton: Princeton University Press, 2005], 103–6) discusses the close association of guardian angels with children, which he traces back to the

seventeenth century, "when these special beings emerged as protectors of children newly identified as innocent." Orsi notes that the aforementioned image of the angel guarding children on a bridge appeared on a popular Catholic holy card.

3. Carlos M. N. Eire, *War Against the Idols: The Reformation of Worship from Erasmus to Calvin* (Cambridge: Cambridge University Press, 1986), 1.

4. See Gen 19:1–23; 24:7, 40; 1 Kgs 19:5, 7; Ps 91:11–12; Tob 5:4. Even in these passages it is not clear whether the angels are viewed as long-term (birth-to-death) guardians over individuals, or as protectors specially assigned for particular shorter-term missions.

5. RSV translation. The standard text (based on Hebrew [Masoretic] manuscripts from the ninth century CE) actually reads "he fixed the boundaries of the peoples according to the number of the *sons of Israel*" (emphasis added). But the Septuagint (an ancient Greek translation) reads "according to the number of the angels of God," and this ancient variant is supported by a fragment of Deuteronomy found at Qumran, which reads "sons of God" (i.e., lesser deities or angels, as at Gen 6:2). The reading "sons of Israel" in the Hebrew (Masoretic) text probably reflects a scribal alteration, made because the original "sons of God" was found to be offensive. See Darrell D. Hannah, *Michael and Christ: Michael Traditions and Angel Christology in Early Christianity* (Tübingen: Mohr [Siebeck], 1999), 18–19.

6. For discussion of the development of the idea of angels of the nations, see ibid., 31–32, 33–38 (on Michael as angelic guardian of Israel); see also John J. Collins, *Daniel* (Minneapolis: Fortress, 1993), 374–76. Collins suggests that the idea derives from the ancient Near Eastern concept of the divine council, and points out that the notion underlies 2 Kgs 18:35 = Isa 36:20. He also discusses the use of the term "prince" to refer to angels (paralleled in Josh 5:14 and in the Dead Sea Scrolls).

7. See *Jub.* 15:31–32; Sir 17:17. For Michael as Israel's guardian, see Dan 10:13, 21; 12:1; *1 En.* 20:5; for discussion with further references, see Hannah, *Michael and Christ*, 33–38. It is possible that the "angels of the churches" mentioned in Rev 2–3 also evolved out of the tradition about angels of nations. For patristic references to the angels of the nations, see J. Michl, "Angels [Theology]" in *New Catholic Encyclopedia* (14 vols.; 2nd edition; Detroit: Thomson/Gale in association with the Catholic University of America, 2002), 1:420.

8. *Jubilees*, trans. O. S. Wintermute, in *OTP* 2:123.

9. Hannah, *Michael and Christ*, 31.

10. *1 Enoch*, trans. E. Isaac, *OTP* 1:81.

11. Pseudo-Philo, *Biblical Antiquities*, trans. Daniel J. Harrington, *OTP* 2:319; cf. 15:5; 59:4. In *OTP* this document is called *Pseudo-Philo*, though it is also known as *Biblical Antiquities* or by the Latin title *Liber Antiquitatum Biblicarum*.

12. *3 Baruch*, trans. H. E. Gaylord, Jr., *OTP* 1:677. The section of *3 Baruch* from which the quoted passage derives was edited by a Christian at an early stage of transmission, but the depiction of guardian angels is not identifiably Christian.

13. On parallels in Mesopotamian religion to Job 33:23 ("Then, if there should be for one of them an angel, a mediator, one of a thousand, one who declares a person upright") see Samuel A. Meier, "Mediator I," *DDD* 555–57; Marvin H. Pope, *Job* (Garden City, N.Y.: Doubleday, 1965), 219. Pope states that the idea behind 33:23 "is clearly related to the concept of guardian angels and interceding saints." See also Job 9:33; 16:19–21; 19:25. On possible links between the personal-god tradition and the Johannine *paraklētos* (John 14:16, 26; 15:26; 16:7), see John Ashton, "Paraclete," *ABD* 5:152 and the works cited therein.

14. *Phaedrus* 242b–c, in *The Collected Dialogues of Plato* (ed. Edith Hamilton and Huntington Cairns; trans. R. Hackforth; Princeton: Princeton University Press, 1961), 489. Other passages referring to Socrates' *daimonion* include *Apology* 40a–b; *Euthydemus* 272e; *Republic* 496c; *Theaetetus* 151a.

15. See *Republic* 620d–e; *Phaedo* 107d–8c; *Laws* 713d–e.

16. See Plutarch, *On the Sign of Socrates,* especially 591–92; in this treatise, characters refer to the philosopher's *daimonion* as if to something out of the ordinary or even unique. Plutarch's explanation (via the character Timarchus) counters this perception: Everyone has such a divine aspect, but most are oblivious to it. See also Maximus of Tyre, *Orations* 8–9, together with M. B. Trapp's discussion in *The Philosophical Orations* (trans. M. B. Trapp; Oxford: Clarendon, 1997), 67–69 (citing other ancient and modern sources). Magicians and diviners in the ancient world were sometimes aided by a "familiar spirit" (*daimōn paredros*), but such spirits were not lifelong companions; rather, the magician summoned one as needed by magical means. See Morton Smith, "Pauline Worship as Seen by Pagans," *Harvard Theological Review* 73 (1980): 241–49.

17. See Chapter 1, n. 39.

18. See the discussion in Steven Chase, *Angelic Spirituality: Medieval Perspectives on the Ways of Angels* (New York: Paulist, 2002), 18–20, 256 n. 31. David Keck (*Angels and Angelology in the Middle Ages* [New York: Oxford University Press, 1998], 17) notes how, in the patristic and medieval eras, Christian theologians wrestled with challenges to orthodoxy posed by such philosophical notions, especially with the troublesome view that spiritual beings who had emanated eternally from God (and thus were themselves uncreated) had participated in the creation of the world.

19. For "little ones" as symbolic of the disciples see especially Matt 10:42; note also that Matthew repeatedly has Jesus use the expression "you of little faith" for the disciples (see Matt 6:30; 8:26; 14:31; 16:8; 17:20). Origen (*Commentary on Matthew,* 13.26) interprets the "little ones" as those who are immature in the faith, who have not yet attained a great measure of spiritual stature, and who have therefore not yet progressed from having angels as their caretakers to having the Lord as caretaker.

20. The disciples may suppose Peter to have died in prison, in which case they are loosely using the term "angel" to refer to Peter's ghost. See Hannah, *Michael and Christ,* 125–26. Crispin H. T. Fletcher-Louis thinks that the disciples infer the caller to be Peter's guardian angel, who not only resembles Peter physically but also has the same voice (*Luke-Acts: Angels, Christology, and Soteriology* [Tübingen: Mohr (Siebeck), 1997], 30).

21. The *Shepherd of Hermas* was written in Rome, probably over the course of several decades up until the mid-second century CE. The book is constituted by a series of visions or revelations, the overarching purpose of which is to offer instruction concerning the possibility of repentance and forgiveness by those who sin after baptism. The revelations fall into three main sections: the "Visions," the "Mandates," and the "Similitudes."

22. *Mandate* 11.9–10, in *The Apostolic Fathers,* trans. Kirsopp Lake, LCL (subsequent quotations of the *Shepherd of Hermas* are also from this translation). On "angel pneumatology," see also Gilles Quispel, "Genius and Spirit," in *Essays on the Nag Hammadi Texts* (ed. M. Krause; Leiden: Brill, 1975), 155–69.

23. Charles A. Gieschen, *Angelomorphic Christology: Antecedents and Early Evidence* (Leiden: Brill, 1998), 224. For helpful guidance through the highly confusing angelology of *Shepherd of Hermas,* see ibid., 214–28.

24. Jean Daniélou, *The Angels and Their Mission* (trans. David Heimann; Westminster,

Md.: Christian Classics [reprint ed.], 1991), 80. Daniélou's small book is a gold mine for quotations and discussion of patristic authors' views of angels (many more than can be cited here). For Origen's teaching on paired opposite angels, see *First Principles* 3.2.4; *Homiliai in Lucam*, 12 and 35. Origen ascribes the idea to Hermas (see *Mandate* 6.2.1–10) and also to *Letter of Barnabas* (see 18.1).

25. Gregory of Nyssa, *Life of Moses*, Patrologia Graeca 44, 337d–340a. Cited in Daniélou, *Angels and Their Mission*, 81.

26. Caesarius was a Cistercian monk from the German Rhineland, and author of *Dialogue on Miracles*, a non-scholarly work. For the view that Caesarius epitomizes the general or popular culture for his era see Aron Gurevich, *Medieval Popular Culture: Problems of Belief and Perception* (trans. János M. Bak and Paul A. Hollingsworth; Cambridge: Cambridge University Press, 1988), 9.

27. Hillary of Poitiers, *Tractatus Super Psalmos* 134. Translation taken from Daniélou, *Angels and Their Mission*, 74–75.

28. The title "angel of peace" is attested also in earlier Jewish apocalyptic literature (*1 En.* 52:5; 53:4; *T. Ash.* 6:6; *T. Dan* 6:5). For patristic references and discussion, see Daniélou, *Angels and Their Mission*, 73–76. Daniélou particularly associates references to "angels of peace" with angelic protection from external dangers and from the devil or demons.

29. Athanasius, *Life of Anthony* 35 (quotation taken from Daniélou, *Angels and Their Mission*, 75).

30. Origen, *Commentary on Matthew* 13.26 (*ANF* 10:490).

31. Ibid. Here Origen is reinterpreting metaphorically Isaiah's prophecy in 49:22–23: "They shall bring your sons in their bosom, and your daughters shall be carried on their shoulders. Kings shall be your foster fathers, and their queens your nursing mothers."

32. On angels' mediation in prayer, see Tob 12:12; Rev 8:3–4; Philo, *On Giants* 3–7; *On Dreams* 1.141–42; for patristic references see Daniélou, *Angels and Their Mission*, 78–79. On angels' effecting of repentance, see *1 En.* 40:7–9 (on the archangel Phanuel); for patristic references see Daniélou, *Angels and Their Mission*, 76–78. In the *Shepherd of Hermas*, the shepherd-angel for whom the book is named is at points identified with the "Angel of Repentance," who tells Hermas to instruct others about the Second Repentance (*Visions* 5.7; *Similitudes* 9.1.1; 9.33.1).

33. Daniélou, *Angels and Their Mission*, 52–53. Daniélou cites Origen's *Commentarii in evangelium Joannis* 6.7 and *Commentarius in Canticum* 12, and notes that the image appears before Origen in the works of Hippolytus. In the Fourth Gospel, John the Baptist uses the metaphor of the "friend of the bridegroom" to describe himself and emphasize his own secondary role in relation to Jesus (John 3:29–30). See also the use of the metaphor of church as "bride" in Eph 5:25–27.

34. Daniélou, throughout his chapter, "The Angels and the Spiritual Life," stresses the preparatory and subsidiary role of the angels (*Angels and Their Mission*, 83–94, especially 91–93). On angels' subsidiary role in the medieval tradition, see Chase, *Angelic Spirituality*, 25–26, 59.

35. Ignatius, *To the Trallians* 5.2. In the New Testament, the power terms are simply listed (for example, Eph 6:12 and Col 1:16). On ideas of angelic hierarchy prior to Pseudo-Dionysius, see Keck, *Angels and Angelology*, 53–55.

36. On the various phases of the influence of Pseudo-Dionysius (which peaked in the thirteenth century), see Keck, *Angels and Angelology*, 49–50, 53–58.

37. Pseudo-Dionysius does not discuss guardian angels explicitly. In his system, members of the higher ranks of angels mediate their influence to the lower levels, working systematically downward through the levels of the hierarchy (with the intensity of the divine light growing weaker at each successive level). Other theologians who wrote about the angelic hierarchy did not conceive of it so rigidly: for example, the twelfth-century theologian Bernard of Clairvaux (drawing on Gregory the Great) conceived of the various choirs of angels as serving different functions in their interactions with humans (Keck, *Angels and Angelology*, 58). John Scotus Eriugena, who translated and commented on *The Celestial Hierarchy* in the ninth century, also differed from Pseudo-Dionysius regarding humans' relationship with the angels. Borrowing from Augustine, Eriugena insisted that no being mediates between humanity and God, and that humans "become peers with the highest angels." According to Pseudo-Dionysius, the angels do mediate. For discussion of this point and excerpts from Eriugena's commentary, see Chase, *Angelic Spirituality*, 161–86.

38. In general, on the remarkable degree of continuity of popular culture (including religion) across the medieval era, see Gurevich, *Medieval Popular Culture*, 9–10, 12. Gurevich argues that for a vast majority of the population, habits of mind were marked by suspicion toward anything novel, and satisfaction from hearing the old and familiar time and again. Specifically, on the great continuity of medieval angelological interpretations of the Scriptures with views of the patristic era, see Keck, *Angels and Angelology*, 13–14. Continuity prevailed, and yet certainly angelology did undergo some change and development in the medieval era. Keck highlights the shifts that occur in the twelfth and thirteenth centuries, when the arrival of competing intellectual systems in medieval Christianity (new syntheses of Neoplatonism and Aristotelian thought) compelled scholastic theologians "to explore the creation of the angels with greater clarity and with more depth than their immediate theological predecessors" (ibid., 19). Keck also discusses developments in angelology resulting from a new scholarly method, namely the *quaestio* (a form and technique for theological investigation that came to dominate scholarly theological discourse by the thirteenth century; see ibid., 75–83). Keck writes, "The development of this particular form of theological inquiry is one of the primary historical reasons for the great expansion of the field of angelology in the twelfth and thirteenth centuries" (ibid., 75). Keck offers a fascinating discussion of how ecclesiastical and urban developments (including the movement of theology from the monastery to the university) fostered changes in angelology (ibid., 75–92).

39. Ibid., 161–62.

40. Chase, *Angelic Spirituality*, 107–8. Other sources of refuge included the sacraments, penance, the Eucharist, and the imitation of the life of Christ. On union with God as the goal of the mystical journey in medieval Latin mystical writers, see Bernard McGinn, "Love, Knowledge, and *Unio Mystica* in the Western Christian Tradition," in *Mystical Union and Monotheistic Faith* (eds. Moshe Idel and Bernard McGinn; New York: Macmillan, 1989), 59–86.

41. From Bernard of Clairvaux, *Sermons on Psalm 90* (Sermon 12). Translation from Chase, *Angelic Spirituality*, 120.

42. From *Sermons on Psalm 90* (Sermon 11). Translation from Chase, *Angelic Spirituality*, 112.

43. On the importance of this use of the *quaestio* style of argumentation for the development of angelology, see Keck, *Angels and Angelology*, 75–83.

44. Thomas Aquinas, *Summa Theologiae* 1a. 113, 6 (see above, n. 1).

45. Chase, *Angelic Spirituality,* 147. I am indebted to Chase's biographical sketch of Umiltà, in ibid., 147–49.

46. Ibid., 151.

47. Ibid., 154.

48. See ibid., 2. Keck (*Angels and Angelology,* 48–49) emphasizes the prevalence in medieval Christendom of what he calls "angelic exegesis": "Prayers, sermons, records of visions, theological textbooks, and iconographic traditions each reveal clerics and lay-people addressing and discussing the angels of Scripture. Moreover, various figurative methods of reading allowed medieval exegetes to read angels into the text even where, at the literal level, they do not occur."

49. Chase (*Angelic Spirituality,* 15) notes that the angels' various ministries "served as a kind of lens that allowed the soul to 'see' the angels, to 'see' the manner in which they participated in God, and thus to 'see' something of the divine mystery itself."

50. Augustine formulated the key questions for angelic spirituality and defined the manner in which they would be addressed (see ibid., 77; includes a list of such questions). Keck (*Angels and Angelology,* 16) likewise observes that "Augustine's interpretation of the creation and the first moments of angelic existence, and his own synthesis of much of patristic angelology, provided the framework for the medieval Christian's understanding of these issues."

51. Chase, *Angelic Spirituality,* 5.

52. For a clear and useful discussion of the relationship of the categories "transcendence" and "immanence" to the apophatic and cataphatic methods in angelic spirituality, see ibid., 34–44 (especially 41–44).

53. From Gregory the Great, *Forty Homilies on the Gospels* (Homily 34); quotation taken from Chase, *Angelic Spirituality,* 103. Chase suggests that, for medieval practitioners of angelic spirituality, the hierarchy of the angelic orders is symbolized best not by a ladder but by an inner journey through concentric circles with God at the center. For explication of medieval notions of the angelic hierarchy, see ibid., 18–25; also Keck, *Angels and Angelology,* 53–58. On how the angelic hierarchy functioned as a model for and confirmation of social and ecclesiastical hierarchies, see ibid., 67; also Bob Hurd, "Angels," in *New Dictionary of Catholic Spirituality* (ed. Michael Downey; Collegeville, Minn.: Liturgical Press, 1993), 39.

54. From Gregory the Great, *Forty Homilies on the Gospels* (Homily 34). Quotation taken from Chase, *Angelic Spirituality,* 104.

55. See Gurevich, *Medieval Popular Culture,* 23.

56. Caesarius of Heisterbach, *The Dialogue on Miracles* (trans. H. von E. Scott and C. C. Swinton Bland; 2 vols.; London: G. Routledge and Sons, 1929). On Caesarius as representative of popular culture from this era, see above, n. 26. Gurevich (*Medieval Popular Culture,* 23) notes that Caesarius and his contemporaries were convinced that interventions from the other, eternal world take place all the time. Gurevich writes, "Hundreds of people see devils; many are being tormented by them. Quite a few people have been allowed to see Christ, the Mother of God, angels or saints face to face, and Caesarius himself knows some of these elect."

57. Keck, *Angels and Angelology,* 117; all of Keck's chapter, "Monks and Mendicants" (ibid., 117–28), is relevant here. Angels exemplified "poverty" because they had no need of material goods, "chastity" because they do not marry (see Matt 22:30), and "obedi-

ence" because the good angels have been confirmed in the grace of glory and so are perfectly obedient.

58. The quotation from Bernard is taken from ibid., 121; the source is Bernard's "Twelfth Sermon on Psalm 90, 'Qui Habitat.' "

59. Ibid., 123.

60. Ibid., 143; cf. 129–59.

61. See ibid., 168–70. More broadly, on the role of angels (not guardian angels specifically) in various regular devotional practices, see Keck's chapter, "Birth, Maturation, and the Regular Religious Practices of Adults" (ibid., 161–88).

62. Ibid., 164. Such desire for a more intimate relationship with one's angel may have been hampered by the church's prohibition against naming one's guardian. Keck (ibid., 163–64) sees the ninth-century prohibition as a probable response "to vestiges of paganism and pagan magical practices that lingered throughout the Carolingian empire." The names Raphael, Gabriel, and Michael were biblical and therefore approved, but these three were understood to be archangels and hence not assigned as guardians to individuals.

63. See *Ignatius of Loyola: The Spiritual Exercises and Selected Works* (ed. George E. Ganss; Mahwah: Paulist, 1991), 201–7 (= sections 313–36; see also the discussion in ibid., 423–24).

64. Online: http://www.catholic-forum.com/saints/saintgak.htm.

65. Eire, *War Against the Idols,* 1.

66. On the centrality of the Eucharist as an organizing symbol in late medieval Catholic theology, society, and politics, and on the Reformed critique thereof, see Christopher Elwood, *The Body Broken: The Calvinist Doctrine of the Eucharist and the Symbolization of Power in Sixteenth-Century France* (New York: Oxford University Press, 1999). Elwood (ibid., 212–13 n. 13) is sympathetic with Eire (*War Against the Idols)* but thinks that the primary impulse for the Reformed resistance was not rejection of Catholic devotion in general (as Eire holds) but rejection of the Catholic Mass.

67. Keck (*Angels and Angelology,* 93–99) discusses the great debate, centered especially in the thirteenth century, on whether angels consisted of both form and matter (a doctrine known as "hylomorphism") or of form only. The metaphysical debate is pertinent to the question of how different parties explained angels' assumed intervention in the material world. On angels as a "tangible link between the sacred and the profane" in the Middle Ages, see ibid., 191.

68. Eire, *War Against the Idols,* 11; Farel's story is summarized on pp. 8–9.

69. Keck, *Angels and Angelology,* 174 (in the discussion, " 'Magic' and the Intercession of Spirits").

70. See Eire, *War Against the Idols,* 197–98. On Plato's influence, see ibid., 200 n. 24; cf. 31–36 (on Platonic/Neoplatonic influence on Erasmus, to whom the Swiss Reformers, including Calvin, were heirs). Luther and the Swiss Reformers broke over this question of the relationship between the spiritual and the material in worship; Luther "strongly rejected any inclination toward body-spirit dualism" (ibid., 72–73). Both the Catholics on the one hand, and Erasmus (together with the Swiss Reformers who built on his work) on the other hand, presupposed a Neoplatonic metaphysics that sharply separated matter and spirit, and taught that humans must strive for emancipation of their spirits from the material world. But the different camps spun out the implications of the spirit/matter separation in different ways. On the Catholic side, Pseudo-Dionysius had proposed that

angels were ranked in a gradation or hierarchy (like the graded emanations of Neopla-tonist thought), and served as buffers between the one God and material creation; only the lower-level angels actually intervened in the material world. Erasmus was also influ-enced by Pseudo-Dionysius, in part through the Catholic devotional program known as the *Devotio Moderna*. But Erasmus rejected a long-standing Catholic argument that combined a Neoplatonic theory of graded reflections or emanations and a strong in-carnational principle, and according to which matter can convey spiritual power and presence. According to Erasmus, the material is of no help in reaching the spiritual. The leaders of the Reformed tradition followed Erasmus in this rejection (ibid., 35–36). See, however, Elwood (*The Body Broken*, 186–87 n. 96), who cautions against overestimating the philosophical influence on the Reformers' critique of Catholic piety and neglecting the influence of ideas derived from their reading of Scripture.

71. Author's translation from the German text of the prayer as reported in Michael Plathow, "Dein heiliger Engel sei mit mir: Martin Luthers Engelpredigten," in *Lutherjahr-buch: Organ der internationalen Lutherforschung* (Göttingen: Vandenhoeck & Ruprecht, 1994), 47.

72. Eric W. Gritsch, *Martin, God's Court Jester: Luther in Retrospect* (Philadelphia: For-tress, 1983), 43. For more reliable information about Luther's perspective on the devil, see Carlos M. N. Eire, "Bite This Satan! The Devil in Luther's Table Talk," in *Piety and Family in Early Modern Europe: Essays in Honour of Steven Ozment* (ed. Marc R. Forster and Benjamin J. Kaplan; Ashgate, 2005), 70–93.

73. John Calvin, *Institutes of the Christian Religion* (ed. John T. McNeill; trans. Ford Lewis Battles; 2 vols.; Philadelphia: Westminster, 1960), 2:166.

74. The comment is made in "Sendbrief vom Dolmetschen" ("An Open Letter on Translating"). An English translation of this letter (trans. Gary Mann; revised by Michael D. Barlowe) is available online: http://www.bible-researcher.com/luther01.html.

75. Luther wrote, "But for my part . . . to accord so much credit to this Dionysius, whoever he was, altogether displeases me, for there is virtually no sound learning in him" (From Luther's *Babylonish Captivity*, section on Ordination; quotation taken from Calvin, *Institutes*, 2:164 n. 14).

76. Ibid., 2:164–65.

77. Ibid., 2:164.

78. Ibid., 2:167.

79. Calvin also cites Luke 16:22, which tells of angels bearing Lazarus to Abraham's bosom; and 2 Kgs 6:17, which tells of Elisha and his servant's vision of the many fiery chariots sent to protect them (ibid., 2:167).

80. Ibid., 2:170.

81. Ibid., 2:169

82. Ibid., 2:171; emphasis added.

83. Ibid., 2:171.

84. The reference occurs in chap. 7 of the *Second Helvetic Confession*. The brevity of references to angels in this document is interesting because its author, Heinrich Bullinger, does discuss angels at greater length elsewhere. In a treatise on good and evil spirits, Bullinger affirmed the angels' protective function, and even ventures cautiously into some of the ancient speculative questions about angels. He discusses Matt 10:18, but (intriguingly) declines to mention the traditional interpretation of this verse as a refer-ence to guardian angels (*The Decades of Henry Bullinger: The Fourth Decade* [ed. Thomas

Harding; trans. H. I.; 4 vols.; Cambridge: The University Press (reprint edition), 1968],
3:327–65).

85. *Westminster Confession of Faith,* 3.3–4 (= 6.016–17 in *The Constitution of the
Presbyterian Church [USA]. Part I: Book of Confessions* [Louisville: Office of the General
Assembly, 2002]); 5.4 (= 6.027); 23.2 (= 6.113); 35.1 (= 6.180); *Larger Catechism,* Q. 123
(= 7.123); Q. 126 (= 7.126); Q. 129 (= 7.129); Q. 215 (= 7.215).

86. Elwood, *The Body Broken,* 141.

87. See Eire's discussion of Calvin's view of miracles, in *War Against the Idols,* 221–24,
230. Calvin downplayed the role of miracles, even those in biblical times, arguing that
their purpose then was not to alter the fabric of material reality but to strengthen the
authority of God's messengers. Moreover, he contended, miracles had ceased at the end
of the Apostolic Age. The so-called miracles claimed by Catholics were, in Calvin's view,
heinous deceptions. On the influence from humanist metaphysics of Calvin's era on his
arguments about what events were "reasonable" or "unreasonable," see ibid., 231. In correspondence, Amy Plantinga Pauw has suggested to me that Calvin's suspicion of accounts of miracles stems in part from his concern that they "smack of superstition and
distract believers from the central good news of God's sustaining and redemptive mercy
in Christ" (personal correspondence, undated). Plantinga Pauw insists further (coun-
tering Eire) that Calvin did not so cleanly separate the spiritual and physical realms, but
saw the whole world infused with the personal presence of God.

88. Amy Plantinga Pauw, "Where Theologians Fear to Tread," *Modern Theology* 16:1
(January 2000): 45. In the article, Plantinga Pauw discusses the coherence of Edwards'
angelology with the rest of his theology.

89. From Edwards' sermon, "Children Ought to Love the Lord Jesus Christ," in Jonathan Edwards, *Sermons and Discourses, 1739–1742* (ed. Harry S. Stout and Nathan O.
Hatch with Kyle P. Farley; New Haven: Yale University Press, 2003), 22:178.

90. Plantinga Pauw, "Where Theologians Fear to Tread," 47.

91. In Edwards' 1734 sermon, "A Divine and Supernatural Light" (in *The Sermons of
Jonathan Edwards: A Reader* [ed. Wilson H. Kimnach et al.; New Haven: Yale University
Press, 1999], 121–40), Edwards distinguishes carefully between God's use of proximate
causes to educate the mind about doctrine and God's unmediated conveyance of actual
knowledge of divine things (the "sense of the divine excellency of [said doctrines] in our
hearts" [ibid., 130–31]). In defending the Great Awakening, Edwards did not insist that
the movement's more excessive manifestations (tears, trembling, groans, loud outcries,
ravishing visions) were necessarily of God; by themselves such signs were ambiguous.
The true evidences of the work of the Spirit were "signs such as love to Jesus, renouncing
of worldly lusts and ambitions, a love of Scripture, a Spirit of truth, and true Christian
love" (George M. Marsden, *Jonathan Edwards: A Life* [New Haven: Yale University Press,
2003], 234–35; see also Marsden's discussion of Edwards' important work *Treatise on
Religious Affections,* published in 1746, in ibid., 285–90).

92. Increase Mather (1639–1723) wrote a book on angelology, published a few years
before Edwards' birth; in the work, Mather affirmed many of the traditional roles of
good and evil angels (Increase Mather, *Angelographia* [Boston: B. Green & J. Allen, for
Samuel Phillips, 1696]; the work is discussed in Ludwig, *Graven Images,* 223–25). John
Wesley (1703–1791) preached sermons on good and evil angels, which likewise affirmed
all the traditional roles of both good and evil angels; Wesley was dubious about the existence of guardian angels, but did not rule out the possibility (sermons available online:

http://new.gbgm-umc.org/umhistory/wesley/sermons/71, and http://new.gbgm-umc .org/umhistory/wesley/sermons/72). For a history of Protestant angelology after the eighteenth century, see Karl Barth, *Church Dogmatics,* vol. 3, part 3: *The Doctrine of Creation* (trans. G. W. Bromiley and R. J. Ehrlich; Edinburgh: T. & T. Clark, 1960), 405–9 and 413–18. Barth describes two tendencies in Protestant theologians' reflections on angels from the eighteenth through the mid-twentieth centuries. One category of theologians had quite a lot to say about the topic. The "modern dogmaticians" in the other category either rejected angels outright, based on the presumed obsolescence of the worldview that gave rise to them (W. M. L. de Wette; D. F. Strauss); or insisted for like reason that angels have nothing to do with central Christian doctrine, but nonetheless weakly permitted the continuing presence of angels in the language (for example, in the hymnody) of Christian practice (F. Schleiermacher and others). Barth thinks that nearly all the theologians he describes—indeed, nearly all theologians since the Bible itself (with only the most thoroughgoing skeptics, such as D. F. Strauss, excepted)—committed the intolerable error of allowing nonbiblical considerations to corrupt their reflections. These nonbiblical considerations included presuppositions drawn from philosophy and reasoned arguments about what "must" be the case. Barth in turn presents his own interpretation of angels, which excludes all nonbiblical evidence and views angels as beings so bound to the will and activity of God that they lack all independent personhood and serve as virtual extensions of the very presence and power of God. Barth writes, "Where an angel appears and is and speaks and works, God Himself appears and is and speaks and works" (ibid., 480). On Barth's view of angels, see the helpful analysis by Amy Plantinga Pauw, "Where Theologians Fear to Tread."

93. Orsi, *Between Heaven and Earth,* 103.

94. The notion that guardian angels act as informants is at least as old as the Rule of Saint Benedict (sixth century): see the discussion in Keck, *Angels and Angelology,* 85.

95. Orsi, *Between Heaven and Earth,* 103–6.

96. Ann Taves, *The Household of Faith: Roman Catholic Devotions in Mid-Nineteenth Century America* (Notre Dame: University of Notre Dame Press, 1986), 125. On the international Catholic revival in the nineteenth century, see John T. McGreevy, *Catholicism and American Freedom: A History* (New York: W. W. Norton & Co., 2003), 19–42.

97. Taves, *Household of Faith,* 113, 132–33.

98. These and other examples of "graces and favors" from mid-nineteenth century Catholicism in the United States are described in ibid., 41–63.

99. Ibid., 64. Taves comments, "Because most Protestant apologists rejected both the idea of modern miracles and the means which Catholics used to obtain them, all miracles recognized by nineteenth-century Catholics had inherent propaganda value." But, although Protestant *leaders* often contended that the age of miracles had passed, many Protestant *lay persons* continued to believe in their possibility, especially in the possibility of miraculous medical cures (ibid., 56–57).

100. Ibid., 60–61.

101. Ibid., 59.

102. Joseph P. Chinnici, *Living Stones: The History and Structure of Catholic Spiritual Life in the United States* (Maryknoll, N.Y.: Orbis Books, 1996), 74.

103. Ibid. The passage is from Neumann's journal, which covered the years 1834–39. Chinnici thinks that Neumann embodied the understanding of sanctity dominant in the immigrant Catholic church.

104. Quoted in Taves, *Household of Faith*, 83.

105. "History of the Sodalities," published in the magazine *Ave Maria* in 1866, and excerpted in *Prayer and Practice in the American Catholic Community* (ed. Joseph P. Chinnici and Angelyn Dries; Maryknoll, N.Y.: Orbis Books, 2000), 64. Taves (*Household of Faith,* 125) comments on the importance of sodalities in the nineteenth century, as social spaces that helped to maintain "the subjective reality of that other, supernatural world with which Catholics communicated through prayer."

106. Discussed in the Baltimore Catechism, question 43. Online: http://www.true catholic.org/baltp1.htm.

107. The quotations are from John T. McGreevy, *Parish Boundaries: The Catholic Encounter with Race in the Twentieth-Century Urban North* (Chicago: University of Chicago Press, 1996), 79–80. The suggestion about the decline of belief in guardian angels as a reflection of worldwide developments in Catholicism was communicated to me by Dr. McGreevy in personal correspondence. Also in personal correspondence, historian Joseph Chinnici similarly stressed the need to look at developments in Catholicism as practiced in the United States in continuity with mutations in Western Christianity in other developed countries. Chinnici suggested further that because "angels represent the invisible connections and intercessions relating heaven and earth," changes in angel piety may be linked to such elusive factors as transformations in Catholics' sense of group solidarity, communal dependence, and kinship.

108. Joseph Chinnici, in personal correspondence. The new catechism of the Catholic Church affirms the existence of angels and describes their nature; recounts their roles in the biblical story; and describes their benefits to the whole life of the Church, including their adoration of God, in which the Church joins through the liturgy, and their watchful care and intercession for humans from infancy to death. Guardian angels are mentioned in passing, but are not the topic of explicit discussion (*Catechism of the Catholic Church* [New York: Doubleday, 1995], 95–98 [= Part one, paragraph 5.1]). In his extended catechesis on angels (given as a six-part General Audience at St. Peter's Square in Rome, from July 9, 1986 to August 20, 1986; online: http://www.ewtn.com/library/PAPALDOC/JP2ANGEL.HTM), Pope John Paul II noted that the modern mentality does not see the importance of angels; he included only a few lines specifically about guardian angels, though he did more generally reaffirm angels' special care and solicitude for people. Bob Hurd ("Angels," 40) sees a connection between the decline of angel piety and "Vatican II's call for the full and active participation of the faithful," which provoked reassessment of the previous "disenfranchisement of the ordinary believer in all areas of Church life. As the priesthood of all believers is reasserted and faith as a whole becomes more Christ-centered, the relevance of mediating higher powers (saints, angels, and even Mary) for spirituality recedes more and more into the background."

109. Orsi, *Between Heaven and Earth,* 152.

110. Ibid., 157.

111. See especially ibid., 155–157, and also Robert A. Orsi, *Thank You, Saint Jude: Women's Devotion to the Patron Saint of Hopeless Causes* (New Haven: Yale University Press, 1996). For an example of continuing devotion to the angels, see the Web site www.opusangelorum.org, representing an international confraternity devoted to the work of the Holy Angels, founded in Innsbruck, Austria in 1961 and with an office in Detroit.

112. Joseph Chinnici, in personal correspondence.

113. Many of the examples in the text were taken from Joan Wester Anderson, *Where*

Angels Walk: True Stories of Heavenly Visitors (New York: Ballantine, 1992); more recently, see J. Anderson, *In the Arms of Angels: True Stories of Heavenly Guardians* (Chicago: Loyola, 2004). Anderson was raised Catholic, and many of her informants were Catholic. *Where Angels Walk* was on the *New York Times* bestseller list for over a year; it sold nearly 2,000,000 copies and has been translated into fourteen languages. Other such stories may be found at http://www.opusangelorum.org/English/Guardian.html (on this Web site, see above, n. 111).

114. Doreen Virtue, *Divine Guidance: How to Have a Dialogue with God and Your Guardian Angels* (Los Angeles: Renaissance Books, 1998), 26.

115. Ibid., 41, 43–44.

116. Ibid., 34.

117. Denny Sargent, *Your Guardian Angel and You* (Boston: Weiser Books, 2004), 40.

118. Virtue (*Divine Guidance,* xviii, xxi–xxii) indicates that many of the clientele in her angel therapy and spiritual healing practice feel alienated from traditional religion. But she also has some "Christian-oriented clients," who sometimes need reassurance that seeking angelic guidance is acceptable Christian practice.

119. Elijah: 2 Kgs 1:1–18; Elisha: 2 Kgs 6:14–17; Daniel: Dan 6:22; Joseph: Matt 2:13; Peter: Acts 12:7–10; Jesus in the wilderness: Mark 1:13; Jesus in Gethsemane (Mount of Olives): Luke 22:39–46.

120. *Angels on Earth* (Sept./Oct. 1998): 3–6. The stories in this Guideposts publication typically do not make the rescuer's angelic identity explicit; rather, the people receiving aid are prompted by the amazing synchronicities to ask whether their helper *might* have been an angel of God. Nor do the stories typically describe events that defy natural law (though they may have been unusual or unlikely). These narrative tendencies probably reflect the origins of the Guideposts organization in the Protestant "positive thinking" theology of Dr. Norman Vincent Peale.

121. The difference of emphasis seems to be correlated with theological orientation: Catholics seem generally more likely to emphasize the otherworldliness of the rescuer, or the violation of natural laws. For illustration, see the works of Catholic writer Joan Wester Anderson (*Where Angels Walk; In the Arms of Angels*), which are replete with natural-law-bending accounts. Regarding a more typically Protestant approach to angel stories, see the preceding note.

122. Online: http://www.opusangelorum.org/English/Guardian.html.

123. Ibid.

124. Ibid.

125. J. Anderson, *Where Angels Walk,* 92–95.

126. On early Christian interpretations of suffering, see pp. 115–26, 132–35; see also Charles H. Talbert, *Learning through Suffering: The Educational Value of Suffering in the New Testament and in Its Milieu* (Collegeville, Minn.: Liturgical Press, 1991).

127. Here I am especially influenced by Mark's Gospel, which poignantly underscores the tension between God's *power* to take away Jesus' cup of suffering (14:36) and the *choice not to do so* (on this tension, see Sharyn Dowd, *Prayer, Power, and the Problem of Suffering: Mark 11:22–25 in the Context of Markan Theology* [Atlanta: Scholars, 1988]). This tension is reduced in Matthew's portrayal (Jesus could have appealed to angels to save him; see Matt 26:53) and in John's portrayal (Jesus freely finishes the work God gave him to do and thereby glorifies God; see John 17:1–5).

128. On the angel as "cipher or symbol of God's own presence," see Hurd, "Angels," 40.

129. On Jesus' cry of dereliction in Mark's Gospel, see Susan R. Garrett, *The Temptations of Jesus in Mark's Gospel* (Grand Rapids: Eerdmans, 1998), 130–33. I argue therein that Mark thinks of God as "hiding God's face" from Jesus at this terrible moment, but not as truly absent from the scene.

130. See above, n. 117.

131. Sargent, *Your Guardian Angel*, 34.

132. Ibid., 52. In his references to "True Will" (and in his discussion of the Holy Guardian Angel more generally), Sargent draws on the Thelema mystical system, which was developed early in the twentieth century by English occultist Aleister Crowley. See the article "Holy Guardian Angel," online: http://en.wikipedia.org/wiki/Holy_Guardian_Angel.

133. Sargent, *Your Guardian Angel*, 19. See also the discussion on p. 150.

134. Athanasius, *Life of Anthony* 35; see above, n. 29.

135. Sargent, *Your Guardian Angel*, 83. On this matter Sargent's position differs from the all-affirming ("I'm OK, God's OK") mentality of many angelic self-help books, on which see pp. 58–62.

136. See above, n. 53.

137. See pp. 146–47. This was always the orthodox view, though in practice it was not always adhered to.

138. Tara Brach, *Radical Acceptance: Embracing Your Life with the Heart of a Buddha* (New York: Bantam Books, 2003).

139. Ibid., 3.

140. Ibid., 11–12.

141. Ibid., 220.

142. Sargent, *Your Guardian Angel*, 136.

143. For a revisionist Christian interpretation of the traditional doctrine of sin from a perspective that is strongly influenced by Buddhism, see Wendy Farley, *The Wounding and Healing of Desire: Weaving Heaven and Earth* (Louisville: Westminster John Knox, 2005), 22–26 and passim. Here I am comparing core Christian beliefs not to Buddhism in all its antiquity and complexity, but to Western adaptations of Buddhism such as are found in some New Age teachings. Still, in thinking about traditional Buddhism I have been helped by Rita M. Gross and Terry C. Muck, eds., *Buddhists Talk about Jesus, Christians Talk about the Buddha* (New York: Continuum, 2005).

144. Farley (*Wounding and Healing of Desire*, 29) writes, "It is not that belief in Jesus makes redemption available. It is rather the reverse: when the always-unbelievable miracle of release from evil burns through a psyche, a family, a church, a community, a political situation, or the endless chaos of nothingness, Christians give it the name handed to us through our tradition. The eternal and limitless power of God Beyond Being is everywhere and always; it cannot coincide with the story of Jesus of Nazareth or the church sprung up in his name. But that is the shard of power that illuminates the corner of space and time Christians inhabit."

145. Buddhist author Bokin Kim ("Christ as the Truth, the Light, the Life, but a Way?" in *Buddhists Talk about Jesus, Christians Talk about the Buddha*, 57) summarizes this point of contrast between Buddhism and Christianity: "A Christian's faith is based on God's grace, where believers totally rely on God. . . . That is, Christians go beyond their ego-boundary while relying on *other power*. On the other hand, Buddhists can reach radical awakening by their strenuous effort of practice. Practice leads them to realize the

true nature of self and to achieve freedom from the ego-boundary. That is, Buddhists rely on *self power* for radical awakening" [emphasis added]. See also Bonnie Thurston, "The Buddha Offered Me a Raft," in ibid., 118–28.

146. David E. Fredrickson, "Paul, Hardships, and Suffering," in J. Paul Sampley, ed., *Paul in the Greco-Roman World: A Handbook* (Harrisburg: Trinity Press International, 2003), 185–90.

147. From Bernard of Clairvaux, *Sermons on Psalm 90* (Sermon 11). Translation from Chase, *Angelic Spirituality,* 112.

148. On the "de-centering" and "re-centering" of the self that discipleship demands, see Miroslav Volf, *Exclusion and Embrace: A Theological Exploration of Identity, Otherness, and Reconciliation* (Nashville: Abingdon, 1996), 69–71.

149. Brian K. Blount and Gary W. Charles, *Preaching Mark in Two Voices* (Louisville: Westminster John Knox, 2002), 31–32.

150. Luke Timothy Johnson, *Living Jesus: Learning the Heart of the Gospel* (San Francisco: HarperSanFrancisco, 2000), 16. Cf. Kathryn Tanner, *God and Creation in Christian Theology: Tyranny or Empowerment?* [Oxford: Basil Blackwell, 1988], 79: "A self-determined transcendence does not limit God's relation with the world to one of distance. A radical transcendence does not exclude God's positive fellowship with the world or presence within it. Only created beings, which remain themselves over and against others, risk the distinctness of their own natures by entering into intimate relations with another. God's transcendence alone is one that may be properly exercised in the radical immanence by which God is said to be nearer to us than we are to ourselves."

151. Here I am influenced by ibid., 99–102.

CHAPTER 6: ANGELS AND DEATH

1. In this chapter, "Death" is capitalized whenever it refers to a personified being as depicted in literature or visual representations. The tombstone quotation was taken from James Deetz and Edwin S. Dethlefsen, "The Plymouth Colony Archive Project: Death's Head, Cherub, Urn and Willow," *Natural History* 76:3 (1967): 29–37 [online: http://etext.lib.virginia.edu/users/deetz/Plymouth/deathshead.html]. See also Allan I. Ludwig, *Graven Images: New England Stone Carving and Its Symbols, 1650–1815* (3rd ed.; Hanover, N.H.: Wesleyan University Press, 1999), which includes photographs not only of gravestones adorned with the death's head, but also of markers featuring skeletal images of Death with a scythe, and death imps. Some speculate that the death's head symbolizes the remains of the mortal buried below (with wings symbolizing immortality), but this is surely wrong: The image is a carryover from prolific images of Death dating back centuries. The cherubic faces on eighteenth-century stones seem in part to have evolved from the death's head; see Deetz and Dethlefsen, "Plymouth Colony Archive Project." The cherub may have symbolized the soul taking flight. In the (mostly) earlier death's head carvings, the soul's passage through death and rebirth into new life was sometimes symbolized in other ways: for example, by a small human profile in the place where the skull's mouth should have been. For information on the iconography of death dating back to the early Christian era, see Philippe Ariès, *Images of Man and Death* (trans. Janet Lloyd; Cambridge, Mass.: Harvard University Press, 1985). Pertinent to the New England gravestone images, Ariès traces the evolution of representations of Death from that of a *transi* (a partially decomposed corpse) common in the fourteenth and fifteenth centu-

ries, to that of a clean, dry skeleton common by the end of the sixteenth century. Winged skeletons or skulls appear on Italian and French tombs of the seventeenth century (ibid., 93 [fig. 143], 188 [fig. 271]). Ariès ties the trend toward clean skeletons to changes in cultural norms surrounding death and budding scientific interest in human anatomy.

2. Some works from this era do, however, seem deliberately gruesome; see, for example, the carved statue of a recumbent corpse from the fifteenth century, and of personified Death (holding an hourglass) from the sixteenth century, both French (photographs in Ariès, *Images of Man and Death,* 156–57). Ariès (176–215) traces the rise of a new world-view beginning in the sixteenth century, a world in which Death "was not of the earth or heaven or hell. He had an indefinable world of his own, a theatrical world in which he was the principal, indeed the only actor" (176). In this new era, themes of eroticism and violence often made their way into the iconography of death.

3. Deetz and Dethlefsen, "Plymouth Colony Archive Project." In the late eighteenth or early nineteenth century (depending on locale), the winged cherubs dropped out of popularity and pictures of urns and willows began to appear. Deetz and Dethlefsen associate this development with the rise of "more intellectual religions, such as Unitarianism and Methodism," and with the larger Greek Revival going on at that time. On the difficulty of distinguishing between created angels and glorified human souls as carved on some of the gravestones, see Ludwig, *Graven Images,* 216–25.

4. Ernest Becker, *The Denial of Death* (New York: The Free Press, 1973). Becker won the Pulitzer Prize in general nonfiction in 1974, two months after his death at 49. Much of the book describes how our strategies for coping with death go awry, leading to neuroses of one sort or another. There is still a great deal of value in this insightful work. See also the documentary film based on Becker's book, entitled *Flight from Death: The Quest for Immortality,* produced by Go-Kart Records and directed by Patrick Shen, 85 minutes, 2003.

5. See, for example, the Underworld vampire-movies, starring Kate Beckinsale (*Underworld,* produced by Robert Bernacchi et al., directed by Len Wiseman, 2003; and *Underworld: Evolution,* produced by Lakeshore Entertainment and Screen Gems, Inc., directed by Len Wiseman, 2006). I cannot comment at length on the current cultural fascination with the undead, especially in the burgeoning vampire mythology. Many of these mythological expressions in print and film or on television offer complex reflections on the meaning of life and death. Becker (*Denial of Death,* 129) analyzes the vampire phenomenon under the heading of personal thralldom; he writes, "The continuing vogue of vampire movies may be a clue to how close to the surface our repressed fears are: the anxiety of losing control, of coming completely under someone's spell, of not really being in command of ourselves. One intense look, one mysterious song, and our lives may be lost forever." On the current popularity of romance novels about vampires, see Belinda Luscombe, "Well, Hello, Suckers," *Time* 167:9 (February 27, 2006, http://www.time.com/time/magazine/article/0,9171,1161234,00.html); Luscombe writes, "As swoony romantic heroes go, vampires are made to order: brooding, dangerous, mysterious, snappily dressed (although, alas, the cape has largely been dispensed with) with eye-catching dentition." Concerning the great popularity of the genre of the zombie horror movie, see n. 6 below.

6. Carol Zaleski (*The Life of the World to Come: Near-Death Experience and Christian Hope* [New York: Oxford University Press, 1996], 9), notes the paradox that we are shielded by medical and funeral technology from direct contact with death, but bom-

barded with shockingly graphic images of the deaths of strangers. These include images of real-life deaths observed in the news-media, and also the overabundance of special-effects images of death and gore given us by the film and entertainment industries. The complex reasons for the popularity of such entertainment certainly include the obvious thrill of adrenalin that violent images provoke, but may also include a widely-felt impulse to immerse oneself in (and thereby desensitize oneself to) that which is most feared, that is, death. Regarding vampire films, see the preceding note. Regarding social critique in the zombie horror films of George Romero (*Night of the Living Dead* and others), see Kim Paffenroth, *Gospel of the Living Dead: George Romero's Visions of Hell on Earth* (Waco, Tex.: Baylor University Press, 2006); Paffenroth examines Romero's use of imagery from the Bible and Dante. See also Jake TenPas, "Better Off Undead," *Corvallis Gazette-Times* for July 1, 2005 (online: http://www.gtconnect.com/articles/2005/06/30/entertainment/columnists/night_rider/tenpas.txt).

7. Here I borrow from William Stringfellow's description of the "reign of death," in *Instead of Death* (New and expanded ed.; New York: Seabury, 1976), 112.

8. Becker, *Denial of Death*, 50. Zaleski (*Life of the World to Come*, 17) comments that overcoming the denial of death can mean many different things: "The implications of death awareness are as various as the definitions of the good life." On the obsolescence of the theories of Freud and others that religion originated as a compensatory mechanism to cope with the fear of death, see John Bowker, *The Meanings of Death* (Cambridge: Cambridge University Press, 1991). Wendy Farley (*The Wounding and Healing of Desire: Weaving Heaven and Earth* [Louisville: Westminster John Knox, 2005], 58–60) discusses the human experience of *terror,* noting that "Søren Kierkegaard, Martin Heidegger, Karl Rahner, Reinhold Niebuhr, Paul Tilllich, Rudolf Bultmann, and others have argued that our precognitive awareness of death, indeterminacy, danger, and meaninglessness constitute a structural component of the human psyche. . . . This pervasive, usually unconscious, awareness of vulnerability that others have analyzed as anxiety might be understood as a dimension of terror" (58).

9. David F. Ford, *The Shape of Living: Spiritual Directions for Everyday Life* (Grand Rapids: Baker Book House, 1998), 65–66.

10. For a comprehensive overview of ancient views of death and afterlife, see especially the important work by Alan F. Segal, *Life After Death: A History of the Afterlife in the Religions of the West* (New York: Doubleday, 2004); Segal situates the various ideas he describes in their respective social and cultural locations. Two other very helpful works are N. T. Wright, *The Resurrection of the Son of God* (Minneapolis: Augsburg Fortress, 2003); and Jaime Clark-Soles, *Death and Afterlife in the New Testament* (New York: T. & T. Clark, 2006).

11. Scholars debate whether Sheol was viewed as the abode of all the dead, without regard for their status or moral character while alive, or as the abode of only the wicked. See Theodore J. Lewis, "Dead, Abode of the," *ABD* 2:104. Segal (*Life After Death,* 139) takes the view that "wherever Sheol is mentioned, evil (*böse*), untimely death is invariably at hand." By contrast, when biblical authors tell of a person being "gathered to the ancestors," the implication is that the person will die and be buried in peace (see ibid., 138–40 for a detailed discussion of "gathering to the ancestors"). Jon D. Levenson (*Resurrection and the Restoration of Israel: The Ultimate Victory of the God of Life* [New Haven: Yale University Press, 2006], 67–81) argues that the Hebrew Bible displays a tension between an older view of Sheol as the gloomy destination of all (a view that comports well with

ancient Mesopotamian and Canaanite notions of human destiny, and that is exhibited especially in the Wisdom literature), and the more prevalent view that distinguishes between those who go to Sheol and those who die blessed, like Abraham, Moses, and Job.

12. With regard to Jesus' glorification see, for example, Matt 25:31 and Heb 1:4; with regard to his followers' end-time status as like, among, or above the angels, see, for example, Matt 13:43; Heb 12:22; 1 Cor 6:3. On believers' conformation to the image of Christ, see Rom 8:29; 1 Cor 15:49; 2 Cor 3:18; Col 3:10.

13. This traditional Appalachian song is sung by Ralph Stanley, on the album, *O Brother, Where Art Thou?* (Lost Highway: 2000). The lyrics are widely available, in slightly varying versions, on the Internet.

14. P. W. van der Horst ("Thanatos," in *DDD*, 854–56) cites Homer's *Iliad* 16.667–75 and Euripides *Alcestis* (438 BCE). He notes that in some ancient references to Thanatos as a deity it is hard to know whether the figure is "a poetic metaphor or a real figure of popular belief." He also remarks that the functions of Thanatos were gradually taken over by Hades and Charon.

15. For an overview of the long history of scholarly debate over the etymology of the word *Sheol*, see Theodore J. Lewis, "Dead, Abode of the," *ABD* 2:102. One Hebrew word for death, *mawet*, derives from the same root as the name of the ancient Ugaritic (Canaanite) god of the underworld, Mot. In general, on death as personified in the Hebrew Scriptures and ancient Near Eastern literature, see Nicholas J. Tromp, *Primitive Conceptions of Death and the Nether World in the Old Testament* (Rome: Pontifical Biblical Institute, 1969), 99–128; pertinent biblical passages include Jer 9:20–22 (note the comparison of death to a "reaper"); Hab 2:5; Hosea 13:14; Ps 33:19; Isa 25:8 (Death, "the Swallower," is himself swallowed); LXX Job 20:15. Other passages apply personal qualities or physical characteristics to Sheol rather than to death itself, for example, Prov 1:12; 30:16; Ps 49:14–15; Isa 5:14. See also Dale C. Allison, *Testament of Abraham* (Berlin: Walter de Gruyter), 323–24 for citations of images of Death in later Christian writings and Greco-Roman mythology. In ibid., 353, Allison refers to a text from Qumran (frg. 1 of 4Q Amram[b]) in which the terrifying figure of a "watcher" appears to Moses' father, possibly as he is dying. The figure wears a cloak and has the face of an asp or a viper.

16. Tromp writes, "Biblical statements about the after-life generally tend to suppress this aspect of Sheol which is copiously depicted in Egyptian sources" (*Primitive Conceptions*, 120).

17. Marvin H. Pope, *Job* (Garden City, N.Y.: Doubleday, 1965), 126. The translation of Job 18:13–14 is from ibid., 123. Pope writes that the most common explanation of the obscure phrase, "Death's firstborn" is as a reference to the malady that afflicts Job.

18. Richard Bauckham, "Descent to the Underworld," *ABD* 2:148; cf. John J. Collins, *Daniel* (Minneapolis: Fortress, 1993), 394–95; Levenson, *Resurrection*, 75 and passim.

19. The variety of formulations used to refer to this agent of God indicates that in biblical times its identity was still in flux. In Exod 12:23 the destroyer kills the firstborn males, but in 12:13, 27, and 29, the LORD is the slayer. In Ps 78:49–51 the story is retold, but here it is a "company of destroying angels" that executes the plague. The author of *Jubilees* blames both "the powers of Mastema" (the name for the Satan figure) for carrying out this execution, and also "the host of the Lord" (*Jub.* 49:2, 4). Finally, in the mention of the slaughter of the Egyptian firstborn in Heb 11:28, the author refers ambiguously to "the one destroying." On the figure of "the destroyer," see Duane F. Watson, "Destroyer,"

ABD 2:159–60; also S. A. Meier, "Destroyer," *DDD*, 240–44. Meier (ibid., 244) points out that although the destroyer originally was conceived as executing persons *en masse,* in later tradition the figure began to merge with the angel of death (who accosts individuals). For example, the "destroying angel" of 2 Sam 24:16 becomes the "angel of death" in the Peshitta (the ancient Syriac translation). Meier also discusses other passages in the Hebrew Scriptures where the destroyer is not explicitly mentioned but probably implied.

20. Note that 2 Sam 24:11–25 is paralleled in 1 Chr 21:9–22:1, but with an expanded role for the angel.

21. Paul may have Satan in view as the destoyer (Gk. *olothreutēs*): he uses a related term in an earlier passage in the letter, when he refers to Satan's "destruction [Gk. *olethros*] of the flesh" of a certain wrongdoer (1 Cor 5:5). Near contemporaries of Paul who harked back to the incident from Num 16:41–50 refer, as Paul does, to a single being distinct from God (4 Macc 7:11, which refers to "an angel" or "the fiery angel"; and Wis 18:20–25, which refers to "the punisher"). On ways that sources from this era portray the working relationship between God and Satan, see Susan R. Garrett, *The Temptations of Jesus in Mark's Gospel* (Grand Rapids: Eerdmans, 1998), 44–48.

22. *Dogma,* produced by Scott Mosier, directed by Kevin Smith, 128 minutes, 1999.

23. Eugene Boring, "Matthew," *NIB* 8:146, 148–50.

24. On the development of traditions about Satan, see pp. 86–88 and Chapter 4. Specifically on the combat myths and beliefs about Satan see also S. Garrett, *Temptations of Jesus,* 36–40.

25. The etymology of the term *belial* is debated among scholars; according to Theodore J. Lewis ("Belial," *ABD* 1:654–56), theories are that *belial* is: (1) the negation of a word meaning "to be profitable or useful"; (2) the negation of a word meaning "to go up"; or (3) a derivation from a word meaning "to swallow." The second and third of these etymologies connote the underworld: Sheol and Mot were both said to "swallow" persons in death, and the idea of "not going up" suggests Sheol, the place "from which one does not go up" or "the land of no return," as in Job 7:9 (ibid., 654). Connotation of the underworld is also evident in 2 Sam 22:5–6 (parallel at Ps 18:4–5), where the "torrents of *belial*" (NRSV: "torrents of perdition") are compared to the "cords of Sheol" and the "snares of death." In the New Testament the term *belial* occurs only in 2 Cor 6:1 (in the Gk. variation *beliar*), but it is used frequently as a name for the Satan figure in the Dead Sea Scrolls, the *Testaments of the Twelve Patriarchs,* and other noncanonical literature. On the Satan figure in the Dead Sea Scrolls see Maxwell J. Davidson, *Angels at Qumran: A Comparative Study of 1 Enoch 1–36, 72–108, and Sectarian Writings from Qumran* (Sheffield: JSOT, 1992), 162–65.

26. Cf. Bauckham, "Descent," 2:147: "In the expectation of resurrection there was a sense of death and its realm as a power which had to be broken by God." Texts cited include *2 Bar.* 21:23 (mentions the angel of death) and 42:8; Matt 16:18; 1 Cor 15:54–55; Rev 20:14; 4 Ezra 8:53.

27. On the transition to Satan as master of hell see Bauckham, "Descent," 2:157 (and Bauckham, *The Fate of the Dead: Studies on the Jewish and Christian Apocalypses* [Leiden: Brill, 1998], 225]; Allison, *Testament of Abraham,* 327. Note that in Rev 6:8, Death and Hades are personified but *not* identical to Satan. In the *Testament of Abraham* (which probably dates from early in the Common Era: see n. 64 below), Death is a character but Satan is not; Anitra Bingham Kolenkow ("The Angelology of the Testament of Abraham,"

in *Studies on the Testament of Abraham* [ed. George W. E. Nickelsburg; Missoula, Mont.: Scholars, 1976], 157) too readily conflates the two.

28. Segal, *Life After Death,* 261. Segal sees a shift beginning with Ecclesiastes, the author of which seems to know and reject a doctrine of a beatific afterlife (ibid., 249–55). Segal notes that the idea of resurrection begins to surface in the Latter Prophets and the Psalms (including especially Ezek 37 [Ezekiel's vision of the valley of "dry bones"] and Isa 25:8–9 [the promise that God "will swallow up death forever"]). But Segal does not find either of these to be "a clear and impressive prophecy of literal future bodily resurrection" (ibid., 261). Still, he argues, the passages do furnish a reservoir of images that will be used by later authors to illustrate what bodily resurrection means. See also Levenson, *Resurrection;* Levenson argues that virtually all modern readers who look for a "doctrine of the afterlife" in Scripture are forcing it into a conceptual framework that would have been foreign to the biblical writers themselves. First, as moderns we view life and death disjunctively, whereas biblical writers viewed them as on a continuum. Therefore, when biblical writers tell of God raising "the dead" from Sheol (referring to ones whom we would identify as extremely ill, or who for other reasons had lost all hope of fulfilled life), we assume the writers are being *metaphorical.* But in the writers' view God *really was* raising the dead to life. Second, today we assume that resurrection means exclusively resurrection of the individual, but in the more social or communal view of biblical authors, renewal of a whole people (through the granting of fertility and progeny, for example) really *did* count as the miracle of resurrection. Even in Daniel and subsequent writings, the doctrine of resurrection did not merely effect God's justice for each individual: it was God's great act of the restoration of the whole people of God, and would be accompanied by *recreation* of those people so that they could live a life of true obedience.

29. See n. 11 above.

30. On the dating of Daniel, see Chapter 2, n. 43. On possible earlier references to resurrection see n. 28 above; see also Wright, *Resurrection,* 85–109; Collins, *Daniel,* 394–98. George W. E. Nickelsburg (*Resurrection, Immortality, and Eternal Life in Intertestamental Judaism* [Cambridge: Harvard University Press, 1972]) engages in close analysis of several key intertestamental Jewish texts pertaining to eschatological events and shows their considerable variety on such matters as the timing, process, and cast of characters at the judgment; immediate immortality versus end-time resurrection (and who will be the recipients in either case); whether resurrection will be bodily or spiritual; and the nature of the interim existence of the dead. Nickelsburg effectively refutes Oscar Cullmann's influential Harvard University Ingersoll Lecture, "The Immortality of Man," in which Cullmann argued that the Jewish/New Testament understanding of bodily resurrection at the end time was incompatible with Greek belief in immortality of soul. (Cullmann's lecture was first published in *Harvard Divinity School Bulletin* 21 [1955/56]: 5–36; was published in monograph form in 1958; and finally appeared [with an afterword] as "Immortality of the Soul or Resurrection of the Dead?" in *Immortality and Resurrection* [ed. Krister Stendahl; New York: Macmillan, 1965], 9–53; references in this chapter are to the last of these). Nickelsburg writes, "The evidence indicates that in the intertestamental period there was no single Jewish orthodoxy on the time, mode, and place of resurrection, immortality, and eternal life. By excluding any discussion of specific Jewish texts, Cullmann has approached the New Testament presupposing a unitary Jewish view which is a pure fiction" (*Resurrection, Immortality, and Eternal Life,* 177–80 [quotation from 180]). On beliefs among the church fathers about the order of eschatological events, see Segal, *Life*

After Death, 536–37; Segal argues that the general trend among the "Orthodox" in early Christianity was to support a fleshly resurrection; immortality of soul was viewed as the doctrine to defeat (ibid., 532–95).

31. Segal, *Life After Death,* 265. So, Dan 12 "seemingly leaves the ordinary people dead forever" (ibid., 279). Segal argues that the prophecy of Dan 12 is based on a visionary interpretation of Isa 66 (ibid., 264–65).

32. Segal, *Life After Death,* 266–69 (includes discussion of 2 Maccabees). On the connection between the expectation of divine justice and doctrines of hell, see Bauckham, *The Fate of the Dead,* 132–48; on resurrection as a "revolutionary doctrine" which undermined the status quo, see Wright, *Resurrection,* 138.

33. Segal, *Life After Death,* 265 (see the discussion of "astral transformation," 265–66); see also Martha Himmelfarb, *Ascent to Heaven in Jewish and Christian Apocalypses* (New York: Oxford University Press, 1993), 50–51; Collins, *Daniel,* 393–94. Wright (*Resurrection,* 110–13) acknowledges that scholarly construal of Dan 12:3 as a reference to astral immortality has become widespread in recent years, but he sees "serious problems with this interpretation." Perceived problems center on the lack of close correspondence between Daniel's wording and Platonic or other Hellenistic expressions of belief in astral immortality. But Wright gives insufficient weight in his consideration to the many Jewish texts (some quite early) that interpret Dan 12:3 as a description of transformation to existence as stars/angels; Segal is more persuasive on these texts.

34. On the association of stars and angels, see Introduction, n. 12. See also *1 En.* 104:2–6, which Collins (*Daniel,* 393) dates to 100 BCE and possibly to pre-Maccabean times: "You will shine like the lights of heaven and will be seen, and the gate of heaven will be opened to you . . . you will have great joy like the angels of heaven . . . for you will be associates of the host of heaven" (translation from ibid.). Later apocryphal and pseudepigraphic references to the righteous as stars include Wis 3:7; *2 En.* 66:7; *T. Mos.* 10:9; 4 Macc 17:5; *2 Bar.* 51:10. In the New Testament, see Matt 13:43.

35. Philo, *Creation* 144; *Dreams* 1.135–37, 138–45; *Giants* 7; *Questions and Answers on Exodus* 2.114; *Moses* 2.108. For Philo's important role in the development of Jewish ideas of immortality, see Segal, *Life After Death,* 368–75. More generally, on astral transformation, see ibid., 265–66; Wright, *Resurrection,* 55–60; Dale B. Martin, *The Corinthian Body* (New Haven: Yale University Press, 1995), 117–20 (on astral immortality specifically; on death and afterlife in Greco-Roman culture more generally, see ibid., 108–17; on Philo, see ibid., 118); Alan Scott, *Origen and the Life of the Stars: A History of an Idea* (New York: Oxford University Press, 1991).

36. *First Enoch* 22:1–5, trans. E. Isaac, *OTP* 1:24–25. George W. E. Nickelsburg (*1 Enoch 1: A Commentary on the Book of 1 Enoch, Chapters 1–36; 81–108* [ed. Klaus Baltzer; Minneapolis: Fortress, 2001], 300–303) dates *1 Enoch* 22 to the third century BCE, which makes it one of the earliest Jewish testimonies to belief in postmortem judgment, and one of the earliest such treatments of the fate of the dead. He accounts for the inconsistencies of the passage (for example, as to whether there are three hollows or four) by positing different stages of composition and redaction. See also Segal, *Life After Death,* 272–81 (arguing, with other scholars, for Babylonian influence).

37. Segal, *Life After Death,* 142–45. Segal argues against John W. Cooper and James Barr, who question the consensus (with which Segal agrees) that the Hebrew Scriptures do not give a doctrine of the afterlife. In Segal's view, scriptural references to the *refa* or *nefesh* surviving death mark the continuing identity of a person but do not imply a judg-

ment or beatific afterlife: "The ancient Hebrew notion of 'soul' has no relationship to the Pythagorean and Platonic notion of an immortal soul, which is deathless by nature and capable of attaining bodiless felicity" (145). Segal discusses Greek and classical views of life after death more fully in ibid., 204–47.

38. Segal, *Life After Death,* 145. Martin (*Corinthian Body,* 115–17) shows that a body/soul dualism and deprecation of the fleshly body were widespread in the early Roman Empire, "especially in philosophical circles, though also among ordinary folk." He argues that this body/soul dualism was not, however, equivalent to a Cartesian dualism of matter/non-matter or physical/spiritual. On the way the Cartesian dualism is taken for granted in popular spirituality today, see p. 81.

39. Segal, *Life After Death,* 279–80, 491–94.

40. On what the historical Jesus may have taught about hell, see Dale C. Allison's fine analysis and provocative set of reflections, in *Resurrecting Jesus: The Earliest Christian Tradition and Its Interpreters* (New York: T. & T. Clark, 2005), 56–110.

41. In Luke 20:27–40, the evangelist edits this controversy story so as to imply that Christians may attain to the immortal angelic life here and now, in part through foregoing marriage. See Crispin H. T. Fletcher-Louis, *Luke-Acts: Angels, Christology, and Soteriology* (Tübingen: Mohr [Siebeck], 1997), 78–86, 219–22. Fletcher-Louis complements the work of Turid Karlsen Seim (*The Double Message: Patterns of Gender in Luke-Acts* [Nashville: Abingdon, 1994], 185–248) by showing how Luke's angelomorphic portrayal of the Christian community (which Seim also detected) is strongly rooted in pre-Christian Judaism.

42. See the summary and discussion of the work of Hugo Gressmann calling attention to the Egyptian folktale, in Joseph A. Fitzmyer, *The Gospel According to Luke* (2 vols.; Garden City, N.Y.: Doubleday, 1985), 2:1126–27. Richard Bauckham (*The Fate of the Dead,* 97–118) qualifies Gressmann's argument, noting that other ancient texts provide closer parallels to some aspects of Luke's story.

43. In Luke 2:11; 4:21; and 5:26, the Greek word *sēmeron* is used in a similarly ambiguous manner, to refer to an event that signifies the dawn of a new era but that also transpires literally on a particular day. The word "paradise" (Gk. *paradeisos*) is a loanword from Persian. In early Jewish and Christian sources it refers to the Garden of Eden, thought still to exist in heaven and sometimes construed as the place of reward after death. In the New Testament the word is used in Luke 23:43; 2 Cor 12:4 (where it is equated with the "third heaven" [12:2]: the notion of a multi-tiered heaven was by Paul's time already ancient, going back to the Sumerians), and Rev 2:7. In the *Testament of Abraham* the term is used repeatedly to designate the place of postmortem reward; see especially 20:14. Segal (*Life After Death,* 467) downplays any implication of immortality of soul in Luke 23:43, consistent with his thesis that the Gospels (and earliest Christian testimony generally) emphasized bodily resurrection. But Segal's thesis does not hold very well for Luke, who accepted the doctrine of a general resurrection (Acts 24:15), yet presupposed that the faithful would enter into the beatific life before that—certainly at death (Luke 16:19–31; 23:43), and perhaps already at conversion (Luke 20:37–40, on which see Fletcher-Louis, *Luke-Acts,* 78–86, 219–22).

44. See 2 Cor 5:8; Phil 1:23; 3:20; Rom 14:8–9.

45. See 1 Cor 3:12–15 (see also Rom 2:5; 14:10). On 2 Cor 5:6–10 see Wright, *Resurrection,* 369–70 (see also 216, 226–27); more generally on beliefs in Judaism of the Second Temple era about the intermediate state of the dead, see ibid., 129–206; also Richard

Bauckham, "Life, Death, and the Afterlife in Second Temple Judaism," in *Life in the Face of Death: The Resurrection Message of the New Testament* (Grand Rapids: Eerdmans, 1998), 88–89. Cullmann's essay "Immortality of the Soul or Resurrection of the Dead" (despite its problems, on which see n. 30 above) also contains insightful reflections on New Testament authors' conception of this intermediate state (ibid., 36–45). Cullmann concedes that the notion of an intermediate state exhibits "a kind of *approximation* to the Greek teaching" of immortality, but with key differences (ibid., 44). On Paul's language about the nature of the resurrected body in 1 Cor 15, see especially Martin, *Corinthian Body*, 123–36; Martin's treatment of the passage is superior to others because of its especially adept philological analysis of contemporaneous popular and philosophical notions relevant to Paul's discussion.

46. See Bauckham, "Descent," 2:146. Bauckham notes that the Gilgamesh tale is "of great interest as the earliest instance of a description of the state of the dead given by someone who had been to the underworld and had returned." Bauckham also summarizes the other cultural traditions of descent to the underworld listed in the text.

47. On the apocalyptic visions or tours of heaven and hell and their relationship to other ancient traditions (including other apocalyptic traditions), see especially Martha Himmelfarb, *Tours of Hell: An Apocalyptic Form in Jewish and Christian Literature* (Philadelphia: Fortress, 1983); Himmelfarb, *Ascent to Heaven;* also Bauckham, "Descent." Mary Dean-Otting (*Heavenly Journeys: A Study of the Motif in Hellenistic Jewish Literature* [Frankfurt: Verlag Peter Lang, 1984]) stresses the influence of biblical portrayals of deity in Exod 24, Isa 6, Ezek 1 and 43 upon the ascent texts. The location of the dead in ancient accounts varies: In Greek literature the realm of the dead (including the blessed) was subterranean; in Jewish and Christian literature, the location of the blessed and/or damned is variously at the western edge of the world, in one of the seven heavens, or under the earth. In many accounts it is hard to determine the presumed geographic location (see Bauckham, "Descent," 2:154; also Dean-Otting, *Heavenly Journeys*, 122–24).

48. The "watchers" were the angels who had descended to earth and mated with human women (Gen 6:1–4); see the discussion of this text and its ancient interpretations in Chapter 3. "Gehenna" is derived from a Hebrew term designating the "Valley of Hinnom" running south-southwest of Jerusalem. During the intertestamental period, Gehenna came to be identified as the place where the fiery judgment or eternal punishment would occur (see Duane F. Watson, "Gehenna," *ABD* 2:926–28; Allison, *Resurrecting Jesus*, 56–110).

49. See Himmelfarb, *Tours of Hell*, for discussion of early Christian apocalyptic tours of hell. On pages 7, 38–39, and 48–49, Himmelfarb discusses the work of Dante scholars in identifying apocalyptic influences on his work.

50. Himmelfarb (ibid., 8) dates the *Apocalypse of Peter* to no later than the middle of the second century CE. She contends that this document is not the original in the genre of "tours of hell," but only the earliest surviving member (ibid., 27–139). Richard Bauckham (*The Fate of the Dead*, 160–258) ties the origin of the *Apocalypse of Peter* to the Bar Kokhba war of 132–35 CE and argues that the document is an important source of knowledge of Jewish (and not just Christian) apocalyptic traditions.

51. *Apocalypse of Peter*, trans. to English by David Hill (from German translation of Ethiopic by H. Duensing), in E. Hennecke, *New Testament Apocrypha* (ed. Wilhelm Schneemelcher; English translation ed. R. McL. Wilson; Philadelphia: Westminster, 1965; 2 vols.), 2:670. Subsequent quotations of the *Apocalypse of Peter* are also from this translation.

52. See Himmelfarb's interesting discussion (*Tours of Hell*, 107–15) of the motif of postmortem punishment by fire and the evolution in the tradition from Sheol (conceived as a dark and miry bog or pit) to a fiery hell (first associated with Gehenna, on which see n. 48 above). Although Sheol was not traditionally depicted as fiery, Old Testament passages describing divine punishment by fire include Ps 21:9, Isa 33:11–14; 66:24; and Mal 4:1; in the New Testament see, Matt 3:12; 18:8, 9; 25:41; 1 Cor 3:13–15; see also 4 Macc 9:9; 12:12. On the angels of judgment in the *Apocalypse of Peter*, see Richard Bauckham's detailed discussion in *The Fate of the Dead*, 221–26. He writes, "Thus the general picture that emerges is that two named angels—Ezrael and Tartarouchos—are in overall charge of hell and its inhabitants, while numerous subordinate angels of punishment take charge of the specific punishments of specific groups of the damned" (226). This picture is not, however, presented systematically in the document; it emerges piecemeal.

53. On the motif of measure-for-measure punishments in the apocalyptic tours of hell and other ancient literature, see Himmelfarb, *Tours of Hell*, 68–105.

54. The *Apocalypse of Zephaniah* is difficult to date; O. S. Wintermute places it somewhere between 100 BCE and 175 CE (*Apocalypse of Zephaniah*, *OTP* 1:500–515; Wintermute's translation is used in quotations here). The author of the *Apocalypse of Zephaniah* appears to have been a Jew and there are no notable Christian interpolations, even though the document was clearly transcribed and preserved by Christian monks (ibid., 501; cf. Himmelfarb, *Tours of Hell*, 13–16, 151–53). Himmelfarb (*Ascent to Heaven*, 51–55) theorizes that the revelation to the seer in *Apocalypse of Zephaniah* reflects "the triumph of an ordinary soul [after death] that can serve as a model for all readers"; cf. Bauckham, "Descent," 2:155.

55. On the identity of this angel and his relation to similarly named angels in other ancient apocalyptic literature, see Himmelfarb, *Tours of Hell*, 151–52.

56. On the great variety in portrayals of the nature of the afterlife and the process of judgment in even the earliest Jewish sources, see Nickelsburg, *Resurrection, Immortality, and Eternal Life*. Nickelsburg argues that the presence of opposing angels as judicial accuser and advocate is a constituent theme of early Jewish traditions about judgment and resurrection, and that Dan 12:1–3 and Zech 3 (in which Satan accuses and the Angel of the LORD defends Joshua) are important exemplars of this tradition (ibid., 11–42 [especially 39–40]; see also Nickelsburg, "Eschatology in the Testament of Abraham: A Study of the Judgment Scene in the Two Recensions," in *Studies on the Testament of Abraham* [ed. George W. E. Nickelsburg; Missoula, Mont.: Scholars, 1976], 36–39).

57. *1 En.* 53:3–5; see also 10:12; 18:10–19:2; 21; 56:1–4; 62:11; 63:1; 66:1; 90:21–24; 100:4; for other references from outside the canon see Allison, *Testament of Abraham*, 262. For angels of punishment in the Old Testament, see Gen 19:13; 2 Sam 24:15; 2 Kgs 19:35; 1 Chr 21:9–22:1 (retells 2 Sam 24:11–25, but with an expanded role for the angel of the LORD, who is identified with the destroyer); 2 Chr 32:21; Isa 37:36; Ps 35:5–6; 78:49; 1 Macc 7:41; 3 Macc 6:18–19; Sus 1:55, 59. On the merging of the figures of the "destroyer" and the "angel of the LORD," see Meier, "Destroyer," in *DDD*, 240–44. On the punishing "angels of destruction" at Qumran, see Davidson, *Angels at Qumran*, 157–58.

58. On angels and humans in the *War Scroll* see Davidson, *Angels at Qumran*, 212–34. He writes that "fundamental to the nature of 1QM 1, and indeed, to the whole *War Scroll*, is the interdependence of the heavenly and earthly realms" (ibid., 216). Later he observes that "just how the angels of the lots of God and Belial help the corresponding human armies is not explained" (ibid., 228 n. 1).

59. See Himmelfarb's discussion (*Tours of Hell,* 120–21) of the development in intertestamental Judaism of the tradition of angels of torture. To account for notable differences from more traditional portraits of punishing angels in the Hebrew Scriptures, Himmelfarb posits Greek influence on this emerging tradition (though she contends that A. Dieterich has overstated the case for such influence). See also Segal, *Life After Death,* 488–89. Segal sees the development as connected in part to the increasingly popular synthesis of resurrection of the dead with immortality of the soul. "Once the soul was immortal and all souls survived forever, then punishment had to be eternal as well, otherwise sinners would appear to get away with their dastardly deeds" (489). For evidence of early impulses to limit punishment, see Allison, *Resurrecting Jesus,* 62, 95; see also Richard Bauckham, *The Fate of the Dead,* 132–48.

60. Allison, *Resurrecting Jesus,* 95 (includes the Holocaust comparison, ascribed to George Steiner). Allison offers a trenchant theological critique of the notion of hell (ibid., 91–100). He recognizes how the severe injustices of the world and "moral reflection within a theological context" seem to drive us to a notion of hell (ibid., 99); he also concedes the positive functions of the doctrine of hell, for example, the notion that "what we do really matters, and our accountability does not forsake us" (ibid., 97). Yet, he argues that the difficulties created by the doctrine of hell are insuperable. The notion of "a God who loves all yet insatiably tortures some" is not "an irreducible tension to be tolerated but a plain inconsistency to be dissolved. Genuine mystery is one thing, stark contradiction another" (ibid., 94). He finds especially repugnant the idea, well established in the tradition, that in the hereafter the righteous will witness the eternal punishment inflicted on their enemies and that doing so will increase their love, joy, and praise of God (ibid., 94–95). Such later Christian lore about hell "goes far beyond anything that the biblical texts and Jesus, both innocent of sadism, taught." Further, Jesus' "characteristic teaching about nonviolence and love of enemy deconstructs the retributive postmortem torture chamber of our tradition" (ibid., 96). See also Bauckham, *Fate of the Dead,* 132–48.

61. On Hermes and Charon, see Segal, *Life After Death,* 210–11; on Helios conducting the emperor's soul, see ibid., 246; on psychopomps in Zoroastrianism, see ibid., 186; on Michael and others as psychopomps in ancient Greco-Roman, Jewish, and Christian sources, see Allison, *Testament of Abraham,* 76, 397–99. An article in Wikipedia (online: http://en.wikipedia.org/wiki/Psychopomp) lists psychopomps from many cultures, not just those in Judeo-Christian-Islamic mythology.

62. Bauckham ("Descent," 2:155) suggests that the shift to belief in immediate postmortem punishment, which transpired over the first two centuries CE and is attested in the apocalyptic "tours of hell," reflects influence from Greek accounts of postmortem recompense. Here Bauckham is qualifying the important finding of Martha Himmelfarb (*Tours of Hell*) that the Jewish and Christian tours of hell are chiefly indebted to Jewish apocalyptic antecedents (rather than to ancient Orphic-Pythagorean traditions, as argued by A. Dieterich; see also Bauckham, *The Fate of the Dead,* 208–9). Dean-Otting (*Heavenly Journeys,* 122–23) argues that the beginning of the idea of punishment in Sheol (previously not a place of punishment) was facilitated by the use of *hades* to translate *sheol* in the Septuagint; on this subject see also Bauckham, "Hades," *ABD* 3:14–15. Note that *4 Ezra*'s detailed description of the fate of the dead in the intermediate state (*4 Ezra* 7:75–101, written in the late first century CE) still does not include any mention of a psychopomp.

63. *Testament of Job,* trans. R. P. Spittler, *OTP* 1:867–68.

64. The *Testament of Abraham* has been preserved in two main recensions: the longer Recension A (preserved in Greek and Rumanian versions), and the shorter Recension B (preserved in Greek, Slavonic, and several other versions). The relationship between the two recensions is complicated; Allison (*Testament of Abraham*, 15) judges that, on the whole, Recension B's shorter story line is secondary, yet he acknowledges that "the issue remains very complex" (see ibid., 4–27 for a full listing of the various manuscripts and discussion of the relationship between the two main recensions). References in this chapter are to Recension A. Allison holds that the original work was of Jewish authorship, but underwent thorough Christian editing over the centuries; he sees good evidence for the work's origin in Egypt somewhere near the turn of the Era (ibid., 28–39).

65. *Testament of Abraham*, trans. E. P. Sanders, *OTP* 1:882; all quotations of the *Testament of Abraham* here are from Sanders' translation.

66. See Nickelsburg, "Eschatology in the *Testament of Abraham*," 41–47 for an illuminating analysis of this judgment scene.

67. Allison, *Testament of Abraham*, 50 (citing Becker, *The Denial of Death*). Bauckham ("Descent," 2:155) regards the scene in which Abraham is taken to see the place in the East where the dead are judged (*T. Ab.* 11–14 [Recension A]; or 8–11 [Recension B]) as strongly reminiscent of Plato's myth of Er in *Republic* 10.614B–621B. The myth of Er (on which see ibid., 2:151; see also Dean-Otting, *Heavenly Journeys*, 15–16) constitutes the most influential ancient account of a near-death experience.

68. Allison (*Testament of Abraham*, 324–25, 329) makes the case that in the *Testament of Abraham*, the patriarch is implied to be an angel though this identity is never made explicit.

69. Ibid., 322.

70. On the notion of death's many faces in worldwide mythology and in Judaism, see ibid., 347–48; cf. 327–28. Allison thinks that the motif in the *Testament of Abraham* may derive from a rabbinic legend that originated in imaginative reflection on the Hebrew text of Gen 23:3.

71. On the motif of a multitude of angels appearing at death, see ibid., 397–98. Allison thinks the motif is "typically Christian," though it may well derive from Judaism; he cites a number of parallels from early Christian literature.

72. Allison (ibid., 42) notes that the repeated commands that Abraham put his house in order lead the reader to expect a testament, which Abraham never provides. "So [*Testament of Abraham*] is a parody. This is why it is so full of comic elements . . . and why it looks like and does not look like other testaments. Perhaps one should call it an 'anti-testament.'"

73. For parallels to the notion of the different deaths (and different guises of the angel of death) experienced by the wicked and the righteous, see ibid., 327, 343; Allison notes that Iranian literature, in particular, offers parallels to this idea, and even to very specific elements in the *Testament of Abraham*.

74. Van der Horst ("Thanatos," 855) sees Euripides' portrayal of the deity Thanatos in the *Alcestis* as an especially important influence on the portrayal of Death in the *Testament of Abraham*. Allison (*Testament of Abraham*, 324 n. 6) tentatively concurs, and suggests that this influence may account for the *Testament*'s referring to the figure as "Death" rather than as "the Angel of Death." Allison also stresses the importance of traditions about the death of Moses (which also involved resistance of the angel of death) as sources for the *Testament of Abraham* (ibid., 24, 175, 185, 189, 388). Dean-Otting (*Heav-*

enly Journeys, 213) acknowledges Egyptian, Greek, and Jewish influences on the *Testament of Abraham's* portrayal of the figure of Death, but comments that the final product is certainly "the product of a fertile imagination."

75. *Ghost,* produced by Steve-Charles Jaffe and Bruce Joel Rubin, directed by Jerry Zucker, 127 minutes, 1990; Howard Storm, *My Descent into Death: A Second Chance at Life* (New York: Doubleday, 2005), 10–25.

76. *Death Takes a Holiday,* produced by Paramount Pictures, directed by Mitchell Leisen, 79 minutes, 1934; *The Seventh Seal,* produced by Allan Ekelund, directed by Ingmar Bergman, 92 minutes, 1957; *Bill and Ted's Bogus Journey,* produced by Scott Kroopf, directed by Peter Hewitt, 93 minutes, 1991; *Monty Python's The Meaning of Life,* produced by John Goldstone, directed by Terry Jones and Terry Gilliam, 103 minutes, 1983; "Reaper Madness," segment in "Treehouse of Horror XIV" of *The Simpsons,* November 2, 2003. For a long list of films and fiction featuring death as a character see "Death (Personification)" (online: http://en.wikipedia.org/wiki/Personified_death).

77. See Ariès, *Images of Man and Death,* 147–55 (includes numerous images).

78. Ibid., 157.

79. See ibid., especially chaps. 5 and 6, for changes in the representation of Death from the fourteenth through nineteenth centuries. See also Web site by Patrick Polleyfeys, "Death in Art" (online: http://www.lamortdanslart.com/danse/Manuscrit/Holbein/dd_holbein.htm).

80. *Testament of Abraham* 4:11; 8:9, 10; see also Jer 9:22, which may have given rise to this motif; LXX Zech 5:1–4 (the seer beholds a giant flying sickle; in the Hebrew it was a flying scroll); Rev 14:15–20. The motif of the sickle is discussed in Allison, *Testament of Abraham,* 145. The notion that Death is a reaper of souls depended on development of belief in the soul as an enduring aspect of the human self, which is destined for postmortem existence.

81. The reference is to the Babylonian Talmud, tractate *Avodah Zarah* 20b; see Allison, *Testament of Abraham,* 73, 325 (includes a list of rabbinic references to the angel of death). Allison points out that in rabbinic sources the angel of death "is often called Sam(m)ael, which may mean 'poison of God' "; he compares the reference to the "bitter cup of death" in the *T. Ab.* 1:3 and 16:11, 12. For a general overview of rabbinic notions of the afterlife, see Segal, *Life After Death,* 596–638.

82. A robed, scythe-bearing skeleton (not hooded) appears in a fourteenth century illustration from Boccaccio's *Decameron* (reproduced in Ariès, *Images of Man and Death,* 96), and in Lorenzo Costa's 1490 painting "The Triumph of Death" (ibid., 205).

83. Charles Dickens, *A Christmas Carol,* Stave 4, "The Last of the Spirits" (online: http://www.cedmagic.com/featured/christmas-carol/1951-xmas-future.html).

84. The edition illustrated by Doré was published by Harper & Brothers in 1883, a year after Doré's death; the illustrations are reproduced (along with a standard edition of the poem) in Edgar Allan Poe, *The Raven* (New York: Dover Publications, 1996). The picture of the Grim Reaper appears in ibid., 21; the figure holds a scythe and an hourglass and looks as though he is taking respite from his work. Doré also depicted personified Death in his 1870 illustrations for Samuel Taylor Coleridge's *The Rime of the Ancient Mariner.* It is not certain when the word "grim" became attached to the figure of the Reaper, but it seems to have been sometime during the early twentieth century. See Loyd Auerbach, "Don't Fear the Reaper" (the October 1996 edition of Auerbach's column "Psychic Frontiers," which appeared in *Fate* Magazine; online: http://www.mindreader.com/fate/articles/Fate1096.doc).

85. See the informative discussion of Holbein's *The Dance of Death* in Pollefeys, "Death in Art." Pollefeys helpfully relates Holbein's "dance of death" to earlier forms of the genre and to other death-motifs in art from about the same time period, including "the legend of the three living and the three dead," "death and the maiden," and "the triumph of death." Pollefeys notes how Holbein's work critiqued the powerful (both secular and religious), often through the use of irony.

86. *Dead Poets Society,* produced by Silverscreen Partners IV and Touchstone Pictures, directed by Peter Weir, 128 minutes, 1989.

87. From "The Voice of Generation Hex," an interview by Chad Hensley (online: http://www.esoterra.org/manson.htm). On social critique in the zombie horror films of George A. Romero (*Night of the Living Dead* and numerous others), see the works cited in n. 6 above.

88. The Gothic cultural phenomenon began in the 1980s, in conjunction with Punk and New Wave music; today the term encompasses various subcultures that share some elements (though they evince notable differences and disagreements). There are various (and in some cases ephemeral) Web sites that are helpful for understanding the Gothic movement(s), including: http://en.wikipedia.org/wiki/Gothic_subculture (includes numerous links). There is often an erotic dimension in Gothic representations of death, present already in Bram Stoker's story of Count Dracula and in visual depictions of personified Death going back centuries (see Ariès, *Images of Man and Death,* 178–79, 181 for illustrations; also the treatment of "death and the maiden" in Pollefeys, "Death in Art"). The erotic theme was present in the 1934 film *Death Takes a Holiday,* in which the beautiful young Grazia willingly becomes Death's consort (other women in the story are likewise fascinated by Death, at least at first).

89. *My First Mister,* produced by Carol Baum et al., directed by Christine Lahti, 109 minutes, 2001.

90. The film's two main characters offer a study in contrasts. J's friend Randall cannot live joyfully because he is socially paralyzed by his fear of death; J herself seems more afraid of plunging into life. Becker commented on both sorts of fear. Regarding fearfulness about life he wrote, "Life can suck one up, sap his energies, submerge him, take away his self-control, give so much new experience so quickly that he will burst; make him stick out among others, emerge onto dangerous ground, load him up with new responsibilities which need great strength to bear, expose him to new contingencies, new chances. Above all there is the danger of a slip-up, an accident, a chance disease, and of course of death, the final sucking up, the total submergence and negation" (*Denial of Death,* 54). My thanks go to Professors Jeff Greenberg and Sheldon Solomon for their help in understanding how fear of death might relate to the proliferation of death-imagery in popular culture.

91. See Ludwig, *Graven Images,* 108–109, 202–216 and passim (includes many photographs of gravestones featuring symbols of eternal life and victory over death, including, for example, crowns of glory and palms of victory).

92. Perhaps it is a question of how one defines "spirituality." Thriving industries center on the occult, the paranormal, and even necrophilia (as a search on the Internet will easily demonstrate); the angel of death plays a greater role in these contexts.

93. See Harold Bloom, *Omens of Millennium: The Gnosis of Angels, Dreams, and Resurrection* (New York: Riverhead Books, 1996), 125–215. Bloom notes that Raymond Moody cited Saint Paul, the *Tibetan Book of the Dead,* and Emanuel Swedenborg as analogues

to recent near-death experiences; Bloom argues that closer analogues are to be found in Christian gnosticism, Shi'ite Sufism, and Kabbalah.

94. Raymond A. Moody, *Life After Life: The Investigation of a Phenomenon—Survival of Bodily Death* (2nd ed.; San Francisco: HarperSanFrancisco, 2001; originally published in 1975). See Moody's Web site (online: http://www.lifeafterlife.com; see also http://www .near-death.com [a gateway to many near-death related sites]).

95. See Williams' introduction to the Web site (online: http://www.near-death.com/ about.html). On the theme of "separation" in current popular spirituality, see p. 81.

96. Zaleski, *Life of the World to Come,* 32–33.

97. From the summary of Ritchie's near-death experience (online: http://www.near -death.com/ritch.html).

98. James Van Praagh, *Heaven and Earth: Making the Psychic Connection* (New York: Simon & Schuster, 2001), 23. On the practice of spiritualism (communing with the dead), see the works cited in n. 102 below.

99. From a summary of Brodsky's near-death experience (online: http://www.near -death.com/experiences/judaism02.html).

100. Betty J. Eadie, "In God We Trust" (online: http://www.embracedbythelight.com/ wakeup/articles.htm).

101. See the account of the beginnings of the near-death movement in Michael Sabom, *Light and Death* (Grand Rapids: Zondervan, 1998), 131–41. Much of the near-death lit- erature features themes consistent with those of New Age spirituality (for example, the problem of separation, the need for universal and unconditional love, the conviction that everything happens according to·a cosmic or divine plan). Sabom argues that this consistency derives not from the near-death experiences themselves, but from ideolog- ical commitments of the tightly-knit core group of researchers in the beginning years of the movement and the influence they exercised over interviewees. Sabom was originally part of this group of researchers but veered away because his own conservative Christian commitments were at odds with them, and because he thought that members were al- lowing ideology to bias their research findings.

102. On the American spiritualist movement and its influence on the present-day phe- nomenon of channeling, see Michael F. Brown, *The Channeling Zone* (Cambridge, Mass.: Harvard University Press, 1997), 11, 58–62. For a fascinating account of the history and current happenings in the town of Lily Dale, New York (a mecca for American spiritual- ists), see Christine Wicker, *Lily Dale: The True Story of the Town That Talks to the Dead* (San Francisco: HarperSanFrancisco, 2003). This and other recent works on the history of spiritualism are reviewed in Jason Byassee, "If Death Is No Barrier," *Books and Cul- ture* 13:1 (2007): 16–21. On the theosophical movement, see "Theosophy," online: http:// en.wikipedia.org/wiki/Theosophy#Reincarnation_is_universal. Sabom (*Light and Death,* 143–63) critiques the interest of some near-death researchers in spiritualism and other psychic phenomena. He describes a public lecture in which Raymond Moody advocated a practice of communing with the dead, following which another speaker randomly se- lected members of the audience for "live readings as directed by the Other Side." Sabom notes with irony that in an earlier published statement, Moody had warned against using near-death experiences "as an excuse for allowing the entrance of spiritualism, with all its bizarre trappings, into medicine," since "the history of the fraud and fakery associated with such dealings is too well known (and too ancient!) to bear repeating" (quoted in *Light and Death,* 144–45).

103. Zaleski, *Life of the World to Come,* 25–26; cf. Segal, *Life After Death,* 205–6; Bauckham, "Descent," 2:152–54; Dean-Otting, *Heavenly Journeys,* 13–20.

104. The passage is attributed to Plutarch in Stobaeus, *Anthologion* 4.52.49; the quoted lines are taken from Zaleski (*Life of the World to Come,* 26–27), who ascribes it to Marvin W. Meyer, ed., *The Ancient Mysteries: A Sourcebook* (New York: Harper and Row, 1987), 9; the quotation is discussed in Zaleski, *Life of the World to Come,* 25–26; also Segal, *Life After Death,* 217 (see ibid., 214–18 on the mystery religions).

105. *Acts of Thomas,* trans. to English (from G. Bornkamm's German translation) by R. McL. Wilson, in Hennecke-Schneemelcher, *New Testament Apocrypha,* 2:473. The incident occurs in Act 6. Himmelfarb (*Tours of Hell,* 11) notes that the earliest form of this text is usually dated to the first half of the third century CE. She rejects the conclusion of M. R. James and G. Bornkamm that *Acts of Thomas* borrows from the *Apocalypse of Peter:* "Both texts drew on the same early traditions as the later Hebrew texts and the Latin Elijah fragment" (ibid.). In general on accounts of near-death experiences in ancient Greece and Rome, see Bauckham, "Descent," 2:150–51.

106. In addition to the chasms where punishment is carried out, there is one cave or chasm where souls are held while awaiting punishment or when punishment is completed. "And some are entirely consumed, and [some] are handed over to other punishments." In a general way these chasms seem to go back to the "chasms" envisioned in *1 En.* 22. As Himmelfarb notes, in the tours of hell, directions and geographic markers are often quite confused (*Tours of Hell,* 107). On the motif of "measure-for-measure punishments," see ibid., 68–105.

107. Zaleski, *Life of the World to Come,* 20–21.

108. Ibid. Cf. Bowker's comment (*Meanings of Death,* 39) on how religious explorations of death raise questions about values for life.

109. Zaleski, *Life of the World to Come,* 13.

110. "Psalm 151," episode 508 of *Touched by an Angel,* November 15, 1998.

111. Zaleski, *Life of the World to Come,* 22.

112. For a similar view expressed by Socrates and also by Epictetus, see Wright, *Resurrection,* 53–54.

113. Zaleski, *Life of the World to Come,* 22.

114. From an interview with Nicholas Wolterstorf, in the Mars Hill audio report: "Best-Selling Spirituality: American Cultural Change and the New Shape of Faith" (audio recording; written and produced by Andrew Witmer; narrated and ed. by Ken Myers; Powhatan, Va.: Mars Hill Audio, 1999).

115. See pp. 122–26. Cf. the remark by William Stringfellow: "The principalities claim, in other words, sovereignty over human life and history. Therefore, they not only compete and conflict with one another for the possession and domination of the lives of human beings, but they also deny and denounce the sovereignty of God. But do not let the arrogance of the idols conceal this fact: when a principality claims moral preeminence in history or over a person's life, it represents an aspiration for salvation from death and a hope that service to the idol will give existence a meaning somehow transcending death" (from *A Keeper of the Word: Selected Writings of William Stringfellow* [edited and with introduction by Bill Wylie Kellerman; Grand Rapids: Eerdmans, 1994], 200).

116. Betty J. Eadie, "In God We Trust."

117. From Kevin Williams' Web site summarizing near-death authors' views on the fu-

ture (online: http://www.near-death.com/experiences/research32.html). Williams relates that earlier in his life he was influenced by fundamentalist Christianity.

118. Such analysis can be carried out using different discourses than the spiritual/ biblical discourse about principalities and powers employed here; for example, one could use the terms and tools of psychology, sociology, or political science. For such analysis using the discipline of psychology (among others), see Becker, *The Denial of Death,* especially 127–58 (on the phenomenon of thralldom to charismatic leaders).

119. The variables for analysis identified here are drawn from a worksheet designed by Bill Wylie Kellermann. The questions are influenced by the work of William Stringfellow.

120. Stringfellow, *Keeper of the Word,* 201.

121. See the discussion in ibid., 201.

122. Cullmann, "Immortality of the Soul or Resurrection of the Dead," 26.

123. Stringfellow, *Instead of Death,* 107.

124. The full text of Tazewell's *The Littlest Angel,* originally published in 1946, is available online, at http://www.geocities.com/Athens/Acropolis/6182/thelittlestangel.html. Print versions are available in various editions. The television movie *The Littlest Angel* was directed by Joe Layton, 1969.

125. On this notion of an angelic afterlife, see the references (including those to discussions of astral immortality) in nn. 33–35 above; see also Segal, *Life After Death,* 292–93, 303–8, 357–58, 372, 412–40, 466, 580, passim; Kevin P. Sullivan, *Wrestling with Angels: A Study of the Relationship Between Angels and Humans in Ancient Jewish Literature and the New Testament* (Leiden: Brill, 2004), 131–39. Wright (*Resurrection,* 422) categorically rejects all arguments that early Christians believed in an angelic afterlife.

126. Segal (*Life After Death,* 356–57) suggests that *1 En.* 39 has been influenced by Dan 12. In *1 En.* 70–71, Enoch is transformed into the Son of Man (also an angelic figure); Segal regards this passage as "a first-person, confessional report of the very experience of undergoing the astral transformation" prophesied in Dan 12 (ibid., 358). All these passages derive from the section of *1 Enoch* known as the Parables or Similitudes (= *1 En.* 37–71), which is difficult to date but may be first century CE (see ibid., 356–59).

127. The date of composition and provenance of *2 Enoch* are very elusive; see the discussion in the introduction to the translation by F. I. Andersen, in *OTP* 1:94–97. Andersen leans toward a date early in the Common Era, and a Jewish (albeit a fringe Jewish) rather than Christian community. Cf. Himmelfarb, *Ascent to Heaven,* 37–38.

128. *Second Baruch,* trans. A. F. J. Klijn, *OTP* 1:638; the work likely originated sometime during the first three centuries CE. See Segal's discussion (focusing on the theme of the angelic afterlife), in *Life After Death,* 495–97; on the relationship of the passage to other apocalyptic traditions, see Nickelsburg, *Resurrection, Immortality, and Eternal Life,* 84–85. On particularly righteous individuals as transformed into angels, see James H. Charlesworth, "The Portrayal of the Righteous as an Angel," in *Ideal Figures in Ancient Judaism: Profiles and Paradigms* (eds. John J. Collins and George W. E. Nickelsburg; Chico, Calif.: Scholars, 1980), 135–51. On the idea that all the righteous (and not just certain individuals) would be elevated and glorified, see Sullivan, *Wrestling with Angels,* 132; Segal, *Life After Death,* 356–59; Himmelfarb, *Ascent to Heaven,* 47–71.

129. The question of when the angelic afterlife will commence is hard to pin down for many of the texts in question. Luke 20:35; Acts 23:6–8; Rev 6:9–11; *Martyrdom and Ascension of Isaiah* 8:15–17; 9:39; 11:35; and *Shepherd of Hermas, Visions* 2:2:7 and *Simili-*

tudes 9:25:2 could all be interpreted to imply immediate translation to angelic existence at death (rather than only at the time of the resurrection). All these passages are analyzed in Sullivan, *Wrestling with Angels,* 131–39.

130. Segal, *Life After Death,* 307.

131. Segal (ibid., 307) contends that at the very least the *leaders* at Qumran may have been regarded by their fellows as angels or as semidivine. The leaders mediated between heaven and earth, and were "exemplars of the perfection which the group emulated and revered" (see the entire discussion of angelomorphism at Qumran in ibid., 303–8; also 414). In taking this position Segal allies himself with Fletcher-Louis, *Luke-Acts,* 184–98; Fletcher-Louis, *All the Glory of Adam: Liturgical Anthropology in the Dead Sea Scrolls* (Leiden: Brill, 2002); cf. Himmelfarb, *Ascent to Heaven,* 49; Davidson, *Angels at Qumran,* 316–19. Fletcher-Louis (*All the Glory of Adam,* 1–32) includes a useful discussion of "angelomorphism in late Second Temple Judaism." Sullivan (*Wrestling with Angels,* 147–78) agrees with the evidence that the Essenes and Paul believed that they mingled with angels in their respective communities (specifically in the Corinthian church, in Paul's case), but he strenuously rejects the suggestion of Fletcher-Louis that any supposed they were actually being transformed into angels.

132. Fletcher-Louis, *Luke-Acts,* 33–107, 216–50.

133. See Luke 20:27–40, discussed in Seim, *The Double Message,* 185–248; Fletcher-Louis, *Luke-Acts,* 78–86, 219–22. The passage was the single most important warrant for the ideal of virginity in the early church; see Robin Lane Fox, *Pagans and Christians* (San Francisco: Harper & Row, 1986), 363, 366.

134. Fletcher-Louis, *Luke-Acts,* 96–106. The phrase *eis diatagas aggelōn* in Acts 7:53 is translated "as ordained by angels" in the NRSV (similarly in other published translations), but Fletcher-Louis shows that this translation is problematic on two separate grounds (the translation of the preposition, and the meaning of *diatagē*). He renders the phrase "with a view to creating an angelic constitution" (ibid., 98–106).

135. See Segal's discussion of Paul, in *Life After Death,* 399–440 (especially 415, 416–21, 424, 430–31, 439).

136. Other texts illustrating the conviction that Christians are being or will be transformed into the image of Christ include Rom 8:29; 1 Cor 15:49; 2 Cor 3:18; and Col 3:10. Of these, 2 Cor 3:18 and Col 3:10 seem to imply that the transformation has already begun. Segal (*Life After Death,* 418) calls attention to "how completely the theophanic language from Greek and Jewish mystical piety has been appropriated for discussing what we today call conversion." This language coheres with Paul's experience of transformation and divinization (or angelification) stemming from his personal encounter with the risen Christ. Segal further insists that the "transformation and angelification is authenticated in communal life, in social transactions (for instance, I Cor 12–14, also I Cor 5:1–5)" (ibid., 419).

137. Here I follow N. T. Wright's suggestive argument (in *The Climax of the Covenant: Christ and the Law in Pauline Theology* [Minneapolis: Fortress Press. 1991], 175–92) that the "mirror" in which Christians behold the glory of the Lord (2 Cor 3:17–18) is not the Gospel or even Jesus but *one another.*

138. The NRSV is superior to many other translations here because by rendering *en hymin* as "among you" instead of "in you" it makes clear that the "you" in question is plural.

139. On 2 Cor 4:4, see Susan R. Garrett, "The God of This World and the Affliction of

Paul: 2 Cor 4:1–12," in *Greeks, Romans, and Christians* (ed. David Balch et al.; Minneapolis: Fortress, 1990), 99–117. On the connection between suffering and transformation, see Segal, *Life After Death,* 437–38.

140. Miroslav Volf, *Exclusion and Embrace: A Theological Exploration of Identity, Otherness, and Reconciliation* (Nashville: Abingdon, 1996), 71.

141. Timothy B. Tyson, *Blood Done Sign My Name: A True Story* (New York: Crown, 2004).

142. Luke's portrayal of the early Christian community in Jerusalem (see Acts 2:44–47; 4:34–37) is an idealization, influenced not only by ideas of angelic community but also by popular philosophical notions about friendship. All in all, this is a rather more complex portrait of community than may be realized by the casual reader.

143. Garrison Keillor, interviewed by Bill McNabb, in *TheDoorMagazine Interviews: Take Two* (ed. Robert Darden; Dallas: TheDoorMagazine, 2002), 104.

144. Volf, *Exclusion and Embrace,* 28.

145. Ibid.

146. Stringfellow, *Instead of Death,* 12.

147. For astute reflection on the continuing worth of dualistic language about "spirit" and "flesh" (when used with discernment), see Zaleski, *Life of the World to Come,* 58–61. For an historical count of the move in liberal Christianity of the late nineteenth and early twentieth centuries away from "the sting of death," see James M. Moorhead, *World without End: Mainstream American Protestant Visions of the Last Things, 1880–1925* (Bloomington: Indiana University Press, 1999), 69–76.

148. Henri J. M. Nouwen, *Bread for the Journey: A Daybook of Wisdom and Faith* (San Francisco: HarperSanFrancisco, 1997), entry for January 16.

CONCLUSION

1. Carol Zaleski, *The Life of the World to Come: Near-Death Experience and Christian Hope* (New York: Oxford University Press, 1996), 34–35.

2. Michael Welker, "Angels in the Biblical Tradition," *Theology Today* 51 (1994): 369–70.

3. The phrase is of Jonathan Edwards, from his sermon "Heaven Is a World of Love."

BIBLIOGRAPHY

Abrams, Michael. *The Evolution Angel: An Emergency Physician's Lessons with Death and the Divine.* Boulder: Abundance Media, 2000.

Allison, Dale C. *Resurrecting Jesus: The Earliest Christian Tradition and Its Interpreters.* New York: T. & T. Clark, 2005.

———. *Testament of Abraham.* Commentaries on Early Jewish Literature. Berlin: Walter de Gruyter, 2003.

Alsup, John E. *The Post-Resurrection Appearance Stories of the Gospel Tradition: A History-of-Tradition Analysis; with Text-Synopsis.* Stuttgart: Calwer-Verlag, 1975.

Andersen, F. I., trans. *2 Enoch.* Pages 91–213 in vol. 1 of *The Old Testament Pseudepigrapha.* Edited by James H. Charlesworth. 2 vols. Anchor Bible Reference Library. Garden City, N.Y.: 2003, 2005.

Anderson, Bernhard W. "Sin and the Powers of Chaos." Pages 71–84 in *Sin, Salvation, and the Spirit.* Edited by Daniel Durken. Collegeville, Minn.: Liturgical Press, 1979.

Anderson, Gary A. *The Genesis of Perfection: Adam and Eve in Jewish and Christian Imagination.* Louisville: Westminster John Knox, 2001.

Anderson, Joan Wester. *In the Arms of Angels: True Stories of Heavenly Guardians.* Chicago: Loyola, 2004.

———. *Where Angels Walk: True Stories of Heavenly Visitors.* Sea Cliff, N.Y.: Barton & Brett, 1992.

The Ante-Nicene Fathers: Translations of the Writings of the Fathers Down to A. D. 325. Edited by Alexander Roberts and James Donaldson. 10 vols. 5th ed. Grand Rapids: Eerdmans, 1974.

The Apostolic Fathers. Translated by Kirsopp Lake. 2 vols. LCL. Cambridge, Mass.: Harvard University Press, 1948.

Ariès, Philippe. *Images of Man and Death.* Translated by Janet Lloyd. Cambridge, Mass.: Harvard University Press, 1985.

Arnold, Clinton E. *3 Crucial Questions about Spiritual Warfare.* Grand Rapids: Baker, 1997.

Ashley, Timothy R. *The Book of Numbers*. The New International Commentary on the Old Testament. Grand Rapids: Eerdmans, 1993.

Ashton, John. "Paraclete." Pages 152–54 in vol. 5 of *The Anchor Bible Dictionary*. Edited by David Noel Freedman. 6 vols. New York: Doubleday, 1992.

Attridge, Harold W. *The Epistle to the Hebrews: A Commentary on the Epistle to the Hebrews*. Edited by Helmut Koester. Hermeneia 53. Philadelphia: Fortress, 1989.

Auerbach, Loyd. "Don't Fear the Reaper." *Fate Magazine* (October, 1999). Cited March 29, 2007. Online: http://www.mindreader.com/fate/articles/Fate1096.doc.

Augustine. *The Confessions*. Edited by John E. Rotelle. Introduction, translation, and notes by Maria Boulding. The Works of Saint Augustine: A Translation for the 21st Century I/1. Hyde Park, N.Y.: New City Press, 1997.

Balentine, Samuel E. "For No Reason." *Interpretation* 57 (2003): 349–69.

Baltimore Catechism No. 2, Revised ed., "Confraternity of Christian Doctrine, 1941." Cited March 29, 2007. Online: http://www.truecatholic.org/baltp1.htm.

Barth, Karl. *Church Dogmatics*. Vol. 3, part 3 of The Doctrine of Creation. Edited by G. W. Bromiley and T. F. Torrance. Edinburgh: T. & T. Clark, 1960.

Bauckham, Richard. "Descent to the Underworld." Pages 145–59 in vol. 2 of *The Anchor Bible Dictionary*. Edited by David Noel Freedman. 6 vols. New York: Doubleday, 1992.

———. *The Fate of the Dead: Studies on the Jewish and Christian Apocalypses*. Supplements to Novum Testamentum 93. Leiden: Brill, 1998.

———. "Hades." Pages 14–15 in vol. 3 of *The Anchor Bible Dictionary*. Edited by David Noel Freedman. 6 vols. New York: Doubleday, 1992.

———. "Life, Death, and the Afterlife in Second Temple Judaism." Pages 80–95 in *Life in the Face of Death: The Resurrection Message of the New Testament*. Edited by Richard N. Longenecker. Grand Rapids: Eerdmans, 1998.

Beck, Martha Nibley. *Expecting Adam: A True Story of Birth, Rebirth, and Everyday Magic*. New York: Times Books, 1999.

Becker, Ernest. *The Denial of Death*. New York: The Free Press, 1973.

Bednarowski, Mary Farrell. *The Religious Imagination of American Women*. Religion in North America. Bloomington: Indiana University Press, 1999.

Bellah, Robert Neelly, Richard Madsen, William M. Sullivan, Ann Swidler, and Steven M. Tipton. *Habits of the Heart: Individualism and Commitment in American Life*. Berkeley: University of California Press, 1985.

Berger, Peter L. *A Rumor of Angels: Modern Society and the Rediscovery of the Supernatural*. Garden City, N.Y.: Doubleday, 1970.

Berkhof, H. *Christ and the Powers*. Translated by John H. Yoder. 2nd ed. Scottdale, Pa.: Herald, 1977.

———. *Christian Faith: An Introduction to the Study of the Faith*. Translated by Sierd Woudstra. Grand Rapids: Eerdmans, 1979.

Bill and Ted's Bogus Journey. Produced by Scott Kroopf and directed by Peter Hewitt. 93 minutes. 1991. DVD by MGM, 2001.

The Bishop's Wife. Produced by Samuel Goldwyn and directed by Henry Koster. 109 minutes, 1948. DVD by MGM, 2001.

Bloom, Harold. *Omens of Millennium: The Gnosis of Angels, Dreams, and Resurrection*. New York: Riverhead Books, 1996.

Blount, Brian K., and Gary W. Charles. *Preaching Mark in Two Voices.* Louisville: Westminster John Knox, 2002.

Bonhoeffer, Dietrich. *Creation and Fall: A Theological Interpretation of Genesis 1–3.* New York: Macmillan, 1959.

Boring, M. Eugene. "The Gospel of Matthew: Introduction, Commentary, and Reflections." Pages 87–505 in vol. 8 of *The New Interpreter's Bible.* Edited by Leander E. Keck et al. 12 vols. Nashville: Abingdon, 1995.

Bowker, John. *The Meanings of Death.* Cambridge: Cambridge University Press, 1991.

Brach, Tara. *Radical Acceptance: Embracing Your Life with the Heart of a Buddha.* New York: Bantam Books, 2003.

Brown, Michael F. *The Channeling Zone: American Spirituality in an Anxious Age.* Cambridge, Mass.: Harvard University Press, 1997.

Bullinger, Heinrich, et al. *The Decades of Henry Bullinger.* Edited by Thomas Harding. Translated by 'H. I.' 4 vols. Reprint ed. Cambidge: The University Press, 1968.

Bulman, Raymond F. *The Lure of the Millennium: The Year 2000 and Beyond.* Maryknoll, N.Y.: Orbis Books, 1999.

Bultmann, Rudolf Karl. *Jesus Christ and Mythology.* New York: Scribner, 1958.

Burnham, Sophy. *A Book of Angels: Reflections on Angels Past and Present and True Stories of How They Touch Our Lives.* New York: Ballantine Books, 1990.

Byassee, Jason. "If Death Is No Barrier." *Books and Culture* 13:1 (2007): 16–21.

Caesarius of Heisterbach. *The Dialogue on Miracles.* Translated by H. von E. Scott and C. C. Swinton Bland. Introduction by G. G. Coulton. London: G. Routledge & Sons, 1929.

Calvin, Jean. *Institutes of the Christian Religion.* Edited by John T. McNeill. Translated by Ford Lewis Battles. The Library of Christian Classics 20–21. Philadelphia: Westminster, 1960.

Carlton, Clark, and Dmitri Royster. *The Faith: Understanding Orthodox Christianity: An Orthodox Catechism.* The Faith Series. Salisbury, Mass.: Regina Orthodox Press, 1997.

Catholic Church. *Catechism of the Catholic Church.* New York: Doubleday, 1995.

Charlesworth, James H., ed. *The Old Testament Pseudepigrapha.* 2 vols. Anchor Bible Reference Library. Garden City, N.Y.: 2003, 2005.

———. "The Portrayal of the Righteous as an Angel." Pages 135–51 in *Ideal Figures in Ancient Judaism: Profiles and Paradigms.* Edited by John J. Collins and George W. E. Nickelsburg. Chico, Calif.: Scholars, 1980.

Chase, Steven, trans. *Angelic Spirituality: Medieval Perspectives on the Ways of Angels.* Introduction by Steven Chase. Preface by Ewert H. Cousins. The Classics of Western Spirituality. New York: Paulist, 2002.

Childs, Brevard S. *The Book of Exodus: A Critical, Theological Commentary.* The Old Testament Library. Philadelphia: Westminster, 1974.

Chinnici, Joseph P. *Living Stones: The History and Structure of Catholic Spiritual Life in the United States.* 2nd ed. Maryknoll, N.Y.: Orbis Books, 1996.

Chinnici, Joseph P., and Angelyn Dries, eds. *Prayer and Practice in the American Catholic Community.* American Catholic Identities. Maryknoll, N.Y.: Orbis Books, 2000.

City of Angels. Produced by Charles Roven and Dawn Steel and directed by Brad Silberling. 115 minutes, 1998. DVD by Warner Home Video, 1998.

Clark, Lynn Schofield. *From Angels to Aliens: Teenagers, the Media, and the Supernatural.* Oxford: Oxford University Press, 2003.

Clark-Soles, Jaime. *Death and Afterlife in the New Testament.* New York: T. & T. Clark, 2006.

Clifford, Richard J. "Isaiah, Book of [Second Isaiah]." Pages 490–501 in vol. 3 of *The Anchor Bible Dictionary.* Edited by David Noel Freedman. 6 vols. New York: Doubleday, 1992.

Collins, John J. *The Apocalyptic Vision of the Book of Daniel.* Harvard Semitic Monographs 16. Missoula, Mont.: Scholars Press, for Harvard Semitic Museum, 1977.

———. *Daniel: A Commentary on the Book of Daniel.* Edited by Frank Moore Cross. Hermeneia 24. Minneapolis: Fortress, 1993.

———. "Daniel, Book of." Pages 29–37 in vol. 2 of *The Anchor Bible Dictionary.* Edited by David Noel Freedman. 6 vols. New York: Doubleday, 1992.

———. "The Mythology of Holy War in Daniel and the Qumran War Scroll: A Point of Transition in Jewish Apocalyptic." *Vetus Testamentum* 25:3 (1975): 596–612.

———. "Patterns of Eschatology at Qumran." Pages 351–75 in *Traditions in Transformation: Turning Points in Biblical Faith.* Edited by Baruch Halpern and Jon D. Levenson. Winona Lake, Ind.: Eisenbrauns, 1981.

Cullman, Oscar. "Immortality of the Soul or Resurrection of the Dead?" Pages 9–53 in *Immortality and Resurrection; Four Essays by Oscar Cullman, Harry A. Wolfson, Werner Jaeger, and Henry J. Cadbury.* Edited by Krister Stendahl. New York: Macmillan, 1965.

Dahl, Nils Alstrup. "Ephesians." Pages 1212–19 in *The Harper's Bible Commentary.* Edited by James L. Mays. San Francisco: Harper & Row, 1988.

Dallas Theological Seminary. "Full Doctrinal Statement: Article V: The Dispensations." Cited March 29, 2007. Online: http://www.dts.edu/about/doctrinalstatement.

Daniel, Alma, Timothy Wyllie, and Andrew Ramer. *Ask Your Angels.* New York: Ballantine Books, 1992.

Daniélou, Jean. *The Angels and Their Mission: According to the Fathers of the Church.* Translated by David Heimann. Reprint ed. Westminster, Md.: Christian Classics, 1991.

Darr, Katheryn Pfisterer. "The Book of Ezekiel: Introduction, Commentary, and Reflections." Pages 1073–1607 in vol. 6 of *The New Interpreter's Bible.* Edited by Leander E. Keck et al. 12 vols. Nashville: Abingdon, 2001.

Davidson, Maxwell J. *Angels at Qumran: A Comparative Study of 1 Enoch 1–36, 72–108, and Sectarian Writings from Qumran.* Journal for the Study of the Pseudepigrapha Supplement Series 11. Sheffield: JSOT, 1992.

Davila, James R. *Liturgical Works: Eerdmans Commentaries on the Dead Sea Scrolls.* Grand Rapids: Eerdmans, 2000.

Dawson, David. "Why Are We So Indifferent about Our Spiritual Lives?" Pages 17–39 in *Why Are We Here? Everyday Questions and the Spiritual Life.* Edited by Ronald F. Thieman and William C. Placher. Harrisburg: Trinity Press International, 1998.

Day, Peggy Lynne. *An Adversary in Heaven: Śāṭān in the Hebrew Bible.* Harvard Semitic Monographs 43. Atlanta: Scholars, 1988.

Dead Poets Society. Produced by Silverscreen Partners IV and Touchstone Pictures and directed by Peter Weir. 128 minutes. 1989. DVD by Buena Vista Home Entertainment, 1998.

Dean-Otting, Mary. *Heavenly Journeys: A Study of the Motif in Hellenistic Jewish Literature*. Frankfurt: Verlag Peter Lang, 1984.

"Death (Personification)." Cited March 29, 2007. Online: http://en.wikipedia.org/wiki/Personified_death).

Death Takes a Holiday. Produced by Paramount Pictures, directed by Mitchell Leisen. 79 minutes. 1934. VHS by Universal Studios, 1991.

Deetz, James, and Edwin S. Dethlefsen. "The Plymouth Colony Archive Project: Death's Head, Cherub, Urn and Willow." *Natural History* 76:3 (1967): 29–37. Cited March 29, 2007. Online: http://etext.lib.virginia.edu/users/deetz/Plymouth/deathshead.html.

Dickens, Charles. *A Christmas Carol*. Cited March 29, 2007. Excerpt online: http://www.cedmagic.com/featured/christmas-carol/1951-xmas-future.html).

Dio Chrysostom. Translated by J. W. Cohoon (vols. 1–2), J. W. Cohoon and H. Lamar Crosby (vol. 3), and H. Lamar Crosby (vol. 5). 5 vols. LCL. Cambridge, Mass.: Harvard University Press, 1949–56.

Dogma. Produced by Scott Mosier, directed by Kevin Smith. 128 minutes. 1999. DVD by Sony Pictures, 2002.

Dowd, Sharyn Echols. *Prayer, Power, and the Problem of Suffering: Mark 11:22–25 in the Context of Markan Theology*. Society of Biblical Literature Dissertation Series 105. Atlanta: Scholars, 1988.

Eadie, Betty J. *Embraced by the Light*. Reprint ed. New York: Bantam, 1994.

———. "In God We Trust." Cited March 29, 2007. Online: http://www.embracedbythelight.com/wakeup/articles.htm.

Edwards, Jonathan. *Sermons and Discourses, 1739–1742*. Edited by Harry S. Stout and Nathan O. Hatch, with Kyle P. Farley. New Haven: Yale University Press, 2003.

———. *The Sermons of Jonathan Edwards: A Reader*. Edited by Wilson H. Kimnach, Kenneth P. Minkema, and Douglas A. Sweeney. New Haven: Yale University Press, 1999.

Eire, Carlos M. N. "Bite This Satan!: The Devil in Luther's Table Talk." Pages 70–93 in *Piety and Family in Early Modern Europe: Essays in Honour of Steven Ozment*. Edited by Marc R. Forster and Benjamin J. Kaplan. Burlington, Vt.: Ashgate, 2005.

———. *War Against the Idols: The Reformation of Worship from Erasmus to Calvin*. Cambridge: Cambridge University Press, 1986.

Elwood, Christopher. *The Body Broken: The Calvinist Doctrine of the Eucharist and the Symbolization of Power in Sixteenth-Century France*. Oxford Studies in Historical Theology. New York: Oxford University Press, 1999.

Evans, Richard Paul. *The Christmas Box*. New York: Simon & Schuster, 1993.

Farley, Wendy. *The Wounding and Healing of Desire: Weaving Heaven and Earth*. Louisville: Westminster John Knox, 2005.

"Feast of Guardian Angels." Cited March 29, 2007. Online: http://www.catholic-forum.com/saints/saintgak.htm.

Fitzmyer, Joseph A. *The Gospel According to Luke: Introduction, Translation, and Notes*. 2 vols. Anchor Bible 28–28A. Garden City, N.Y.: Doubleday, 1981, 1985.

Fletcher-Louis, Crispin H. T. *All the Glory of Adam: Liturgical Anthropology in the Dead Sea Scrolls*. Studies on the Texts of the Desert of Judah 42. Leiden: Brill, 2002.

———. *Luke-Acts: Angels, Christology, and Soteriology*. Wissenschaftliche Untersuchungen zum Neuen Testament 94. Tübingen: Mohr (Siebeck), 1997.

Flight from Death: The Quest for Immortality. Produced by Go-Kart Records, directed by Patrick Shen. 85 minutes. 2003. DVD by Go-Cart Records, 2005.

Ford, David F. *The Shape of Living: Spiritual Directions for Everyday Life.* Grand Rapids: Baker Books, 1998.

Forsyth, Neil. *The Old Enemy: Satan and the Combat Myth.* Princeton: Princeton University Press, 1987.

Fox, Robin Lane. *Pagans and Christians.* San Francisco: Harper & Row, 1986.

Frangipane, Francis. *The Three Battlegrounds.* Cedar Rapids, Iowa: Arrow Publications, 1989.

Fredrickson, David E. "Paul, Hardships, and Suffering." Pages 172–97 in *Paul in the Greco-Roman World: A Handbook* (Harrisburg: Trinity Press International, 2003).

Freedman, David Noel, B. E. Willoughby, H. Ringgren, and H. J. Fabry. *"mal'āk."* Pages 302–325 in vol. 8 of *Theological Dictionary of the Old Testament.* Edited by G. Johannes Botterweck and Helmer Ringgren. Translated by John T. Willis. 15 vols. Grand Rapids: Eerdmans, 1997.

Freeman, Eileen E. *Touched by Angels: True Cases of Close Encounters of the Celestial Kind.* New York: Warner Books, 1993.

Fretheim, Terence E. "The Book of Genesis: Introduction, Commentary, and Reflections." Pages 319–674 in vol. 1 of *The New Interpreter's Bible.* Edited by Leander E. Keck et al. 12 vols. Nashville: Abingdon, 1994.

Garrett, Duane A. *Angels and the New Spirituality.* Nashville: Broadman & Holman, 1995.

Garrett, Susan R. "Christ and the Present Evil Age." *Interpretation* 57 (2003): 370–83.

———. *The Demise of the Devil: Magic and the Demonic in Luke's Writings.* Minneapolis: Fortress, 1989.

———. "Exodus from Bondage: Luke 9:31 and Acts 12:1–24." *Catholic Biblical Quarterly* 52 (1990): 666–67.

———. "The God of This World and the Affliction of Paul: 2 Cor 4:1–12," Pages 99–117 in *Greeks, Romans, and Christians.* Edited by David L. Balch, Everett Ferguson, and Wayne A. Meeks. Minneapolis: Fortress, 1990.

———. "New Creation." Pages 192–93 in *Dictionary of Feminist Theologies.* Edited by Letty M. Russell and J. Shannon Clarkson. Louisville: Westminster John Knox, 1996.

———. "The Patience of Job and the Patience of Jesus." *Interpretation* 53:3 (1999): 254–64.

———. "Paul's Thorn and Cultural Models of Affliction." Pages 82–99 in *The Social World of the First Christians: Essays in Honor of Wayne A. Meeks.* Edited by L. Michael White and O. Larry Yarbrough. Minneapolis: Fortress, 1995.

———. *The Temptations of Jesus in Mark's Gospel.* Grand Rapids: Eerdmans, 1998.

———. "The Weaker Sex in the *Testament of Job.*" *Journal of Biblical Literature* 112 (1993): 55–70.

Gaster, Theodore H. "Host of Heaven." Pages 566–67 in vol. 9 of *Encyclopaedia Judaica.* Edited by Michael Berenbaum and Fred Skolnik. 22 vols. 2nd ed. Detroit: Macmillan Reference USA, 2007.

Gates, David. "The New Prophets of Revelation." *Newsweek* (May 24, 2004).

Gerstner, John H., and Don Kistler. *Wrongly Dividing the Word of Truth: A Critique of Dispensationalism.* Morgan, Pa.: Soli Deo Gloria Publications, 2000.

Ghost. Produced by Steve-Charles Jaffe and Bruce Joel Rubin, directed by Jerry Zucker. 127 minutes. 1990. DVD by Paramount, 2001.

Gieschen, Charles A. *Angelomorphic Christology: Antecedents and Early Evidence.* Arbeiten zur Geschichte des antiken Judentums und des Urchristentums 42. Leiden: Brill, 1998.

Gorenberg, Gershom. "Intolerance: The Bestseller" (Review of the Left Behind series). *The American Prospect* 13:17 (September 23, 2002). Cited March 29, 2007. Online: http://www.prospect.org/print/V13/17/gorenberg-g.html.

"Goth Subculture." Cited March 29, 2007. Online: http://en.wikipedia.org/wiki/Gothic_subculture.

Graham, Billy. *Angels: God's Secret Agents.* Dallas: Word, 1994.

Gritsch, Eric W. *Martin—God's Court Jester: Luther in Retrospect.* Philadelphia: Fortress, 1983.

Gurevich, Aron. *Medieval Popular Culture: Problems of Belief and Perception.* Cambridge Studies in Oral and Literate Culture 14. Cambridge: Cambridge University Press, 1988.

Hackett, Jo Ann. "Balaam." Pages 569–72 in vol. 1 of *The Anchor Bible Dictionary.* Edited by David Noel Freedman. 6 vols. New York: Doubleday, 1992.

———. Critical notes to the book of Numbers. Pages 194–254 in *HarperCollins Study Bible.* Edited by Harold W. Attridge and Wayne A. Meeks. Rev. ed. San Francisco: HarperSanFrancisco, 2006.

Halperin, David J. *The Faces of the Chariot: Early Jewish Responses to Ezekiel's Vision.* Texte und Studien zum antiken Judentum 16. Tübingen: Mohr, 1988.

Handy, Lowell K. "Dissenting Deities or Obedient Angels: Divine Hierarchies in Ugarit and the Bible." *Biblical Research* 35 (1990): 18–35.

Hanegraaff, Wouter J. *New Age Religion and Western Culture: Esotericism in the Mirror of Secular Thought.* Albany: State University of New York Press, 1998.

Hannah, Darrell D. *Michael and Christ: Michael Traditions and Angel Christology in Early Christianity.* Wissenschaftliche Untersuchungen zum Neuen Testament 109. Tübingen: Mohr (Siebeck), 1999.

Hanson, Paul D. "Rebellion in Heaven, Azazel, and Euhemeristic Heroes in *1 Enoch* 6–11." *Journal of Biblical Literature* 96 (1977): 195–233.

Harper, Ralph. *On Presence: Variations and Reflections.* Philadelphia: Trinity Press International, 1991.

Hengel, Martin. *Judaism and Hellenism: Studies in Their Encounter in Palestine during the Early Hellenistic Period.* 2 vols. Philadelphia: Fortress, 1974.

Hennecke, E. *New Testament Apocrypha.* Edited by Wilhelm Schneemelcher. Translated by A. J. B. Higgins et al. Translation edited by R. McL. Wilson. 2 vols. Philadelphia: Westminster, 1965.

Hensley, Chad. "The Voice of Generation Hex." Cited March 29, 2007. Online: http://www.esoterra.org/manson.htm.

Hill, Craig C. *In God's Time: The Bible and the Future.* Grand Rapids: Eerdmans, 2002.

Himmelfarb, Martha. *Ascent to Heaven in Jewish and Christian Apocalypses.* New York: Oxford University Press, 1993.

———. *Tours of Hell: An Apocalyptic Form in Jewish and Christian Literature.* Philadelphia: Fortress, 1983.

Hoeller, Stephan A. "Angels, Holy and Unholy: The Gnostic Alternative to Mainstream

Angelology." Pages 97–105 in *Angels and Mortals: Their Co-Creative Power*. Edited by Maria Parise. Wheaten, Ill.: Quest Books, 1990.

"Holy Guardian Angel." Cited March 29, 2007. Online: http://en.wikipedia.org/wiki/Holy_Guardian_Angel.

Horst, Pieter W. van der. "Thanatos." Pages 854–56 in *Dictionary of Deities and Demons in the Bible*. Edited by Karel van der Toorn, Bob Becking, and Pieter W. van der Horst. 2nd ed. Leiden: Brill, 1999.

Huffines, Launa. *Healing Yourself with Light: How to Connect with the Angelic Healers*. Tiburon, Calif.: H J Kramer, 1995.

Hurd, Bob. "Angels." Pages 38–41 in *New Dictionary of Catholic Spirituality*. Edited by Michael Downey; Collegeville, Minn.: Liturgical Press, 1993.

Hurtado, Larry W. *One God, One Lord: Early Christian Devotion and Ancient Jewish Monotheism*. Philadelphia: Fortress, 1988.

Ignatius. *Ignatius of Loyola: The Spiritual Exercises and Selected Works*. Edited by George E. Ganss et al. Classics of Western Spirituality. Mahwah, N. J.: Paulist, 1991.

Isaac, E., trans. *1 Enoch*. Pages 5–89 in vol. 1 of *The Old Testament Pseudepigrapha*. Edited by James H. Charlesworth. 2 vols. Anchor Bible Reference Library. Garden City, N.Y.: Doubleday, 2003, 2005.

Johnson, Luke T. *The Letter of James: A New Translation with Introduction and Commentary*. Anchor Bible 37A. New York: Doubleday, 1995.

———. *Living Jesus: Learning the Heart of the Gospel*. San Francisco: HarperSanFrancisco, 1999.

———. *The Real Jesus: The Misguided Quest for the Historical Jesus and the Truth of the Traditional Gospels*. San Francisco: HarperSanFrancisco, 1996.

Joines, K. R. "The Serpent in Genesis 3." *Zeitschrift für die Alttestamentliche Wissenschaft* 87 (1975): 1–11.

Jones, Gregory Knox. *Play the Ball Where the Monkey Drops It: Why We Suffer and How We Can Hope*. San Francisco: HarperSanFrancisco, 2001.

Keck, David. *Angels and Angelology in the Middle Ages*. New York: Oxford University Press, 1998.

Keillor, Garrison. Interview by Bill McNabb. In *TheDoorMagazine Interviews: Take Two*. Edited by Robert Darden. Dallas: TheDoorMagazine, 2002.

Kelly, Henry Ansgar. *The Devil, Demonology, and Witchcraft: The Development of Christian Beliefs in Evil Spirits*. Rev. ed. Garden City, N.Y.: Doubleday, 1974.

———. "The Devil in the Desert." *Catholic Biblical Quarterly* 26 (1964): 190–220.

Kim, Bokin. "Christ as the Truth, the Light, the Life, but a Way?" Pages 52–58 in *Buddhists Talk about Jesus, Christians Talk about the Buddha*. Edited by Rita M. Gross and Terry C. Muck. New York: Continuum, 2000.

Knibb, Michael A. *The Qumran Community*. Cambridge Commentaries on Writings of the Jewish and Christian World, 200 BC to AD 200, no. 2. Cambridge: Cambridge University Press, 1987.

Kolenkow, Anitra Bingham. "The Angelology of the Testament of Abraham." Pages 153–62 in *Studies on the Testament of Abraham*. Edited by George W. E. Nickelsburg. Society of Biblical Literature Septuagint and Cognate Studies 6. Missoula, Mont.: Scholars, 1976.

Kugel, James L. *The Bible As It Was*. Cambridge, Mass.: Belknap/Harvard University Press, 1997.

——. *The God of Old: Inside the Lost World of the Bible.* New York: The Free Press, 2003.

——. *Traditions of the Bible: A Guide to the Bible as It Was at the Start of the Common Era.* Cambridge, Mass.: Harvard University Press, 1998.

LaHaye, Tim, and Jerry B. Jenkins, *Are We Living in the End Times? Current Events Foretold in Scripture . . . and What They Mean* (Wheaton, Ill.: Tyndale House, 1999).

——. *Glorious Appearing: The End of Days.* Wheaton, Ill.: Tyndale House, 2004.

——. *The Indwelling: The Beast Takes Possession.* Wheaton, Ill.: Tyndale House, 2000.

——. *Left Behind: A Novel of the Earth's Last Days.* Wheaton, Ill.: Tyndale House, 1995.

——. *The Remnant: On the Brink of Armageddon.* Wheaton, Ill.: Tyndale House, 2002.

The Last Temptation of Christ. Produced by Barbara DaFina, directed by Martin Scorsese. 164 minutes. 1988.

Layton, Bentley. *The Gnostic Scriptures: A New Translation with Annotations and Introduction.* Garden City, N.Y.: Doubleday, 1987.

Levenson, Jon D. *Creation and the Persistence of Evil: The Jewish Drama of Divine Omnipotence.* San Francisco: Harper & Row, 1988.

——. *Resurrection and the Restoration of Israel: The Ultimate Victory of the God of Life.* New Haven: Yale University Press, 2006.

Levison, John R. "The Prophetic Spirit as an Angel According to Philo." *Harvard Theological Review* 88 (1995): 189–207.

Lewis, Theodore J. "Belial." Pages 654–56 in vol. 1 of *The Anchor Bible Dictionary.* Edited by David Noel Freedman. 6 vols. New York: Doubleday, 1992.

——. "Dead, Abode of the." Pages 101–5 in vol. 2 of *The Anchor Bible Dictionary.* Edited by David Noel Freedman. 6 vols. New York: Doubleday, 1992.

"Life After Life: The Official Online Presence of Dr. Raymond A. Moody—Author, Lecturer, Counselor." Cited March 29, 2007. Online: http://www.lifeafterlife.com.

Longenecker, Richard N. "Some Distinctive Early Christological Motifs." *New Testament Studies* 14 (1967–68): 536–41.

Ludwig, Allan I. *Graven Images: New England Stone Carving and Its Symbols, 1650–1815.* 3rd ed. Hanover, N.H.: Wesleyan University Press, 1999.

Luscombe, Belinda. "Well, Hello, Suckers." *Time* 167:9 (February 27, 2006). Cited March 29, 2007. Online: http://www.time.com/time/magazine/article/0,9171,1161234 ,00.html.

Luther, Martin. "An Open Letter on Translating." Translated by Gary Mann, revised by Michael D. Barlowe. Cited March 29, 2007. Online: http://www.bible-researcher .com/luther01.html.

Maloney, George A. *Gold, Frankincense, and Myrrh: An Introduction to Eastern Christian Spirituality.* New York: Crossroad, 1997.

Mark, Barbara, and Trudy Griswold. *The Angelspeake Book of Prayer and Healing.* New York: Simon & Schuster, 1997.

——. *Angelspeake: How to Talk with Your Angels.* New York: Simon & Schuster, 1995.

Marsden, George M. *Jonathan Edwards: A Life.* New Haven: Yale University Press, 2003.

Martin, Dale B. *The Corinthian Body.* New Haven: Yale University Press, 1995.

Maximus of Tyre, *The Philosophical Orations.* Translated with an introduction by M. B. Trapp. Oxford: Clarendon, 1997.

McAlpine, Thomas H. *Facing the Powers: What Are the Options?* Monrovia, Calif.: MARC, 1991.

McDonald, Marci. "The New Spirituality." *McLeans* (October 10, 1994): 44–48.

McFague, Sallie. *Life Abundant: Rethinking Theology and Economy for a Planet in Peril.* Minneapolis: Fortress, 2001.

McGinn, Bernard. "Love, Knowledge, and *Unio Mystica* in the Western Christian Tradition." Pages 59–86 in *Mystical Union and Monotheistic Faith.* Edited by Moshe Idel and Bernard McGinn. New York: Macmillan, 1989.

McGreevy, John T. *Catholicism and American Freedom: A History.* New York: Norton, 2003.

———. *Parish Boundaries: The Catholic Encounter with Race in the Twentieth-Century Urban North.* Chicago: University of Chicago Press, 1996.

Meier, Samuel A. "Destroyer." Pages 240–44 in *Dictionary of Deities and Demons in the Bible.* Edited by Karel van der Toorn, Bob Becking, and Pieter W. van der Horst. 2nd ed. Leiden: Brill, 1999.

———. "Mediator I." Pages 554–57 in *Dictionary of Deities and Demons in the Bible.* Edited by Karel van der Toorn, Bob Becking, and Pieter W. van der Horst. 2nd ed. Leiden: Brill, 1999.

Michael, produced by Ethan Coen, directed by Nora Ephron. 106 minutes, 1996. DVD by Turner Home Entertainment, 1997.

Michl, J. "Angels [Theology]." Pages 418–23 in vol. 1 of *New Catholic Encyclopedia.* 14 vols. 2nd ed. Detroit: Thomson/Gale in association with the Catholic University of America, 2003.

Millar, William R. "Isaiah 24–27 [Little Apocalypse]." Pages 488–490 in vol. 3 of *The Anchor Bible Dictionary.* Edited by David Noel Freedman. 6 vols. New York: Doubleday, 1992.

Miller, Patrick D., Jr. *The Divine Warrior in Early Israel.* Harvard Semitic Monographs 5. Cambridge, Mass.: Harvard University Press, 1973.

Moltmann, Jürgen. "In the End Is My Beginning: A Hope for Life—A Life for Hope." Address, Louisville Presbyterian Theological Seminary, April, 2000.

———. *The Source of Life: The Holy Spirit and the Theology of Life.* Translated by Margaret Kohl. Minneapolis: Fortress, 1997.

Monty Python's The Meaning of Life. Produced by John Goldstone, directed by Terry Jones and Terry Gilliam. 103 minutes. 1983. DVD by Universal Studios Home Entertainment, 2005.

Moody, Raymond A. *Life After Life: The Investigation of a Phenomenon—Survival of Bodily Death.* 2nd ed. San Francisco: HarperSanFrancisco, 2001.

Moore, Michael S. *Balaam Traditions: Their Character and Development.* Society of Biblical Literature Dissertation Series 113. Atlanta: Scholars, 1990.

Moorhead, James M. *World without End: Mainstream American Protestant Visions of the Last Things, 1880–1925.* Bloomington: Indiana University Press, 1999.

Morray-Jones, Christopher R. A. "Paradise Revisited (2 Cor 12:1–12): The Jewish Mystical Background of Paul's Apostolate." *Harvard Theological Review* 86 (1993): 177–217 and 265–92.

Mullen, Brendan. "To Know God: A Post-New Age Dialogue with Dr. Stephan Hoeller." *LA Weekly* (May 7–13, 1999). Cited March 29, 2007. Online: http://www.laweekly .com/general/features/to-know-god/11959/.

Mullen, E. T. "Divine Assembly." Pages 214–17 in vol. 2 of *The Anchor Bible Dictionary.* Edited by David Noel Freedman. 6 vols. New York: Doubleday, 1992.

Murphy, Ed. *The Handbook for Spiritual Warfare.* Rev. ed. Nashville: Thomas Nelson Publishers, 1996.

My First Mister. Produced by Carol Baum et al., directed by Christine Lahti. 109 minutes. 2001. DVD by Paramount, 2002.

"Near-Death Experiences and the Afterlife." Cited March 29, 2007. Online: http://www .near-death.com.

Newman, Carey C. *Paul's Glory-Christology: Tradition and Rhetoric.* Supplements to Novum Testamentum 69. Leiden: E.J. Brill, 1992.

Newsom, Carol A. "Angels: Old Testament." Pages 248–53 in vol. 1 of *The Anchor Bible Dictionary.* Edited by David Noel Freedman. 6 vols. New York: Doubleday, 1992.

———. "The Book of Job: Introduction, Commentary, and Reflections." Pages 317–637 in vol. 4 of *The New Interpreter's Bible.* Edited by Leander E. Keck et al. 12 vols. Nashville: Abingdon, 1996.

———. "The Development of *1 Enoch* 6–19: Cosmology and Judgment." *Catholic Biblical Quarterly* 42 (1980): 313–14.

Nickelsburg, George W. E. Critical notes to the Book of Tobit. Pages 1293–1312 in *Harper-Collins Study Bible.* Edited by Harold W. Attridge and Wayne A. Meeks. Rev. ed. San Francisco: HarperSanFrancisco, 2006.

———. "Eschatology in the *Testament of Abraham:* A Study of the Judgment Scene in the Two Recensions." Pages 23–64 in *Studies on the Testament of Abraham.* Edited by George W. E. Nickelsburg. Society of Biblical Literature Septuagint and Cognate Studies 6. Missoula, Mont.: Scholars, 1976.

———. *1 Enoch 1: A Commentary on the Book of 1 Enoch, Chapters 1–36; 81–108.* Edited by Klaus Baltzer. Minneapolis: Fortress, 2001.

———. *Resurrection, Immortality, and Eternal Life in Intertestamental Judaism.* Cambridge, Mass.: Harvard University Press, 1972.

Noll, Stephen F. *Angels of Light, Powers of Darkness: Thinking Biblically about Angels, Satan, and Principalities.* Downers Grove, Ill.: InterVarsity, 1998.

Nouwen, Henri J. M. *Bread for the Journey: A Daybook of Wisdom and Faith.* San Francisco: HarperSanFrancisco, 1997.

Nowell, Irene. "Tobit." Pages 568–71 in *New Jerome Biblical Commentary.* Englewood Cliffs, N.J.: Prentice-Hall, 1990.

Nussbaum, Martha C. *The Therapy of Desire: Theory and Practice in Hellenistic Ethics.* Princeton: Princeton University Press, 1994.

O'Neill, Kim. *How to Talk with Your Angels.* New York: Avon Books, 1995.

"Opus Sanctorum Angelorum: Work of the Holy Angels." Cited March 29, 2007. Online: http://www.opusangelorum.org/.

Orsi, Robert A. *Between Heaven and Earth: The Religious Worlds People Make and the Scholars Who Study Them.* Princeton: Princeton University Press, 2005.

———. *Thank You, Saint Jude: Women's Devotion to the Patron Saint of Hopeless Causes.* New Haven: Yale University Press, 1996.

Paffenroth, Kim. *Gospel of the Living Dead: George Romero's Visions of Hell on Earth.* Waco, Tex.: Baylor University Press, 2006.

Pauw, Amy Plantinga. "Where Theologians Fear to Tread." *Modern Theology* 16:1 (January 2000): 39–59.

Peretti, Frank. *Piercing the Darkness.* Westchester, Ill.: Crossway Books, 1989.

———. *This Present Darkness.* Westchester, Ill.: Crossway Books, 1986.

Pfitzner, Victor C. "Worshipping with the Angels." *Lutheran Theological Journal* 29 (1995): 50–60.

Philo Judaeus of Alexandria. Translated by F. H. Colson and G. H. Whitaker. 10 vols. LCL. Cambridge, Mass.: Harvard University Press, 1929–62.

Placher, William C. *Jesus the Savior: The Meaning of Jesus Christ for Christian Faith.* Louisville: Westminster John Knox, 2001.

Plantinga, Cornelius. *Engaging God's World: A Reformed Vision of Faith, Learning, and Living.* Grand Rapids: Eerdmans, 2002.

Plathow, Michael. "Dein heiliger Engel sei mit mir: Martin Luthers Engelpredigten." Pages 45–70 in *Lutherjahrbuch: Organ der internationalen Lutherforschung.* Göttingen: Vandenhoeck & Ruprecht, 1994.

Plato. *The Collected Dialogues of Plato, including the Letters.* Edited, with introduction and prefatory notes by Edith Hamilton and Huntington Cairns. Bollingen Series 71. Princeton: Princeton University Press, 1963.

Poe, Edgar Allan. *The Raven.* New York: Dover Publications, 1996.

Polleyfeys, Patrick. "Death in Art." Cited March 29, 2007. Online: http://.lamortdanslart .com/main.htm.

Pope, Marvin H. *Job: Introduction, Translation, and Notes.* Anchor Bible 15. Garden City, N.Y.: Doubleday, 1965.

Porter, F. C. "The Yeçer Hara." Pages 151–52 in *Biblical and Semitic Studies: Yale Bicentennial Publications.* New York: Scribner, 1902.

Poythress, Vern S. *Understanding Dispensationalists.* 2nd ed.. Phillipsburg, N.J.: P. & R. Publishing, 1993.

The Preacher's Wife. Produced by Debra Martin Chase, directed by Penny Marshall. 124 minutes, 1996. DVD by Buena Vista Home Entertainment, 2002.

Presbyterian Church (USA). *The Constitution of the Presbyterian Church (U.S.A.) Part I: Book of Confessions.* Louisville: Office of the General Assembly, 2002.

———. *The Presbyterian Hymnal: Hymns, Psalms, and Spiritual Songs.* Louisville: Westminster John Knox, 1990.

The Prophecy. Produced by Joel Soisson, directed by Gregory Widen. 1995. DVD by Dimension, 1999.

"Psalm 151." Episode 508 of *Touched by an Angel.* Original air date: November 15, 1998.

Quispel, Gilles. "Genius and Spirit." Pages 155–69 in *Essays on the Nag Hammadi Texts.* Edited by M. Krause. Leiden: Brill, 1975.

Rabey, Steve. "Apocalyptic Sales Out of This World." *Christianity Today* 43 (March 1, 1999): 19.

Rad, Gerhard von. *Genesis: A Commentary.* Translated by John H. Marks. Philadelphia: Westminster, 1961.

Rad, Gerhard von, with Gerhard Kittel and W. Grundmann. *"angelos."* Pages 74–87 in vol. 1 of *Theological Dictionary of the New Testament.* Edited by Gerhard Kittel. Translated and edited by Geoffrey W. Bromiley. 10 vols. Grand Rapids: Eerdmans, 1964–1976.

Ray, Stephen G. *Do No Harm: Social Sin and Christian Responsibility.* Minneapolis: Fortress, 2002.

"Reaper Madness." Segment of episode "Treehouse of Horror XIV" of *The Simpsons.* Original air date: November 2, 2003.

Redfield, James. *The Celestine Prophecies: An Adventure.* New York: Warner Books, 1993.

Riley, Greg J. "Demon." Pages 235–40 in *Dictionary of Deities and Demons in the Bible.* Edited by Karel van der Toorn, Bob Becking, and Pieter W. van der Horst. 2nd ed. Leiden: Brill, 1999.

Rosenbaum, Ron. "Staring into the Heart of the Heart of Darkness." *New York Times Magazine* (June 4, 1995), 36–44, 50, 58, 61, 72.

Rossing, Barbara. *The Rapture Exposed: The Message of Hope in the Book of Revelation.* Boulder: Westview, 2004.

Rowland, Christopher. *Christian Origins: An Account of the Setting and Character of the Most Important Messianic Sect of Judaism.* 2nd ed. London: SPCK, 2002.

———. "The Vision of the Risen Christ in Rev. i.13ff.: The Debt of an Early Christology to an Aspect of Jewish Angelology." *Journal of Theological Studies* 31 (1980): 1–11.

Royalty, Robert M., Jr. "Dwelling on Visions: On the Nature of the So-Called 'Colossians Heresy,'" *Biblica* 83 (2002): 329–57.

Rudolph, Kurt. "Gnosticism." Pages 1033–40 in vol. 2 of *The Anchor Bible Dictionary.* Edited by David Noel Freedman. 6 vols. New York: Doubleday, 1992.

Russell, D. S. *The Method and Message of Jewish Apocalyptic.* Philadelphia: Westminster, 1964.

Russell, Jeffrey Burton. *A History of Heaven: The Singing Silence.* Princeton: Princeton University Press, 1997.

Sabom, Michael. *Light and Death.* Grand Rapids: Zondervan, 1998.

Sargent, Denny. *Your Guardian Angel and You.* Boston: Weiser Books, 2004.

Savran, George. "Beastly Speech: Intertextuality, Balaam's Ass and the Garden of Eden." *Journal for the Study of the Old Testament* 64 (1994): 33–55.

Scholem, Gershom. "Merkabah Mysticism or Ma'aseh Merkavah." Pages 66–67 in vol. 14 of *Encyclopaedia Judaica.* Edited by Michael Berenbaum and Fred Skolnik. 22 vols. 2nd ed. Detroit: Macmillan Reference USA, 2007.

Schucman, Helen. *A Course in Miracles.* Tiburon, Calif.: Foundation for Inner Peace, 1995.

Scott, Alan. *Origen and the Life of the Stars: A History of an Idea.* New York: Oxford University Press, 1991.

Segal, Alan F. *Life After Death: A History of the Afterlife in the Religions of the West.* Anchor Bible Reference Library. New York: Doubleday, 2004.

———. *Paul the Convert: The Apostolate and Apostasy of Saul the Pharisee.* New Haven: Yale University Press, 1990.

Seim, Turid Karlsen. *The Double Message: Patterns of Gender in Luke-Acts.* Nashville: Abingdon, 1994.

The Seventh Seal. Produced by Allan Ekelund, directed by Ingmar Bergman. 92 minutes. 1957. DVD by Criterion, 1999.

Smith, Christian, and Melinda Lundquist Denton. *Soul Searching: The Religious and Spiritual Lives of American Teenagers.* New York: Oxford University Press, 2005.

Smith, Jonathan Z., trans. *Prayer of Joseph.* Pages 699–714 in vol. 2 of *The Old Testament Pseudepigrapha.* Edited by James H. Charlesworth. 2 vols. Anchor Bible Reference Library. Garden City, N.Y.: 2003, 2005.

Smith, Morton. "Pauline Worship as Seen by Pagans." *Harvard Theological Review* 73 (1980): 241–49.

Spangler, David. "The Movement toward the Divine." Pages 79–105 in *New Age Spiritu-*

ality: An Assessment. Edited by Duncan S. Ferguson; Louisville: Westminster John Knox, 1993.

Stone, Michael E. *Fourth Ezra: A Commentary on the Book of Fourth Ezra.* Edited by Frank Moore Cross. Hermeneia 60 part 2. Minneapolis: Fortress, 1990.

Storm, Howard. *My Descent into Death: A Second Chance at Life.* New York: Doubleday, 2005.

Stowers, Stanley K. *A Rereading of Romans: Justice, Jews, and Gentiles.* New Haven: Yale University Press, 1994, 42–82.

Stringfellow, William. *Instead of Death.* New and expanded ed. New York: Seabury, 1976.

———. *A Keeper of the Word: Selected Writings of William Stringfellow.* Edited and with introduction by Bill Wylie Kellerman. Grand Rapids: Eerdmans, 1994.

Stuckenbruck, Loren T. *Angel Veneration and Christology: A Study in Early Judaism and in the Christology of the Apocalypse of John.* Wissenschaftliche Untersuchungen zum Neuen Testament. 2nd Series 70. Tübingen: Mohr, 1995.

Sullivan, Kevin P. *Wrestling with Angels: A Study of the Relationship between Angels and Humans in Ancient Jewish Literature and the New Testament.* Arbeiten zur Geschichte des antiken Judentums und des Urchristentums 55. Leiden: Brill, 2004.

Sweeney, Marvin A. "Habakkuk," Pages 668–70 in *The HarperCollins Bible Commentary.* Edited by James L. Mays. Rev. ed. San Francisco: HarperSanFrancisco, 2000.

Talbert, Charles H. *Learning through Suffering: The Educational Value of Suffering in the New Testament and in Its Milieu.* Collegeville, Minn.: Liturgical Press, 1991.

Tanner, Kathryn. *God and Creation in Christian Theology: Tyranny or Empowerment?* Oxford: Basil Blackwell, 1988.

———. *Jesus, Humanity, and the Trinity: A Brief Systematic Theology.* Minneapolis: Fortress, 2001.

Taves, Ann. *The Household of Faith: Roman Catholic Devotions in Mid-Nineteenth Century America.* Notre Dame: University of Notre Dame Press, 1986.

Taylor, Eugene. "Desperately Seeking Spirituality." *Psychology Today* (November/December, 1994): 55–68.

Taylor, Terry Lynn. *Guardians of Hope: The Angels' Guide to Personal Growth.* Tiburon, Calif.: H J Kramer, 1992.

Tazewell, Charles. "The Littlest Angel." Cited March 29, 2007. Online: http://www.geocities.com/Athens/Acropolis/6182/thelittlestangel.html.

TenPas, Jake. "Better Off Undead." *Corvallis Gazette-Times.* 1 July 2005. Cited March 29, 2007. Online: http://www.gtconnect.com/articles/2005/06/30/entertainment/columnists/night_rider/tenpas.txt.

"Theosophy." Cited March 29, 2007. Online: http://en.wikipedia.org/wiki/Theosophy#Reincarnation_is_universal.

Thomas Aquinas. *Summa theologiae. Latin text and English Translation, Introductions, Notes, Appendices, and Glossaries.* 61 vols. Cambridge: Blackfriars; New York: McGraw-Hill; London: Eyre & Spottiswoode, 1964.

Thurston, Bonnie. "The Buddha Offered Me a Raft." Pages 118–28 in *Buddhists Talk about Jesus, Christians Talk about the Buddha.* Edited by Rita M. Gross and Terry C. Muck. New York: Continuum, 2000.

Tobin, Thomas H. "Logos." Pages 348–56 in vol. 4 of *The Anchor Bible Dictionary.* Edited by David Noel Freedman. 6 vols. New York: Doubleday, 1992.

Tromp, Nicholas J. *Primitive Conceptions of Death and the Nether World in the Old Testament.* Rome: Pontifical Biblical Institute, 1969.

Tyson, Timothy B. *Blood Done Sign My Name: A True Story.* New York: Crown, 2004.

Underworld. Produced by Robert Bernacchi et al., directed by Len Wiseman. 2003. DVD by Sony Pictures, 2004.

Underworld: Evolution. Produced by Lakeshore Entertainment and Screen Gems, Inc., directed by Len Wiseman. 2006. DVD by Sony Pictures, 2006.

VanderKam, James C. "1 Enoch, Enochic Motifs, and Enoch in Early Christian Literature." Pages 60–88 in *The Jewish Apocalyptic Heritage in Early Christianity.* Edited by James C. VanderKam and William Adler. Assen, Netherlands: Van Gorcum; Minneapolis: Fortress, 1996.

Van Praagh, James. *Heaven and Earth: Making the Psychic Connection.* New York: Simon & Schuster, 2001.

Vermes, Geza, trans. *The Dead Sea Scrolls in English.* 3rd ed. London: Penguin, 1987.

Virtue, Doreen. *Divine Guidance: How to Have a Dialogue with God and Your Guardian Angels.* Los Angeles: Renaissance Books, 1998.

Vogel, Marta. "Looking for Reverence in All the Wrong Pews." *Washington Post,* May 11, 1997.

Volf, Miroslav. *Exclusion and Embrace: A Theological Exploration of Identity, Otherness, and Reconciliation.* Nashville: Abingdon, 1996.

Wagner, Donald E. "Short Fuse to Apocalypse?" *Sojourners* 32 (July/August 2003): 20–21.

Walsch, Neale Donald. *Friendship with God: An Uncommon Dialogue.* New York: G. P. Putnam's Sons, 1999.

Watson, Duane F. "Angels: New Testament." Pages 253–55 in vol. 1 of *The Anchor Bible Dictionary.* Edited by David Noel Freedman. 6 vols. New York: Doubleday, 1992.

———. "Destroyer." Pages 159–60 in vol. 2 of *The Anchor Bible Dictionary.* Edited by David Noel Freedman. 6 vols. New York: Doubleday, 1992.

———. "Gehenna." Pages 926–28 in vol. 2 of *The Anchor Bible Dictionary.* Edited by David Noel Freedman. 6 vols. New York: Doubleday, 1992.

Wauters, Ambika. *The Angel Oracle: Working with the Angels for Guidance, Inspiration, and Love.* New York: St. Martin's, 1995.

Weber, Timothy P. *On the Road to Armageddon: How Evangelicals Became Israel's Best Friend.* Grand Rapids: Baker Academic, 2004.

Welker, Michael. "Angels in the Biblical Traditions." *Theology Today* 51 (1994): 367–80.

Wesley, John. "The Sermons of John Wesley." Cited March 29, 2007. Online: http://new .gbgm-umc.org/umhistory/wesley/sermons/.

Westermann, Claus. *Genesis 12–36.* Translated by John J. Scullion. Minneapolis: Augsburg, 1985.

Wicker, Christine. *Lily Dale: The True Story of the Town That Talks to the Dead.* San Francisco: HarperSanFrancisco, 2003.

Widengren, Geo. "Iran and Israel in Parthian Times with Special Regard to the Ethiopic Book of Enoch." Pages 85–129 in *Religious Syncretism in Antiquity.* Edited by Birger A. Pearson. Missoula, Mont.: Scholars, 1975.

Wilson, Robert R. "Ezekiel." Pages 583–622 in *The HarperCollins Bible Commentary.* Edited by James L. Mays. Rev. ed. San Francisco: HarperSanFrancisco, 2000.

Wings of Desire. Produced by Wim Wenders and Anatole Dauman, directed by Wim Wenders. 128 minutes, 1987. DVD by MGM, 2003.

Wink, Walter. *Engaging the Powers: Discernment and Resistance in a World of Domination.* Minneapolis: Fortress, 1992.

———. *Naming the Powers: The Language of Power in the New Testament.* Philadelphia: Fortress, 1984.

———. *The Powers That Be: Theology for a New Millennium.* New York: Galilee, 1999.

———. *Unmasking the Powers: The Invisible Forces that Determine Human Existence.* Philadelphia: Fortress, 1986.

Winston, David. "The Iranian Component in the Bible, Apocrypha, and Qumran: A Review of the Evidence." *History of Religions* 5:2 (1966): 183–216.

Wintermute, O. S., trans. *Apocalypse of Zephaniah.* Pages 497–515 in vol. 1 of *The Old Testament Pseudepigrapha.* Edited by James H. Charlesworth. 2 vols. Anchor Bible Reference Library. Garden City, N.Y.: 2003, 2005.

Wire, Antoinette Clark. *The Corinthian Women Prophets: A Reconstruction through Paul's Rhetoric.* Minneapolis: Fortress, 1990.

Witmer, Andrew. "Best-Selling Spirituality: American Cultural Change and the New Shape of Faith." Produced by Andrew Witmer. Edited and narrated by Ken Myers. Powhatan, Va., 1999. Sound Recording.

Wojtyła, Karol Józef. "Catechesis on the Angels." Catechesis on the Holy Angels by Pope John Paul II, given at 6 General Audiences from July 9 to August 20, 1986. Cited March 29, 2007. Online: http://www.ewtn.com/library/PAPALDOC/JP2ANGEL.HTM.

Wright, N. T. *The Climax of the Covenant: Christ and the Law in Pauline Theology.* Minneapolis: Fortress, 1991.

———. *The Resurrection of the Son of God.* Minneapolis: Augsburg Fortress, 2003.

Wuthnow, Robert. *After Heaven: Spirituality in America since the 1950s.* Berkeley: University of California Press, 1998.

———. *America and the Challenges of Religious Diversity.* Princeton: Princeton University Press, 2005.

———. "To Dwell or To Seek: Where and How Do We Find Spirituality in Our Lives?" *In Trust* (New Year 1999).

Zaehner, R. C. *The Dawn and Twilight of Zoroastrianism.* New York: G. P. Putnam's Sons, 1961.

Zaleski, Carol. *The Life of the World to Come: Near-Death Experience and Christian Hope.* New York: Oxford University Press, 1996.

Zoloth-Dorfman, Laurie. "Traveling with Children: Mothering and the Ethics of the Ordinary World." *Tikkun* 10:4 (1995): 25–29, 78.

GENERAL INDEX

access to divine world. *See* divine world, human access to

accounts of angels, nonfictional vs. fictional, 13–14

afterlife: angelic community after death for Christians, 223–32; in biblical world, 194–202; humans becoming angels after death, 201–2, 223–32; intermediate existence, 195–99, 293–94, 296; resurrection of the dead, 187, 189, 191, 194–202, 212, 217, 219, 222, 224, 225, 232, 236, 290, 291, 292, 293, 294, 295, 296; worshipping with angels in, 62–63. *See also* death and angels; near-death experiences

"the angel of the LORD," 21–27, 30, 31, 37, 48, 53–55, 57, 58, 60, 67, 74, 98, 127, 191, 201, 204, 238, 246–47, 248–50, 295

"angelification" of humans after death, 201–2, 223–32

angels, 1–16; accessing divine world by (*see* divine world, human access to); accounts of, 13–14; desire for human women (*see* desire); existence, evidence for, 2–5; as figures of light guiding souls to heaven, 212–23; modern interest in, 1–2, 12–16; significance of, 237–42; self-help angels, 12, 29–30, 36, 38, 43–46, 75–76, 169–74. *See also* "the angel of the LORD"; biblical world, angels in; death and angels; films about angels; guardian angel(s); messenger(s) from God; Satan and his angels

Augustine, 150, 277, 278; *Confessions,* 8, 94–95, 99

awe, angels inspiring. *See* fear and awe: angelic inspiration of

biblical world, angels in, 6–12, 14; afterlife, angels associated with, 194–202; Balaam and his ass, 20–21; death and angels, 190–202; chief angelic mediator, 11, 57, 127, 175, 226, 249; death figures in Old Testament, 190–93; Ezekiel's vision, 49–54; guardian angels, 142–47; Jacob and the angels, 46–49; Second Temple era belief in angels, 30–31; messengers from God (*see* "the angel of the LORD"); "the sons of God and the daughters of men" (*see* desire); worshipping with angels, 62–69, 74–75, 257, 259. *See also* "the glory of the LORD"; guardian angel(s); Satan and his angels

boundaries, angels' crossing of, 78–81

Buddhism, 5, 171–74

Caesarius of Heisterbach (*Dialogue on Miracles),* 146, 151, 166, 276, 278

Calvin, John, 23, 153–56, 181–82, 281, 248, 279, 280, 281

Catholicism: belief in angels, importance of, 16; guardian angels, 140–41, 181–83; in Middle Ages, 142–47; Protestant critique of, 153–61; rescuers, angels as, 164, 165

Christianity: coping with evil as disciples of Jesus, 132–35; death and angelic community, 223–32; desire for God and the world, 97–100; "the glory of the LORD," 55–57; Jesus as "the angel of the LORD," 26–27; Jesus as healing messenger from God, 33–37; the sacred vs. the everyday for, 71–73; theodicy problem, acuteness of, 104; worshipping with angels, 63–69. *See also* guardian angel(s)

Christmas and angels, 19, 63, 209–10

Christology, 11–12, 33–37, 49, 126–35, 174–80. *See also* "the glory of the LORD": manifested in Christ; king of angels, Jesus as; Transfiguration

City of Angels, 19, 78, 80–81, 85, 90, 93, 100, 212

community, angelic, 223–32

cosmic order, importance of, 88–90

321

Darby, John Nelson, 108–9, 265, 266
Dead Sea Scrolls. *See* Qumran (and Dead Sea Scrolls)
death and angels, 16, 186–236; afterlife, angels associated with, 194–202; in biblical world, 190–202; Christians and angelic community after death, 223–32; discussion of death, modern tendency to avoid, 187–88; humans becoming angels after death, 223–32; roles of angels in death, 189–90; tombstones, death's heads on, 186–87; worshipping with angels, 62–69, 74–75, 257, 259. *See also* reapers of souls, angels as
Death Takes a Holiday, 208
desire: of angels for human women 15, 79–81; celebration of desire and its fulfillment, 90–92; Christian desire for the world, 97–100; as delight and danger, 90–97; motives and consequences of angelic desire, 84–88; ordering of desires, concern with, 88–90, 93–97; power of desire, 77–79. *See also* boundaries, angels' crossing of; cosmic order, importance of; knowledge, angels' revelation of
destroyer, in Old Testament, 191–93, 249, 289–90, 295
Devil. *See* Satan and his angels
Dionysius the Areopagite. *See* Pseudo-Dionysius
dispensationalists and Satan, 106–12
divine knowledge. *See* knowledge, angels' revelation of
divine world, human access to, 15, 40–76; Ezekiel's vision, 49–54; fear and awe vs. chumminess with God, 58–62; "the glory of the Lord," 54–58; Jacob and the angels, 46–49; in popular thought, 41–46; the sacred vs. the everyday, 69–73; worship, 62–69
dualism, 81, 83, 101, 121. *See also* separation

Eastern Orthodox church, worshipping with angels in, 63
Edwards, Jonathan, 156–57, 281
evil, problem of, 103–6, 124–25, 165–66; coping with evil as disciples of Jesus, 132–35; overview of biblical understandings, 112–15. *See also* Satan and his angels
evil inclination, 118–120, 269
existence of angels, evidence for, 2–5

fallen angels: in human world (*see* desire: of angels for human women); Satan (*see* Satan and his angels)

fear and awe: angelic inspiration of, 21–27; balanced by trust in God's grace, 58–62; death figures in Old Testament, 190–93
fictional vs. nonfictional accounts of angels, 13–14
films about angels: *City of Angels*, 19, 78, 80–81, 85, 90, 93, 100, 212; *Death Takes a Holiday*, 208; *It's a Wonderful Life*, 13, 19, 29, 93, 223; *Michael*, 19, 78, 81–84, 93, 101; *Monty Python's the Meaning of Life*, 208; *My First Mister*, 211; *The Preacher's Wife*, 78, 89; *Wings of Desire*, 78, 80, 81

Gabriel, 84, 114, 123, 202
"the glory of the Lord," 53–58, 59, 64–69, 73, 76, 102, 125, 140, 154, 197, 229, 236, 242, 255, 256, 279, 303; manifested in Christ, 55–58, 67–69, 71–72, 74, 75, 98–99, 123, 127, 175, 190, 225–27, 238–39, 268
gnosticism, 45–46, 83, 162, 234, 235
God. *See* messenger(s) from God; divine world, human access to; guardian angel(s): doctrine as means of asking theological questions; transcendence v. immanence of God
Gothic subculture, 211, 299
grim reaper, 202–12. *See also* death and angels
guardian angel(s), 16, 139–85; biblical and early Christian views of, 142–47; and children, 140, 144, 154, 156, 157–58, 182, 273–74; doctrine as means of asking theological questions, 140; interior v. exterior dimension of, 150; Jesus as shepherd and guardian of souls, 146–47, 174–80; medieval opinions on, 147–53; in modern thought, 164–74; Protestant vs. Catholic views of, 140–41, 153–61, 181–83; as psychological helpers, 146, 148, 150, 162–63, 169–74; as rescuers or protectors, 146, 148–49, 150, 162–63, 164–69

heaven, changing views of, 63–66, 74–75
healing: angels as messengers of, 17–20; Jesus, miracles of, 33–37. *See also* messenger(s) from God
hierarchy, angelic, 42, 124, 141,144, 147, 149, 150, 151, 154, 181, 183, 258, 259, 276, 277, 278, 280
Higher Self, 44–45, 169, 173, 239, 252
Holbein, Hans the Younger, woodcuts of death by, 210
Holy Spirit, 3, 61–62, 66, 71, 76, 111, 130, 144, 145, 150, 168, 174, 177, 222, 231, 240, 244

human access to divine world. *See* divine world, human access to

Ignatius of Loyola, 152, 279
individualism, cultural model of, 28–30, 32, 36, 37, 38–39, 76, 214, 220, 249, 259

Jesus. *See* Christianity; Christology
Judaism. *See* biblical world, angels in

king of angels, Jesus as, 126–35; deconstructing the powers in relationship to, 128–32; opposed by the powers, 126–28
knowledge, angels' revelation of, 82–84
Left Behind series, 106–12
light, going into (dying), 212–23
love and peace, angels inspiring, 42–43, 58–62, 146, 170
Lucifer. *See* Satan and his angels
Luther, Martin, 153–54, 181, 279, 280

messenger(s) from God, 14, 17–39; Balaam and his ass, 20–21; Jesus as, 26–27, 33–37; as reshapers or revealers of values, 28–32. *See also* "the angel of the LORD"
merkabah mysticism, 49, 254, 259
Michael (archangel), 54, 55, 87, 107, 142–43, 164, 202, 204–8, 234, 238
Michael (film), 19, 78, 81–84, 93, 101
miracles of Jesus, 33–37
monism, 44–45
Monty Python's the Meaning of Life, 208
movies about angels. *See* films about angels
My First Mister, 211

near-death experiences, 5,2 9, 31, 42–43, 62–63, 83–84, 212–23, 233, 234, 237, 297, 300, 301
Neoplatonism, 144, 146, 153, 183, 277, 279, 280
New England tombstones, death's heads on, 186–87
New Testament. *See* biblical world, angels in; Christianity

Old Testament. *See* biblical world, angels in
order, concern with, 88–90, 93–97
Orthodox church, worshipping with angels in, 63

peace and love, angels inspiring, 42–43, 58–62, 146, 170; figures of light guiding souls to heaven, 212–23; Jesus as bringer of peace, 177–80, 185, 228

Philo of Alexandria, 55, 56, 74, 91, 97, 127, 195, 238, 246, 254, 256, 263, 272, 276, 292
Plato, 45, 143, 194, 196, 279, 297
the powers. *See* principalities and powers
The Preacher's Wife, 78, 89
presence of God, 15, 16, 27, 33, 38, 44–76, 95, 102, 138, 141, 152, 158, 168, 176, 183, 184, 222, 226, 237–39, 241, 242, 247, 253, 260, 281, 282, 284, 286. *See also* transcendence v. immanence of God
principalities and powers: concept of, 122–26; deconstructing, 128–32; Jesus as king of angels opposed by, 126–28
Prayer of Joseph, 49, 56, 254
Protestantism: divine world, human access to, 63, 68; guardian angels, doctrine of, 140–41, 153–61, 181–83
providence, doctrine of, 138, 149, 156, 163, 165–67, 182, 184, 240
Pseudo-Dionysius, 124, 147, 149, 154, 183, 270–71, 276, 277, 279, 280
psychological helpers, guardian angels as, 169–74
psychopomps, angels as, 16, 203, 212–23, 296

Qumran (and Dead Sea Scrolls), 66, 121, 202, 224, 257, 267, 269, 270, 271, 274, 289, 290, 295, 303

Raphael, 14, 30, 31–34, 84, 98, 146, 202, 237
reapers of souls, angels as: figures of light guiding souls to heaven, 212–23; grim reapers, 202–12
Reformation critique of guardian angels, 140–41, 153–61
Reformed Protestantism (Calvinism): beliefs about divine immanence, 141, 153, 155–56, 157, 183
rescuers, guardian angels as, 164–69
resurrection of the dead. *See* afterlife: resurrection of the dead
Roman Catholicism. *See* Catholicism

Satan and his angels, 15–16, 103–38; coping with evil as disciples of Jesus, 132–35; emerging biblical perspective on, 115–22; deconstructing the powers in relationship to, 128–32; evil, problem of, 103–6; in *Left Behind* series, 106–12; opposed by the powers, 126–28; and the power of death, 193; "principalities and powers," concept of, 122–26; versus Jesus as king of angels 126–35 separation, 81, 90, 93–95, 101, 119, 173, 211, 261, 279, 300

The Simpsons, 208

sin, awareness of, 34, 60–61, 173–74, 285

"the sons of God and the daughters of men." *See* desire: of angels for human women

spiritual warfare, 110–12, 266, 267, 270, 272

television shows about angels, 208, 213

theodicy problem. *See* evil, problem of; Satan and his angels

Thomas Aquinas, 139, 148–49, 166; *Summa Theologiae,* 139, 166

Touched by an Angel, 19, 213

transcendence v. immanence of God, 23–26, 33, 38, 54, 73–74, 95, 101, 141, 170, 171, 240, 244, 278, 286; doctrine among medieval mystics, 150; doctrine among Protestant Reformers, 153–57, 183

Transfiguration, 34, 39, 57, 72, 239

truth, angels as messengers of, 17–20. *See also* messenger(s) from God

Uriel, 89, 196, 200

values, angels reshaping or revealing, 28–32

warfare. *See* spiritual warfare

Wings of Desire, 58, 80–81

worshipping with angels, 62–69, 74–75, 257, 259

yetser hara ("evil inclination"), 118–20, 269

Zoroastrianism, 30, 115, 121, 250, 270, 272, 296

INDEX OF MODERN AUTHORS

Abrams, Michael, 83
Allison, Dale C., 202, 205, 206, 289, 293
Alsup, John E., 34
Andersen F. I., 302
Anderson, Bernhard W., 122, 267
Anderson, Gary A., 85, 262
Anderson, Joan Wester, 165, 245, 283, 284
Ariès, Phillipe, 209
Arnold, Clinton E., 111, 265–67
Ashley, Timothy R., 247
Ashton, John, 274
Attridge, Harold W., 255
Auerbach, Loyd, 298

Balentine, Samuel L., 271
Beck, Martha Nibley, 18, 28, 28, 41, 93, 246, 249
Becker, Ernest, 188, 287, 288, 297, 299, 302
Bednarowski, Mary Farrell, 24, 248, 259
Bellah, Robert Neelly, 29, 249
Berger, Peter L., 2, 3, 243
Berkhof, H., 118, 119, 122, 137, 247, 248, 269, 271, 272–73
Bloom, Harold, 253, 299, 300
Blount, Brian K., 180
Bonhoeffer, Dietrich, 118, 269
Boring, M. Eugene, 192, 290
Bowker, John, 288, 301
Brach, Tara, 171–72, 173, 178, 285
Brown, Michael F., 252, 253, 259, 261, 300
Bullinger, Heinrich, 155, 280
Bulman, Raymond F., 109, 265, 266
Bultmann, Rudolf Karl, 128–30, 131, 161, 244, 272, 288
Burnham, Sophy, 165, 245
Byassee, Jason, 300

Carlton, Clark, 257
Charles, Gary W., 180, 286
Charlesworth, James H., 258, 302

Chase, Steven, 149, 259, 271, 275, 276, 277, 278, 286
Childs, Brevard S., 247
Chinnici, Joseph P., 282–83
Clark, Lynn Schofield, 243
Clark-Soles, Jaime, 288
Clifford, Richard J., 245
Collins, John J., 244, 250, 255, 256, 257, 267, 269, 270, 271, 274, 289, 302
Cullman, Oscar, 222, 291, 294, 302

Dahl, Nils Alstrup, 273
Daniel, Alma, 44, 244, 249, 252
Daniélou, Jean, 257, 262, 275–76
Darr, Katheryn Pfisterer, 255
Davidson, Maxwell J., 257, 290, 295, 303
Davila, James R., 258
Dawson, David, 263, 264
Day, Peggy Lynne, 268
Dean-Otting, Mary, 294, 296, 297, 301
Deetz, James, 286–87
Denton, Melinda Lundquist, 243
Dickens, Charles A., 209, 298
Dowd, Sharyn Echols, 284
Dries, Angelyn, 282–83

Eadie, Betty J., 42–43, 46, 58, 70, 83, 212, 215, 220, 252, 253, 261, 300, 301
Eire, Carlos M. N., 141, 153, 274, 279, 280, 281
Elwood, Christopher, 279, 280, 281
Evans, Richard Paul, 246

Fabry, H. J., 247, 267
Farley, Wendy, 264, 273, 281, 285, 288
Fitzmyer, Joseph A., 293
Fletcher-Louis, Crispin H. T., 33–34, 36, 225, 248, 251, 257, 259, 263, 275, 293, 303
Ford, David F., 13, 35, 36, 37, 77, 99, 109, 229, 245, 251, 260, 264, 288
Forsyth, Neil, 262, 267

Fox, Robin Lane, 303
Frangipane, Francis, 266, 267, 272
Fredrickson, David E., 178, 286
Freedman, David Noel, 247, 267
Freeman, Eileen E., 41–42, 43–44, 70, 244, 252
Fretheim, Terrence E., 253

Garrett, Duane A., 267, 270
Garrett, Susan R., 251, 258, 260, 263, 264, 267, 268, 269, 270, 271, 272, 285, 290, 303
Gaster, Theodore H., 244, 245
Gates, David, 265
Gerstner, John H., 266
Gieschen, Charles A., 145, 245, 247, 249, 254, 255, 256, 259, 275
Gorenberg, Gershom, 108, 110, 265, 266
Graham, Billy, 3, 6, 243
Griswold, Trudy, 58, 244, 251, 252, 257
Gritsch, Eric W., 280
Grundmann, W., 260
Gurevich, Aron, 276, 277, 278

Hackett, Jo Ann, 246
Halperin, David J., 50, 254, 255
Handy, Lowell K., 258
Hanegraaff, Wouter J., 261
Hannah, Darrell D., 248, 249, 256, 273, 275
Hanson, Paul D., 262
Harper, Ralph, 58, 72, 257, 289
Hengel, Martin, 250
Hennecke, E., 294, 301
Hensley, Chad, 299
Hill, Craig C., 266
Himmelfarb, Martha, 64, 257–58, 259, 260, 263, 292, 294–95, 296, 301, 302, 303
Hoeller, Stephan A., 253, 261
Horst, Pieter W. van der, 289, 297
Huffines, Launa, 252
Hurd, Bob, 278, 283, 284
Hurtado, Larry W., 249

Isaac, E., 261, 263, 274, 292

Jenkins, Jerry B., 16, 104, 105, 106, 109–11, 128, 130–32, 137, 245, 265, 266, 273
Johnson, Luke T., 184, 256, 263, 273, 286
Joines, K. R., 268
Jones, Gregory Knox, 271

Keck, David, 147, 148, 151–52, 249, 257, 261, 275, 276, 277–79, 282
Keillor, Garrison, 230, 304
Kelly, Henry Ansgar, 262
Kim, Bokin, 285

Kistler, Don, 266
Kittel, Gerhard, 260
Knibb, Michael A., 271
Kolenkow, Anita Bingham, 290
Kugel, James L., 23, 47, 247, 249, 250, 253–54, 262, 272

LaHaye, Tim, 16, 104, 105, 106, 109–11, 128, 130–32, 137, 245, 265, 266, 273
Layton, Bentley, 253, 302
Levenson, Jon D., 254, 267, 269, 288, 289, 291
Levison, John R., 256
Lewis, Theodore J., 280, 288, 289, 290
Longenecker, Richard M., 249, 272
Ludwig, Allan I., 281, 286, 287, 299
Luscombe, Belinda, 287

Madsen, Richard, 29, 249
Maloney, George A., 257
Mark, Barbara, 58, 244, 251, 252, 257
Marsden, George M., 281
Martin, Dale B., 81, 92, 260
McAlpine, Thomas H., 266, 272, 273
McDonald, Marci, 252
McFague, Sallie, 95–96, 101, 264
McGinn, Bernard, 277
McGreevy, John T., 160, 282, 283
Meier, Samuel L., 274, 290, 295
Michl, J., 274
Millar, William R., 245
Moltmann, Jürgen, 58, 61, 62, 99, 257, 264
Moody, Raymond A., 213, 214, 299, 300
Moore, Michael S., 246
Moorhead, James M., 304
Morray-Jones, Christopher R. A., 259
Mullen, Brendan, 253
Mullen, E. T., 248
Murphy, Ed, 266

Newman, Carey C., 256
Newsom, Carol A., 64, 88, 247, 248, 250, 258, 261, 262, 263
Nickelsburg, George W. E., 250, 258, 261, 263, 291, 292, 295, 297, 302
Noll, Stephen F., 246
Nouwen, Henri J. M., 235, 251, 264, 304
Nowell, Irene, 251
Nussbaum, Martha C., 263

O'Neill, Kim, 252
Orsi, Robert A., 157, 161, 273, 274, 282, 283

Paffenroth, Kim, 288
Pauw, Amy Plantinga, 156, 281, 282

Peretti, Frank, 6, 13, 16, 104, 105, 111
Pfitzner, Victor C., 63, 257
Placher, William C., 264, 269
Plantinga, Cornelius, 265
Plathow, Michael, 280
Poe, Edgar Allan, 210, 298
Polleyfeys, Patrick, 298
Pope, Marvin H., 191, 274, 289
Porter, F. C., 269
Poythress, Vern S., 266

Quispel, Gilles, 275

Rabey, Steve, 265
Rad, Gerhard von, 247, 260
Ramer, Andrew, 44, 244, 249, 252
Ray, Stephen G., 273
Redfield, James, 244, 257
Riley, Greg J., 271
Rosenbaum, Ron, 268
Rossing, Barbara, 266
Rowland, Christopher, 249, 254, 256
Royalty, Robert M., Jr., 259, 272
Royster, Dmitri, 257
Rudolph, Kurt, 253
Russell, D. S., 250, 262
Russell, Jeffrey Burton, 7, 244

Sabom, Michael, 300
Sargent, Denny, 163, 169–70, 171, 172, 244,
    252, 284, 285
Savran, George, 246
Scholem, Gershom, 254
Schucman, Helen, 252
Scott, Alan, 292
Segal, Alan F., 54, 55, 56, 190, 194, 196, 224,
    225, 249, 254, 255, 256, 259, 288, 291–93,
    296, 298, 301, 302, 303, 304
Seim, Turid Karlsen, 293, 303
Smith, Christian, 243
Smith, Jonathan Z., 254
Smith, Morton, 275
Spangler, David, 252–53
Stone, Michael E., 268–69
Storm, Howard, 62, 63, 68, 83, 208, 213, 257,
    261, 298
Stowers, Stanley K., 263
Stringfellow, William, 222, 234, 272, 288,
    301–2, 304
Stuckenbruck, Loren T., 256

Sullivan, Kevin P., 302–3
Sullivan, William M., 29, 249
Sweeney, Marvin A., 267
Swidler, Ann, 29, 249

Talbert, Charles H., 284
Tanner, Kathryn, 243, 244, 248, 264, 286
Taves, Ann, 158, 282–83
Taylor, Eugene, 252
Tazewell, Charles, 223, 302
TenPas, Jake, 288
Thurston, Bonnie, 286
Tipton, Stephen M., 29, 249
Tobin, Thomas H., 248
Tromp, Nicholas J., 289
Tyson, Timothy B., 229, 304

VanderKam, James C., 262, 271
Van Praagh, James, 214, 300
Vermes, Geza, 257
Virtue, Doreen, 162–63, 252, 284
Vogel, Marta, 69–70, 259
Volf, Miroslav, 134, 228, 230, 257, 260, 273,
    286, 304

Wagner, Donald E., 266
Walsch, Neale Donald, 25, 45, 248, 252, 253,
    260
Watson, Duane F., 289, 294
Wauters, Ambika, 244, 252
Weber, Timothy P., 266
Welker, Michael, 24, 238, 248, 249, 257, 304
Wesley, John, 281–82, 286
Westermann, Claus, 247
Wicker, Christine, 300
Widengren, Geo, 250
Willoughby, H. Ringgren, 247, 267
Wilson, Robert R., 254, 281, 294, 301
Wink, Walter, 16, 123, 128, 129–30, 131, 132,
    267, 270, 272–73
Winston, David, 270
Wintermute, O. S., 268, 274, 295
Wire, Anoinette Clark, 66, 258
Witmer, Andrew, 301
Wojtyła, Karol Józef, 283

Zaehner, R. C., 270
Zaleski, Carol, 214, 215, 216, 217, 218, 238,
    287, 288, 300–301, 304
Zoloth-Dorfman, Laurie, 70, 259

INDEX OF SCRIPTURE AND OTHER ANCIENT WRITINGS

SCRIPTURE

OLD TESTAMENT

Genesis
chs. 1–11, 112
2:7, 80
ch. 3, 117, 268
3:5, 79, 120
3:17–19, 271
3:19, 268
3:22, 79
ch. 6, 76
6:1–4, 9, 15, 78, 79, 80,
85, 86, 115, 258, 271,
294
6:2, 274
6:3, 80, 81
6:4, 262
9:29, 260
11:1–9, 79
11:6, 79
14:18–19, 67
ch. 15, 247
15:4–5, 247
15:6, 81
16:7–10, 22
16:7–11, 246
16:13b, 59
chs. 18–19, 34
18:16–33, 113
19:1–23, 274
19:13, 295
21:17, 246
21:17–19, 27
22:2, 22
22:11–15, 246
23:3, 297
24:7, 274
24:40, 274
27:41–45, 46

28:12, 1, 46, 253
28:13, 253
28:13–15, 254
28:17, 1
32:1–2, 47
32:22–32, 47
32:24–30, 246
32:28, 254
32:28–31, 47
32:30b, 59
35:9–15, 47, 254
37:35, 194

Exodus
3:2, 22, 23, 246
3:6, 23
3:14, 23
4:2–4, 246
4:11–12, 37
4:22, 254
12:23, 191, 289
14:19, 24, 246
14:24, 24
16:7–10, 22
16:7–11, 246
16:10, 255
16:13b, 59
19:12, 23
19:18–21, 59
19:21, 23
19:22, 23
19:24, 23
20:20, 60
ch. 23, 256
23:20, 248
23:20–21, 247
23:21, 55
23:23, 24, 246
ch. 24, 294
24:9–11, 247
24:15–17, 54
25:18–22, 254

32:34, 246, 248
33:2, 248
33:3, 24
33:11, 247
33:18–23, 54, 255
33:20, 9, 23
33:22, 23
37:7–9, 254
40:34, 255

Numbers
11:24–29, 248
16:41–50, 191, 290
20:6, 255
20:16, 248
chs. 22–24, 246
22:2–24:25, 246
22:5–6, 20
22:23–35, 246
22:31–35, 21
24:2–3, 248
27:5–11, 251
31:8, 246
31:16, 246
36:2–12, 251

Deuteronomy
30:15–16, 112
30:19–20, 112
32:8, 142
33:2, 126

Joshua
5:14, 274
10:12–13, 245
10:12–23, 9

Judges
2:1–4, 246

3:10, 248
5:20, 9, 194, 245
5:3, 246
6:11–12, 246
6:23, 60
13:3–21, 246
13:22, 23

1 Samuel
2:1–10, 85
4:4, 254

2 Samuel
6:2, 254
7:4–17, 113
22:5–6, 290
22:11, 51
24:11–16, 191
24:11–25, 290
24:15, 295
24:16, 290

1 Kings
6:23–28, 254
8:6–7, 254
18:46, 254
ch. 19, 247
19:5, 274
19:7, 246, 274
22:19, 26

2 Kings
1:1–18, 284
1:3, 246
1:15, 246
2:9–15, 248
6:14–17, 284
6:17, 280
17:6, 250
18:35, 274
19:35, 246, 295
20:13, 88

1 Chronicles
ch. 21, 135
21:9–22:1, 290
21:15–16, 249
21:15–29, 246

2 Chronicles
32:21, 295

Ezra
8:53, 290

Job
chs. 1–2, 65, 116, 127, 135,
    136, 262, 268
1:7–12, 116, 248
1:20–21, 116
1:22, 267
ch. 2, 116, 265
2:1–7, 248
ch. 3, 268
7:9, 194, 290
9:33, 274
15:8, 248
16:19–21, 274
18:13–14, 191, 289
19:25, 274
20:15, 289
27:1–7, 263
33:23, 274
38:7, 194

Psalms
9:13, 191
18:4–5, 290
18:10, 51
21:9, 295
24:7–10, 255
29:1, 248
30:3, 191
31:8, 61
33:5–6, 295
33:19, 289
Ps. 44, 114
49:14–15, 289
78:49–51, 289, 295
78:60–61, 255
Ps. 82, 64, 248
84:7, 50
84:10, 50
86:13, 191
89:6–9, 248
89:10, 126
89:30–34, 113
89:47–48, 189
90:10, 148
91:11–12, 274
97:7, 65
99:1, 51
103:15–16, 189
110:4, 67
Ps. 139, 254
139:2–5, 48, 167
139:8–10, 53
139:9–10a, 167
142:2, 139
Ps. 148, 65

Proverbs
1:12, 289
30:16, 289

Isaiah
chs. 1–39, 245
5:14, 194, 289
ch. 6, 294
6:1–8, 7, 56, 248
6:2–4, 65
6:5, 59
11:2, 248
ch. 14, 121, 262
14:2, 87
14:9, 121
14:11, 121
14:13–14, 120
14:15, 121
14:19, 121
chs. 24–27, 245
24:1–27:13, 11
24:21–23, 10, 245
25:8, 289, 291
27:1, 126
33:11–14, 295
36:20, 274
37:36, 295
38:16–18, 191
chs. 40–66, 245
40:26, 11
42:1, 248
49:22–23, 276
51:9, 126
58:6, 33
61:1–2, 33, 248
63:9, 248
chs. 66, 292

Jeremiah
4:18, 113
9:20–22, 289, 298
23:18, 248
23:22, 248

Ezekiel
ch. 1, 255, 294
1:1, 50
1:26–28, 49, 51, 238
2:2, 248
3:12–13, 53, 255
3:15, 59
3:22, 254
8:1, 254
chs. 9–10, 52, 255
10:3–5, 52

Ezekiel (*cont.*)
10:4, 255
10:9–17, 256
chs. 28–32, 86, 115, 121, 262
28:11–19, 86, 254
28:12, 87
28:22, 255
32:27, 262
36:27, 269
ch. 37, 291
37:1, 254
chs. 40–48, 258
40:1, 254
40:3–4, 248
43:2–5, 255

Daniel
chs. 1–6, 266
3:28, 246
6:22, 284
ch. 7, 34, 54–55, 115, 256
7:9–14, 248
7:10, 65
7:13, 54
8:16, 250
9:1–27, 114
9:21, 250
ch. 10, 34, 142, 256
10:12–21, 123
10:13, 154, 250, 267, 274
10:19, 60, 179
10:20–21, 154, 250, 267,
   274
ch. 12, 195, 292, 302
12:1, 250, 274, 295
12:2, 189, 194, 198, 224
12:3, 292

Hosea
12:3–4, 48
13:14, 289

Joel
2:28–29, 248

Jonah
2:2–9, 191

Habakkuk
1:13, 114
2:5, 289
3:11, 245

Haggai
1:13, 246

1:14, 248
2:5, 248

Zechariah
chs. 1–6, 246, 248
ch. 3, 127, 135, 136, 248, 295
4:6, 248
5:1–4, 298
7:12, 248

Malachi
3:1, 248
4:1, 295

OLD TESTAMENT
APOCRYPHA

Tobit
1:3–22, 250
2:2, 250
3:14–15, 251
4:3–21, 250
4:12–13, 251
chs. 5–12, 34
5:4, 274
5:17, 31
7:11, 31
12:6–10, 250
12:9–10, 32, 250
12:11–15, 31
12:12, 276
12:15, 31
12:19, 98
12:21, 34
14:2, 250
14:8–9, 250
14:10–11, 250

Wisdom
2:23–34, 268
2:24, 193
3:7, 292
18:14–16, 238, 249
18:20–25, 290

Sirach (Ecclesiasticus)
17:17, 274
51:5–12, 191

Susanna
1:55, 295
1:59, 295

1 Maccabees
7:41, 295

3 Maccabees
6:18–19, 295

4 Maccabees
7:11, 290
9:9, 295
12:12, 295
17:5, 290

2 Esdras
chs. 3–14, 269

NEW TESTAMENT

Matthew
2:13, 284
2:16–18, 192
2:23, 33
3:12, 295
4:8–9, 262
5:21–22, 134
5:43–45, 134
6:13, 273
6:20, 99
6:30, 275
8:26, 275
10:16, 232
10:18, 280
10:29–30, 235
10:30, 167
10:38, 36
10:42, 275
13:36–43, 197, 289
13:43, 292
13:45, 36
14:31, 275
16:8, 275
16:18, 290
16:22, 97
17:1–8, 33
17:2, 72
17:20, 275
18:8, 295
18:9, 295
18:10, 144, 148, 154,
   181
22:23–33, 197
22:30, 278
ch. 25, 197
25:31–46, 197, 289
25:37–40, 175
25:41, 295
26:53, 174, 284
26:64, 272
26:69, 126

Mark
1:13, 284
1:24, 127
3:27, 105
5:8, 134
8:22–26, 33
11:23, 167
14:33–35, 189
14:36, 98
14:38, 133, 176, 273
14:62, 272
15:34, 73
16:19, 272

Luke
1:11, 250
1:19, 250
1:26, 250
2:11, 293
4:6–8, 88, 125, 262
4:18–19, 33
4:21, 293
5:1–11, 33
5:8, 59, 179
5:26, 293
8:12, 271
9:24, 222
9:31, 269
10:18, 121, 127
10:19, 132
13:2–5, 271
15:4–9, 49
15:7, 154
16:19–31, 197, 293
16:22, 232
20:27–40, 293, 303
20:37–40, 293
22:39–46, 284
22:42, 167, 168
22:53, 124
23:43, 293
24:30–31, 34
24:41–43, 239

John
1:1–18, 26
1:3, 56, 272
1:9, 177
1:14, 56, 98
1:50–51, 253
3:18–21, 177
3:29–30, 276
5:19, 106
5:19–47, 256
5:28–29, 197

6:8, 199
6:9–11, 196
6:40, 197
7:4–17, 199
8:58, 56
11:35, 189
12:31, 127
12:41, 56
14:16, 274
14:23, 49
14:26, 274
14:27, 177
15:26, 274
16:7, 274
17:1–5, 284
20:13–14, 199

Acts
1:9, 34
2:25, 272
2:33–34, 272
2:44–47, 230, 304
5:1–10, 230
5:31, 272
6:15, 225
7:53, 225, 303
7:55–56, 272
ch. 9, 259
9:1–19, 34
9:3–5, 59
9:9, 35
9:16, 36
10:38, 105
12:1–24, 269
12:7–10, 284
12:15, 144, 154, 181
17:25, 168
17:34, 124, 147
ch. 22, 259
22:6–16, 34
22:17–22, 71, 259
23:6–8, 302
24:15, 293
ch. 26, 259
26:12–18, 34
26:15–18, 35

Romans
4:17, 227
5:1–11, 99, 179
5:5, 71, 178, 235
5:12, 118, 124, 193
5:18–19, 120, 128
5:21, 118
6:6, 118

6:12, 118
6:13, 128
6:14, 118
6:16, 118
6:17, 118
ch. 7, 119
7:8, 118
7:11, 118
ch. 8, 127
8:18–23, 192, 227
8:20, 125, 271
8:21, 125, 178
8:22, 189
8:28, 257
8:29, 272, 289, 303
8:34, 128, 272
8:38, 124, 136
12:9, 273
12:15, 273
12:17, 273
12:21, 272
ch. 13, 123
13:4, 136
14:8–9, 293
14:17, 177

1 Corinthians
2:6–8, 270
2:8, 226
3:12–15, 293, 295
5:5, 271, 290
6:3, 289
7:5, 92
10:10, 191
10:13, 100
11:7, 258
11:10, 9, 66
11:29–30, 271
12:24, 75
12:26, 71, 273
14:18, 71
14:27–31, 71
ch. 15, 294
15:24–26, 128, 192
15:25–28, 219
15:26, 193
15:28, 76
15:49, 289, 303
15:52, 232
15:54–55, 290

2 Corinthians
1:8b–10, 222
2:6–8, 100
2:11, 121, 136

2 Corinthians (*cont.*)
3:14–16, 227
3:17–18, 67, 71, 226, 228,
    303
3:18, 225, 227, 259, 289, 303
4:1–12, 268, 304
4:3–4, 268
4:4, 303
4:4–6, 33, 227
4:6, 55, 239
4:7, 227
4:11, 189
4:17, 227
5:6–10, 198, 293
5:8, 218, 293
5:13–15, 179
5:14, 72, 222
5:17, 226
5:19, 228
6:1, 290
6:15, 271
11:3, 119
11:14, 118, 268, 271
11:15, 121
12:1–12, 259
12:2–4, 71, 216, 259
12:4, 293
12:7, 121, 271
12:8, 176
12:9, 176

Galatians
1:4, 176
1:8, 136
1:11–12, 71
2:20, 11
3:23–24, 136
4:13–14, 175, 227
4:14, 11, 245
6:1, 100

Ephesians
1:20–21, 106, 138, 272
2:2, 273
2:6, 68
3:20, 106
5:25–27, 276
ch. 6, 110
6:10–13, 110
6:12, 105, 123, 272, 276
6:14–18, 110
6:16, 273

Philippians
1:6, 226
1:23, 293
2:5–11, 85
2:6, 56
2:7, 56
2:8, 185
3:7, 35
3:10, 226
3:14, 35
3:20, 293
4:7, 177
4:13, 133

Colossians
1:15–20, 49, 56, 272
1:16, 272, 276
2:18, 68, 259
3:1, 272
3:9–15, 259–60
3:10, 225, 289, 303

1 Thessalonians
3:5, 271
4:13, 189
4:16–17, 107
5:5, 125

Hebrews
1:1, 26
1:2, 272
1:3, 56, 75, 226, 272
1:4, 57, 239, 289
1:6, 49, 272
2:8, 128, 242
2:14–15, 106, 188, 193,
    212
4:12–13, 17, 177, 249
4:16, 67
5:7–9, 175
8:1, 67
9:12, 67
9:24, 67
11:28, 289
12:22–24, 67, 289

James
1:6–7, 119
1:14–15, 91

1 Peter
2:25, 142, 177

3:9–12, 273
3:22, 104, 272
5:8, 127

2 Peter
1:16, 72

1 John
2:9–14, 134
3:15, 134
5:19, 124

3 John
v. 11, 273

Jude
v. 6, 88
v. 9, 250

Revelation
ch. 1, 245
1:5, 272
1:13–16, 55
chs. 2–3, 274
2:7, 293
3:19, 271
6:8, 199, 204, 290
6:9–11, 198, 302
7:4–17, 199
7:9–12, 68
7:14, 68
8:4, 68, 276
9:22, 191
ch. 12, 128
12:7–9, 202, 250
12:9, 119, 121
12:10, 127
12:12, 125
ch. 13, 115, 121
14:1–3, 255
14:15–20, 298
ch. 17, 248
19:6, 255
19:11–16, 249
20:1–3, 202
20:4, 198
20:6, 108
20:11–13, 198
20:13–14, 199, 290
21:9–22:6, 248
22:8, 248
22:16, 248

OTHER EARLY JEWISH AND CHRISTIAN WRITINGS

Acts of Thomas, 216, 217
Apocalypse of Peter, 200
Apocalypse of Zephaniah, 200–201, 203–4, 217
Biblical Antiquities (Pseudo-Philo)
  11:12, 143
2 Baruch
  21:23, 290
  42:8, 290
  51:10, 224, 292
3 Baruch
  13:3, 143
1 Enoch
  5:9, 260
  chs. *6–11*, 84, 261, 262
  8:1–2, 82
  10:4–6, 262
  10:12–14, 262
  12:4, 262
  14:5, 85, 262
  15:2–10, 262
  15:6, 81, 261
  15:8–9, 271
  16:3, 82
  16:6, 85
  chs. *17–19*, 85, 262
  18:4–19:1, 262
  20:5, 274
  ch. *22*, 195, 196, 292, 301
  22:1–5, 195
  ch. *39*, 302
  40:7–9, 276
  ch. *47*, 259
  52:5, 276
  53:4, 276
  chs. *70–71*, 302
  chs. *72–82*, 263
  75:1–2, 89
  100:5, 142
  104:2–6, 292
2 Enoch
  9:19, 258
  22:6–10, 224
  66:7, 292
Jubilees
  5:1, 271
  10:1–6, 260, 271
  12:20, 124
  15:31–32, 142, 274
  17:15–18:19, 263
  17:16, 117, 268
  35:17, 142
  49:2, 289
  49:4, 289

Life of Adam and Eve
  14:3, 87, 135
Martyrdom and Ascension of Isaiah
  8:15–17, 302
  9:39, 302
  11:35, 302
Philo
  Creation: 144, 292
  Dreams: 1.135–37, 138–45, 292; *1.141–42*, 276
  Giants: 3–7, 276; *7*, 292
  Moses: 2.108, 292
  On the Special Laws: 4.79, 91; *4.79–94*, 263; *4.95*, 91
  Questions and Answers on Exodus: 2.114, 292
  Questions and Answers on Genesis: 4.97, 127, 272
Prayer of Joseph, 49, 56, 254
Shepherd of Hermas
  Visions: 2.2.7, 302; *5.2–3*, 144
  Mandates: 11.9–10, 145, 275
  Similitudes: 9.25.2, 302–3
Songs of the Sabbath Sacrifice, 66
Testament of Abraham (Recension A)
  1:7, 204
  4:11, 298
  6:8, 204
  7:9, 12, 204
  8:9–10, 298
  8:9–12, 204–5
  16:1, 4–6, 205
  16:12, 16, 206
  17:6, 7–8, 13, 14–17, 19, 206
  20:3, 7, 8, 10, 206
  20:14, 207
Testament of Job
  27:1–7, 263
  33:3–9, 203
  40:3, 203
  48:2–3, 66
  52:8–12, 203
Testament of Moses
  10:9, 292
Testaments of the Twelve Patriarchs
  Testament of Reuben: 5:1–6, 260
  Testament of Dan: 6:5, 276
  Testament of Asher: 6:6, 276
Thanksgiving Hymns
  3.21–22, 63, 257
  10.3–6, 60
War Scroll, 202